Astrology and Reformation

Astrology
and
Reformation

ROBIN B. BARNES

OXFORD
UNIVERSITY PRESS

UNIVERSITY PRESS

Oxford University Press is a department of the University of Oxford. It furthers the
University's objective of excellence in research, scholarship, and education by publishing
worldwide. Oxford is a registered trademark of Oxford University Press in the UK and in
certain other countries.

Published in the United States of America by Oxford University Press
198 Madison Avenue, New York, NY 10016, United States of America

© Oxford University Press 2016

Library of Congress Cataloging-in-Publication Data
Barnes, Robin Bruce, 1951—
Astrology and Reformation / Robin B. Barnes.
pages cm
Includes index.
ISBN 978–0–19–973605–8 (cloth : alk. paper) 1. Reformation. 2. Church history—
16th century. 3. Astrology. 4. Evangelicalism. 5. Evangelicalism—Germany.
I. Title.
BR307.B37 2015
261.5′13—dc23
2015009980

1 3 5 7 9 8 6 4 2
Printed in the United States of America
on acid-free paper

For ALB, MLB, MBB, and THF

Contents

Acknowledgments

THIS BOOK HAS been a long time in the making. I can never offer thanks enough to my wife, Ann Lee Bressler, and our now grown children, Molly Leeanna Barnes and Morgan Bruce Barnes, for their infinite loving indulgence through many trying phases and interruptions of the work. To my friend and former doctoral adviser H. C. Erik Midelfort, Professor Emeritus of History at the University of Virginia, I owe deep gratitude for countless helpful reactions to drafts of my chapters, and for unflagging encouragement. Long-time fellow members of both the Sixteenth Century Society and Conference and the Society for Reformation Research have aided me with their questions and comments at scholarly meetings as well as other venues. My colleagues in the Department of History and in the Humanities Program at Davidson College have graced me with ongoing scholarly stimulation and collegiality. I am grateful for research support from the American Philosophical Society and the National Endowment for the Humanities; at a crucial stage of the work I benefited from an American Council of Learned Societies Fellowship.

Many family members and other friends have helped me, often in ways they do not realize. Among them are George Barnes, Kit and Candace Barnes, Bill and Linda Bressler, William Brown and Mary Jo Clark, Richard and Jane Gawthrop, John Headley, Charles Hogan and Juliet Kingsmill, Kevin Moll, Roger Munsick, Gerda Nischan, Anthony and Françoise Papalas, Joanne and Tom Ratchford, Tom Robisheaux and Angelique Drossaert, R. Brooks Sherman and Shauna MacLaughlin, and Price and Margaret Zimmermann. Finally, my editor at Oxford University Press, Cynthia Read, has been the picture of perfect patience and generosity; she too has my most sincere thanks.

Davidson, NC
March 2015

A Note on Sources

SINCE I BEGAN work on this book the digital revolution has dramatically transformed the landscape of historical research. Many of the primary sources I had accessed physically or via microfilm are now readily available online, and soon virtually every page printed in the early modern era will be accessible in this way. In particular, the online collections of the Bavarian State Library (www.bsb-muenchen.de) and the Herzog August Bibliothek, Wolfenbüttel (www.hab.de) have led the way in making available German printed sources from the fifteenth to eighteenth centuries. Most of the annual calendars, practicas, and other primary works I have consulted are listed in one of two major bibliographic databases: the *Verzeichnis der im deutschen Sprachbereich erschienenen Drucke des 16. Jahrhunderts* (VD16) and the *Verzeichnis der im deutschen Sprachbereich erschienenen Drucke des 17. Jahrhunderts* (VD17). In turn, these and other major collections are now covered by the bibliographic databases of the Consortium of European Research Libraries (CERL: www.cerl.org), which include records of both printed and manuscript materials from major European as well as North American institutions; I have benefitted above all from access to the *Heritage of the Printed Book* (HPB) database. Finally, I have drawn on Ernst Zinner's massive *Geschichte und Bibliographie der Astronomischen Literatur in Deutschland zur Zeit der Renaissance* (Stuttgart, 1964), which includes works now lost or not yet listed in the online databases.

I have cited astrological forecasts or "practicas" for a single year by the author's last name followed immediately by the year for which the work was reckoned (e.g., Virdung 1497; Gasser 1547; Herlicius 1617). Nearly all these works appeared under titles such as *Practica Deutsch, Prognosticon Astrologicum*, or variations such as *Practica auff das Jar* .... Because these works remained quite brief through most of the period under study, I have often foregone signature and leaf citations, especially when the references are to points found in prefatory sections.

This book is essentially an interpretative essay. I have drawn heavily on recent secondary sources, but often in ways that do not echo their arguments. Moreover, recognizing that historical interpretations are always in flux and that recent and current trends have not always brought refinement, I have not hesitated to cite studies going back to the nineteenth century. My main concern has been to offer an original and provocative synthesis that might contribute to the overall vitality of studies on the German Reformation.

Astrology and Reformation

Introduction

The heavens are telling the glory of God;
and the firmament proclaims his handiwork.
Day to day pours forth speech,
and night to night declares knowledge.
There is no speech, nor are there words;
their voice is not heard;
yet their voice goes out through all the earth,
and their words to the end of the world.

PSALM 19

IN 1557 THE Calvinist physician Thomas Erastus expressed both wonder and dismay that "the vicious superstition of astrology should hold broader sway, in the very places where God's Word has been truly preached these many years now, than anywhere else in Christendom." The renowned medical scholar was referring to the Protestant cities and lands of the Holy Roman Empire, where the Lutheran evangelical movement had grown so strong that two years earlier, in 1555, it had gained legal status in the Peace of Augsburg. Like many other Calvinists, Erastus had the highest respect for Martin Luther and the reform he had inspired; indeed he saw his own faith as directly heir to that restoration of the gospel. He was thus baffled as well as disturbed to observe that nowhere else was it so very common as it was among otherwise enlightened Germans for men and women to govern their doings according to the stars, even in the smallest matters. Many people, he lamented, evidently took these notions and habits from their teachers, and thus questioned them "as little as they question the grammar they have learned."[1]

Nearly four centuries later, the great German Jewish art historian Aby Warburg experienced a similar deep puzzlement as he considered essentially the same apparent paradox: the simultaneous flowering, in early sixteenth-century Germany, of pagan astrological myths and the Reformation ideal of the fully free human conscience.² In Warburg's eyes, Martin Luther's struggle was fundamentally about human spiritual freedom, the liberation of the individual from all moral or mental enslavement. Yet all around the Reformer, in the very minds that were drawn most strongly to his teaching, swirled fears of planetary demons, feelings of dread stoked by the revived Hellenistic fatalism of his day. Warburg spent no small part of his scholarly life seeking to understand the dramatic coexistence of these cultural forces, which seemed to him inherently contradictory. Yet today, nearly a century after he wrote, this same basic historical conundrum still looms, a puzzle that many postmodern explorers of that distant age seem to have forgotten, or are perhaps reluctant to confront.

No less today than in the sixteenth century or in the early twentieth, the picture begs for illumination: how was it that a culture in which such powerful and pervasive astrological preoccupations flourished was the very same in which the evangelical movement found its cradle and home? But more to the point is another question: How is it that most major studies of the Reformation as a religious and social movement, including many published within the last generation, do not even begin to address this striking juxtaposition, and often include no more than one or two cursory mentions of belief in the force of the stars? Looking over the dozens of books, collections, and articles on early modern European culture that appear every year, especially those published in English, we might easily be led to conclude that the whole burgeoning sixteenth-century galaxy of star-inspired images, ideas, and practices had no implications at all for early Protestant religious sensibilities. And those studies that have taken the art of reading the stars as a subject of serious historical investigation have rarely encouraged us to consider the broader implications of their findings for the religious culture of the Reformation. It is almost as if we are looking at two parallel early modern cultural universes, evolving in close proximity but without touching one another in a more than superficial way. When we do find contacts acknowledged, we most often encounter the presupposition that we are dealing with two deeply conflicting conceptions of reality, which could coexist at best in a state of precarious truce.³

Directly challenging all such approaches, *Astrology and Reformation* argues that over the "long sixteenth century" (c. 1480–1620) in Germany, the symbolic worlds of astrology and evangelical faith were interrelated in

basic ways. The central theme of this book is that the prodigious propagation of astrological ideas and symbolism in the cities of the Holy Roman
Empire produced a star-saturated culture that helped both to prepare the
ground for Luther's evangelical movement, and to shape the distinctive
features of the German Reformation world through its first century. Most
Europeans of that time actually neither could nor wanted to make any
sharp separation between the lessons to be drawn from the physical heavens and the truths of the Christian faith, but in the towns of the Empire
these two aspects of experience evolved in an especially close and potent
dynamic. Before, during, and after the period of Luther's reforming career
(c. 1517–1546), burghers from Lübeck to Lindau were caught up in the science of the stars in ways that did much to mold their broader outlook,
including their religious perspective and their piety.[4]

Many of the ideas and a good deal of the evidence I present in this
book are far from new. In fact, along with Aby Warburg, numerous other
German cultural historians who wrote in the late nineteenth century and
the first half of the twentieth took seriously the pervasive influence of
astrological imagery and assumptions in the Reformation era. Few if any
followed the lead of Johann Friedrich, whose 1864 work *Astrologie und
Reformation* presented a wildly overdrawn argument linking astrological prophecies to both the Reformation and the Peasants' War.[5] But in
studies by Friedrich von Bezold, Willy Andreas, and Will Erich Peuckert,
among others, we find the recognition that the stars carried enormous
cultural weight that bore on many realms of experience, including religious outlooks, throughout that era.[6] These scholars well understood that
the Renaissance debate over stellar science, the intellectual quarrels so
famously spurred by Giovanni Pico's *Disputationes contra astrologiam divi-
natricem* (1494), had virtually no braking effect on the surging advance
of astrology that came with the spread of vernacular printing, especially
in the towns. They also acknowledged, at least in general terms, that this
advance could not be disentangled from the religious currents of the age.

With the "Luther Renaissance" of the early twentieth century, however, and especially after the Second World War, this recognition tended
to fade from the general historiography; meanwhile it remained all but
entirely absent from Anglo-American studies of the Reformation. Not that
astrology ceased to figure in work on other dimensions of life in the early
modern West. For a few art historians following in the path of Warburg,
as well as for a handful of historians of science such as Lynn Thorndike,
sixteenth-century interpretations of the heavens continued to draw serious

attention. Students of late medieval prophetic traditions also produced a notable body of work that took the subject into account.[7] But among scholars of the religious reforms and accompanying social transformations of that age, the subject dropped almost completely out of sight for several decades. To church historians it seemed irrelevant to the central issues of theology and ecclesiology; for many social historians the whole phenomenon was nothing more than a superficial froth of the imagination. One of the few branches of German Reformation studies in which the subject remained alive was that of scholarship on Philipp Melanchthon; it was simply impossible to overlook the deep and sustained interest of Luther's most important Wittenberg colleague in stellar study and prediction. But even here the topic long remained mostly marginal, often written off as a largely irrelevant sidelight in the thought world of this leading evangelical humanist.[8]

A thickening flurry of studies over the past couple of generations has in fact helped create a much-enriched picture of late medieval and Renaissance astrology. Those efforts that bear in any significant way on German Reformation, however, tend to be relatively specialized, without the sort of accessibility and broad resonance to be found, for instance, in Anthony Grafton's work on Girolamo Cardano (1501–1576), which allows us to see the life and labors of this legendary Italian stargazer in the context of sixteenth-century social networks, humanism, and explorations of the self.[9] Some of these recent explorations have focused on topics to which the older cultural historians had already devoted attention, such as the uproar over astrological predictions of a second universal flood to come in 1524. The discussion in this realm has followed some new vectors under the influence of work in communications theory and the concept of an emerging "public sphere."[10] In addition, scholars have ably expanded the inherited stream of attention to the astrological teachings of Melanchthon, providing essential insights into their importance in shaping Lutheran approaches to natural philosophy, medicine, theology, and education. Claudia Brosseder's detailed study of the Wittenberg astrologers stands out as an especially impressive achievement. These inquiries are related to a broader flowering in the history of science that has included attention to Reformation ideas and attitudes; here we should note in particular the dauntingly erudite work of Robert Westman. Taking another and still wider perspective, Euan Cameron's *Enchanted Europe* offers a valuable discussion of Protestant attraction to stellar science as a weapon in the campaign against medieval ritual superstition. On the whole, however, the insights afforded by these and other contributions have remained marginal in most approaches to the sixteenth-century movements of religious and social reform.[11]

One reason many historians have had trouble placing astrology together in the same picture with these movements is the continuing tendency to view the art of reading the heavens in terms of abstract polarities: Athens versus Alexandria, West versus East, the rational versus the mythical, science versus superstition, religion versus magic, free will versus fatalism, modern versus medieval. In Reformation studies, the most pervasive of all such polarities lies in the metahistorical assumption that astrology was essentially incompatible with, and hence ultimately irrelevant to, Christian belief: faith and fatalism were inherently at odds. This unhelpful preconception surfaces in a good deal of otherwise sophisticated scholarship. Related notions often creep in quietly but firmly: astrology was essentially ahistorical and opposed any vision of meaningful historical movement because of its attention to cyclical patterns, or the art was fundamentally unbiblical because it supposedly limited God's omnipotence. We often meet with the implication that Christians who put stock in stellar prediction were unconsciously caught up in a logical contradiction that more enlightened outlooks have long since rejected.

But human history has never been a logical affair, and what we conceive as contradictory was not necessarily so in the past. In order to avoid imposing a metahistorical logic, we need to resist the temptation to reduce either "astrology" or "Christianity" to an abstract category. In the sixteenth century there were indeed grounds for competition and conflict between certain religious doctrines and the science of the stars. But conflict was by no means inevitable, either in principle or in practice. Whether an astrologer stood in alliance with prevailing ecclesiastical teachings or in antagonism toward them depended entirely on particular beliefs, attitudes, and circumstances. And in premodern Europe, cases of cooperation were by all indications more prevalent than instances of conflict. The engagement of numerous medieval and Renaissance popes with stargazers became a popular theme years ago mainly because in modern eyes it was likely to appear scandalously incongruous. But the simple fact is that the overwhelming majority of those who made use of the art saw themselves as orthodox believers. The practice of interpreting the heavens was far more often propounded than attacked on Christian grounds.

The tendency to speak of astrology as if the term has an essential, superhistorical meaning has been especially persistent. An historian

of science might perhaps usefully denote it as "that branch of knowledge that aims at predicting and/or studying the power of celestial
bodies on earth," yet such a broad definition as this is not very useful
in historical analysis, and may even fail to capture some significant
dimensions.[12] Eugenio Garin refers to Renaissance astrology as "not
so much a technique of prediction as a general conception of reality
and of history," but here too we are left with the task of clarifying the
particular historical circumstances, assumptions, concepts, and practices in question.[13] Similar issues accompany the title of "astrologer."
The stereotype of the professional stargazer, dedicated mainly or even
exclusively to constructing horoscopes and making sweeping, delphic
predictions about the lives and deaths of kingdoms and great persons,
has at best a slim basis in early modern realities. It may come closest to fitting a handful of high-profile diviners such as the Frenchman
Nostradamus (1503–1566), the Italian Girolamo Cardano (1501–1576),
or even the Englishman John Dee (1527–1608). But such figures were
hardly typical; in fact they gained much of their fame as notorious
mavericks. The astrologers through whom the art gained exceptional
cultural weight in early modern Germany were mainly lesser-known
professors, physicians, surgeons, barbers, midwives, priests and pastors, calendar-makers, courtiers, and nearly endless ranks of amateur
practitioners.

Some historians of science have tried to define astrology at least
partly by separating it sharply from the supposedly scientific enterprise
of astronomy, arguing that by the sixteenth century if not earlier, these
disciplines were clearly distinguished: astronomy studied the planetary movements, while astrology interpreted their meaning. In this
view the mythological and nonmythological aspects of celestial observation were thus already identified in a way that facilitated the evolution of modern scientific cosmology. But most recent studies insist
that no such conceptual division was generally recognized before the
seventeenth century.[14] The Greek concept of *astrologia* had incorporated
both astronomy and astrology, and the terms continued to be basically
interchangeable. If any meaningful difference obtained, we might say
it was simply between the theoretical and practical aspects of a single
art. But as Stephen Vanden Broecke has pointed out, even this catego-
rization may be misleading, for both branches of stellar investigation
had practical as well as theoretical dimensions.[15] Down through the
Reformation era, the student of the stars was most commonly called

a "mathematician," one who both measured and read the celestial motions.

As a general set of cosmological concepts as well as a diagnostic and predictive art, astrology has always combined scientific and religious impulses. On the one hand, as historians of science have long understood, astrology in the ancient, medieval, and early modern worlds contributed in basic ways to an emphasis on precise observation, to the systematization of natural knowledge, to mathematical theory, and to concepts of natural law. Yet both as theory and as practical art it was also fundamentally religious in the sense that it sought to take the very pulse of the universe, to grasp the essential links between the individual and the cosmos, to orient the self in the world. According to C. G. Jung, "the first knowledge of psychic law and order was found in the stars," and however else we might judge Jung's engagement with astrology, we can hardly reject his discernment of an original spark to both understanding and reverence in the common urge to contemplate the heavens.[16]

Even as premodern astrology had inherent religious dimensions, premodern Christianity was never entirely without cosmological dimensions. Despite the general hostility of the ancient Church Fathers toward any and all forms of pagan divination, important elements of the ancient astrological world-picture had carried over into Christian thought. Scholars disagree about the status of the stellar art in the early medieval West; while the usual assumption has been that "scientific" astrology lay mostly dormant during this period, it is far from clear that this neglect resulted from the opposition of Church leaders. Valerie Flint argues that early medieval churchmen actually promoted a simplified form of astrology in order to combat more threatening forms of popular magic.[17] In any case, no formal prohibition could stop the new learned interest that was spreading by the eleventh century, and that exploded in the twelfth. With the growth of the schools and especially with the translation of key Arabic and classical texts into Latin, Europeans embarked on an insistent quest to develop a logical and comprehensive understanding of the universe, an astrologically founded cosmology. The most influential medieval scholastic thinkers, including Thomas Aquinas, contributed to this integrated, elegant, and enduring structure.

Naturally, medieval Christian astrology assumed both divine and human freedom. On the human side, this principle was summed up in the pseudo-Ptolemaic formula "astra inclinant, sed non necessitant" (the stars incline, but they do not force). Throughout the high and late

Middle Ages, most European astrological writers were careful to guard against the perceived dangers of the Arabic tradition, which leaned in the direction of an outright philosophical determinism. Disavowing the more extreme claims about natural causation, Christian thinkers felt generally comfortable subsuming the stellar art under theology, as a form of natural philosophy. For Aquinas and for the scholastic tradition generally, the heavenly bodies exercised a powerful control over terrestrial nature, but could not directly affect the human intellect or will. At the same time, Christian doctrine required principles of natural and moral order as well as of freedom; God's creation had a structure, after all. And the dangers of anarchy, worldly or spiritual, were at least as great as those of suffocating enslavement.

Thus for Christian thinkers the matter was not merely one of accommodating non-Christian ideas in suitably domesticated form. From Roger Bacon and Albertus Magnus to Dante and Chaucer, astrology was not a watered-down foreign import, but an integral element in the balance of reason and revelation. The Book of Nature idea, which saw Creation itself as a source of revelation complementing scripture, was rooted securely in orthodox medieval thought and imagery, although its full flowering would not come until the Reformation era. In the hands of a respected Churchman such as Pierre D'Ailly (1351–1420), the art could become a key instrument of Christian prophecy.[18] A good deal of religious iconography points not merely to accommodation or compromise, but rather to deliberate, positive syntheses of assumptions and ideas; images related to an astrological cosmology were often worked into medieval art in ways that were far from peripheral. Associations abounded between the planets and signs of the Zodiac on the one hand, and biblical figures and passages on the other. As Theodore Wedel recognized long ago, "after the middle of the thirteenth century a sane science had no longer anything to fear at the hands of the Church." And John North can assert without hesitation that in the later Middle Ages "the flirtation of Mother Church with astrology in all its guises was [both] a matter of the heart . . . and an affair of the head."[19]

On the other hand, basic questions remained about the boundary between legitimate and illegitimate astrological knowledge and practice. During the fourteenth and fifteenth centuries anything smacking of "pagan divination" was liable to suspicion among Church authorities. Since the planets had represented the gods of antiquity, who were actually demons in some Christian eyes, engagement with them in order to gain knowledge of the future could appear at the very least idolatrous, and at worst an alliance with Satan's minions. Increasingly, attempts to foresee particular human events were classed with demonic magic. The broader late medieval intensification of fears about magic and divination has received a good deal of study, especially from scholars interested in the intellectual and cultural conditions that nourished growing fears of witchcraft.[20] Among those who pursued knowledge of the stars, the main result lay in increasingly insistent efforts to draw a sharp line between defensible "natural" forms and prohibited "judicial" forecasts. To oversimplify: natural astrology was supposed to consider the planetary influences on the terrestrial elements, and was thus useful above all in medicine and meteorology, while judicial astrology sought to predict particular events, especially those that affected individual human lives.

A long-standing historical generalization holds that nearly everyone in late medieval and Renaissance Europe accepted the natural art, while judicial interpretations were almost always more or less suspect because they implicitly denied individual free will. Since early modern practitioners often used these categories, historians have sometimes adopted them as if they were unambiguous. Yet no clear divide was possible here. If predictions about the workings of terrestrial nature were permissible, how could the fates of individuals, who were partly natural creatures, be left entirely out of the picture? Where was one to draw the line between the general and the particular? Precisely how far could the astrologer go in making legitimate forecasts on the basis of observed natural patterns? This very broad grey area was the ground on which countless debates played out.

Eugenio Garin has shown that these Renaissance quarrels over sidereal science were essentially efforts to come to grips with unanswerable riddles of human nature and knowledge: "If human science is to be valid, iron laws of nature are necessary; but if universal and necessary laws of nature exist, how is free and creative human activity possible? If everything is already written in the heavens, what sense has the work of man?"[21] Astrology posed in stark and disturbing terms the inescapable paradox of freedom and order; the very possibility of knowledge assumes some sort of knowable order, but what is the point of knowledge if human beings, as parts of that order, can do nothing to change it? Inevitably we yearn to understand our world in terms of regularities, but as Immanuel Kant made clear in the eighteenth century, we are simply forced to acknowledge our existential liberty—our sense of being free—even if we cannot explain how it is possible. Astrology shared this central ambiguity with every other systematic effort to understand reality. It was closely parallel to the paradox that lay at the heart of Christian theology: If God is omnipotent then how are humans endowed with free choice at all, and whence arises sin? Because even the strictest theory of stellar determinism could never obviate the human need to make choices, the association of astrology with fatalism has always been—to use Tamsyn Barton's words—"something of a red herring."[22]

By a similar token, the habit of seeing the art as a form of premodern magic, or as inherently occultist or esoteric, has long distorted historical perceptions. At its worst, this tendency is driven by the assumption that the medieval and early modern debate over the art was essentially a struggle between Western enlightenment and oriental superstition. The main currents of astrological thought and practice had little to do with the dreams of the magical adept, but were grounded in relatively straightforward concepts of natural law. These ideas and methods were not magical for the simple reason that they were not operational; they sought not to manipulate or control nature, but merely to understand and adapt to it. While many magical schemes and rituals did build on a foundation of astrological principles, those principles themselves cannot therefore be called magical. Nor can we properly call the main currents occultist, since the basic reality of planetary influence was plainly manifest in the effects of the sun and the moon, and the common assumption was that the interpretative rules were derived from centuries of careful observation. Most medieval and early modern astrologers saw theirs as a natural rather than an occultist or esoteric pursuit, even though they never gained a full understanding of the forces at work.[23]

One major strain of Renaissance astrology did indeed have a pronounced magical aspect. The learned form of the art cultivated most famously by the Florentine Neoplatonist Marsilio Ficino (1433–1499) offered human beings potent tools for operating within the web of cosmic influences; it was thus a source of active power and even spiritual transformation. Building on the basic vision of a "great chain of being," a cosmic hierarchy that was negotiable by the worthy adept, Neoplatonic astrology offered potentially enormous freedom and agency to individuals. In this tradition the practitioner undertook not only to understand cosmic forces, but to employ them. It thus remained a principal foundation for magical theory and practice throughout the sixteenth and seventeenth centuries. Before the later sixteenth century, however, such Platonizing ideas gained relatively little traction north of the Alps. We can find them in a few thinkers such as Cornelius Agrippa, the Abbot Trithemius, and Paracelsus, but in their own day these figures stood well outside the astrological mainstream.

As the following chapters will illustrate, what prevailed in the swelling realm of popular astrology were the more straightforward, down-to-earth principles of Aristotelian/Ptolemaic cosmology, fortified with strong doses of Arabic doctrine. This form of the art was geared primarily to practical matters such as medical treatments, weather predictions, and the activities of everyday life. It did include horoscopes and other forms of prediction that bore directly on the fates of individuals, but the personal focus of such readings, not to mention the costs of private consultations, tended to limit their public visibility and social weight. At its most expansive this kind of astrology could be—and very often was—used to forecast events of political, world-historical, and prophetic or apocalyptic dimensions. But at every level this most common form of stellar study was fundamentally about understanding rather than agency. While its representatives were always careful to disavow fatalism, their endeavor presumed that earthly nature was for all practical purposes governed by universal planetary forces, which were finally an expression of providential power. Insight into those forces, at once natural and divine, was of the essence for the most public and powerful currents of sixteenth-century Christian astrology. What this sort of comprehension offered was mainly the possibility that humans might adapt to celestial influences, might maintain a certain equilibrium in a world where imbalance constantly threatened.

The complexities and ambiguities of the relationship between Christian teachings and astrology make it hard to avoid the conclusion that scholars have generally read too much into the Renaissance debate between supposed friends and foes of the art. For the most part, the disagreements were not over the legitimacy of the art per se, but rather over its limits. It was as little possible to reject all astrology in the sixteenth century as it would be to reject the discipline of economics in our own time; one might question particular models or predictions, but it was virtually impossible to doubt the basic validity of the questions. Even D. C. Allen, who wrote one of the classic pro and con studies, acknowledged that the lines between opponents and defenders were far from clearly drawn; the more moderate figures on each side shared a great deal of common ground.[24] Moreover, while the intellectual debates did accelerate rapidly from the late fifteenth century on, they had little or no effect on the even quicker and far more visible dissemination of astrological ideas and images in the public market. We therefore need to focus less on theoretical controversies than on this powerful movement, on the particular social and cultural contexts in which it flourished, and on its significance in the lives and outlooks of early modern people.[25]

In particular, questions about the relationship between the massive expansion of popular astrology and broader shifts in religious outlook and identity remain largely unexplored. While assumptions about inevitable conflicts between the metahistorical categories of astrology and Christianity are counterproductive, we can ask fruitful questions about how a booming aspect of lay culture bore on particular medieval traditions, practices, and assumptions. The religious landscape of the German towns was already shifting and volatile in the decades before Luther's appearance; it makes perfect sense to inquire into the ways in which the tremendous penetration of stellar science figured in this scene, and its broader effects as a pervasive feature of that culture through the sixteenth century. *Astrology and Reformation* represents my effort to bring this large complex of problems closer to center stage.

This study is grounded mainly in a large selection of the cheapest and most common of all early modern publications: over three hundred printed annual calendars (or "almanacs") and prognostications (or "practicas") from c. 1480 to 1620.[26] While my selection is only a fraction of the thousands of such ephemera issued in Germany over that period, it offers a substantial cross-section. These early ancestors of the modern yearly almanac, a genre that would eventually come to combine calendrical and astronomical data, astrological predictions, and various other "new, useful and entertaining matter," remained throughout this period the central media for the dissemination of astrological ideas and images to the public; indeed we have good reasons to see them as among the very broadest channels of publicity overall. "No kind of book under the sun," wrote the Lutheran mathematician Johannes Kepler, "sells so many copies, each and every year, as the calendars and prognostications of a celebrated astrologer."[27] From the late fifteenth century through at least the early seventeenth, the cities of the Empire were inundated with these mass printings; no other place in Europe came close to matching the production and distribution rates that obtained here. Often accompanied by dramatic woodcuts full of astrological symbols, these works were explicitly aimed at everyman, and their contribution to the spread of lay literacy and numeracy should not be underestimated.[28] Bearing on matters from personal health, to weather forecasts, to harvest prospects, to likely dangers for hometowns, princes, peoples, Christendom, and for the cause of the gospel itself, these ubiquitous printings supplied nearly endless grist for everyday conversation, even when their readers and hearers understood next to nothing of the science on which they were supposedly based. In addition to these most humble of printed sources, I have made use of scores of longer-range prognostications, popular planet books, comet tracts, weather treatises, medical manuals, theoretical and instructional books, polemical pamphlets, sermons, orations, and other writings in an effort to round out this picture. I have also attempted to synthesize much of the best secondary literature, both old and new.

The pattern of organization in what follows is partly chronological, partly thematic. Chapter 1 sets the scene by examining the massive proliferation of astrological ideas and images in the cities of the Holy Roman Empire during the fifteenth and early sixteenth centuries, and the main channels by which this process took place. No other setting in the Christian West, not even the sophisticated urban centers of Italy, experienced such a rapid and dramatic appropriation of this new language, which had far-reaching consequences. The second chapter argues that this vigorous dissemination of astrological symbolism promoted a newly universal and transcendent vision of God, offered German townsfolk a systematic and potentially liberating way to order their world, and thus worked to undermine medieval ecclesiastical assumptions about time, nature, divine action, and clerical authority.[29] Chapter 3 proposes that even as the popular astrologers sought to provide a liberating form of natural knowledge, by relentlessly drawing attention to future dangers they paradoxically expressed and fueled a widespread anxiety and a sense of imminent catastrophe among pre-Reformation burghers. The mushrooming astrological discourse of the era was the main spur to the infamous flood panic that came in the early 1520s, a great tide of apocalyptic expectancy that forcefully buoyed the reception of the early Reformation message.

To some biblically oriented reforming spirits, astrology represented a form of mental enslavement that went hand in hand with the spiritual blindness and perversity of the Roman Church. All the more striking, then, is the speed and ease with which influential followers of Luther appropriated the main genres of popular astrology, and came to regard the properly understood art as a godly gift for use in the daily lives of Christians. This is the central theme of Chapter 4. Luther's general distrust of the art would prove insignificant in comparison with the influence of Philipp Melanchthon, "the teacher of Germany," who led the establishment of a flourishing program of astrological learning at the Lutheran universities. Scores of Wittenberg-trained students carried these teachings to a broader public through the ever more ubiquitous almanacs and practicas, nearly perfect vehicles for preaching and propaganda in the service of a new order. As Chapter 5 seeks to show, this program of astrologically based order was essentially unique in Christendom. While among both Catholics and Calvinists clerical opposition tended more and more to restrict the art to elites, German Lutheran culture proved positively hospitable to the perpetuation and intensification of a popularized stellar science. In the second half of the sixteenth century a majority of Lutheran clerics indulged and even promoted a form of astrology that complemented their own biblical preaching and their vision of proper Christian discipline.

As the century progressed, the authors of the almanacs and prognostications worked to sustain a sense of prophetic certainty among evangelicals; their reading of the heavens became a basic means by which Luther's heirs sought to reassure themselves that an all-powerful God was fulfilling his plan for the world. Yet assurance in a positive mode proved difficult to sustain. Chapter 6 argues that even as popular astrology retained its mundane and largely local goals of bodily health, practical virtue, and social stability, this form of publicity manifested and reinforced a deepening historical pessimism among Luther's heirs, a growing disgust with a hopelessly problem-ridden social order. Indeed the "calendar men" played a significant role in perpetuating and intensifying the apocalyptic expectancy that was central to the German Reformation from the start. Conceived as a major instrument of prophetic warning for a world on the very eve of destruction and Judgment, the evangelical art of the stars helped cultivate a profoundly conservative and defensive outlook; it legitimized established authority as a final bulwark of order, but distrusted all new forms of political or social control. The culture of popular astrology thus did much to shape the original Lutheran confessional identity.

By the turn of the century, however, the synthesis of popular astrology and evangelical teaching was showing signs of strain. Soon it began to unravel, and by the era of the Thirty Years' War (1618–1648) it would collapse altogether. Chapter 7 undertakes to analyze the main factors that led to this breakdown by looking at the context of an early-seventeenth-century "crisis of piety" among Lutherans, a mounting showdown between mystical seekers and magical pansophists on one hand, and the voices of a new biblicism and skepticism on the other. Increasingly under assault from at least two broad fronts, the last preachers of a full-fledged evangelical astrology struggled to maintain the now-traditional combination of everyday orientation with urgent stellar and scriptural meanings. Their efforts faded in the face of a successful orthodox campaign to divorce Lutheran teachings from stellar prediction and prophecy, a movement reinforced by the chaos and disillusionment of war. Far from bringing the recovery of a presumably pure and original evangelical perspective, these developments marked a new departure, a major reorientation of Lutheran teaching and piety.

The synthetic worldview explored in this study represents a particularly distinctive sixteenth-century cultural pattern, neither medieval nor modern. Since postmodern historians have recognized the uniqueness of early modern outlooks in so many other ways, it seems strange that this aspect of German Reformation culture has continued in such general eclipse, especially among Anglo-American scholars. Few issues in the complex story of that movement have escaped close scrutiny, new approaches, and reinterpretation at the hands of historians, so that even the picture presented in basic textbooks has been expanded and enriched in basic ways. Ironically, one part of the scene that remains too much in the shadows, begging for new and brighter illumination, is the realm of the sun, moon, and stars.

I

From Athens to Augsburg

A Welcome Invasion

The general quickening of spiritual, intellectual, and artistic life in late medieval Europe included a momentous expansion of interest in astrological ideas and images. The science of the stars, revived and cultivated in the schools and universities since the twelfth century, began to penetrate the broader culture of Western Christendom and became for many Europeans a feature of everyday life. Hilary Carey rightly points out that in the period between 1300 and 1500 "astrology was transformed from a learned science into the basis of a popular movement," which had profound influence over notions of "cosmology, weather, medicine, the destinies of princes and nations, and the formulation of individual character."[1] With the expansion of lay literacy, to which in turn it gave a swift boost, and above all with the new mass medium of printing, the stargazer's art surged quickly beyond the bounds of scholarly and courtly circles.

As Aby Warburg recognized long ago, however, this surge was far more forceful in some European lands than in others. Warburg sought to map out the major migrations of the ancient stargazers' art down through the centuries, first from Athens to Alexandria, then with the Islamic scholars to medieval Iberia, thence later to Renaissance Florence, and on across the Alps to sixteenth-century Augsburg, Erfurt, and Wittenberg.[2] This picture, though surely oversimplified, was essentially accurate. In fourteenth-century Europe an astrological movement extending beyond the schools and the princely courts was most evident in Italy; in this as in other ways, the tide of obsession with ancient learning rose earliest in the land of Petrarch and Boccaccio. Yet only slightly later, soon after 1400, the German-language regions saw the beginnings of a reception at least equally remarkable. In both the German and the Italian cities, a still more dramatic takeoff of popular astrology would come with the advance of the new printing technology after midcentury. And we will see that by the time the Luther affair exploded in the 1520s this accelerating engagement had shifted its main weight to the north, to the towns of the Holy Roman Empire. Here the art would remain pervasive at all cultural levels throughout the Reformation era.

Even a quick glance at the sorts of materials that became available to German townsfolk in the first half of the fifteenth century reveals a remarkable advance of interest in the stars and in questions of celestial influence. At Ulm around 1405, Johannes Wissbier of Gmünd composed an early and influential vernacular digest of astronomical and astrological theory that survives in some thirty South German manuscripts. In the same period, vernacular translations of medieval astrological handbooks such as that of Michael Scotus began to appear.[3] Extracts from John of Sacrobosco's *De sphaera mundi,* the most widely used medieval cosmological textbook, made their way into shorter, more accessible writings. The German *Lucidarius,* a hugely popular encyclopedic work, incorporated sections that conveyed in simplified, nonmathematical form the fundamental elements of the Aristotelian/Ptolemaic world model, including the planetary motions in the Zodiac.[4] Moving well beyond the sphere of common inherited notions, these vernacular writings reveal a newly intense interest in systematic concepts with the power to explain a wide range of earthly phenomena. From the cities of southern Germany above all, we have evidence of heavy demand for such literature among the more educated laity.

Some of the strongest signs of a forceful new phase in the popularization of astrological knowledge come from vernacular songs and poems. Although it is likely that many of these versified works were originally performed at courts, they soon reached a broader lay public, disseminating concepts more sophisticated and powerful than anything inherited forms of folk belief could offer. We find here, for instance, the earliest articulation of a full-fledged doctrine of the "planetary children." The notion that each planet had its natural offspring, people who were born under its influence and who thus shared common characteristics, had been formulated only vaguely in ancient and medieval astrology. It now began to undergo an elaboration that added new dimensions and possibilities to the astrologer's tasks. In greatly oversimplified terms, Jupiter governed rulers (both worldly and spiritual);

Saturn held sway over old people, peasants, monks, and nuns; Mars over knights, soldiers, and smiths; Mercury over intellectuals, students, and creative artists; Venus over women, children, and poets; the moon over sailors, fishermen, travelers, and common folk. The sun's reign extended to all. Already by around 1400 the idea began cropping up in vernacular works probably meant for oral recital, such as the verses attributed to an anonymous "Monk of Salzburg." In seven stanzas this poem sang of the planets, their natures, and their children. Although the author included virtually no theory and no technical details at all, his direct associations between planetary powers and specific human types helped disseminate this potent conceptual scheme among lay-folk. Before long other popular lyrical works presented these connections in fuller and more detailed ways. A 1422 versified work by the South Tyrolean poet Oswald von Wolkenstein, for instance, amounted to an instructional text not only on the planetary progeny but also on the Zodiac, the terrestrial houses, and the nature and limits of stellar influence. Even if such songs and poems were originally performed mainly at courts, they were clearly aimed at a broader lay public.[5]

It was just at this point that the goal of reaching larger audiences was mightily furthered by the advent of the block book, which allowed a mass-produced union of image and text. No set of ideas was better suited to this medium than the teachings of the astrologers. Woodcuts and accompanying texts now worked to reinforce one another, pressing ideas about cosmic powers still more forcefully upon audiences extending well beyond learned and privileged chambers. The block-book form was crucial in promoting a new iconography of the planets and the planetary children, innovative depictions that that would become standard for centuries in Western astrology. This imagery had begun to circulate slowly at first in various early fifteenth-century manuscripts. But it surfaced with a splash in a work of around 1430 from Basel, a series of twenty-four woodcuts accompanied by detailed verses. Here each planet, as a naked human form, addressed the reader directly, giving its name, basic characteristics, related houses, and course through the heavens. Each went on to describe its earthly children, with their typical features and activities. A pronounced gulf between the celestial realm of the planets above and the earthly habitation of mortal creatures below conveyed a strongly dualist cosmology in which all power flowed downward. This iconography was not simply taken over from classical or Italian models; it was an original synthesis, with the newly explicit goal of popularizing this knowledge.[6]

Images of this kind soon found their way into larger composite works known as "planet books." Drawing on the teachings of masters such as Ptolemy, Aristotle, and various Arabic authorities, as well as more recent writers such as Sacrobosco, Guido Bonatti (c. 1230–1296), and Konrad von Megenburg (1309–1374), the typical planet book was a wide-ranging compilation of practical information presented within a broad astrological-cosmological framework. Most such collections taught a stripped-down version of Ptolemaic cosmology, presented basic calendrical data for each month including saints' and feast days, gave basic astrological rules for health and hygiene (especially for phlebotomy), explained the workings of the four bodily humors, described the inherent characteristics of each sign of the Zodiac, discussed the nature and powers of each planet, and listed "unlucky" (or "Egyptian") days on which certain important activities, including phlebotomy, were to be avoided.[7] This genre did not really take off until the middle decades of the fifteenth century, as the new woodcut depictions of the planets and their children became standard. Although most early manuscript copies were probably owned by physicians, the goal of these collections was to guide any literate layman through both the natural and the liturgical year with a variety of practical and devotional materials; indeed these handbooks touched on virtually all aspects of daily life.

Open didacticism was nearly everywhere in these texts, whether in manuscript or printed form. The cosmological section, for example, often stressed the sphericity of the Earth, arguing that if it appeared to be flat, this could only be owing to its immensity. Even mountains did not affect its basic shape, "any more than does a millet seed placed on the surface of a skittleball."[8] The didactic aspect included everything from the most mundane details of daily life to the very largest cosmological matters. The devotional element, though not always explicit, was equally pervasive. The lessons of nature spoke to the eternal wisdom and goodness of an all-powerful God; the cosmos was a mirror of divine glory and power. These works sought in various ways to integrate astrological and biblical lore, to find connections, for instance, between "unlucky days" and the less-happy events of the Old and New Testaments. Copies were often bound with the Bible or other devotional works; such juxtapositions mirrored the widely shared medieval assumption that the messages of nature and scripture were complementary. A printed planet book first appeared at Augsburg in 1481; this was the *Teutsch Kalender* of Johann Blaubirer, which went through no fewer than thirty-two subsequent editions before 1522. In

1508 a typical section offering folkloric rules for weather prediction first surfaced separately; known as the *Bauernkalender* or *Bauernpractica,* this humble genre saw motley variations throughout the sixteenth century.[9]

The planet books revealed a new level of systematization and sophistication in lay conceptions of nature and the heavens. At the same time, they contributed to an increasingly swift popularization of astrological images and concepts. But ultimately far more important in this regard were briefer and cheaper genres of the annual calendar and prognostication, explicitly practical works usually composed by a physician or university professor. While ephemeral texts of this general sort had begun to appear as early as the fourteenth century, not until the later fifteenth did they emerge as a ubiquitous feature of the urban cultural landscape in the German lands. In this as in other ways the printing industry, which sprouted earliest and grew the fastest in these towns, would radically accelerate developments that were already in motion.

Professors and Princes

Before wading into the paper avalanche of the annual ephemera, we need to take heed of the world of learning that sanctioned it and set it in motion. The most important sowers of a more powerful and pervasive astrological culture were those who studied and taught the science of the stars. University foundations had begun relatively late in German-speaking central Europe, but between the mid-fourteenth century and the early sixteenth, no fewer than fifteen new schools sprang up in this region—sixteen if we include the university of Crakow in Poland, which was tied closely both economically and culturally to the eastern parts of the Empire. In the scholastic tradition adopted by these schools, astrology had long been regarded as essential to the study of medicine in particular. But a knowledge of stellar influences had a respected place among the seven liberal arts as a branch of astronomy as well, and in many of the newer German foundations mathematics, or astronomy and astrology, came to enjoy equally high favor. Over the course of the fifteenth century the older and more prestigious Italian universities drew rising numbers of German students, especially those seeking advanced degrees in medicine or law; scholars who took Italian doctorates then typically recrossed the Alps to take up posts in the northern schools. For the study of astronomy and astrology, however, Crakow became the leading European institution by the latter half of the century; many aspiring German mathematicians studied here.[10] By this time several schools within the Empire, such as Vienna and Leipzig, were quickly gaining renown as centers for this sort of learning as well.

The waxing regard for mathematics in the universities during this period was closely related to the first stirrings of humanism in Germany. The relationship between humanism and the science of the stars was highly complex. On one hand, the recovery and study of ancient texts drew attention to skeptical views, cogent criticisms, and outright dismissals of the art by both classical and Christian thinkers. Giovanni Pico's *Disputationes* of 1494, the most famous Renaissance critique of astrology, drew heavily on such revived perspectives, and in turn did much to spread them. On the other hand, the ongoing recovery and study of ancient texts led to a more sophisticated understanding of many aspects of celestial science, and a desire to regain mastery of its evident complexities. There were, moreover, strong and deep links between the art and humanist interests. The whole theme of "renovatio," renewal, was closely related to astrological notions about temporal cycles, as in the revival that came with each new year.[11]

In Germany, humanism was never as alien to the universities as it had been in Italy. In the early phases of German humanism, the mathematician and the poet emerged as the men of learning most deserving of respect, and both were welcomed in the faculties. Scholars have long recognized the great importance placed on mathematics, which broadly conceived included cosmology and geography, in the German schools; these were to become "distinctively German sciences," according to Paul Joachimsen. The high status of these studies offered evidence of "that blend of imaginative speculation and technical application so typical of the Germans," one prominent example of which was Albrecht Dürer's "spiritual preoccupation with both the divine and the created." Joachimsen could even suggest that a complementary interest in theological and mathematical problems was a key feature of German humanism that set it apart from its Italian counterpart. The celebrated poet Conrad Celtis, a leader of early humanist literary culture north of the Alps, had eagerly studied astronomy and astrology at Krakow, and remained a lifelong devotee of the stellar art.[12]

Well before humanism took shape as a self-conscious movement in Germany, however, men of learning had grown excited over the recovery of ancient astronomical and astrological teachings, and the hope of clarifying them through exact observation. Most famous in this regard are the great scholars of Vienna, starting with Johannes von Gmunden (c. 1380–1442), "the founder of astronomy in the German lands," who not only brought close attention to the classical texts but also engaged in careful observation. Following in his train but far better known today were Georg Peurbach (1423–1461) and his student Johannes Müller von Königsberg, known as Regiomontanus (1436–1476). Peurbach was a leader of early efforts to illuminate the teachings of Ptolemy, and thus to reestablish what mathematical minds of the day conceived as a fully scientific astrology. His *Theoricae novae planetarum*, an impressive attempt to reconcile the Ptolemaic theory of epicycles with more recent observations and theories, would remain a central text for scholars well into the sixteenth century. Building on Peurbach's accomplishments, Regiomontanus would become Europe's most renowned astronomer before Copernicus, for whose insights he did much to prepare the way.[13] Regiomontanus's most productive years (1471–1475) were spent in Nuremberg, which thus gained its early reputation as a beacon of mathematical learning. Here with the help of the wealthy merchant and scholar Bernard Walther he established not only an observatory, but also his own press for the publication of astronomical works.[14]

Regiomontanus was the first scholar to issue technical yet relatively accessible astronomical and calendrical works that supplied powerful new tools for astrological prediction. His booklet-form *Kalender*, appearing in 1474 in German, presented astronomical data covering three lunar cycles of nineteen years (1475–1532). Reprinted many times, this compilation remained a key source for stellar forecasters over several generations; it helped open the way for physicians and other practitioners to engage in their own reckonings, on the basis of expert professional calculations, for the purpose of medical treatments, weather predictions, personal horoscopes, or general planning.[15] Regiomontanus himself was a producer of prognostications as well as a caster of nativities; for him as for all students of the heavens at that time, astronomy and astrology could not be separated in any practical sense. The weight of his reputation over the following generations would be difficult to overestimate; his name and achievements would take on immense importance in the eyes of those who took pride in German intellectual culture.

Efforts to propagate essential astronomical data would be pushed further by scholars such as Jacob Pflaum of Ulm and Johannes Stöffler of Tübingen, who issued *Ephemerides* or astronomical tables covering several decades to come; these publications included instructions for the practical use of their projections, and were marketed with tremendous success. Pflaum's German *Kalender* of 1478 amounted to a sophisticated planet book, packed with the basics of astrological, calendrical, and medical knowledge.[16] Johannes Stabius, who worked in the early sixteenth century to revive the great Viennese astronomical tradition, published various paper "instruments," graphic tools intended mainly to facilitate the calculation of horoscopes. His successor Andreas Perlach, who like Stabius lectured extensively on the use of the almanac, produced an instructional guide for the horoscopic art and its everyday applications.[17] Johannes Essler of Leipzig issued in 1508 a Latin *Speculum Astrologorum*, a work fully in the scientific line of Peurbach and Regiomontanus, that not only provided instruction but argued forcefully for the full complementarity of mathematics and theology. These and other prominent German astronomers of the pre-Reformation era contributed directly to the articulation and dissemination of a natural-philosophical vision that was inherently astrological.[18]

As initiators of a campaign to reform celestial science by returning to its purest ancient forms, humanist astronomers also worked with printers to edit and publish the writings of classical astrological authorities. While important ancient texts had been studied in the schools since at least the thirteenth century, the fifteenth century brought a host of new recoveries. The appearance of both newly and not-so-newly recovered texts in standardized printed editions forcefully propelled the circulation of key tools and concepts. As early as 1472 Regiomontanus produced an edition of the verse-form *Astronomicon* of the Roman writer Manilius. Ptolemy's *Quadripartitum* first went to press in 1484, along with the pseudo-Ptolemaic *Centiloquium*. The earliest edition of Ptolemy's famous *Almagest* was a Latin abridgement completed by Regiomontanus already in the 1460s, but not published until 1496; it long remained the standard reference for Ptolemaic principles.[19] Although humanistic reformers tried to stand aloof from the medieval Arabic writers whose works had gained such high regard among earlier schoolmen, in the 1480s and 1490s publishers attuned to the market produced texts by major Arab authorities such as Albumasar and Haly Abenragel. Most influential overall was no doubt Albumasar's *De magnis conjunctionibus (On the Great Conjunctions)*, first printed by Erhard Ratdolt at Augsburg in 1489. This work served to broadcast the idea that periodic conjunctions of the upper planets, namely Jupiter and Saturn, had profound importance and could in fact be used to understand the unfolding of world history. Many classical and Arabic works were first published in Italy, but by far the most active early printer of such books south of the Alps was Ratdolt, who worked for almost a decade in Venice (1476–1486) before returning to set up shop in his native Augsburg. Ratdolt in fact nearly monopolized the market in Latin texts in this field until well into the 1490s.[20]

Almost as eagerly consulted as these classical and Arabic volumes were editions of various high- and late medieval sources. Always in high demand, John of Sacrobosco's *De sphaera mundi* appeared in print as early as 1472. Ratdolt issued in 1490 a much-admired treatise on the concordance of astrology and theology by the French churchman Pierre D'Ailly (1350–1420). A major work by the Italian Guido Bonatti (c. 1220–1290), *Decem tractatus astronomiae*, came out at Augsburg in 1491.[21] While learned works such as these were hardly aimed at a large lay readership, their new availability in print was both cause and sign of a rapidly intensifying astrological discourse, which would soak quickly into the common life of the German towns through ever-widening channels of mass publication.

Until the late fifteenth century, the most prominent employers of the astrological and medical expertise cultivated in the schools and universities had been the princely courts. In the high Middle Ages the court astrologer was already a well-established figure, but the practice of patronizing and consulting stargazers became far more common in ruling orbits by the fifteenth century, and nowhere was this more obviously true than in the Empire. Here the most prominent example was the Habsburg court at Vienna, where astrologers received especially generous and consistent support and encouragement from the emperors Frederick III (r. 1452–1493) and Maximilian I (r. 1493–1519). But such consultations grew ever more frequent at a swarm of ducal, electoral, and smaller princely and ecclesiastical courts as well. At Heidelberg, for instance, Johann Virdung von Hassfurt (1463–c. 1538), the most celebrated astrologer in Germany by around 1500, was employed by the Elector of the Palatinate. In this case as in most others, the prince's astrological consultant also served as his physician; very often he held a university post, as Virdung did at Heidelberg.[22]

Inevitably, rulers looked to their court astrologers not only for medical expertise but for other sorts of insight and advice as well; in fact the stargazers' role as political consultants stands among the most often noted and studied aspects of their art in the medieval and early modern eras. The ongoing expansion of princely patronage naturally helped to inflate the public status and renown of astrologers. But the process of reputation-building would gain momentum above all through the explosion of printed calendars, prognostications, and other relatively humble astrological works that began in the decades prior to 1500. These mass-produced forms were aimed primarily not at princes, but at the urban layman.

Mass Media

While elements of a systematic astrology that went well beyond customary folk beliefs had made definite inroads into the world of the German burgher before Gutenberg's breakthrough, this process was speeded exponentially by the business of printing. The instruments and data supplied by scholars such as Regiomontanus, together with the published versions of classical, Arabic, and scholastic texts, marked one step in this development. But only through the mass production of cheap practical works could the revived systematic science of the stars begin to influence the very fabric of life among layfolk in the central European cities and towns. Decades ago, students of early printing argued that the rise of typographical culture "changed the channel" in which Europeans thought, from mainly oral and communal to mainly visual and individual.[23] More recent studies have all but buried this argument under the weight of a thousand qualifications and nuances, yet the presumption that truly profound changes in outlook followed from the introduction of moveable metal type has rightly survived. The blizzard of astrological broadsheets and pamphlets that swept over central Europe in the pre-Reformation era played a largely unexplored role in effecting those changes.[24]

The annual almanacs and prognostications were by all indications the most common printed vernacular materials during the half-century before the explosion of the Reformation movement; indeed from the very start they were basic staples of the business. These works were essentially practical tools that employed the symbols and concepts that the planet books had already done much to popularize. While they sometimes included instructional passages, on the whole they assumed a basic level of astronomical and astrological knowledge. In general they were more directly informed than the planet books by the mathematical learning of the universities, and thus demanded a somewhat more technical understanding. Both forms came to include a greater variety of information and interpretive materials as time passed. These annual works would far surpass the larger planet books in popularity by 1500, and would soon nearly displace them altogether. While the older-style compendia would survive and even enjoy a resurgence by the 1530s, they lacked the nearly limitless market potential of the yearly calendars and forecasts.[25]

The derivation of the term "almanac" is uncertain, but most likely went back to the Arabic *al manach*, literally a counting or reckoning. Most of the earliest printed broadsheet almanacs were not really calendars as we tend to think of them. While they did typically begin by giving data for the coming year such as the date of Easter, the golden number (indicating the year's place in the nineteen-year lunar cycle), the dominical letter (a letter from A through G determined by the first Sunday of the new year), and the solar number (denoting the year's place in a calendrical period of twenty-eight years), they did not place each day in an ordered series. Rather, these were essentially lunar tables, indicating the times of new and full moons throughout the coming year. The central concern was to determine the best times for phlebotomy, or therapeutic bleeding, but the potential uses for the data supplied were much more varied. Almost always the days and times of expected eclipses for the coming year were indicated; these general harbingers of bad fortune also brought dangerous times for any medical treatment or bathing. Since their timing varied according to location, each calendar edition was reckoned for a particular city or region. The eclipses in particular were often illustrated with woodcuts designed to catch the eye.[26]

The earliest surviving printed astrological calendar came from Gutenberg's press at Mainz around 1457; it was probably intended to aid lay stargazers in reckoning horoscopes. We also have a German phlebotomy calendar for 1462, produced by Ulrich Han at Vienna. But only after 1470 did the printed broadsheet form emerge in force.[27] The genre's growth was obviously spurred in part by the newly published data made available by scholars such as Regiomontanus, but the calendar writers appealed more often to the mainstays of classical and Arabic learning: Aristotle, Ptolemy, Albumasar, and Avicenna, among others. The basic form soon underwent considerable elaboration. From the 1480s on many calendars began to list every day of the year, and noted the coming planetary conjunctions as well as eclipses, thus including Zodiacal as well as lunar data. While editions were calculated for particular locations, some authors began to achieve broader appeal by including data for several cities, or by showing how users could make adjustments for other regions. Jakob Honiger's 1494 calendar gave lunar reckonings not only for Erfurt, but for nine neighboring towns as well.[28] Increasingly these works offered brief weather forecasts and addressed matters of general husbandry, indicating propitious times for sowing, planting, reaping, butchering, bathing, purging, fishing, cutting hair and nails, pulling teeth, weaning children, and the like. In fact the calendar had uses bearing on virtually all aspects of daily life, including traveling, building, and beginning new enterprises. In an astrological calendar that incorporated the Christian ideal of love for one's neighbor, the Zurich city physician Eberhard Schleusinger (d. 1499) even indicated the best days and hours in which to begin friendships and make social connections.[29]

As the scope of the astrological reckoning and forecasting in the calendars expanded, graphic images became more elaborate. Typical illustrations began regularly to include not only eclipses but also the well-known zodiacal man, illustrating the correspondences between the parts of the body and the twelve signs. But other graphic elements, such as new year's greetings depicting the Virgin with the Christ child, evolved notably as well. Shortly after 1500 the broadsheets were commonly enlarged into a two-sheet form, which made it easier to add an even wider array of practical information, illustrations, and textual matter, including fuller warnings about times of adversity and suffering to come. Only later, in the mid-sixteenth century, would these broadsheet calendars be replaced in Germany by booklet-form calendars, which offered separate pages for each month, and which typically left room blank for daily notes by the owner. This highly popular form would become known as the *Schreibkalender*.[30]

Along with the broadsheet calendar, the closely related genre of the printed "practica," a more comprehensive prognostication for the coming year, began to take shape in the 1470s. As their manuscript precursors were highly varied, so the first printed examples of these small booklets showed little uniformity of organization; indeed one relatively early edition has been called "an exercise in chaos." The 1480s brought some significant movement toward standardization, especially through the efforts of the most prominent member of the first generation of popular authors, the Leipzig professor Wenzel Faber von Budweis. Not until the 1490s, however, did the practica take on the basic common format it would retain for many decades to come. As Jonathan Green has shown, it was Faber's younger contemporary Johann Virdung, the author of over sixty annual practica editions, who did more than any other astrological writer to establish the prevailing model.[31]

The typical *Practica Teutsch* for any given year was a simple quarto pamphlet of around eight leaves. A title page identified the year and the author, depicted the ruling planets for the coming twelve months in human forms similar to those in the planet books, and often cited the city for which the work was mainly reckoned. Following a prefatory letter to a prince, noble, or city council, and sometimes a preface to the reader, an early section explained the ruling planets and expected astronomical events such as eclipses and conjunctions. Then in no particular order came short chapters on the outlook for general fertility and the harvest, illness and health, war and peace, and each of the seven groups of planetary children, as well as the expected fortunes of various princes, lands, cities, and social classes. Many practicas continued to offer predictions for the three great religious followings: Christians, Jews, and Muslims (generally called "Turks," "Saracens," or simply "heathens"). Often last but certainly not least came the calendar of lunar phases with weather forecasts through the four seasons, and sometimes the work was rounded out with a short conclusion. The lengths and arrangements of these various sections were highly variable.

At the simplest level, the annual practica appealed to the fundamental need for a secure orientation in nature and in time: what conditions would prevail over the coming year, and what dangers and promises awaited in the months immediately ahead? Here, just as in the astrological calendars, the primary purposes were practical; the data provided a basis on which to plan in accordance with natural influences and conditions. But if astrological medicine and hygiene were the core purposes of the calendars, the central attraction of the typical German practica was undoubtedly the weather forecast. Astrometeorology was certainly among the very earliest applications of celestial study, going back to the Babylonians. Yearly meteorological predictions in manuscript form had circulated in Italy at least as early as the later fourteenth century; the earliest we have from Germany date from the early to mid-fifteenth century.[32] With the printed practica, however, expectations and speculations about the state of the earthly atmosphere in the coming year found a powerful new vehicle, which made them a central channel in the quickly broadening stream of mass publicity.

Keith Thomas probingly observed that in premodern society "it was not possible for a weather forecast to remain simply a weather forecast."[33] Meteorological interest had a close and natural connection with cosmology, thus too with larger questions of social and political order, and ultimately with spiritual and prophetic realms. Nearly everyone shared an interest in predictions about the weather, the crops, sickness, and health; but one could hardly separate such matters from questions about war and peace, and how various cities, lands, and classes of people could be expected to fare. These booklets ranged widely over human subjects, from the Erfurters to the Bavarians, from cardinals to merchants, from women to the common folk, from the pope to the King of Poland. Inevitably, conjectures about what was in store for a city or region, for the high clergy, or for all Christendom drew sprinklings of prophetic material from the Bible or from medieval traditions; for even among sober physicians, the science of the stars could not be separated from larger questions of meaning. Moreover, the forecasts of the practica writers would grow more threatening over time, more and more often presenting dire warnings of disasters to come. Such features helped insure a virtually irresistible product. No wonder that by the turn of the century the practicas of the leading writers often went through several printing runs, and that pirated editions began to pop up. Competition to exploit the popular demand for such works grew more and more intense; printers' agents and booksellers hawked editions by the best-known authors in cities throughout Germany, and even in the era of incunabula translations for publication elsewhere were not unknown.[34]

The astrological calendars, prognostications, and related publications reached a larger audience in the German cities than anywhere else in pre-Reformation Europe. Remarkably, in the period before 1520 we find virtually no examples of broadsheet almanacs from Italy, France, Spain, the Netherlands, or England; nowhere outside the German-speaking lands did this form become established, while within the Empire it became all but ubiquitous. The German towns also became leaders in the early production of annual prognostications. It appears that only in Italy were more of these works published during the first decades of printing. But the balance would soon shift; and as we will see, other circumstances would tend to dampen the effects of stellar forecasting on lay culture south of the Alps.[35]

Because calendars and practicas counted among the most ephemeral of all printed works, they were also among the most likely to disappear forever. Without doubt printers produced far more editions in the late fifteenth and early sixteenth centuries than survive; oblivion likely claimed an especially high percentage of works issued in the years immediately after 1500. Nineteenth- and twentieth-century archivists rescued every printed incunabular scrap they could find, but generally ignored similar materials from subsequent decades. For this reason we should take with several grains of salt the claim that a market crash came early in the new century. In many cases we have no more than a small handful of examples from writers who in all likelihood produced them serially over many years.[36] Printers often used the paper from outdated calendars and practicas in the bindings of larger books, from which traces of lost originals sometimes still peek out at modern scholars. Once the year for which it was reckoned was over, a work of this sort was as likely as not to end up kindling flames in a fireplace, or in crumpled, reeky pieces at the bottom of a latrine.

We know of around 390 single-leaf astrological calendars from before 1501. If we add the more than 210 attested annual prognostications from Germany in this period, we reach a total of some 600 works.[37] Since these ephemera were so prone to be lost altogether, a very conservative estimate of the actual number published might add half again as many. If we make another conservative guess of a thousand copies per issue on average, we can conclude that within a single generation before 1501 nearly a million copies had circulated in the German towns; for the period before 1520, the likely total would be multiples higher. These rough figures do not include the many editions of calendars or prognostications for more than one year. Nor do they include the many other forms of literature that contributed to the phenomenal intensification of a popular astrological culture.[38]

The numbers from Germany dwarf those from almost every other European region. Undoubtedly one reason for the early predominance of German cities in this realm was simply that printing in almost all its forms spread most rapidly here. In France, for example, the slow growth of a popular press naturally retarded the development of the almanac. Closer clerical control over publication as well as narrower channels of distribution restricted the dissemination of astrological ideas and imagery. The famous Simon de Phares (c. 1440–c. 1499) may have had a thriving private practice as well as dealings with the king himself, but like other French stargazers he failed to exploit the new media in promoting his art.[39] Well into the sixteenth century, most French almanacs were not cheap works aimed at a mass market. Across the Channel even fewer avenues allowed astrology to penetrate the larger culture. Among the earliest writers of annual printed prognostications in England was William Parron, who worked for Henry VII between c. 1490 and 1503. Yet Parron inspired few imitators, and sixteenth-century England has justly been called "an astrological backwater."[40] Only toward the end of that century did the art receive much attention here, and its great popular flowering did not come until after 1600. Most of the earliest English vernacular astrological publications were in fact translations of continental works. Among the popular writings that made the crossing by 1500 were annual prognostications by members of the Laet family, a line of highly successful Antwerp astrologers. Joannes Laet may have issued his first booklet of this sort before 1470, and he soon became the best known among several popular writers in the Low Countries. Annual practicas under the Laet name continued to appear into the mid-sixteenth century, and regularly made their way into English. The Laet publications represent the most notable continuous tradition of this sort outside the German-speaking lands in pre-Reformation northern Europe.[41]

Nowhere except in Italy can we find a market in astrological publications comparable to that of the German cities during this early period. Here, printed prognostications multiplied quickly in the late fifteenth century, and probably outnumbered works of the same sort issued in Germany. But by the first decades of the sixteenth century, German printers were apparently taking the lead. More important is that the proportion of vernacular prognostications was evidently much higher in the North than in Italy. Of some 390 known German calendars from before 1501, almost 75 percent were aimed at non-Latinate readers. Even before 1480, in the very first decades of the commercial press, over half the known broadsheet calendars were in German. As we have seen, the printing of annual practicas was in general a little slower to gain momentum, but of something over 200 works of this sort from German-speaking lands in the fifteenth century, well over half were directly available to a non-Latinate readership.[42] The already high proportion of calendars and practicas published in the vernacular continued to increase after 1500; German editions became more and more predominant. Here was another reason for the apparent drop in the number of practica editions at this time: many authors simply stopped bothering with a Latin version, and concentrated fully on the popular market.

These trends become all the more striking if we realize that among all books of any kind printed in this period, the great majority were in Latin. In Germany, for instance, Latin texts comprised over 80 percent of all works published before 1501. Studies of early sixteenth-century German popular pamphlets (a designation that has traditionally excluded the astrological ephemera) show that only from 1520 on did vernacular writings begin to outnumber Latin ones.[43] We lack bibliographical data for Italy comparable to what we have for the German lands, especially regarding more ephemeral forms, but we do have a large collection of Italian practicas from the library of Christopher Columbus and his heirs, avid gatherers of astrological and astronomical publications. On the basis of this major cluster of some 250 editions from around 1490 to 1530, it appears that south of the Alps, vernacular works did not outpace Latin ones until the second or third decade of the sixteenth century. Thus while more astrological practicas may have been published in Italy before 1520, far fewer of them were aimed at a truly popular market. Even if we ignore the largest genre of all—namely the broadsheet almanacs produced exclusively in the cities of the Holy Roman Empire—we can hardly escape the conclusion that astrological symbols and ideas had far broader channels through which to reach layfolk in Germany than in any other part of Christendom during these pre-Reformation decades.[44]

The production of almanacs and prognostications was also much more decentralized in Germany than in Italy and other lands. To a certain extent this was true of the German printing industry as a whole; numerous presses were established in smaller cities, each publishing at least in part for a local market while looking for larger opportunities. The main centers of calendar and practica production were the famous towns of the early printing industry: Augsburg, Nuremberg, Strasbourg, Ulm, Leipzig, and Erfurt were among the most notable. The first leader in this realm was Augsburg; by 1500 Nuremberg was even more active, and would remain dominant for more than a century thereafter. Other places of early production included Reutlingen, Bamberg, Basel, Frankfurt am Main, Passau, Heidelberg, Regensburg, Munich, Lübeck, Mainz, Magdeburg, Eichstatt, Würzburg, and Ingolstadt. This list is far from exhaustive; in fact many towns not known as particularly prolific centers of early printing saw the early production of calendars and practicas, a point that helps to confirm our picture of widespread demand in Germany. At least sixty-nine German printers of these annual predictive works were active between 1470 and 1501; they worked in no fewer than twenty-five cities.[45]

The demand included other forms of astrological literature, most of which had circulated, like the annual works, in manuscript or block-book form well before the quantum leap in production that came with printing. We have noted the role of the planet books, which instructed laymen in a broad range of natural doctrines and practices. Cheap printed versions of these collections, along with popular works such as the *Lucidarius* and

Konrad von Megenburg's *Buch der Natur,* were in wide circulation by 1500. Most tracts on health and hygiene, including works on the new "French disease" (syphilis) as well as the plague, included astrological analyses; so too did broadsheets and pamphlets on natural wonders. Historical and chronological works such as the famous *Nuremberg Chronicle* of Hartmann Schedel (1494) often incorporated astrological references. And finally this picture needs to include works that combined astrology with ancient and medieval prophetic traditions, presenting forecasts that bore on issues of profound consequence for the fate of whole peoples and indeed the entire world. Such prophetic dimensions were by no means entirely absent from the annual ephemera, but they took top billing in a tome such as Johann Lichtenberger's sensational bestseller of 1488, the *Pronosticatio,* then as now the most famous astrological work of the pre-Reformation era. All these types of publication worked together with the massive spread of the calendars and practicas to promote a star-saturated atmosphere in the cities of the Empire.

Authors, Printers, and Publics

Just who were the publicists who showered the German towns with a popularized science of the stars? Most of these writers hardly fit today's usual image of the Renaissance astrologer, a priest of occult science living a dangerous, roller-coaster life of adventure and intrigue. The stereotypical portrait formed from such flamboyant and controversial figures as the Frenchman Nostradamus, the Englishman John Dee, and Italians such as Luca Gaurico and Girolamo Cardano continues to influence even scholarly approaches to premodern astrology. Among pre-Reformation figures, perhaps the one who fits this stereotype most closely was the nearly legendary Lichtenberger (c. 1440–1503). Rising from an obscure background in the Rhine Palatinate, this ambitious interpreter may have attended the court of the emperor Frederick III in the 1470s, but for most of his career he served in a humble pastorate. In 1488 he made an enormous splash with his *magnum opus,* a large folio volume published in both Latin and German versions. Except for a small handful of earlier works such as the Gutenberg Bible this was the original European blockbuster, going through no fewer than eighteen editions in Germany and another twelve in Italy by 1530.[46] A grab-bag of ostensibly planetary forecasts about terrible changes to come, late medieval prophetic visions of trial and triumph, and imperial propaganda, the *Pronosticatio* unquestionably had an important role in advancing a rising tide of prophetic expectancy and a sense of social crisis over several decades. Yet its importance is easy to overestimate, and it would be misleading to see it as representing the predominant pattern in German astrological thinking or publicity. In fact the book owed much of its great success to the culture of popular astrology that was already flourishing through the humbler annual calendars, prognostications, and astrological handbooks.

Less obviously colorful than Lichtenberger, but more representative of common trends, were the university professors and city physicians who seized upon the new commercial opportunities opened up by regular printings for the urban market. Not a few of these men wore multiple hats, combining the roles of professional scholar, court physician-astrologer, urban practitioner, and mass publicist. Strikingly enough, though, in the very first years of printing the personal identities of contemporary astrologers played a very limited role in the marketing of practical annual works; these names would have meant little to most purchasers. In fact, with the exception of a few figures such as Jobst Hord, "Master at Augsburg," most of the earliest calendar authors remained anonymous; the reputation of the writer was entirely subordinate to that of the revered Greek and Arab scientific authorities. These works often recommended their contents with an invocation of unquestioned authority: "Aristotle tells us," "Avicenna says," or the like. Increasingly in the last ten to fifteen years of the century, however, especially with the rapid emergence of the annual practica, calendar authors began to identify themselves, to give their names a distinguishing and advertising role.[47]

Since the main purposes of the calendars had to do with astrological medicine, it is no surprise that physicians ranked among their most common early producers. Often these men held appointed posts as city physicians. By the late fifteenth century many local councils had made it a standard practice to name at least one official *physicus*, who served as an overseer to the city's various health workers such as surgeons, barbers, and midwives. The responsibilities of the position also typically included providing medical diagnoses and prescriptions, helping to establish and enforce sanitary regulations, and making forensic judgments. With the swift multiplication of competing calendars for the same year, conflicting calculations and predictions led local governments to impose regulations about which one medical practitioners were to follow. Thus especially in the larger cities, an appointed physician was assigned to issue a sanctioned calendar in order to supply regular guidance to local barbers and citizens in the correct timing and administration of various treatments.[48] Increasingly, too, city governments and territorial princes came to expect a yearly practica to complement the official calendar, and this task likewise often fell to a city physician. Yet formal duties of this sort were rarely the main impetus to the production of calendars and practicas, which authors most often undertook willingly and independently.

Just like the calendar-makers, practica writers regularly invoked the authority of Greek and Arabic authorities. These were the masters; "if they erred, so also do we err," wrote the Cologne stargazer Sigismund Fabri in a forecast for 1496. But unlike the calendars, the practicas generally appeared under an author's name right from the start. The sorts of predictions they offered required a higher order of interpretation; hence they fell more obviously within the bailiwick of credentialed experts. An astrologer's name gained special drawing power when he could claim association with a university or a court, and accordingly the figures who gained greatest prominence by the 1490s were those who could boast professorial status, princely patronage, or both. Among the early writers who advertised a university connection was John of Glogau (d. 1507), a mathematician at Crakow whose lectures drew a young mathematician named Nicholas Copernicus.[49] Practica title pages in particular tended to flaunt an author's faculty status whenever possible. Martin Pollich von Mellerstadt (d. 1513) billed himself "doctor of three faculties" at Leipzig. Pollich was supposed to have drawn up the horoscope for the 1502 foundation of the University of Wittenberg, where he served as the first rector. His prestige benefited as well from his role as a consultant to the Saxon Elector, and he would eventually serve as personal physician to Frederick the Wise.[50]

Pollich typified an emerging breed of scholars and physicians who pursued what John North calls "a new profession of astrologer to Everyman."[51] The growing predominance of the vernacular in their writings reflected an increasingly deliberate program of popularization; in fact these yearly publications in the everyday tongue represented the first printed materials addressed explicitly to the "common man." Wenzel Faber's practica for 1492 helped define the trend, announcing its design for the use and benefit of the common man and its aim to serve the "common good." Johann Engel offered his predictions for 1497 in praise of God, to honor the good name of the University of Ingolstadt, and "for the benefit of the common people."[52] Most historians concur that such terms were generally meant to apply to the middling classes of the towns rather than to the peasants or the lower urban orders. Still, the authors and publishers of these cheap ephemera managed to reach an audience far larger than any before, and it is hard to doubt that in so doing they created a powerful new stimulus to basic literacy and numeracy.

Already in the 1470s printers in many German towns regarded the yearly astrological guides as a guaranteed cash cow, an almost sure-fire way of getting a start in the business and assuring a base-level income. The famous Anton Koberger of Nuremberg, for instance, got his press established partly by issuing such works; he was later able to produce the sort of humanistic writings that were his main interest.[53] By the following decade printers in the major publishing centers were scrambling for shares of a swelling market; indeed Koberger soon abandoned this humble if remunerative enterprise to energetic competitors such as Johann Sensenschmidt, Friedrich Creussner, Hans Folz, and Peter Wagner. Among the most active early printers of calendars was Gunther Zainer, whose business did much to make Augsburg the leading center of early almanac production, but who likewise faced stiff competition there from Johann Baemler, Anton Sorg, Johann Blaubirer, and Erhard Ratdolt, among others.[54]

In producing these ephemera most printers were not much worried about aesthetic niceties; they cranked out these works quickly and cheaply, and priced them to sell. In the early sixteenth century a typical broadsheet calendar cost about six German pence, about the price of a couple of chickens; a short quarto pamphlet of a few leaves might have sold for as little as three to four pence, perhaps a quarter of the typical day-laborer's wages.[55] At these rates, printers needed to sell in massive volume in order to turn a profit. We have limited evidence about the size of the typical print run, but it appears likely that editions of a thousand copies or more were not unusual. Pirated editions sold even more cheaply, despite efforts to prevent them. Local governments prosecuted unauthorized printing operations when they were discovered, and a famously successful writer such as Johann Virdung might even obtain an Imperial privilege for his annual ephemera, but in both cases the effects were minimal. The demand was so great that by the 1490s an aspiring humanist such as Thomas Murner could compose an annual practica as a quick and easy way to make a name for himself while still cutting his literary teeth.[56]

That the market witnessed early and open competition is clear from a public row that erupted in 1489 between the Leipzig professor

Wenzel Faber, whose annual forecasts were a hot commodity in the Saxon towns, and another figure who had begun publishing practicas in the city, Paul Eck. Some years earlier, Faber had already publicly criticized the predictions of his colleague Martin Pollich, now he had come to regard the outsider Eck as an especially unwelcome upstart and threat. The two writers denounced one another in a series of printed broadsides that traded accusations of greed, dishonor, and incompetence. The university faculty predictably sided with its own, and helped Faber fight off Eck's challenge to his local monopoly. This stargazers' spat was the first significant publicity battle ever carried on in print; it would not be long before such disputes were regular features of life among authors and publishers.[57] Eck's challenge was in fact testimony to Faber's role in the popularization of early calendars and practicas; indeed Faber's published calculations for Leipzig were becoming models for other writers. He led the way in popularizing the main printed symbols for the planets and heavenly aspects, which remain standard to this day. His soaring fame led numerous would-be imitators to advertise their works as "following the style of Master Wenzel von Budweis."[58] Such blatant jockeying for reputation was already in full swing well before the turn of the century. Marcus Schynnagel, another astrologer who advertised his connection with "the dear University of Crakow," fought for his piece of the pie by boldly dismissing other writers' forecasts as worthless. Faber, Schynnagel, and their rival calendar and practica writers were certainly among the very first commercial media stars. With the aid and encouragement of their publishers, they threw themselves into the competitive mass marketing of their writings and reputations.[59]

By the 1490s members of a rising generation could claim renown not just regionally, but across much of the Empire and even beyond. Burghers who lived hundreds of miles apart were increasingly likely to be familiar with the names of practica writers such as Faber and Engel, whose annual predictions drew more attention with each new issue. Soon to achieve even greater renown than these figures was Johann Virdung, whom we met above as a physician and professor serving the Palatine Elector. Virdung took the Bachelor's degree at Crakow in 1486, and proudly announced this status on the title pages of his practicas even after he received the Masters at Leipzig in 1491. His first annual prognostication appeared in 1487; before his death in 1538 he would go on to publish over eighty astrological writings. Virdung was said to have cast the horoscope at Philipp Melanchthon's birth in 1497. In the eyes of admirers he eventually became "the prince of

German astrologers," a title that attested to his successful combination of academic prestige and princely favor with the new power to disseminate astrological concepts to the lay public as never before.[60]

The commercial success and rising fame of Virdung and a handful of other writers can probably help explain the lower numbers of surviving calendar and practica editions from the years immediately after 1500; the prospects for would-be competitors were daunting. Not a few aspiring authors evidently tried to break into the market with little or no success; so for instance Bernhard Lutz, "sometime student at the praiseworthy University of Leipzig," issued a *Practica Teutsch* for 1512 and another for 1513, after which we never hear from him again.[61] But enterprising publicists were not deterred for long. Those who jumped into the business early in the new century included Georg Tannstetter, a serious scholar and teacher at Vienna who lectured tirelessly on the principles and applications of his art. With the patronage of Emperor Maximilian, whom he eventually served as a personal physician, Tannstetter consciously sought to revive the glory days of Peuerbach and Regiomontanus at the university; in his calendars he proudly identified himself as a master in the arts faculty. Tannstetter was only the most prominent among several mathematical scholars active at Vienna in the first decades of the new century, and was not alone among them in entering the mass market.[62] Meanwhile, eager younger scholars elsewhere ventured into the field. At Leipzig, for instance, the mathematics professor Simon Eyssenmann followed in the footsteps of Faber, emerging as a prolific practica writer in the years immediately before the eruption of the Luther affair. Others not quite so young proved equally ready to leap on this lucrative bandwagon. The Nuremberg cartographer and instrument-maker Erhard Etzlaub was well over fifty when he began to issue annual calendars in the fifteen-teens, shortly after he added the practice of medicine to his already impressive professional resumé. By 1520 his annual works appeared in no fewer than four variants reckoned for different cities and regions of the Empire.[63] With successes like this, the world of the lay consumer appeared to offer almost limitless possibilities.

But just what sort of world was this? What sort of public opinion, if that term can be used at all, went with this wave of popular printed materials, the first in Western history? Some scholars have expressed doubts about whether these works had any role in the emergence of a public discourse with significant social or political implications. One recent study claims that the "communicative framework" of the astrological practicas amounted to a private conversation between the author and a prince or other powerful patron, making the common reader a passive and silent outside observer, a mere subject.[64] Others have pointed out that while the astrological writers sought to present an open and public face, their art retained a secret, hidden, private aspect as well; even as they enjoyed leaping commercial success and popularity, they continued to depend on elements of gnostic secrecy in their pursuit. The stargazer's personal experience and insights were always in play, thus insuring an aura of mysterious authority in his work.[65]

The notion that the typical practica writer was engaged in some sort of implicitly exclusive relationship with a ruler or patron need not detain us. Nearly everything we have noted about the authors' backgrounds and goals makes this suggestion unsustainable. The annual forecasts were manifestly intended as guides for everyman. The related and often overlapping contents of the calendars and the practicas demonstrate that both these genres were anchored far more in the mundane civic concerns of townsfolk than in courtly political stratagems. To be sure, some of our authors were engaged in the inherently risky business of giving political counsel to those in positions of power, but they did this mainly in person or in unpublished writings. In this regard the writers of the annual forecasts were anticipating a broader trend: the gradual retreat of political astrology into the realm of private princely consultation has become a generally recognized feature of sixteenth-century astrological publicity and practice.[66]

On the other hand, the aspect of mystery and personal authority did unquestionably play some role, even when astrology was presented as a purely natural art. The mathematical learning that formed the basis of astrology was far beyond the ken of most laymen. Especially in these earliest decades, most popular calendars and practicas explained the technical reasoning behind particular predictions only briefly and vaguely, if at all. A certain awe toward those who dispensed knowledge gained from the stars was thus inevitable. In more expansively conceived prophetic writings such as Lichtenberger's *Pronosticatio*, the practical and sober aspects of sidereal science were all but fully crowded out by a sense that the stargazer was an explorer of profound and hidden truths. Yet even the more modest annual ephemera could foster the perception of astrology as a form of arcane knowledge, a quasi-spiritual pursuit, even a realm of wizardry. We know that in the eyes of many Church officials and heresy hunters, prediction from the stars always retained something of a dangerous

quality, potentially suspect as a kind of pagan divination involving secret
commerce with demons. Thus even hard-headed mathematicians were
never entirely free of an aura that could evoke fascination, fear, or a combination of both.

In spite of these legitimate points, it would be seriously misleading
to see most publicists of stellar science as contributing to the spread of
occultism, an atmosphere of mystification, or a sense of public exclusion
from a realm of high secrets. Recent scholarship has found a significant realm of public awareness and discourse emerging at the end of the
Middle Ages in connection with the circulation of astrological predictions
and prophetic expectancy. Gert Mentgen argues that the sorts of astrological materials with which we are engaged contributed to the advent of the
first genuinely open public exchanges in western history, in the sense
that the materials were directed not to closed circles of any sort but to the
broadest possible audience.[67] This perspective agrees with all we know
about the contents and marketing of the annual ephemera, including
the sort of public battling over competence, reputation, and market share
that broke out between Eck and Faber in 1489. The vast majority of these
authors were anything but wild-eyed wizards probing forbidden secrets;
they were professors, physicians, and humanists whose goals included the
broad dissemination of a useful natural understanding.

We have noted that close ties linked scholars, practitioners, and publicists of the art, and that these hats were very often worn by the same
person. Respected professorial experts were in fact among the best-known
popularizers, and in Germany few hesitated to publish their annual
instruments in the common tongue, aimed directly and purposefully
at lay readers. They remained on the whole remarkably uninfluenced
by Renaissance Neoplatonism and Hermeticism, by the lure of hidden
knowledge, or by the temptation to experiment with astral magic of the
sort described in the notorious medieval Arabic text *Picatrix*. Drawing on
a comparatively modest scholastic framework of natural philosophy, their
overriding goal was to supply the common man with basic tools for practical orientation in the world. As they worked to address the broadest possible market, the authors of calendars and practicas sought consistently
to emphasize the concrete personal and civic usefulness of their efforts.
They were essentially publicists of a practical science rather than adepts
of a secret art.[68]

Again a comparison with the Italian scene can be helpful, for the
evidence strongly suggests that here scientific astrology remained more

fully restricted to the cultural elites. Studies of Italian prognostications indicate that in general their authors provided more in the way of technical astrological reasoning than did the Germans. Several scholars have also pointed out that the southern authors tended to focus more on political prophecy, while in the North, medical and meteorological concerns were often more prominent.[69] We can reasonably link both the higher level of technical detail and the greater interest in politics to the much lower proportion of vernacular publication among the Italians. The technical explanations were likely to be understandable only to more learned readers, while the obvious dangers of trumpeting political forecasts among the common folk likewise made Latin preferable. Also fitting within this picture are Aby Warburg's now century-old observations about differences in the prevailing images of the planets north and south of the Alps. In Italy, imagery connecting the seven "wandering" stars with the antique deities became markedly more prominent under the influence of humanist aesthetic ideals, a trend suggestive of elite interests. To the north the planets far more rarely took on Olympian traits, but appeared most often as contemporary social types and embodiments of natural forces.[70]

Preoccupied mainly with these natural forces and with mundane conditions, the German calendar and practica writers engaged directly with the common life of their communities; on the whole they proved ready to employ their art openly, for practical benefit and the public welfare. Already in his 1474 *Ephemerides*, Peurbach had referred explicitly to the civic uses of astronomy and astrology; in doing so he was appealing to the prevailing communal ethos among central European townsfolk in the late Middle Ages, a sense of the common good that included an ideal of shared knowledge.[71] General forecasts bearing on meteorological and medical matters aided both individuals and communities to plan ahead, to exercise special caution in some circumstances and to embrace opportunities for health and bounty. Admonitions to peace and cooperation were common. Among the more obvious expressions of civic concern were frequent warnings to usurers not to take advantage of forecasts for a poor or mediocre harvest, such as Thomas Murner issued in his stereotypical practica for 1498; any food hoarded on this basis, he declared, would quickly spoil. Johann Virdung denounced the usurers for fastening on his words as if they were holy gospel whenever he predicted dearth or bad harvests.[72] These forecasters saw their art as an instrument for the benefit of the Christian community, and hoped to guard against abuses.

Inevitably we are left with some frustratingly difficult questions about audience and reception. Just who was buying, reading, or hearing the popular astrological literature? What elements were of greatest interest, and to whom? Precisely how and to what extent did consumers actually make use of the planetary data or forecasts? While fully satisfying answers to these issues lie beyond our reach, the evidence points to a powerful, widespread, and ever-growing interest in these works among those townsfolk who could begin to understand them and put them to use. Inventories of lay libraries from the years around 1500 help confirm that these ephemera were very widely disseminated in the cities.[73] Sold by tens of thousands each year, and no doubt read aloud and discussed both in homes and in public gathering spots, they appealed to the most basic concerns of an ever-expanding world of readers and hearers.

Testimonies to Success

The public and civic character of popular astrology as presented in the calendars and practicas tended to dampen controversy over the art. Whatever debates were starting to heat up among humanists and churchmen drew minimal attention among those who engaged with stellar study in the German towns; Pico's famous work of 1494 and the resulting back-and-forth were largely dismissed or simply ignored by German schoolmen, physicians, and calendar writers. The first significant German answer to Pico, a 1502 *Apologia astrologiae* by the mathematician and physician Jakob Schonheintz, was anything but a soberly reasoned defense; rather it was a visceral lashing out, expressing utter incomprehension that anyone could actually question this most noble of human arts. Astrology was a God-given gift of natural knowledge. Its practitioners stood on the rock-solid foundations of scripture and the wisest authorities. In Schonheintz's mind this indispensable practical study was simply not to be questioned.[74]

To be sure, the massive expansion of stellar science into the realm of everyday living could not fail to evoke some critical reaction among German observers. Like the teachings of the astrologers themselves, the views of a handful of skeptics and mockers inevitably gained visibility through the new channels of print. But it is hard to find much serious or sustained opposition even among German intellectuals and clerical leaders. Official sanctions of any sort against stargazers remained extremely rare. Many of the objections that did surface were largely standard medieval fare, easily countered with no less standard justifications. Newer humanistic and biblical criticisms surely owed something to the revival of Augustinian and broader Patristic traditions, but attested above all to simple unease over the pervasive spread of the art into the realm of everyday living. A great deal of wavering and uncertainty marked the attitude of most critics. The most common reaction was simply amazement at the way astrology was coming to penetrate all dimensions of life.

The few known cases of clerical persecution of astrologers originated mainly in Cologne. Ruled by a powerful elector-archbishop, the city was a bastion of the Dominican Observant movement in the late fifteenth century, home of the Empire's most influential theological faculty, and a center for the veneration of saints. The first official clerical censorship of printed materials began here, with Papal approval, in 1475, and although the city was an important early center of printing, it produced remarkably few calendars and practicas.[75] In 1488 the Cologne theological faculty censored an otherwise unknown astrological writer named Hartung Gernod; in the early 1490s the same body asked the Inquisitor to arrest the already famous Johannes Lichtenberger, apparently on the basis of his horoscopic prediction of a death by killing or hanging. But the matter fizzled, which made it very unlike the harsh actions of the Paris theological faculty against the renowned French stargazer Simon de Phares just a couple of years later.[76] The issues in these cases had little if anything to do with the validity of the art itself, and even such minor cases of official questioning were apparently exceptional.

Formal published attacks on stellar prediction offered little or nothing new. Around 1490 Benedikt Ellwanger of Nürnberg issued a *Judicia vel prognostica astrologorum superstitiosa*, essentially a summary of patristic and medieval arguments in defense of astronomy and against astrology, a limited natural use of the stars over against demon-haunted superstition.[77] Likely provoked above all by the sudden sensation of Lichtenberger's 1488 *Pronosticatio*, Ellwanger's work had little applicability to the popular prognostications that were becoming more pervasive each year. We have no reason to suppose that this Latin rehearsal of traditional arguments gained much attention among the emerging ranks of the calendar and practica writers, virtually all of whom saw their art as a study of natural influences. Preachers and theologians had always been concerned to defend freedom, both human and divine, but they could hardly reject the astrological cosmology that had long since become integrated into Christian thought. Like Ellwanger, the Erfurt Augustinian Johannes von Paltz sought to denounce astrology only in those forms that could be unambiguously labeled superstitious. His negative judgments on the stellar art remained weak and formal, quite unlike his heated assaults on various forms of popular operative magic.[78]

The feeble ambivalence of numerous humanist Churchmen and scholars was perfectly exemplified in a figure such as the Franciscan Thomas Murner, later to become one of Martin Luther's most outspoken opponents. Murner's 1499 *Invectio contra Astrologos* was somewhat subtler than earlier works such as Ellwanger's, but his approach was fundamentally no different. The work represented not an invective against astrologers generally, but against popular writers who stepped over the line to make too-definite individual forecasts—in this case those especially who had predicted the defeat or death of Emperor Maximilian in his ultimately fruitless war against the rebelling Swiss. As we saw earlier Murner was certainly no principled enemy of the stargazers, having tried his hand at practica-writing only shortly before he produced the *Invectio*. He prefaced his forecast for 1498 with complaints about self-proclaimed astrologers who had introduced all sorts of errors, thus spreading disdain for the study of the stars. He pointedly kept his pronouncements on a very general level: "These are scientific; particular predictions are not."[79] One tremendous advantage of this position, of course, was that the more general the prediction, the more difficult it was for critics or mockers to show that it had missed its mark. Like others, then, Murner limited his criticisms to what he saw as popular misuses of the art as it spread among his German contemporaries.

In very few cases did this sort of prudent skepticism evolve into a broader and deeper questioning, although such instances were not unknown. In a prognostication for 1490 Martin Pollich, later the first chancellor of the University of Wittenberg, took pains to distance himself from astrologers who tried to forecast the fortunes and deaths of particular princes from their nativities. Several years later, a public dispute with his Leipzig colleague Simon Pistorius over the causes of the new scourge of the French disease led Pollich to question the usefulness of the art in medicine, and in his last years he could even propose that the true faith of the Church pre-empted belief in the influence of the stars. But doubts of this order were certainly unusual. Far more typical was the Nuremberg chronicler Hartmann Schedel, himself trained in medicine, who declared that anyone ignorant of astrology was entirely unqualified to be a physician, and deserved rather to be called an enemy of nature.[80]

More often than not it was astrologers such as Pollich who criticized their fellow practitioners. Regiomontanus himself, though a heroic figure to German stargazers at all levels, was a leader of early reform efforts, a sharp critic of what he already saw as popular errors and abuses, including the tendency to too-precise predictions, and the basic contradictions and confusions that often marked the annual forecasts. Varying methods of determining the ruling planets for the coming year, for instance, led to stark contradictions that were obvious to the most casual observer who compared title pages. Authors were fully aware that this sort of discordance was rife; almost all of them fell back on the argument that the fault lay not in the principles of the art, but rather in a general lack of mastery. The renowned Wenzel Faber did not hesitate to point out disagreements among various authorities, and even inconsistencies in Ptolemy himself; as a result, he freely admitted the difficulty of making forecasts on certain key matters, such as where and when war would break out. An anonymous Nuremberg calendar for 1492 referred to the great contributions Regiomontanus had made to the calendrical science in general, but lamented that too often the ephemeral literature, instead of helping people to order their lives, had actually fostered disorder.[81]

Partly because of such patent discord, the breathtaking expansion of popular astrology in print also inspired numerous parodies, which likewise came mainly from the pens of the art's promoters. Already in a calendar for 1480 by Hans Folz of Nuremberg we find a comical aping of the popular astrological trends.[82] In his famous *Ship of Fools* (1494), the Nuremberg lay poet Sebastian Brant included a chapter ridiculing the ubiquitous practicas and prophecies. Here as in so many other cases, modern interpreters have too often been led to fix their eyes on the evidence of controversy rather than on the more basic fact, namely the quickly advancing saturation of this culture by the stellar art. Moreover, the parodies were anything but outright dismissals; in fact, although he showed a common mistrust of too-specific forecasts, Brant was a zealous believer in celestial prediction and an avid consulter of the annual prognostications.[83] Still, the *Ship of Fools* helped establish a genre of satire that would rarely refrain from mocking the stargazers. A 1501 *Practica Deutsch Doctor Gril vom Kittelperg*, which laced its predictions with off-color cracks and general nonsense, would likewise inspire imitators for decades, including for instance an inanity-filled Swiss pseudopractica of 1509 attributed to one Doctor Johannis Roßschwantz.[84]

In his *Praise of Folly* (1509) Desiderius Erasmus famously pilloried "the Chaldean superstition," although like Brant he softened his blows by making stargazers just one more example of universal human foolishness. Perhaps even more widely read among German burghers on the eve of the Reformation were works such as the *Practica zu Teutsch* issued in 1515 by the playwright and publicist Pamphilus Gengenbach, who used the joking pseudonym "Doctor Nemo." Although like most other critics he was far from rejecting astrological science altogether, Gengenbach here presented verses depicting its popular forms as an unworthy distraction for a Christian. Above all, his semisatirical critique was testimony to the strength of the prevailing obsession.

> *O Lord I am amazed to see*
> *how all the world looks eagerly*
> *each year to know of future things*
> *and what the heavens' course will bring.*
> *Folks read the practica to hear*
> *of how it will go in the coming year,*
> *whether corn or wine will fail and rot,*
> *if war will break out here or not,*
> *or if disease will waste our land;*
> *they think they have these facts in hand* ... [85]

The universal eagerness to consult the annual practicas and calendars would remain an easy target for critics, moralists, and satirists throughout the century of the Reformation, yet the ridiculing attacks witnessed to the tremendous power of such publications and of the symbols and concepts they conveyed. The main reaction of both critics and parodists was a bewildered astonishment at the way astrology was coming to penetrate the outlook of contemporaries. And notably more of the early satires were published in the Empire than anywhere else.[86]

These works of mockery and warning help confirm the view that during the pre-Reformation decades the German towns were fast becoming more deeply immersed in astrological imagery than any other part of Europe. Although in Italy the political elites and more learned classes had seen similar trends, the burghers of the Empire witnessed an especially rapid and pervasive onslaught of stellar ideas and images. No doubt many traditional forms of medieval piety showed an acceleration and intensification in pre-Reformation Germany, including the pursuit of indulgences and a host of marginally orthodox rituals.[87] But we can also find, in the same region and in the same period, an unprecedented reception of new symbols for making sense of the cosmos and of everyday existence. We are dealing here with the rapid rise of what Silvia Pfister has rightly called "a newly powerful consciousness-shaping and publicly influential force," one that carried implications for virtually every aspect of life, including perceptions of time, nature, and the relationship between the human and the divine.[88] Already before the close of the fifteenth century, the astrological writers had blazed their way into the heady new realm of public controversy in a mass medium, leading the way for others who would soon exploit the same means for other ends. Without a clear recognition of this aspect of pre-Reformation culture, we can hardly hope to paint a full picture of the setting in which the religious and social explosions of the 1520s took place.

2

Mathematics and the Sacred

Die hymel vnnd einfluss der stern
Sprechen auss die glori des herrn.
—LEONHARD REYNMANN, *Nativitetskalender* (1515); from
Psalm 19

AT VARIOUS TIMES in various traditions, an advancing interest in the workings of the heavens has brought with it a movement away from religious anthropomorphism toward an enlarged concept of divinity. Scholars have long maintained, for instance, that ancient astrology contributed to a transformation of Greco-Roman polytheism by encouraging more expansive and unitary visions of the cosmos. Efforts to discover universal laws operative in the stars helped evoke belief in a single governing power behind all phenomena, and the growing tendency to see the sun as the key manifestation of that power similarly dampened belief in a plurality of gods. In the ancient Mediterranean world this trend was one important basis for the appeal of Christianity, which adapted and incorporated a great deal of earlier cosmological imagery.[1] Despite the profoundly different setting that obtained in European Christendom over a thousand years later, we can see broadly similar implications in the rapid diffusion of astrological images and notions among laypeople in the German towns during the half-century before the Reformation. Much as in the ancient world astrological myths worked to wean people away from traditional polytheism and to condition them for the universalist claims of Christianity, the mass printing of popular almanacs and related star-centered materials accelerated the breakdown of the inherited medieval economy of the sacred among German burghers of the late fifteenth and early sixteenth centuries, and favored the reception of a simpler, more personal, and more prophetic form of faith.[2]

Charting Time and Space

The late Robert Scribner wrote that the sixteenth-century move away from a sacramental view of the world might have resulted not primarily from the new Reformation theology, but rather from the discovery of "other means by which to order the natural world, without resorting to sacred intervention."[3] Although he was not referring specifically to astrological notions, his words describe one of the main ways in which the science of the stars worked to influence the religious outlook of German townsmen. The popular astrology of the almanacs was the most pervasive manifestation of the early modern mathematization and naturalization of time and space, a gradual and highly uneven process that came into conflict with the sacramental culture of the medieval church. This insistent subjection of nature to measurement helped to evoke new conceptions of both divine power and mundane realities.

Most medieval Europeans lived in a world in which clocks and calendars still played a very marginal role, a world governed by rhythms quite unlike any we know. Christendom had inherited the framework of the Julian calendar from the Romans, but the actual shape of the year derived more immediately from a clerically governed correlation of particular days and periods with biblical events and the lives of the saints. A major responsibility of medieval church leaders was the "computus," the reckoning of Easter's date and the consequent dating of all the other moveable feasts and fasts of the liturgical year. This was a complex matter that few people had the knowledge to solve; each year the crucial dates were promulgated from Rome. The schedule of holy days had evolved partly in connection with the annual agricultural rhythms, so that the medieval Christian calendar reflected a combination of ecclesiastical and common agrarian patterns and values.[4]

By the late Middle Ages the western Christian calendar was packed with religious celebrations or observances, many of which involved abstention from work or business of any kind. Times of communal fasting were frequent; in some bishoprics Christians were officially prohibited from eating meat or milk products for over one hundred days of the year.[5] The annual cycle of feasts and fasts was marked by highly uneven periods; life was a complex mix of profane and sacred times. Even in the cities, many people kept at best a vague count of days, orienting themselves mainly by the schedule of saints' days. Similarly vague was any sense of historical chronology. It is unlikely that even in the fifteenth century most burghers knew the current *Anno Domini*, since it made no great difference to them in their everyday lives.[6] Even among the educated, many people did not know the precise year of their birth; often the date was simply recalled in relation to other events: one might say, for instance, that he was born in the same year the Emperor Sigismund died. In such a world, time was itself measured less by standard patterns of hours, days, and years than by tasks, religious observances, seasonal changes, and memorable events.

In the cities, however, the traditional medieval rhythms were increasingly subjected to new pressures, most obviously those arising from commercial activity. It is too simple to point to an emerging opposition between a "traditional" sense of time and a modern "bourgeois" or "secular" perception. As Jacques Le Goff has noted, in the late Middle Ages there were many kinds of time, corresponding to varying social and economic structures and interests. These different kinds of time could overlap and partially reinforce one another, as happened with agrarian and ecclesiastical time, but they could also unfold in tension and competition, as did traditional and "merchant" time. In any case, control of the calendar, its rhythms, and their meanings was ultimately an issue of power, and conflicts in this realm had major social implications. In a very real sense, control over time and its rhythms meant control over the political and social order.[7]

The historian William Bouwsma argued that astrology was largely an attempt to gain a new measure of control over time. As a reflection of the desire for "the proper regulation and use of time," it eliminated some of the basic unknowns; "it warded off, objectively, the blows of fortune, that comprehensive symbol of the uncertainty of life." In short, astrology was at least in part an effort to reduce the radical unpredictability of human life and history by linking it to the natural and predictable movements of the heavens. This need to reduce the anxiety of existence was especially pronounced in the towns, which had seen "the development of life that was less dependent on natural rhythms, and more dependent on one's radically unpredictable fellow humans."[8] What may loosely be called "astrological time," as it appeared in the calendars and practicas, was far from a modern or secular sense of time, but it did much to help undermine the traditional rhythms, and indeed the whole medieval ritual complex.[9]

The particular significance of astrology in the emergence of a new sense of time has by no means gone unnoticed. Hilary Carey, for example, sees a late medieval struggle to control time in which Church traditions were opposed by "the practical modernizers such as the princes and the astrologers whose judgements they sought." Carey argues that by the fifteenth century at latest, "astrological time" had won out over "Church time" because astrology was "necessary for a reasoned understanding of the way the world worked."[10] Her discussion is limited to England and France, where the art had found its way into the world of the courts, but where a more broadly based astrological culture was relatively slow to develop. The argument applies far more fruitfully to Italy and Germany, where independent cities and regional princes rather than central courts dominated the political landscape. Here, in urban settings where growing numbers of layfolk sought basic orientation in a world filled with dangers and uncertainties, the dissemination of systematic cosmological conceptions had profound consequences. Most suddenly and forcefully among German burghers, astrological images and ideas came to affect everyday lives and outlooks in ways that challenged key aspects of the inherited religious culture.

The vernacular calendars and practicas offered layfolk an alternative way to order the world, especially the world of time. Even in its vulgarized forms, astrology represented a "mathematization" of time that worked to undermine traditional outlooks and habits. As Peter Brown has pointed out, the cult of saints tended to abolish time; the saints were timeless agents, forceful personalities who never changed and who bridged the gulf between heaven and earth. Brown argues that the medieval clergy generally sought to impose "rhythms of work and leisure that ignored the slow turning of the sun, the moon, and the planets through the heavens, and that reflected, instead, a purely human time, linked to the deaths of outstanding individuals."[11] While this campaign was largely successful to the extent that the cult of the saints came to prevail among Europeans, the reception of systematic astrology first among scholastic thinkers, and then among laymen in the late Middle Ages, directed attention back to the stars and thus revived the old conflict. In the world of the popular almanac no condition was "timeless"; the liminal atmosphere of festivals and saints' days was implicitly deflated. In its place arose a perception of natural regularities measuring out calendrical time, an astrological time that flowed without slowdowns or breaks.

The astrologers' measurements of time, though often in error, showed at least the ideal of precision; the lunar quarters, for instance, were almost always indicated by day, hour, and minute. As early as the 1480s, lunar calendars published in Ulm and other Imperial cities gave the center or middle time for an eclipse down to hours, minutes, and seconds for their localities.[12] The simple operation of counting hours and days inevitably reinforced towndwellers' perception of a regular temporal unfolding; indeed the very form of the popular calendars and prognostications, as well as their grounding in natural events, helped to cultivate a new sense of regular temporal order. In looking at a printed calendar, one found different times by looking at evenly ordered spaces. In our own age, which despite the mind-warping global explosion of digital media seems still dominated by direct mental analogies between time and space, it is easy to forget how new and potentially thought-transforming this sort of visual experience was for people of the late Middle Ages. The calendar invited one to envision regular divisions of time, divisions based on specific and predictable astronomical events. The times of the day, month, and year took on their own mathematical order, a quantitatively even unfolding, a measured one-way movement from past to future. The recognition of an ongoing celestial schedule made increasingly impossible the traditional sacred suspensions of time, which had taken shape, for instance, in the belief that one did not grow older in the time spent attending mass.[13]

The counting of days and the precise demarcation of times was greatly facilitated by the rapidly spreading use of Arabic numerals. Many of the earliest calendars used only Roman numerals, but as early as 1472 the new form began to appear, and within a scant generation it had come to prevail. The printed astrological calendars were certainly one of the main means by which basic numeracy spread among urban populations.[14] It bears noting that in the fifteenth century and even later, Church authorities still viewed the new symbols with distrust. The adoption of Arabic numerals among laymen, which made almost all arithmetical calculations infinitely easier, threatened what little remained of the traditional ecclesiastical dominance of education in numeracy. Clerical instruction had favored the abacus, and late medieval defenses of this method represented belated efforts to defend a fast-waning status. But now the calendars and practicas loudly advertised the high status of the new mathematics in the German universities. The vernacular edition of Johann Stöffler's *Great Roman Kalender* could not have made the point more strongly: "He who knows numbers and reckoning / is learned, a master of everything." For Stöffler mathematics stood at the heart of worldly learning; all natural phenomena could be understood through numbers.[15]

The burghers who purchased and used these popular instruments learned to choose times carefully according to the mathematically calculated dictates of nature, which were unmoved by saintly intervention. The early calendars and practicas did often use the traditional method of dating ("Tuesday after St. Michael's Day"), as did even the 1474 *Kalender* of Regiomontanus. But increasingly the saints' days themselves were located according to Zodiacal time. Thus those days became less "timeless" as they became part of a more regular temporal framework. Grounded in calendrical reckoning, numbered days, and carefully calculated intervals, the common astrological publications made the saint's days nearly incidental: "The last [lunar] quarter falls on the day before St. Lawrence, at 7 PM. Saturn will make it cold, wet, and windy; several days thereafter will be fair."[16] As E. F. Bosanquet pointed out with reference to English works from a later period, the user of an astrological calendar, "whether astronomer, astrologer, physician, or student, took no account of the Saints' days and when they fell; but he had to know the months and the number of days in each."[17]

Names of the days of the week, used only rarely in the earliest calendars and practicas, appeared much more often toward the turn of the century: "the following Friday, good for purging." The saints' days were becoming merely days in a series the meaning of which was wholly independent of them: "April's new moon falls on Monday after St. Gregory's day at 9 hours 33 minutes. There will be fairly warm weather on account of Mars and the Moon in Aries." Often the saints' days were left out entirely, especially in the seasonal weather predictions: "The fall begins on the 13th day of September; the first part of the season will be somewhat cool and wet." Already in the later 1480s the weather forecasts in some practicas mentioned no saints' days at all.[18] The older and newer forms were sometimes combined, as in an Ulm practica of 1492: "Winter begins on the 7th day of December, on the eve of St. Luke." But increasingly the days of each month fell into a continuous numbered series. The trend continued into the new century; Jacob Pflaum's almanac for 1510 offered a full calendar, with numbered days of the month; the traditional feasts and fasts were essentially ignored. Numbered dates now also commonly appeared in lists of especially favorable times for sowing, planting, weaning children, and the like.[19]

The astrological guidelines for the timing of medical treatments, eating, bathing, and other tasks often contradicted the dictates of the ecclesiastical calendar. The stars took no notice of Carnival or Lent, or

of particular holy days. The calendar might recommend undertaking
a certain labor or starting a journey on precisely those days that were
sacrosanct in the traditional yearly cycle. Astrological time had its own
qualitative differentiations, of course, with its good and bad times for particular activities; in fact they were its essential import. But these variations
were quite unlike the medieval alternations of sacred and profane time.
Astrology knew no sacred times, days, or seasons; its differentiations were
part of the natural order of things. Time itself was uniform and objectively measureable; only the changing relationships of the stars to one
another and to the terrestrial realm made for propitious or unpropitious
times. It is true that traces of this newer sense of time "punctuated by
the stars" appeared in other genres, such as the books of hours, that were
common outside the German lands. But in devotional works of this sort
the traditional canonical hours, the fluctuating feasts and fasts, and other
carry-overs from earlier clerical practice all greatly outweighed any sense
of time as measurably and inescapably uniform.[20]

In one sense the annual calendars and practicas could reinforce age-old
celebrations of the new year, a cyclical rebirth that was practically a universal human experience. But in more significant ways they worked against
traditional conceptions of time as an ongoing cyclical repetition. For as
Sigismund Fabri explained in his practica for 1496, God had ordered the
influence of the planets so that each year was different from others. Each
annual publication applied only to the coming twelve months, for each
year would see a different weather pattern, a different schedule of eclipses,
different human fortunes, and different threats. If years were all essentially the same no almanacs would be needed at all, for nothing would be
truly new or different. These ephemera thus enlarged the realm of future
possibility, and raised awareness of genuine novelty. A Memmingen
vernacular broadsheet of 1486 gave in tabular form the basic astronomical and chronological data (dominical letter, golden number, sun cycle,
leap-years, etc.) for over ninety future years, up through 1579; this representation of the historical future in terms of measured linear time was
certainly among the first of its kind available to layfolk.[21] Moreover, few
products of the printing press can have done more to evoke a sense of
passing time than an outdated annual calendar, or a newly purchased one.
A much later English jingle made the point bluntly: "Every year thy almanac thou buyest, brings thee one year nearer to the year thou diest." The
almanac was thus a new sort of *memento mori*; as Bernard Capp points
out, each yearly edition reminded the reader of "another step toward the

grave."[22] By the 1490s images of Saturn literally eating his children, a pre-eminent symbol of temporal change and the inconstancy of the world, not infrequently appeared in the popular astrological ephemera. To order time more strictly according to the stars was not only to depart from a temporal economy of sacred and profane times; it was also to become more aware of time as a measure of all earthly things.

As the yearly broadsheets and prognostications evolved and grew more elaborate, they more frequently listed data on planetary conjunctions and other aspects. As early as the 1480s, they began to include at least brief references to the Arabic doctrine of periodic conjunctions. This theory had long been among the more suspect branches of the art, for it seemed in the eyes of some Churchmen to imply a universal historical determin-ism. Although even a highly respected late medieval ecclesiastical figure such as Pierre D'Ailly could employ it with little to no reserve, humanist astronomers such as Regiomontanus made at least some effort to distance themselves from the teaching as a corruption of pure Ptolemaic astrology, which their program of reform sought to recover and reconstruct. Still, they could never stem their own interest in the Arabic texts, which con-tinued to exercise a strong influence in the schools. Most popularizers of learned astrology did not hesitate to retain Albumasar, Alkindi, and other representatives of this tradition among their most revered authorities.

A vastly oversimplified sketch of Arabic conjunction theory begins with the division of the circle of the Zodiac into four "trigons" or "triplicities," each formed by an equilateral triangle whose sides connected signs asso-ciated with one of the basic elements: earth, water, air and fire. Thus for instance the Watery Trigon was formed by the signs of Cancer, Scorpio, and Pisces, the Fiery Trigon by Aries, Leo, and Sagittarius. Conjunctions of the "upper" planets—namely Jupiter and Saturn, those farthest from the earth—occurred at regular intervals of around twenty years, each time having moved just under 120 degrees from the last. Accordingly these plan-etary meetings, most commonly called "great conjunctions," remained within the signs of one trigon for a period, then transitioned into a new one. According to Albumasar's reckoning, these transitions came some 240 years apart; each entry into a new trigon brought a "greater conjunc-tion." A complete cycle through the four trigons thus took place around every 960 years, and the first conjunction in each new cycle marked a "greatest conjunction," an event of major world-historical importance. By the late fifteenth century most interpreters followed a revised reckoning by which the intermediate or "greater" conjunctions were expected to fall around 200 years apart, while the "greatest" happened at intervals just short of 800 years.[23]

References to planetary conjunctions appeared earlier and more often in the practicas than in the calendars, which as we saw required less learning to produce, and which remained on the whole more exclusively concerned with medical and other information for day-to-day use. Still, by 1500 both genres called attention frequently to past and future meetings of the upper heavenly bodies along with their listings of eclipses and other theoretically predictable phenomena. No doubt the theory of the conjunctions and their hierarchy of importance remained beyond the grasp of the typical lay user or reader of the annual ephemera.[24] Yet even authors who only half understood the doctrine could point to periodic great conjunctions as events of particular significance. To publicize the precise dates of these occurrences, both past and future, was again to highlight the irresistible movement of time. Given the great early popularity of the calendars and practicas in the German towns, it may be that the traditional rhythms of ecclesiastical time were already weaker here than in other European societies. In any case, the sudden and dramatic diffusion of the annual ephemera toward the end of the fifteenth century posed an especially insistent challenge to inherited temporal habits and attitudes.

Along with the astrological representation of regular and measurable time, the popular astrological works also approached space in ways that inevitably helped shape the German townsman's basic sense of orientation in the world. Part of this approach was simply to stress the sheer immensity of the cosmos. Popular planet books, for example, presented readers with knowledge that was at once awe-inspiring and humbling. The *Teutsch Kalender* of 1512, falsely but cleverly attributed to Regiomontanus, described each of the heavenly spheres, and explained the sizes and distances of the planets: Saturn was ninety-nine times as large as the earth, and lay over sixty-five million German miles from the earth. The very lowest planet, the Moon, was over two hundred thousand miles away.[25] It was likely almost as hard for German layfolk to imagine such sizes and distances as it is for us to grasp the reality of galaxies separated by billions of light years. Conceptually, the earth itself was inevitably shrinking. Thus the popular astrological and cosmological works contributed to the same imaginative shift that led the Nuremberg astronomer and geographer Martin Behaim to produce the earliest surviving model terrestrial globe in 1492.[26]

More down-to-earth but no less significant were the ways in which the calendars and practicas encouraged a heightened awareness of geographical space. Thus for example calendar writers became gradually more careful to specify the city for which the times of the new and full moons were reckoned. By the end of the fifteenth century some even offered instructions for adjusting the times for regions or towns to the east or west.[27] Many early printed practicas offered forecasts for various lands and cities of Christendom, from France to Saxony, from Swabia to Hungary, from Cologne to Constantinople, with little to no consistency in either the places chosen or the forecasts themselves. Gradually in the years after 1500 forecasters began working with an adapted Ptolemaic doctrine of astrological geography. The Zodiac was divided into three groups of four signs each; each land or city fell under one of the three quadrangles. In addition, each planet held a special rule over particular regions. Here again the stellar publicists remained far from agreement in their groupings of regions and towns under the quadrangles and planetary influences. Yet just as they promoted in principle a newly charted and standardized time, so too they advertised a sense of space that took no account of especially sacred places or objects. The natural law of the stars worked the same everywhere. The more they were exposed to this new conceptual structure, the more likely laymen were to lose confidence in an older web of assumptions about nature and the supernatural.

Stars or Sanctity?

The explosion of cheap stellar literature was intimately connected with the quickly rising public profile of astrological medicine, or "iatromathematics." To be sure, stargazers and medical men were by no means necessarily allied. In fact with the surge of astrological discourse in the fifteenth century, an older learned debate over the practice of astrologically informed healing was revived. While physicians generally recognized that the human body and its humors were subject to celestial influences, the Galenic tradition left room for doubt about the extent to which it was necessary or even possible to understand those influences in order to treat disease. Medical men thus held a range of views about the precise ways in which an understanding of the planetary positions and movements could properly contribute to diagnosis, prognosis, and treatment. At one end of the spectrum was Hartmann Schedel's view that anyone ignorant of astrology "deserves not to be called a physician, but an enemy of nature."[28] But others saw next to no need for celestial science in medical practice; while the celestial bodies undoubtedly influenced general tendencies in the terrestrial world, useful medical understanding was restricted mainly to analysis of more immediate earthly forces and their effects on humoral balance in the human body. The central question in this debate simply echoed the larger problem for astrologers: how was one to draw a clear line between the general and the particular? How definitively could one calculate the celestial influences on the human body and mind? A certain level of ongoing controversy was inevitable, but we can fairly assume that by the late Middle Ages medical astrology figured prominently in the training of most physicians, and that nearly all public practitioners in the German towns accepted at least the basic principles informing the almanacs.

For the majority of physicians, these principles were essentially conservative; theories or treatments with any odor of occultism or magic were to be avoided. Yet powerful preconceptions associating stellar science with magic or divination continue to influence studies of astrological medicine, or iatromathematics. Here, as with astrology generally, we need to distinguish among various strands of iatromathematical theory and practice. Many university-trained physicians saw a knowledge of the stars as prerequisite to any proper diagnosis or prognosis without any thought that their work was magical in any sense, natural or otherwise. It is true that some of the vernacular iatromathematical handbooks that began to circulate toward the end of the Middle Ages incorporated aspects of folk-medicine and a variety of occultist cures, yet these elements do not appear to have carried over into the almanacs and prognostications, which on the whole reflected a fairly straightforward mixture of Galenic principles and astrological timing.[29] As we will see, moreover, by the late fifteenth century physicians were quickly taking on an elevated civic profile that was largely incompatible with claims to occult knowledge. The rapidly expanding public and civic dimensions of medicine would do much to promote the public and civic claims of astrological practitioners more generally.

The urban physicians, surgeons, and barbers were of course not the only agents of healing; throughout the Middle Ages the power of the saints had been partly, in fact largely, the power to heal. The heritage of late-ancient Christianity persisted, in which—to use Brown's words once again—"healing and deliverance ... had to pass through a precise set of interpersonal relations." This healing took place most often at saints' shrines. The shrine, as another scholar has put it, served as "a hospital, even as a casualty ward."[30] As Brown explains, the early medieval scholars who helped build the cult of the saints held that true reverence included a willingness to focus belief on invisible persons—that is, Christ and the saints—in such a way as to commit the believer to definite rhythms in his life. To deny this sort of reverence meant the "failure or positive refusal to give life structure in terms of ceremonious relationships with specific invisible persons." The "rhythm of cure" encouraged by medieval church teachings was thus the rhythm connected with the veneration of saints, whose virtues became linked to specific days and times.[31] And special places of healing were determined by affinities between holy persons and particular abodes, or by the location of saintly remains, holy relics. As archetypal healers, the saints were often depicted as heavenly physicians, and as such they naturally had their fields of specialization. To medieval minds in which conceptions of physical and spiritual health were practically inseparable, the saints were holistic therapists.[32]

The astrological medicine of the popular almanacs posed a powerful if mostly implicit challenge to this older form of reverence, and thus to the whole culture of saintly intervention. Here the stars made for illness as well as healing, and understanding the natural celestial rhythms was basic to hygiene and to all medical treatment. Personal relations had little or nothing to do with healing; rather, both physician and patient were subject to cosmic forces. The close relationship between the science of the stars and the concerns of the physician has provoked the observation that medical diagnosis was "the back door to a transformation in mentalities"; in other words, it was through iatromathematics above all that new astrological conceptions of time and of nature influenced the broader lay culture of the late Middle Ages.[33]

Since they had to do with correct timing, the theories and methods of astrological medicine evolved together with the sense of a regular and measurable temporal unfolding in nature generally. One simple and almost universal rule, for instance, was that a person should take no bodily therapy, and should especially avoid phlebotomy, during the "dog days" of high summer. Closely related was the idea that whenever the moon was in a particular zodiacal sign, the corresponding body part had too much blood, and should not be bled or operated on.[34] The doctrine of correspondences between the signs and the parts of the body, later known as "melothesia," focused on maintaining or restoring the natural humoral balance required for human health; to practice medical healing on this basis was to observe a careful schedule. This approach had long stood in competition, at least implicitly, with the tradition of healing through the intercessory powers of the saints and their relics, indeed with the whole system of sacramental and quasi-sacramental piety. It can hardly be without significance, then, that with the broadsheet almanacs, which were unique to the German lands, the image of the spread-eagled Zodiacal Man and the medical concepts associated with it gained unprecedented recognition at nearly all social levels.[35]

Many of the earliest calendars were little more than bleeding charts that indicated the phases and positions of the moon, along with good, bad, or neutral times for letting blood. But toward 1500 and thereafter, these listings became increasingly elaborate and refined. Johann Virdung's publications show a clear evolution in this respect, including more detailed guidelines as the years passed for a widening variety of treatments. Local calendar makers often depended on learned university authorities; the works of Johann Stöffler, for instance, served as sources on which practitioners learned to count for overall accuracy and consistency. Particularly after the turn of the century, Georg Tannstetter's publications drew high regard for their use of all the planetary aspects to establish precise therapeutic rules. Even so, multiple calendars for the same year and city continued often to contradict one another, indicating entirely different propitious times for bathing, bleeding, hair-cutting, and the like.[36]

Its proponents worked to popularize and legitimize this sort of astrological medicine partly through suggestive iconographic associations between its methods and Christian teachings and rituals. We find such efforts especially in calendars toward the end of the fifteenth century. A number of editions prominently depicted the tree or root of Jesse from the Book of Isaiah, referring to the descent of Christ from David, son of Jesse. This image had close associations with the surge in Marian veneration in the waning Middle Ages, which was in turn related to a trend toward more Christocentric forms of piety. The tree or vine appeared as a border on a number of calendars emerging from the figure of Jesse or David, and then typically one margin of the sheet, depicting the blossoms of the sacred genealogy (see Figure 2.1). In a top corner the vine flowered in glory, issuing as its fruit either the Virgin and child together, or the infant Jesus alone. The image played on the metaphor of Christ as the "fruit of the vine." At the Last Supper Christ spoke directly of the wine, his blood, as "this fruit of the vine" (Mt 26:29, Mk 14:25, Lk 22:18), and a long, potent tradition of Christian eucharistic iconography—one that

FIGURE 2.1 Double-broadsheet lunar calendar for 1494, issued at Strasbourg, with Christ as fruit of the vine. Reproduced from Paul Heitz and Konrad Haebler, *Hundert Kalender-Inkunabeln* (Strasbourg, 1905).

included popular pre-Reformation images—depicted the bleeding Christ in a winepress.[37]

These themes had inescapable significance in works that were primarily guides for phlebotomy. Calendars that employed such imagery evoked an association between Christ's blood, shed to save sinners, and the therapeutic bleeding each person was to undergo with the help of the barber-surgeon or physician. "I am the true vine," says Jesus to the disciples in Luke 15, "and My Father is the vinedresser. Every branch in Me that does not bear fruit He takes away, and every branch that bears fruit he prunes ['purgabit' in the Latin Vulgate, i.e. 'purges'], that it may bear more fruit." Christians who saw strong connections between physical and spiritual healing were unlikely to miss the associations between the sacrifice of Christ's blood to overcome sin and a periodic imitation of that sacrifice through a voluntary bleeding. As Christ saved by shedding his blood, so now the believer should shed blood to sustain life. In this way, spiritual wholeness and bodily health became interrelated in a subtly new and powerful way. In several surviving calendars the message was reinforced through woodcuts showing a practitioner ministering to his patient by bloodletting, cupping, and other treatments. Thus the main therapies of astrological medicine were implicitly presented in these calendars as forms of witness to God's act of self-pruning, perhaps even as a kind of sacramental reenactment. As Christ shed his blood to save the faithful, body and soul, so the bleeding to be undertaken by each person was an aid to both physical and spiritual health. This therapeutic overflow kept one's life in balance, preventing the disastrous overflow of sin/disease. The sacramental links may have been furthered by associations between the terms *Aderlass*, or venesection, and *Ablass*, or indulgence; both denoted a beneficial letting, a healthful release.[38]

This imagery suggested shifting conceptions of the relationship between bodily and spiritual health, and of the best means of pursuing both. We have noted that many early German calendar-makers were physicians; others had at least some training in astrological medicine. The authors of the calendars were implicitly presenting the medical services of the physician as a kind of sacred responsibility for each person, a ritual perhaps more likely to benefit health and wholeness than calling on a saint, going on a pilgrimage, or investing in an indulgence. The speed with which the astrological world picture spread in the German towns was thus one reflection of the intense late medieval quest for "ever-new assurances of salvation," both material and spiritual.[39] While before the

1520s most laymen certainly did not abandon the traditional saintly and sacramental avenues to healing, alternative means were rapidly gaining both visibility and status.

The saints certainly had roles that went beyond issues of individual bodily health. The German lands were home to numerous local weather saints, many of whom were not officially approved by the Church but whose days were nevertheless honored.[40] But these spiritual agents of storm and sun were very rarely mentioned in the calendars or the practicas; forecasting the weather on the basis of the heavens was a very different enterprise from seeking the aid of a weather saint. The stars were not essentially souls or intelligences, but natural forces directly manifesting the power of God, who alone could alter their influence. One could not communicate with the heavenly bodies; one could only read them. To the extent that the astrologers could accurately predict their movements and influence, the earth's atmosphere might itself become more predictable, and a basic source of human insecurity could thus be reduced. Like iatromathematics, then, meteorology was a form of practical cosmological interest that directed attention away from personal mediators between the human and the divine. While it was surely possible to see the stars as causes or predictors of the weather and at the same time to look to the aid of a weather saint in mitigating expected effects, astrological forecasts nonetheless tended to short-circuit the currents of cosmic power, to turn one's spiritual gaze past the incandescent glow of saintly figures, straight to universal natural forces and to the all-powerful generator.

From the start, commercial stargazers in Germany entered into hot competition as weather forecasters. In his practica for 1488, for example, Johann Engel bragged of offering "a new and true forecast of the weather according to the four qualities (cold, moist, warm, and dry); it is of a sort almost unknown to astrologers, none of whom has ever presented forecasts in this daily form according to the calendar." Here he sought to give a weather forecast for every day of the year, somewhat in the style of a modern farmer's almanac.[41] Following such leads, weather predictions tended to become gradually fuller and more detailed in the pre-Reformation decades. Because they were among the most immediate attractions for purchasers of the annual forecasts, they were also the feature that was quickest to draw ridicule or scorn when they proved wrong, or when astrologers' predictions contradicted one another. Yet as with modern stock-market seers, their services were no less in demand as a result.

The intense astrometeorological interest reflected in the practicas soon inspired larger publications that sought to explain the basics of the science. Among the very earliest and most influential of these works was one by Leonhard Reynmann, himself a writer of annual practicas. His *Wetterbuchlein*, first published at Augsburg in 1505, was a vernacular textbook that might have inspired any ambitious reader to think of composing his own forecasts. The author had certainly not misjudged the market; this "people's book" went through eleven editions by 1520, and at least six more in the early Reformation years.[42] So successful was this democratizing venture that potential competition faltered nearly altogether; a Latin meteorological work by the Silesian Johann aus Gross Glogau, published posthumously at Crakow in 1514, remained without a German edition until much later. Equally striking is that except for the scholars at Crakow, not a single writer outside Germany issued a book on weather forecasting until several decades later. The first Italian work of this sort, published in Latin, did not appear until 1540; no vernacular Italian weather-book was printed until 1551.[43] We can reasonably conclude that the works of the astrometeorologists both reflected and helped cultivate a pronounced concern with natural-philosophical and cosmological issues among German townspeople. And this intensified interest in the workings of the heavens was accompanied in turn by mounting awe in the face of the divine ruler who stood behind them. Indeed just as medical bleeding was about more than humoral balance, a weather forecast was always much more than a mere meteorological prediction.

Divine Rule, Human Weakness

The Dutch historian of culture Johan Huizinga once suggested that the rapid propagation of the cult of guardian angels toward the end of the Middle Ages may have been "a sort of unconscious reaction against the motley crowd of popular hagiology," reflecting a desire for a simpler and more elevated connection with the divine.[44] Far more dramatic in the German lands was the propagation of the cult of the stars, in which a movement toward just such a simpler connection is at least as evident, if not more so. Popular astrology worked against the cult of the saints partly because it reinforced, in both implicit and explicit ways, the conception of an omnipotent deity who governed nature through the motion of the heavens. For the authors of the ever-more popular annual forecasts, nature was an immediate expression of divine will rather than a realm in which various spiritual agents were sporadically and unpredictably engaged.[45] Far from leading a return to ancient demonic beliefs, the astrologers encouraged believers to discard the forms of mediate social intercourse between man and the divine that had crept into medieval Christianity. The stars directed attention away from a hierarchy of persons or spirits, toward the absolute sovereignty and majesty of the one true God.

Inevitably a certain tendency to anthropomorphize the planets was revealed in continuing popular depictions of the planets as human figures; indeed these images became ubiquitous through the title pages of the practicas, showing the ruling planets for a given year. Practica writers also frequently resorted to personal characteristics in explaining celestial influences, pointing for example to the likely effects of wrathful Mars or lusty Venus. For both Plato and Aristotle the planets had represented immortal, divine beings, and key Arabic mediators such as Albumasar had perpetuated this notion. For Ptolemy, however, at least by reputation the most important ancient authority of all, they were natural powers only. Among scholastic thinkers, a tendency to de-animate the heavens and to see the cosmos as a unity under a single divine will was already in evidence by the twelfth century. The notion of cosmic oneness increasingly prevailed in late medieval scholastic thought, and emerged strongly in the German vernacular literature. Here, despite their common depiction as human forms, the planets did not actually take on the personal characteristics of the ancient divinities.[46] They were not living beings to be entreated, but natural influences pointing beyond themselves to that single controlling power without which neither heavens nor earth would have any meaning (see Figure 2.2).

Already in the older planet-book tradition, the primary function of cosmological instruction was to stress God's "omnipotence . . . his goodness, and his eternal wisdom."[47] The ideas noted earlier regarding the immensity of the planets and the humbling dimensions of the heavens reinforced such teachings. While it is hard to weigh the effects of these heady notions on the burghers among whom they circulated, it would be a mistake to underestimate their significance. They helped give new meaning to the biblical truth that the stars directly revealed the glory of God. This message remained integral in the new annual printed works. A Mainz calendar of 1482 spoke of the planets as an "instrument of the almighty God" who has endowed them with "powers and virtues." Johannes Goetz began his practica for 1486 by citing Aristotle to the effect that all nature was

FIGURE 2.2 God rules the astrological cosmos, including the terrestrial houses, the zodiacal signs, and the seven planets. Erhard Schön, title page illustration from Leonhard Reynmann's *Nativitet Kalennder* (Nuremberg, 1515). Reproduced from Heinz Artur Strauss, *Der astrologische Gedanke in der deutschen Vergangenheit* (Munich, 1926).

an essential unity; all the heavens and the earth worked together under divine control. Johann Stöffler saw the sun especially as the source and expression of God's omnipresent working in nature, and Virdung wrote that the stars followed their course "by the will of him who created the heavenly spheres, to whom be honor, praise, and thanks in eternity."[48]

The writer of predictions for 1487 similarly stressed that all earthly things were governed by influences from above as determined by the Creator. The Almighty had established the heavenly movements as signs and as influences over the earth so that each and every master of this art might recognize them. Thus to read the stars was in no way to diminish God's glory, but to praise and honor him. The astrologer's task was to help others learn to understand and conform themselves to these forces. This author added that if the reader hoped to see better influences than were forecast in this practica, he should call directly on God that he might strengthen the good, and turn all to the best. A vernacular prognostication for 1502 stated in a similarly explicit way that God stood directly behind every natural event or appearance. Both the regularities and the freaks of nature were direct acts of the universal will. Another popular astrological forecast from the same year opened with the declaration that "the wisdom of God shows us that one God rules all things, illuminates all things." When in 1520 the almanac-writer Simon Eyssenmann referred prominently to "the will of the almighty eternal God" and to the need to trust in that infinite will, he was expressing a resolutely unitary and expansive conception of divinity that had been preached by his fellow stargazers over several decades.[49]

For such authors the art was a form of divinely ordained reason that could and should not only aid believers in their daily lives, but also raise their awareness of God's glory and might as manifest in the natural world. The stars revealed not fate, but providential power. Eyssenmann was among numerous writers who assured their readers that "the heavens can effect no more than God decrees." Johann Seger's 1517 practica made it clear that through "the proper art of astronomy and the influence of the heavens" Christians were to learn of future evils that they might better their lives, calling upon almighty God and the Virgin Mary, who could turn away all corrupting influences. When the stars announced good fortune, this was occasion for thanks to the ruler of Creation, for the heavens could have no influence at all apart from his decrees.[50] As notable here as the affirmation of God and the Virgin was the absence of any other sort of intercessor. Numerous popular forecasts included woodcuts that left no room for doubt about God's omnipotent rule. Georg Tannstetter, a learned professor as well as a writer of almanacs, presented in his *ex libris* the memorable image of a celestial sphere with a pair of heavenly hands before it breaking a staff: God, and only God, could break the power of the stars.[51]

This pervasive emphasis on divine unity and sovereignty in the calendars and practicas reflected in part a broader late medieval acceleration of Christocentric and Mariological forms of piety, a movement especially pronounced in the German lands. These currents were reflected clearly in the common calendar symbolism of Mary as Queen of Heaven and the newborn King as announcer and blesser of the new year. The authors and publishers of the annual astrological works wove astrological ideas together with the new stress on Christ and Mary in several other ways. An anonymous Ulm prognostication for 1495, for instance, concluded with a symbolic woodcut suggesting that the sun, moon, and stars all pointed to Christ. Images of Christ as the sun were equally if not more explicit. The Virgin was easily linked to the zodiacal sign of Virgo, especially since the sun's entry into this sign began the yearly time of fruitful harvest. In medieval prophetic thought the woman of Revelation 12, clothed with the sun and standing on the moon, had long been associated with Mary; an illustration of the connection appeared in a calendar of 1485. Wenzel Faber issued his practica for 1492 in explicit praise of God and the Virgin Mother.[52] The cosmological symbolism associated with both Christ and the Virgin thus reinforced their status above and beyond the crowded market of saints.

While the inherited popular religious culture tended to localize and humanize divine power, the rapidly spreading astrological conceptions tended to make it universal and natural. The astrologers recognized the subjection of all terrestrial life, including human beings, to natural forces. Their teachings could only have helped lead central European townsfolk toward a conception of nature as a reflection of absolute divine power and will. This conception left small scope for sacred suspensions of natural time, for miraculous healings at holy shrines, or for bargaining with saints in order to gain their aid. Instead astrology taught practical ways to adjust to those natural forces, while also focusing religiou attention on the Virgin and her son, the crucial personal mediators w ose transcendent status remained unquestioned.

The main task of the astrologer was to discover the balance between good and ill influences, to understand where, when, and for whom one or the other would prevail. One broad corollary of this concern was the tendency of astrology to build on binary oppositions: good and bad, hot and cold, love and hate, flood and drought. The deepest binary opposition was mainly implicit in the popular media, but it was nonetheless pervasive, in fact inescapable. This was the immense gulf between earthly corruption and the divine majesty that ruled the heavens. This common tendency in astrology had long led some critics to associate the art with the radical dualism of Manichaean or gnostic heresy, the idea that matter itself was evil and had to be escaped.[53] The almanac makers never imagined any such radical gulf between divine goodness and the material creation. Yet by emphasizing time and again that the stars manifested the universal power of a sovereign God they threw into relief the corruption of terrestrial nature, thus underlining human weakness in the face of infinitely greater forces. To be sure, they were careful to acknowledge human freedom, and thus endlessly echoed the pseudo-Ptolemaic dictum that "the wise man rules the stars." In his practica for 1595 Virdung echoed the standard line that what the stars revealed were merely natural tendencies, not rigid laws. Yet as Thomas Murner explained in 1498, among a thousand people scarcely one could be found who actually ruled himself, and who could thus rule the heavens. The implication was clear: the mass of men were sinners who followed their natural instincts.[54]

Here then was a fundamental paradox: while on one level astrology offered layfolk a sense of practical empowerment, on another it served to mirror the limits of human freedom, showing how little control people ultimately had in a universal scheme. Their eager reception of the new science contributed to the process by which, as Peter Blickle puts it, "late medieval people began to take responsibility for their own lives."[55] The science of the stars provided tools by which burghers could liberate themselves from humanly imposed rules, conforming themselves to a higher natural law. But while one might well gain some practical understanding of this law, one could do nothing to change it; only God himself could do that. There could be no mistake about the great gulf between heavenly power and human capacities.[56] To take the power of the stars seriously was to move toward a recognition of practical freedom in human affairs, but bondage in relation to cosmic powers.

Planetary Sociology

As the astrologers' attention to the heavens and their influence encouraged an exalted conception of cosmic reality and of the God who created and sustained the world, it also stimulated the impulse to analyze the world itself, to understand human beings and their relationship to the universal forces. Even in its cruder and more vulgar forms, the science of the stars afforded premodern Europeans a system of categories and concepts that allowed them to look at human life and society from new perspectives. With his usual acuity, the venerable English historian Keith Thomas once suggested that in Renaissance astrology we can detect "the germ of modern sociology."[57] The massive dissemination of astrological ideas and images that came with printing made available a powerful vocabulary for the depiction and analysis of human types, social groups, and their ongoing interactions. The newly popular symbols thus served to draw attention to the ever-present tensions, conflicts, and imbalances of earthly life. Writing with reference to late Antiquity, Peter Brown proposed that "astrology brought down into men's views of their lives and personalities the complexities and conflicts which they saw in the planets."[58] So too in the late medieval setting, by highlighting the faults inherent in a corrupt nature, the starry vault above served to intensify perceptions of this world as a realm of struggle and strife, far removed from the perfect unity and harmony of the divine will. Paradoxically, then, while the goal of the yearly predictions was to offer a basic sense of orientation in time, nature, and the cosmos, the implicit contrast between the sovereign power above the stars and the messy variety of earthly existence fostered an attitude of incipient relativism with regard to all human structures.

In his *Practica von Ingolstadt* of 1486, Johannes Goetz discussed the various ways in which humanity could be divided up in order to analyze the workings of the stars. Prominent among these schemes was the one according to which "every individual person is assigned to a planet." As noted in Chapter 1, the idea of the planetary children, which offered nothing less than a "system of planetary anthropology," had already been established in vernacular literature and iconography well before the swelling tide of printed calendars and practicas arrived.[59] In these annual works, though, it quickly took on a weightier role, and the basic idea of identifying human types was elaborated and extended. Although some of the earliest practicas discussed only the "children" of each planet as traditionally understood, it soon became equally if not more common to make

predictions about the outlook for classes and groups that were more readily associated with late medieval social structures: the nobles, the clergy,
merchants and burghers, craftsmen, and the common people. The identification of types would go yet further; by the 1490s forecasts variously
discussed the pope and his retinue, princes, women, pregnant women,
widows, soldiers, religious orders, musicians, singers, travelers, and the
members of particular trades and occupations, among other slices of
humanity. In addition, the annual ephemera gave massive new currency
to the notion of differing human complexions according to the dominant
bodily humor, referring to melancholy, choleric, sanguinary or phlegmatic
folk, as well as those of mixed complexions; these types were often associated with different colors. Yet another classification was by age group;
although a correlation of the seven ages of man with the seven planets was
rarely explicit in these early printed works, astrologers often made general
forecasts for young children, old people, or middle-aged men.

Geographic and political categories entered the mix as well. Here we
need not dwell on the complexities of ancient astrological geography. The
practica writers played freely with the sundry schemes handed down from
Ptolemy and other ancient and medieval authorities whereby kingdoms,
lands, and cities fell under the special influence of a planet or a particular
sign of the Zodiac. Not all writers included a geographical section, but
those who did might comment on the general outlook for Bohemia or
Spain, Saxony or Hungary, Paris or Erfurt or Constantinople. Most often
the focus fell largely on cities and principalities within the Empire, but
efforts to include locations throughout the known world signal the astrologers' desire to present an expansive image of the terrestrial globe in all
its variety. Even among people who had never seen a map, and for whom
Sicily or Genoa were little more than names, such forecasts probably
increased awareness of the world that lay beyond personal experience, a
world of uniform space and measurable distances, but one that contained
a host of different peoples and places.[60]

Popular astrology not only drew attention to differences, it also supplied
tools to sharpen and intensify them. This sort of reinforcement is evident,
for example, in the stereotypes about women conveyed by the practica
writers. Although females were generally ruled by Venus, traditionally a
symbol of love and sexual generation, the planet's feminine nature most
often evoked associations with weakness, inconstancy and frivolity; thus
too with children, singers, and stage players. Passion and weakness created their own perils; the astrologers regularly warned about the danger

of wives lording it tyrannically over their husbands, or about women who were simply quarrelsome, proud, or uppity. Typical was the forecast of Marcus Schynnagel for 1500 that in the coming year "women will rule over men, and they will cause a great deal of strife and suffering, and they will have little shame."[61] Since comments of this sort were entirely in keeping with widespread prejudices, they are unlikely to surprise us. But their sudden and widespread dissemination in popular print could have had no effect other than to magnify and codify perceptions of gender differences. In his practica for 1488 Johann Engel included not only women among those over whom Venus ruled, but also men "who affect the ways of women." Thomas Murner identified "womanly men" as sharing a distinctive complexion with other children of Venus. Such planetary stereotypes would become if anything more consistent in the early Reformation era: Venus's progeny now included "gay, ridiculous men [frölich, schympflich menschen]," who appeared in a decidedly negative light. The popular astrological works not only reflected inherited perceptions of difference; they also helped to define and shape those perceptions.[62]

Even more sweeping were the divisions of all humanity by religion: Jews, Christians, and "Mahometans" or "Turks." The notion that each of the major faiths had arisen under and was shaped by a particular celestial alignment had come to the Christian West as early as the twelfth century, mainly through Albumasar. Commonly known today as "the horoscope of religions," this doctrine was founded on this Arab thinker's conjunction theory. The basic idea had been taken up by scholars such as Albertus Magnus and by the English Franciscan Roger Bacon, who had correlated major periodic conjunctions with six world religions, believing he could thus confirm Christianity's superiority.[63] Numerous later thinkers chose to focus on the three primary branches of monotheism, and this approach surfaced strongly in the popular forecasts of the late fifteenth century. Although common negative stereotypes sometimes surfaced in predictions about Jews and Turks, more notable is the general evenhandedness with which most writers approached the three followings. It was clear that the stars had different effects on each, yet what strikes the modern reader is the quite neutral language of these predictions. In fact sometimes, as for instance in Wenzel Faber's practica for 1499, the general outlook appeared considerably better for "Mahometans" than for Christians.[64] Forecasts of this sort were only one manifestation of the prevalent sense that Christendom was in crisis, an outlook the practica writers did much to advertise.

Paola Zambelli finds that in a variety of early sixteenth-century texts "the [Arabic] conjunctionist thesis leads imperceptibly and unconsciously to the idea of variability and pluralism in religious and political regimes."[65] Indeed by focusing on natural forces that shaped and affected all the varied persons, groups, and regions on earth, the astrology of the yearly predictions moved more generally in this direction, at least potentially casting into doubt the inherent superiority of any particular human custom or institution. Other scholars have pointed to an implicit relativism in the astrologers' overall approach to worldly conditions. Even as they promoted and reinforced perceptions of human types and differences, these popular works discussed all classes, ranks, nations, regions, and religions. All were subject to the workings of the stars, for both good and evil. Sigismund Fabri's predictions for 1496 about the people of Bavaria were not untypical. In the spring they would experience many losses and much anguish; during the following fall they would undertake religious pilgrimages. Fabri may well have thought these were fairly safe bets, but if even the choice to go on pilgrimage was subject to stellar influence, what were readers to conclude about the status of this practice in relation to a truly universal faith?[66] Banal though they were, such prognoses could easily prompt wonderings about the parochial human origins of common practices.

Eugenio Garin must therefore be at least partially right in saying that certain astrological teachings, including the horoscope of religions, "seemed fundamentally to question the values of faith." In some theologically strict eyes, no doubt, any astrological analysis of religious origins, beliefs, or practices threatened ultimately to strip Christianity of its world historical uniqueness.[67] Although such a radical implication remained far from the minds of those who produced and consumed the popular astrological works, what could come increasingly into question were those visible features of Christian society that most clearly seemed the products not of universal revealed truth, but of human customs, laws, and institutions. Indeed the popular predictive works provided the first true mass medium through which worldly conflicts, failings, and corruption could fall under public scrutiny. The idea that a new public sphere was emerging in the German towns by 1500 gains weight when we consider that the annual astrological works, and especially the practicas, provided a nearly ideal tool for social commentary and criticism.

By itself, the art of reading the stars carried no inherent, metahistorical social or political meaning. In some circumstances it could appear to favor social egalitarianism: "As the grave equals all men, so do celestial influences." On the other hand, interpreters have often argued that the doctrine of the planetary children served mainly to reinforce a traditional social order of higher and lower classes, rulers and ruled.[68] But to restrict ourselves to such starkly polar meanings is naturally misleading; the matter was rarely so simple. We can in fact see both these tendencies at work in the era around 1500. The physicians and scholars who produced astrological works for mass consumption combined a social outlook that was in many ways profoundly conservative, even reactionary, with a vision of personal empowerment for the common man. Popular astrology could thus appeal both to city authorities who looked to consolidate their control and maintain order, and to burghers searching for ways to gain a sense of independence as well as a secure orientation in the world. Both sets of aspirations were compatible with resentment toward the clerical establishment, expressions of which became ever more pronounced in the annual predictions over the half-century or so before 1520.

The anticlerical sentiments that came to mark the practicas in particular can be understood partly as a function of the prominent role of physicians in the production of these works. We have already noted the characteristics of astrological medicine that caused it to pose an implicit challenge to traditional forms of sacramental and saintly healing. But just as significant were the accelerating social and institutional changes that raised the civic profile of the physicians and surgeons, giving both them and their methods of treatment greater weight in the daily lives of the people at large. We have noted the mounting concern of local authorities to name official city physicians and to oversee medical services more generally; the clear trend by 1500 was toward more organized communal attention to public health. As we might expect, this agenda was also pushed by the physicians, who presented themselves as key agents of the common good; they could increasingly regard themselves as public servants, offering practical knowledge and advice for the benefit of all. This ever loftier conception of their own calling as healers dovetailed with the anticlerical outlook of the practica-writing physicians.

Competition between priests and medical men was hardly new at this time, but we have good reasons to think that the strains were becoming more severe and more open as systematic teachings and organized health care gained a new centrality in civic life. It is well known that clerical status and power were already on the decline in the German cities well before the 1520s, as laymen sought to take more control over their own lives. A less well-recognized dimension of this picture lies in the leading role of physicians in this burgher preemption of clerical status. As the tasks of the natural diagnostician or therapist took on greater weight over against those of the priest or the confessor, the contrast loomed larger between traditional clerical privileges and a newly practical ideal of medical service for the common good. The truest public servants and healers, it appeared, were the trained students of bodily health. Moreover, this was no mere professional rivalry, for much broader and deeper issues were at stake. To the extent that townsmen found promise in the newly forming medical and astrological culture of the day, their regard waned not only for the clergy, but for the whole sacramental culture to which priestly authority was intimately tied.

The notion that astrology posed a rival system of meaning to late medieval Christianity has sometimes led to the suggestion that the astrologers themselves constituted a sort of rival priesthood. This view does find some support in the arguments of at least a few mid-millennium stargazers. Johannes Lichtenberger, for example, maintained that in the distant past astrologers had been the priests, and that their descent from this role had been a tragic thing. Although he prudently refrained from expanding on this idea, Lichtenberger certainly hoped to convey the message that he and his fellow forecasters deserved a far higher status than they currently enjoyed relative to members of the clergy. Johannes Indagine, who like Lichtenberger was both a priest and a prognosticator, went even further. "Who then," he asked, "would not be drawn to this art, from the knowledge of which one can be party to the mysteries of God, even as a prophet?"[69] Both these figures, however, engaged in a style of prediction marked by cryptic pronouncements and a general aura of mystery. In seeking to elevate the authority and status of their art, they stood apart from the far more numerous down-to-earth practitioners who presented themselves mainly as dispensers of practical tools for the common good. The calling of the calendar or practica writer did not confer any priest-like authority, for it involved the pursuit of a natural knowledge that could be shared by all. Ultimately the stellar art gave every person direct access to a God-given understanding; it encouraged in this way a culture of individual self-examination and self-help. It is thus less accurate to picture the typical astrologer as aspiring to priestly status than to follow Nicholas Campion's formulation: the astrologers offered "a democratic alternative to the organized priesthood."[70]

So too there is certainly something to be said for the suggestion that late medieval popular astrology had features in common with the openly heretical movements of the age such as those of John Wyclif and Jan Hus. Carey sees the art as one of several "alternative belief systems," the spread of which reflected broad dissatisfaction with the perceptions and assumptions underlying the established religious fabric. The rise of these various alternatives points to "a willingness, even an eagerness, to believe new claimants to truth, new sources of advice, new agents of spiritual and intellectual authority."[71] The major difference, of course, was that neither the purveyors nor the consumers of popular astrology ever conceived of their art as involving a rejection of orthodox faith. And here is one reason why Germany remained largely free of open heresy in the pre-Reformation era. Bernd Moeller points out that currents of mystical piety became quietly domesticated in this period, but that in the process they actually grew more pervasive and powerful. At the same time, believers pursued the traditional outward forms—including indulgences, for instance—more energetically than ever in a fervid and often desperate quest for assurance.[72] Missing from this picture is the eager reception of a system of concepts and imagery that allowed each person a new way to conceive his relationship both to nature and to divinity, to reorder his or her life without consciously rejecting any particular orthodox teaching or ritual custom.

Again, the search for alternatives to traditional sacramental piety went hand in hand with implicit opposition to the powers of the priesthood. Over the pre-Reformation period the popular works contained more and more suggestions of future disasters for the clergy. Already in the 1480s, predictions of coming trials and suffering for the clergy were appearing in the astrological pamphlets and broadsheets. Perhaps the author of an anonymous practica for 1487 thought he was simply making a safe bet in foretelling that clerics would be generally scorned. Equally vague was Wenzel Faber's forecast of general troubles coming for monks, priests, and prelates, but he went on to sound a more pointedly critical note: cardinals, legates, and other high clergy would "create widespread discord, by which the Christian church will be heavily burdened."[73] It is true that predictions for the clergy were often hardly much worse than those for other groups; Johann Engel's outlook for the common people in 1488 was nearly as bleak as his expectations for "the prelates of the Church." Johann Virdung's practica for 1503 included dark admonitions to the churchmen, threatening their downfall, but also severe warnings to the common folk for breaking God's law: "Be careful, I'm warning you." Yet comments on the clergy were on the whole more consistently and bitingly negative than those on other groups, especially when the higher ranks were singled out. Sigismund Fabri did not hesitate to announce in his calendar for 1493 that "in this year the prelates will be caught up in much perversity."[74] In the German practicas of this era we find nothing remotely similar to a passage from an Italian prognostication for 1479, in which the physician Gerolamo Manfredi felt compelled to acknowledge that the Cardinals had more power than the stars.[75]

The pope himself could not escape the anticipated negative influence of the heavens. "The most holy father the Pope will in this year [1493] without doubt be sorely attacked and harried by opposition," ran a typical projection; "he cannot expect much good fortune." Such predictions nearly always meant bad news also for the higher clergy, and for the pope's supporters generally. The same writer foresaw "great upheaval, violent conflict, envy and hate" among the cardinals and other prelates; at the same time "they will draw upon themselves much ridicule and evil repute, and some will give themselves over to death."[76] Such thinly disguised expressions of disillusionment were both a product of and a further spur to the mounting anticlericalism of the pre-Reformation era. In his practica for 1498 the young humanist Thomas Murner may have been merely experimenting with the genre, but in doing so he worked to produce a worthy emulation of all its typical characteristics. The pope stood in great danger; he could be expected to suffer major injury in the coming year, not only personally but also in his wealth and through harm to the standing of the Church. Murner's overall picture matched the usual tendency to gloom, above all in regard to churchly matters: "Those who are experienced in this science have no doubt that this year will bring great wars, not only of the worldly sort, but also among the religious orders. And this war among the orders will be entirely open to public view."[77] An anonymous practica for 1502 predicted that Pope Alexander VI would be punished by God with a horrible death, along with his son Cesare Borgia. Forecasts breathing resentment against the clergy typically foresaw terrible trials for the pope and the whole Church, even as they looked to a final great renewal.[78]

Most practica writers who indicated threats to the clergy were probably influenced to some extent by Johann Lichtenberger's *Pronosticatio*, which became instantly known throughout the Empire after its first appearance in 1488. Lichtenberger predicted that the Church would be rocked by catastrophe of nearly unimaginable proportions in the coming years, but that eventually it would be purified and attain its proper glory. The hoped-for hero of his story was Maximilian I, the Holy Roman Emperor; indeed the final triumph of the Church would come only with the triumph of the House of Habsburg over all the enemies of Christian faith and unity. Although the annual prognostications tended to focus on more immediate expectations, the general pattern of dire forecasts for Church leaders together with hopeful expectations for Imperial authority is evident in many of these humbler works. Indeed practicas from the 1490s through at least the first decade of the new century presented some version of this outlook. The pope, wrote Tannstetter in 1504, would be "severely troubled and anguished," while the "Roman King" would experience good fortune and honor.[79] While we might well expect to find such a view expressed by a well-placed writer who benefited from Maximilian's patronage at Vienna, parallel sentiments surfaced widely.

It is difficult to tell just how much wish fulfillment was at work here on the part of the authors, or to what extent they may have been pursuing a relatively easy form of sensationalism by feeding sentiments that were already widespread. In either case, the very pervasiveness of these cheap works insured that the air grew thicker every year with unfavorable images of prelates, monks, and priests. That wish fulfillment played more than a marginal role is suggested by the views of the contemporary German poet and scholar Conrad Celtis, himself an avid supporter of stellar study. For this "arch-humanist" the appeal of classical nature-religion was related to anti-Romanism, anticlericalism, opposition to saint veneration, and a general desire to escape from the inherited sacramental, ecclesiastical culture.[80] Popular astrology at this time was certainly something other than an ancient nature-religion, but it did offer a language that facilitated a similar if subtler escape for less prominent layfolk. Serving as cultural middlemen, the practica writers did much to disseminate in their mass audience an anticlerical and antisacramental orientation that had taken root among many German humanists and advocates of Imperial reform.

Saturnine Warnings

According to ancient tradition the most confounding celestial influences came from Saturn, the slowest-moving and most distant planet, embodying the powers of time and destiny. Closely associated with sadness, old age, loneliness, misfortune, melancholy, madness, paralysis, decay, and death, its influence could sometimes also inspire the most profound sort of wisdom. The prevalence of Saturnine imagery in the fifteenth and six-teenth centuries has been much studied, and was certainly one expression of growing uncertainty and apprehension in that era. In the popular astrological literature the personified planet often appeared as a reaper, holding a scythe, and sometimes consuming his own children; if there was any suggestion of wisdom here, it was the wisdom that came from sadness and suffering. When this old and cold figure appeared in his own house of Capricorn, and thus as a ruling planet, the forecasts were especially full of darkness and disaster: "The hour of Saturn is the hour of evil. In that hour God was betrayed and delivered to death."[81] According to the prolific Johannes Engel, Saturn's unlucky children included monks, hermits, old people, Jews, peasants, and all who performed "unclean work." The list typically became longer in later years, with more frequent mentions of the poor, the crippled, the ill, and melancholics among others. Fear of Saturnine devastation was thus certainly by no means restricted to a humanist elite; it swiftly became a prominent theme in the world of the townsfolk.[82]

Yet Saturnine influence could not be separated from that of the other planets. In fact the most dramatic and definite effects resulted from the juxtaposed forces that came from eclipses and from planetary conjunctions. Unlike the saints, who represented both earthly and heavenly reconciliation, the stars were not intercessors; instead they evoked a sense of inevitable worldly struggles and strife.[83] The great challenge was to maintain or regain order and balance in a world of cosmic forces where chaos always threatened. The annual calendars and prognostications thus lent themselves from the start to forecasts that were at best mixed, and that more often focused on coming evils than on prospects for stability and prosperity. As the astrologers pointed out, it would hardly be necessary to issue forecasts at all if things could be expected to go well year after year, and in any case it was easier to predict unfortunate events and conditions than happy ones.[84] Indeed beyond their calendrical, medical, and agricultural uses, the main purpose of the annual works was to warn people about future dangers and hardships.

The general sense of foreboding came across most clearly and consistently in the practicas. Conflict, illness, and suffering were always on the horizon. A typical outlook for 1487 was that "many men will show no restraint toward one another, and will hate and chastise one another; and Mercury will cause many lies, forgeries, and the like, as well as many business losses." A calendar for 1496 looked to a frightful prospect for most burghers: a great defeat for the ruling lords, but the peasants would benefit from taking up arms, "for all will go according to their will."[85] Johann Engel's practica for 1497 was echoed many others with its general prediction of "fatal illness for several princes" along with numerous other disasters. Thomas Murner's overall forecast for human health in 1498 epitomized the prevailing tone, vague but bleak: "In short, this year will be full of mortality and illness of every kind," caused by the positions of the Sun, Saturn, and Mercury. Even the annual practicas of Georg Tannstetter, who had close ties to the Emperor Maximilian, have been described as "uniformly pessimistic."[86] Naturally there were occasional exceptions; the force of the stars could and did at least sometimes conduce to earthly peace and harmony. But almost always, forecasts of good fortune were strongly qualified. Wenzel Faber predicted happy conditions for the common man in 1487, but he carefully left himself an out, for it was possible that a predicted eclipse would "turn the whole happy year to unhappiness." Similar equivocations abounded. Another writer's predictions for 1490 foresaw no outbreak of plague in that year; but "on the other hand, we should fear a great mortality for the coming year of 1491." Johann Stabius's *Practica Teutsch* for 1501 foresaw a generally pleasant year, if one could overlook a likely renewed outbreak of the French disease. Predictions for good times, when they did appear, were much less specific than forecasts of evil and suffering. Their tone was often vague: "their affairs will start to improve," or "they will stand in a better way."[87]

This sort of dwelling on future threats was partly a function of the mathematization of time we have noted. As the historian William Bouwsma pointed out, anxiety is largely a function of attitudes toward time. The awareness of time encouraged by the astrologers deflated the traditional enchanted times in which individual and communal psychological pressures had been released; those pressures now built up as hopes and fears about what the future would bring.[88] Warnings of disasters to come became more open and frequent around 1500 and in the years that followed. Growing more pervasive and at the same time taking shape in a few key images as time went on, such expectancy inevitably encouraged a sense of impending divine punishment and judgment. Virdung's practicas typified this trend; more and more, they took on the aspect of repentance sermons. His predictions for 1503 included dire scenarios of great suffering at the hands of the Turks, terrible wars and divisions among the ruling classes, and extreme unrest among the common people. Most people, he complained, failed to call on God until they were faced with imminent death. The time to do so was now; the central lesson of the stars was to repent before it was too late.[89]

Murner's concluding exhortation for 1498 made clear the largest import of his forecasts: "But now let us pray to God, whose punishing judgment stands at our door, that he will be merciful toward us, as the time for his mercy has come." Conrad Tockler's *Practica Lipensis* for 1515 was "based on the natural influence of the heavens," but issued as "a warning to [all] men, that we should zealously and humbly pray to the almighty God to turn away all dangers to our lives and souls." It was by no means merely to use a conventional formula when an astrologer such as Simon Eyssenmann concluded his practicas with the phrase "God have mercy on us."[90] Almost inevitably, many popular astrological writers crossed over into the role of repentance preachers. Some of the earliest surviving manuscript practicas had commented on the world's sinfulness, and the need for repentance in order to escape the divine punishments announced and executed by the stars. This trend grew markedly stronger, and dramatically expanded its social reach, through the popular printed works of the period around 1500. More and more we encounter the thought that in the face of overwhelming worldly problems, the only possible help lay in prayer and repentance.

Chapter 3 will explore more closely the role of popular astrology in fueling and shaping pre-Reformation apocalyptic expectancy, helping to stir up the storm in which Martin Luther's evangelical movement came to life. But we can already see certain elements coming together. The rush of astrological publication over barely more than a generation promoted an accelerated mathematization of time and space, conveyed forms of medical and natural understanding that implicitly bypassed the saints and sacraments, emphasized the providential rule of an all-powerful God, built awareness of human conflicts and contingency, stoked disillusionment with the clergy, and heightened anxiety about the future. All these changes served to cultivate attitudes among German townsmen that would prove favorable to the evangelical preaching of the 1520s. Perhaps the greatest irony of this massive movement of popular astrology was that while it aimed to reduce anxiety by liberating people from artificial human constraints and orienting them securely in the natural cosmos, its larger result was not to allay but to expose and concentrate basic fears, both personal and communal.

3

The Flood

Lord save us, we perish.
—MATTHEW 8:25

Here is the real core of the religious problem: Help! Help!
—WILLIAM JAMES

IN THE LATE nineteenth and early twentieth centuries, students of the Reformation era in Germany were generally agreed that a pervasive, fearful sense of spiritual and social crisis was among the key preconditions of the evangelical explosion of the 1520s. More recently scholars have sought to play down, deny, or simply ignore this view, partly on the basis of the assumptions that every age has its severe critics and doomsayers, and that we cannot legitimately extrapolate the alarmist expressions of a few to a broader public. Peter Blickle, for example, rejects the idea that anxiety and fear drove people to the Reformation "because of a lack of empirical evidence and because the existing interpretative models are not very plausible."[1] Nonetheless, this interpretation continues to enjoy strong currency for the inherently persuasive reason that the testimony of contemporaries overwhelmingly supports it. To cite a lack of empirical evidence is to flirt with absurdity in light of the many thousands of documents, from city council records to private letters to mass-produced pamphlets, that directly reflect or otherwise make reference to common perceptions of breakdown, anticipations of disaster, and visions of an approaching Judgment.[2]

Closely tied up with this issue is that of the role of astrology in stirring up fears and hopes on the eve of Luther's leap to the stage. Friedrich von Bezold was among the historians of a past generation who found close links between popular astrology and the swelling prophetic currents of the pre-Reformation era. In Germany, he wrote, the stargazers became the prophets and way-makers of a great revolution that had been predicted for the Church for centuries; indeed the whole social and political order was shaken by the intensification of prophetic awareness that resulted mainly from the invasion of astrological concepts. The years around 1500 were a time of mounting apocalyptic angst, fueled above all by bleak and threatening stellar forecasts. The most dramatic and notorious predictions looked to a major cluster of planetary conjunctions expected in February of 1524, including a twenty-year great conjunction, which brought speculations about a second universal deluge and possibly the end of the world. Along with many other European cultural historians who wrote before the mid-twentieth century, Bezold was convinced that the upheavals of the 1520s had to be viewed against this background.[3]

This interpretation has evoked both explicit contradictions and a host of qualifications. A few scholars have denied straightforwardly, if arbitrarily, that the science of the stars had any bearing on the Reformation as either a religious or a social phenomenon. Others acknowledge only a negative relationship; in this view the evangelical movement brought a Bible-based rejection of superstitious fears of all sorts, including those hawked by the stargazers. Jonathan Green argues that the usual understanding of the relationship between printed prognostications and widespread fears must be reversed: predictions of a deluge did not lead to panic; rather, anxiety over rapid social changes and epistemological confusion gave rise to forecasts of disaster.[4] Myriad studies discount the topic simply by marginalizing or ignoring it. Despite the growth of a serious and substantial specialized literature on sixteenth-century astrology and the flood panic, deep reservoirs of resistance remain against movements to integrate this material fully into the history of early modern religious movements and sensibilities. This chapter essays not only to reaffirm that the stargazers did much to pump up the atmosphere of fear and anxiety on the eve of Luther's explosive appearance, but also to show that the evangelical message spread less in reaction to the currents of apprehension centering on the flood forecasts than within those currents.

Lichtenberger's Dreams

The relationship between scientific astrology and religious prophecy is a historical problem fraught with unusual complexity. In principle, the two forms of knowing were clearly separate: one was essentially a matter of reason, the other depended on divine revelation. Yet as Green points out, "prophecy and [astrological] prognostication prove to be too closely inter-twined in the fifteenth and sixteenth centuries to be entirely separated from each other, and many contemporaries perceived the two as com-plementary rather than contradictory."[5] As early as the twelfth century, Western thinkers were drawing on classical and Islamic texts to employ astrology as a tool of prophetic and apocalyptic understanding. But this trend became far more pronounced in the late Middle Ages, as systematic astrological concepts gained currency. Indeed, astrology became a major catalyst in the accelerating ferment of prophetic ideas and traditions; in many eyes, the celestial signs offered an objective, scientific basis for spec-ulations and warnings about the prophetic future. A highly varied array of predictive scenarios emerged, expressing outlooks ranging from the deepest worldly pessimism to sanguine anticipation.

Many late medieval apocalyptic visions focused on the coming of the Last Judgment and those fearsome events, such as the coming of the Antichrist, that would usher it in. Others, however, included strong ele-ments of hope for some sort of divinely predestined historical fulfillment before the end. Often such schemes saw the immediate future as filled with terrible catastrophes and suffering, but looked to a final recovery and earthly victory for the faithful. The most powerful tradition of the lat-ter sort grew out of the writings of the Calabrian abbot Joachim of Fiore (c. 1132–1202), whose insights into the prophetic books of scripture led him to break decisively with the long-established Augustinian interpreta-tion of world history. Inspired by Trinitarian visions, Joachim conceived an essentially tripartite scheme in which the past Age of the Father and the current Age of the Son would soon be followed by the birth pangs of a third, culminating historical period, the age of the Holy Spirit, a time of full spiritual enlightenment and peace. From the thirteenth century on, Joachim's understanding nourished a tendency among many Western Christian thinkers to find consolation in the promise of an approaching earthly triumph of the good.[6]

In the realm of systematic astrology, meanwhile, few ideas were more consequential than the Arabic theory of periodic conjunctions of the upper planets, which became a key basis for speculations about the prophetic outlines of world history. Albumasar's teaching about great conjunctions of Jupiter and Saturn had inspired countless learned prophetic calcula-tions since the introduction of his work to Christian Europe around 1150. In the late fifteenth century these notions began to make their way, how-ever superficially, into a broader urban culture. John of Lübeck helped with the advertising, predicting in 1474 that the expected conjunction of 1503 to 1504 would be followed by the birth of the Antichrist. Although consumers of the popular forecasts learned little about the mathematics of conjunction theory, they could easily enough grasp the notion that periodic meetings of the upper planets had extraordinary significance. Each successive twenty-year great conjunction in this era (1464, 1484, 1504, and 1524) gained wider attention and provoked more apocalyptic speculation, especially in Italy and Germany, largely because of the ever-widening reach of the common astrological publications.[7] This waxing regard to major conjunctions by no means displaced the more common predictive concerns of the astrological publicists, but it greatly broadened the potential range of their forecasts.

Joachimist prophecy, Arabic conjunction theory, and a variety of other late medieval prophetic and divinatory currents found a famous confluence in the still-shadowy figure of Johannes Lichtenberger. In his *Pronosticatio*, Lichtenberger used the pseudonym Pilger Ruth, posing as a blind old forest-dwelling hermit with great prophetic gifts. His work adopted a standard medieval concept of three possible sources for knowledge of the future: past experience, astrological art, and divine revelation. But whatever clarity such a division might have promised in theory was lost in the application, for this text proved a motley mash of astrology, biblical prophecy, horrifying visions of coming troubles, and dreams of future peace. Lichtenberger's range of extrabiblical authorities was enormous, from Aristotle and the Persian-Jewish stargazer Messahala to sources such as Birgitta of Sweden and the Sibylline Oracles. Much of his text was in fact plagiarized from a work by the Netherlander Paul of Middleburg, whose attention had centered on the 1484 great conjunction of Jupiter and Saturn in Scorpio. Middelburg himself drew mainly on Albumasar, but probably owed his understanding of this particular conjunction to a German calendar for 1484 by the prolific German physician and astronomer Johannes Engel. Here Engel had predicted that Saturn's predominant influence would result in "great war, dearth, and pestilence," as well as the birth of a false prophet who would oppose true Christian teaching. The 1484 conjunction was supposedly central to the *Pronosticatio*, but that celestial event often became nearly lost in the tangled fabric of these pages.[8]

Unlike many or even most of the calendar and practica writers, Lichtenberger was not a physician. His main goal was not to provide immediate orientation and guidance for everyman, but rather to express fears and hopes for the twin pillars of his world, namely Church and Empire. Drawing more on scriptural and medieval prophetic traditions than on stellar reckoning, he foresaw terrible crises affecting all classes. His most elaborate predictions concerned the clergy, who faced a time of unprecedented upset and suffering. Here he picked up on the Engel-Middelburg expectation of a false prophet who would mislead and oppress Christians; in fact he spoke of several such figures, including one who would appear as a monk and whose words would be received as divine truth. The last of these prophets would be the Antichrist himself, who would mislead almost the entire world. But while the Ship of St. Peter would be badly buffeted by these storms, she would not finally go down. The time of trials would eventually come to an end, and a thorough reformation of the world would follow under a great emperor and a series of angelic popes. The main embodiment of these hopes was Maximilian I, "King of the Romans," who became Emperor in 1493; this aspect of pro-Habsburg propaganda lay very close to the heart of the work. Mainly preoccupied with the German lands of the Empire, Lichtenberger's work was deeply conservative and thoroughly medieval in outlook.[9]

All these ideas emerged in fuzzy outline, and many appeared contradictory; almost none were connected in a clear and precise way with scientific astrological reasoning. Some forty-five large, often cryptic woodcuts accompanied the text. Prominent were images of Christ as ruler and judge of the entire world; others suggested the failings of clergy, rulers, and common people. A storm-tossed Ship of St. Peter represented the Church in peril. The image of a false prophet took the highly charged form of a monk with a devil sitting on his shoulder, a depiction that would inevitably be swept into the propaganda battles surrounding Luther in the 1520s. Only one woodcut, representing the 1484 conjunction of Jupiter and Saturn in Scorpio, included explicit astrological content. It is hard to avoid the conclusion that in the end his readings of the stars remained largely subservient to the author's main goal, namely to marshal a collection of prophetic threats and promises that could serve the cause of Imperial revival and moral renewal.[10]

The practice of combining astrology and medieval prophecy in service to conservative ideals and Habsburg authority found further prominent representatives in the following generation, including the Bavarian Dr. Joseph Grünpeck (c. 1473–c. 1532). In many respects an imitator of Lichtenberger, Grünpeck is a less shadowy figure, a trained physician and scholar who had studied at Crakow in the 1490s, and who served for some years at the court of Maximilian I. His works, like Lichtenberger's, presented hair-raising prospects of imminent calamity along with savior-emperor myths and Joachimist visions of a final time of earthly peace. For both writers, astrology was less a natural and medical tool than a social and political one.[11] Both were ultimately propagandists for the Habsburgs and severe critics of the clergy who felt their world falling apart, feared the terrible and deserved scourge of divine justice, and expected little but suffering and chaos in the near future, even as they called for universal repentance and hoped desperately for the restoration of order.

Perhaps partly because of his medical background, Grünpeck's writings were on the whole less cryptic than Lichtenberger's. His first major work (1498) was on the French disease—venereal disease—which he saw as both a natural illness and a result of worsening human sin. Any proper treatment would require not only the expertise of physicians, but a general reformation of the Church and all classes. The same theme informed his tract on wondrous signs of 1502 to 1507, if yet more soberly: the rush of recent portents warned of the coming end of the world; nothing short of a full renewal of persons, Church, and Empire could possibly avert the punishments to precede it.[12] His best-known work, the *Spiegel*, first appeared in both Latin and German versions in 1508; many further editions followed. Drawing heavily but without acknowledgment on Lichtenberger, Grünpeck delivered an eclectic brew of astrology, prophecy, and the interpretation of natural wonders.[13] Like his wonder tract, the *Spiegel* was essentially an extended repentance-sermon, focusing on the urgent need for both inner personal and outward imperial reform. Grünpeck harped on the lust for money as the greatest current threat to Christian virtue and social order, and excoriated the clergy for manifold failings. His work was packed with Old Testament and historical references illustrating God's dealings with his people, and leaving no doubt about the current condition of eschatological crisis. He adopted from Lichtenberger the image of the storm-threatened Ship of St. Peter, which was at least loosely associated with the story of the biblical deluge and Noah's ark. At some points Grünpeck focused almost exclusively on a biblical message of individual repentance. Still, while he often implied that no improvement could come without a change in human hearts, his *Spiegel* made references to a heroic ruler who would reform the world before the End, revealing hopes much like Lichtenberger's for a universal renewal under Habsburg leadership.[14]

Lichtenberger and Grünpeck were far from the only prominent pre-Reformation German writers to add the potent spice of astrology to the mixed grill of medieval prophetic traditions. The influential mathematician and practica writer Johannes Stabius, who moved from Ingolstadt to a position of high prestige at the University of Vienna in 1502, focused on the expected 1503 conjunction of the upper planets while incorporating Joachimist traditions and medieval hopes for a last world emperor. Drawing heavily on Lichtenberger but engaging in more serious stellar reckonings, his work likewise served as pro-Imperial propaganda. Variations on the theme of terrible trials but final triumph surfaced in numerous other texts of the time, ranging from basically conservative warning tracts by figures such as Johann Virdung to more radical social critiques such the *Book of a Hundred Chapters* (c. 1509–1510) by the anonymous "upper-Rhenish revolutionary."[15] By 1516 the Lichtenbergerian mode took form in a mini-genre of prophetic pamphlets that combined vague astrological references with visions from a stall of famous ancient and medieval prophetic figures, including Joachim of Fiore, Birgitta of Sweden, Hildegard of Bingen, the pseudo-Methodius, Cyril of Alexandria, and the Sybilline oracles. Some thirteen versions of this collection, often known as the "Anonymous Practica," appeared by 1530, though only a few came after 1521. Most of the prophecies followed a now-familiar pattern: heated criticism of the clergy, anticipations of unimaginable suffering, calls for quick and sincere repentance, and dreams of deliverance by a great German hero-figure who would lead a universal reformation and establish worldwide peace. Several versions predicted the birth of a child of evil, a false prophet whose oppressions would affect all classes. But then a purification of the world would follow: "a new reformation, a new law, a new kingdom, an honorable and chaste life in both spiritual and worldly estates." These notions generally floated in seas of cryptic language, once again showing the long shadow of Lichtenberger.[16]

Because in this tradition astrology often became little more than window dressing, some scholars have suggested that in the pre-Reformation era the culture of prophecy absorbed and vitiated serious astrological prediction, at least at the level of vernacular publicity.[17] Yet the interaction between these two broad currents was by no means one-sided. While prophetic hopes and fears may have led to corruptions of astrological science in some strains of popular literature, it is equally true that by the early sixteenth century the mathematical astrology of the calendars and prognostications was helping to deflate the whole realm of medieval compensatory dreams.

Influx and Overflow

Even as they sought to provide a liberating form of natural knowledge, the astrologers who produced the annual forecasts worked relentlessly to expose future dangers. A sober reading of the stars inevitably perceived threats of conflict, disorder, destructive change and breakdown; these were conditions that the serious stargazer could always predict with relative confidence. The greatest perils lay in imbalance—disequilibrium—which was virtually always in prospect. A potent vocabulary for exploring the inescapable flux of time and its constant threats tended to favor the articulation of fears over hopes. As a result, what came to prevail increasingly among German burghers was a discourse of dread, involving not only premonitions of disaster but also deep anxiety and a sense of human helplessness. This outlook tended to favor stark apocalyptic visions of finality over Lichtenberger's style of hope for restored order.[18] The intensification of popular astrology both spurred and evidenced a collective disillusionment with medieval prophetic dreams, a disillusionment that reached a climax in the early 1520s, just as the Luther affair exploded.

Fears of instability and breakdown helped quicken the spread of literature on natural wonders, reflecting an uneasy fascination with irregular, mysterious, and freakish phenomena. Such attention was anything but new in the period around 1500, but it did grow more intense, evincing a new level of curiosity, equally passionate and anxious. As with the astrology of the calendars and practicas, printing certainly helped accelerate this broadening concern with natural oddities. Werner Rolewinck's *Fasciculus Temporum*, a world-chronicle appearing first at Cologne in 1474, exemplified the trend with its many discussions of strange happenings as presages of future events. The very first book printed at Lübeck, the *Rudimentum Novitiorum* (1475), was also a sort of universal history that focused especially on weird and freakish occurrences as indicators of the threats hanging over mankind.[19]

The interpretation of natural wonders had long been part of the art of astrology broadly conceived; attention to the laws of nature and interest in exceptional occurrences were, after all, complementary. Ptolemy and the Arabs had seen comets as astrological phenomena; Albumasar

had studied them as a function of the signs of the Zodiac. This perspective differed from that of Aristotle, who had made a sharper division
between astronomy and the study of the terrestrial atmosphere, yet most
latter-day stargazers adopted it, taking extraordinary phenomena of all
sorts under their purview.[20] This expansive engagement was all the easier because of the prevailing ambiguity about causes and signs. A comet,
like a conjunction, could be the cause of natural events that had not yet
taken place, for the effects took time to be realized; but it might also be
a warning sign from God about an impending punishment. Unusual
celestial phenomena were analyzed in terms of their relationships to
the Zodiac, the terrestrial houses, and the wandering stars, all of which
could bear on their significance. For these reasons it is easy to overemphasize the distinction between systematic astrology and the interpretation of wonders in the early modern era. Not only in practice but even in
theory, the lines often blurred between a science of causes and a theology of signs.[21]

The Strasbourg humanist and poet Sebastian Brant typified the
complementary interests of contemporaries in natural regularities and
irregularities. Brant is certainly best known today for his semisatirical
Ship of Fools, but as Dieter Wuttke makes clear, the very fame of that
work has done much to obscure its author's actual views. The poem
appeared to dismiss both "scientific" astrological prediction and the
reading of natural wonders, yet Brant was himself heavily involved in
these pursuits. Between 1480 and 1521, he issued some thirty-two interpretative reports of at least twenty natural wonders, including eight
pamphlets in 1496 alone. His most widely circulated works included
a commentary on the famous meteor of Ensisheim, which thundered
to earth in southern Alsace on November 7, 1492, and another on the
strangely conjoined Worms twins of 1495. Brant regarded such phenomena with profound seriousness, seeing them as divine warnings to
a world—and particularly a German Empire—in crisis, if still potentially reformable. He gathered his early writings of this kind in a 1497
collection, *Varia carmina*, thus essentially founding the tradition of the
wonder collection. He also published at least three practicas, offering
predictions based on the conjunctions of 1503/04 and 1524, drawing
data from works such as the 1499 *Ephemerides* of Stöffler and Pflaum.
His practicas, like his wonder pamphlets, warned of coming wars,
upheavals in church and state, the appearance of false prophets, floods,
failed harvests, disease, and the nearing the end of the world. Along

with most of his contemporaries, Brant saw no conflict between stellar science and the reading of natural wonders.[22]

During the years immediately preceding the great outburst of religious controversy in Germany, the most sensational spate of celestial wonders appeared in at Urach, in Württemberg, in 1514. They included a large moon with a cross covering its face, flanked by two smaller moons, each with strange protrusions. A pamphlet by Virdung made these appearances widely known, analyzing them in natural terms but also presenting them as an omen of various misfortunes, and as a warning to both the rulers and the common people of Württemberg in the wake of the "Poor Conrad" rising, a bloody but abortive popular revolt against Duke Ulrich. The physician Alexander Seitz, a zealous advocate of astrological medicine, echoed much of Virdung's discussion in a 1516 tract. In the past such signs had often announced massive flooding, earthquakes, and the deaths of great princes. But Seitz went further; these amazing phenomena were also apocalyptic warnings of impending judgment. And as the astronomers knew, appearances of this sort generally portended the worst ills for the lands in which they were seen. Similar portents were multiplying quickly, Seitz warned, and they spoke especially to Germany, "the head and heart of all Christendom."[23]

To mention the threat of flood, as Seitz did, was to hit on an image with especially strong resonance in this star-struck culture. Indeed, astrological associations between images of overflow and threatening disaster went back centuries. A key tradition arose from the Toledo Letter, a document that first appeared around 1084, purporting to be a warning from the astrologers of Toledo about the imminent worldwide destruction by great storms, famines, earthquakes, and other deadly strokes. These calamities would be announced by a terrifying eclipse and effected by a conjunction of all the planets in Libra. Despite the failure of the prediction new permutations appeared, and around 1330 the genre took on a new life, stirring irregular waves of fear. In many versions the original vague references to storms and rising seas were altered to suggest a universal flood, and some became openly apocalyptic, connecting the deluge to the end of the world. The astrological calculations presented in later adaptations became more sophisticated and detailed as the basic elements of Arabic conjunction theory spread beyond the universities. In the second half of the fifteenth century, a series of new Toledo Letters in print reinforced the flood image more and more, especially in Germany and Italy.[24]

As Gert Mentgen has shown, the Toledo-letter tradition was an important part of the background for the flood fears that rose ever higher in the years following 1500. Thus the panic of the early 1520s was at least partly the culmination of a long medieval inheritance that had gained momentum in the preceding decades. These letters helped fuel an expanding realm of public discourse by articulating shared fears.[25] Mentgen emphasizes the role of the princely courts in this process, but we need to take into account the far broader dissemination of astrological concepts and images that came mostly through the annual ephemera. We have seen that the popular science of the calendars and practicas supplied burghers with a new analytical language and practical ways to order their lives. Ironically, however, the very pursuit of this new order evoked higher anxiety and a stronger tendency to view the world in apocalyptic terms. The flood theme became the most prominent current of an apocalyptic discourse that was nourished less by any one tradition of medieval expectancy than by the new mass literature of stellar knowledge and prognostication.

The early star-based calendars, as we noted, were concerned in the first place with scheduled therapeutic bloodlettings to maintain a proper humoral balance. In the annual practicas, a happy forecast promised normal, predictable, and beneficial atmospheric fluctuations. But these very concerns with order and balance evoked ever-closer attention to the dangers anticipated for the coming months, threats to the vital equilibrium. The Moon and Saturn, the highest and lowest planetary bodies, were prominent in this connection. Most obvious in the calendars were the lunar phases and eclipses for the coming year, often strikingly and prominently illustrated. More than any other wandering star, the moon symbolized changefulness; thus too it was often associated with instability, uncertainty, weakness, folly, corruption, decay, and death. The practicas devoted more space to planetary conjunctions and oppositions in the various signs of the zodiac; here then the concern with coming conflicts and imbalance became yet more pervasive and explicit. Hence, while the popular ephemera surely reflected in one sense a quest for order, by their very nature they conveyed fears of disorder, lunar excess, Saturnine chaos, and overflow.

The moon and Saturn both evoked ancient images of time as an incessant and fearsome flushing. Their qualities included the liquidity of putrid ooze and rot, the plethoric moisture of disease; both planets were blamed for unusually high tides, damaging floods, and drownings. Saturn in particular became the ultimate embodiment of extremes, of contradictions;

the Saturnine melancholic might swing violently from tears to laughter and back again.[26] In this sense, the planet epitomized the dangers to equilibrium and the threat of upset and overflow that drew concern in the annual forecasts. Well before 1500 we find a pattern of imagery in these works centering on images of threatening, shocking, death-dealing fluid excess. Wenzel Faber's practica for 1492, to cite one striking example, included a title page woodcut showing a personified Saturn literally vomiting over the entire earth (see Figure 3.1). More general images of planetary superfluity became common; another title page from a Leipzig practica showed Venus and Mars together with Aquarius and Taurus pouring out their liquid effects over the lower realm.[27]

The original chaos (Genesis 1) was watery, but common images of overflow naturally included the bodily humors as well as water. Both blood and water had spurted from the wounded side of the dying Christ (John 19:34). Lyndal Roper points out that from the fifteenth century on, both the "literature of excess" and the "literature of discipline" regularly presented the human body as "a container of fluids, bursting out in every direction."[28] This image had strong roots in astrological theory. Terms such as *überflüssig* (overflowing, overabundant) became more and more common in the calendars and practicas, referring not only to humoral excess but to other forms of dangerous superflux as well. A practica for 1514 by Hans Überling, "Master of the Seven Liberal Arts," typified many others in warning of the dangers of severe sickness brought on by "excess of blood," and in mentioning the danger of terrestrial flooding as well. According to a standard teaching, superabundant moisture was the main cause of putrefaction, and numerous commentators associated contemporary outbreaks of flooding with the spread of deadly maladies.[29]

This connection was especially apparent in reactions to the terrifying spread of the French disease from 1494 on. From the very beginning, the intense discussion on the origins of this scourge included astro-medical interpretations of imbalance and overflow. The Nuremberg physician Dietrich Ulsenius published a verse dream-vision in a 1496 broadsheet according to which the cause of the upset lay in the 1483 to 1484 great conjunction. Albrecht Dürer supplied the famous illustration for this text, depicting an afflicted man with the zodiac-globe above, labeled with the year 1484.[30] Widespread debate broke out on the exact causes and dating of the outbreak; even those who acknowledged the heavy import of the 1484 conjunction disagreed about precisely which planetary aspects were responsible. But virtually all commentators noted the symptomatic oozing

FIGURE 3.1 Saturn vomits disaster upon the earth. Title page woodcut from Wenzel Faber's practica for 1492. Reproduced from Heinz Artur Strauss, *Der astrologische Gedanke in der deutschen Vergangenheit* (Munich, 1926).

sores, stinking pustules, and rotting flesh, and most associated the affliction with a corrupt, overly moist atmosphere and a notable recent rash of
floods in Germany and Italy. The debate, along with the disease itself, was
pan-European, yet nowhere was attention stronger or more sustained than
in the Empire, where observers such as Grünpeck publicized the connections with God's wrath over sin.[31]

Virdung's *German Practica for several years* (1503) helps illustrate the
infiltration of frightful flood imagery even among writers who otherwise
hopefully predicted a final victory for the forces of good. A 1503 to 1504
great conjunction of the upper planets in Cancer, a sign in the "watery"
triplicity, would announce the advent of a dangerous prophet of perversity
and a general collapse of order. Virdung foresaw sicknesses arising from
a coming "raging of waters" with strong winds, thunder, and lightning;
soaking storms would destroy crops, thus bringing dearth and death.
Virdung cited both Ptolemy and Pierre D'Ailly to assert that a conjunction
of Saturn and Jupiter in Cancer and the fourth house had been a clear
sign—or cause—of the biblical flood: "Now if these two planets brought
such tremendous water at that time, what will all three bring when they
meet in Cancer and remain there seven months? Note it well, you men
of learning and intelligence." He also speculated about the period in
which this great conjunction would have its effects, and one of the most
likely possibilities, he thought, was that its influence would begin after
twenty years, or one great conjunction cycle, thus in 1523, lasting into 1524.
Virdung proposed that the conjunction would magnify whatever good or
evil was to come, yet he feared it was "a sign from God that announces
strange, unprecedented, and horrifying things such as never have happened." The only hope lay in prayer and repentance.[32]

Similar nightmares of storm and deluge seem increasingly to surface
everywhere around this time. The *Book of a Hundred Chapters* referred to
conjunctions of Saturn and Jupiter, echoing the now common notion that
when they occurred in a "watery" sign, devastating inundations would follow. Predictions of an invasion by the Turks were most often cast in terms
of a sweeping bloodbath; the rivers would all run red before the end. The
most common depiction of the Church in danger, popularized particularly by Lichtenberger, Grünpeck, and other astrological writers, was the
Ship of St. Peter; it was now tossing badly in angry waves. The popular
poem known as *Die Welsch Gattung* (c. 1512) was thick with storm imagery. This work's anonymous author had a clear reverence for scientific
astrology, and placed heavy emphasis on an eclipse of the sun expected

in 1513. Although he offered no specific calculations, he made it clear that the stars were his main prophetic tool for warning his fellow Germans. The work reflected a sense of deepening frustration regarding a reform of the Empire. Since all efforts had failed, calamity seemed certain. The clouds were gathering over the land, and a horrible tempest was coming over Germany; the future promised only gloom, doom, and destruction. The Ship of St. Peter, in particular, faced unprecedented peril as it tossed on the storm-roiled waters.[33]

Famously, however, the main source of the specific flood predictions for 1524 was the 1499 *Almanach nova plurimis annis* of Johannes Stöffler and Jacob Pflaum, a work later reissued many times. Here Stöffler, a respected scholar and almanac-writer who later became professor of mathematics at Tübingen, made a prediction of twenty conjunctions for February of 1524, no fewer than sixteen of which would occur in the watery sign of Pisces. Among these was the twenty-year great conjunction of the upper planets. Stöffler expected tremendous and unheard-of changes, but did not predict a universal flood. "Lift up your heads, therefore, ye Christian men," he concluded, making plain that these heavenly phenomena held a crucial message.[34]

Students of the era have labored with no little frustration to trace the precise venues by which the Stöffler-Pflaum calculation evolved as the key prediction in a debate that would rage throughout Europe, and most violently in Germany, by the 1520s. Definitive conclusions remain elusive. The Italian astrologer Luca Gaurico may have sharpened the predictions of Stöffler and issued warnings about a flood as early as 1501; he repeated such warnings in numerous works over the following years. Gaurico worked the flood into a larger prophetic scenario that followed the typical late medieval Lichtenbergerian pattern, foreseeing a time of terrible troubles including storms, earthquakes, starvation, deadly epidemics, and the advent of a false prophet. All this was to be followed some time after 1535 by a final reformation of the Church and an age of peace, which only a third of humans would live to see.[35] It seems reasonably certain that the Imperial Diet at Trier in 1512 boosted the discussion to new levels of intensity. Shortly after the meeting, the humanist Johann Aventinus noted scornfully the rapid spread of rumors that an approaching entry of the sun into Libra would herald a great deluge. It is possible, though in some eyes unlikely, that Gaurico was the framer of a now-lost flood prophecy for 1524 that circulated at the Diet. In a Latin *Invectiva* of that year, Virdung rejected this prediction, basing his argument largely on the biblical promise of God not to repeat the flood (Genesis 9:8–17), but using astrological reasoning as well: since the planets did not work on all parts of the earth at once, a general flood under their influence was not possible.[36]

The prophecy that excited the Trier assembly may have been a version of the Toledo Letter. Mentgen proposes that the revival of this tradition had much to do with actual weather conditions in Italy and Germany during the decades surrounding 1500; many reports of serious flooding survive from the period.[37] But if objective climatic conditions were part of the larger picture, their significance in the eyes of contemporaries was tied to the concepts, images, and mental habits disseminated in the popular literature. To buy and to study the calendars and practicas was after all to become an amateur physician and meteorologist, attuned to natural fluctuations, aware of changes in the atmosphere, comparing the accuracy of various forecasts. We noted the instant and enormous popular appeal of Leonhard Reynmann's astrometeorological handbook of 1505; during these same years concern with weather forecasting became more central than ever in the practicas of leading authors such as Tannstetter. In Nuremberg, the mathematician Johannes Werner recorded careful weather observations from 1513 to 1520, and composed aphorisms for weather prediction that were fully grounded in astrological assumptions.[38] The unprecedented public circulation of astrological weather rules, observations, and predictions in a cultural setting where the weather was inseparable from larger cosmological conceptions goes far to explain why popular anxiety increasingly congealed around visions of the ultimate meteorological disaster.

Sirens in the Empire

Well before most Germans had heard the name Martin Luther, fears of what the planetary conjunctions of 1524 would mean had become an ever-present backdrop to the discussion of affairs both public and private in the Empire. We cannot rightly understand the tremendous expansion in vernacular publicity that centered on Luther and his teachings apart from an already widespread discourse of apprehension strongly shaped by popular astrology. By the late fifteen-teens, decades of commercial printing had showered the German cities with layers of star-lore unmatched elsewhere, so that here astrologically inspired fears of an approaching catastrophe gained unique weight and resonance. The annual vernacular practica became the basic model for most of the "flood tracts" of the early 1520s, which despite many of their authors' intentions worked to focus anxiety and bring it to a head.

The evidence is strong that the flood panic was more pervasive and had more dramatic effects in Germany than anywhere else. Scholars have found virtually no echo of the theme in England. From France we have a small handful of references, but nothing that would indicate widespread excitement. In fact the most prominent French astrologer of the time, Pierre Turrel, appears to have deliberately steered clear of the matter. Scattered contributions to the debate from Spanish, Portuguese, Flemish, Netherlandish, and Polish authors do not offer strong justification for see- ing the phenomenon as truly pan-European. As with the earlier spread of popular astrological literature, only Italy shows evidence of concerns at all comparable to what we find in Germany. But here again the Italian authors wrote mainly in Latin, while the Germans overwhelmingly used the vernacular.[39] Ottavia Niccoli argues that Italian writers often reserved their more alarmist flood predictions for their Latin works, consciously presenting a more consoling picture to their less educated readers. Niccoli also proposes that in Italy popular fears about February of 1524 were prob- ably defused, at least in part, by the laughter of Carnival; the powerful tradition of periodic release from mundane burdens and concerns tended to soften the sense of impending doom.[40] Contemporary accounts tend to complement these arguments. In a work of 1523 to 1524 that sought to dampen the panic, for example, the Spanish theologian Petrus Cervelo (Cervol) asserted that predictions of a great flood came mostly from the Germans, while the Italians tended to play down or deny the notion. From 1520 to 1524 some fifty vernacular writings devoted explicitly to the flood projections appeared in the German cities, many in multiple editions; all were aimed at the widest possible audience. No other part of Christendom produced more than a small handful of vernacular writings on the topic.[41]

The first major learned work to address the flood fears attests to their prevalence on the eve of the great religious explosion. In December 1518 appeared the *Defense of Astrology* of Albert Pigghe, astrologer to the French court, member of a humanist circle centered at the university of Louvain, and soon to become one of the most zealous of all defenders of the Papacy and the Roman Church. This book was not primarily concerned with the predictions for 1524, but was mainly an attack on the sort of popular astrology now thriving above all in Germany. Pigghe stood in the line of humanist astrologers, including Peurbach and Regiomontanus, whose ideal was a pure Ptolemaic art unsullied by Arabic additions. Inevitably, then, he discussed the expected conjunctions and the forecasts based on them. For his main target he looked close to home, choosing his fellow Netherlander Gaspar Laet, whose practicas were the best known in France and the Low Countries, and who had helped broadcast the 1524 forecasts. The resulting fears were having lamentable effects, he wrote, especially among common folk who were letting all go to ruin. Pigghe denounced all efforts to make precise predictions, even about the weather, on the bankrupt grounds of conjunction theory.[42]

While Pigghe blamed the popular prognosticators for the rising agitation, events soon thickened the mood of apprehension. In January of 1519 the Emperor Maximilian died. Because the election of his successor was a matter of serious tension and uncertainty, many long-cherished hopes of Imperial as well as churchly rejuvenation threatened to pass away with him. Schemes for meaningful reform were by this time becoming but wistful longings; increasingly, all seemed to depend upon divine mercy. Simon Eyssenmann's predictions for 1520 captured something of the churning mix of anticipations. Although this Leipzig professor's outlook was not without its bright spots, his overall picture was unsettling in the extreme, with the planets indicating "great changes in the world," special dangers for the common man, and death threatening everywhere. "Yet it all stands in the will of the almighty eternal God," he wrote, "in whom one should trust and place his hopes with a ready purpose. For the Almighty will not let his little ship be lost, as the Holy Scriptures show and the gospel teaches."[43]

The second major learned response to fears of diluvian disaster appeared late in 1519; this was *On the False Flood Prediction* by the Italian Agostino Nifo, court astrologer to Pope Leo X. Like Pigghe, Nifo favored Greek over Arabic teachings, though he did not reject conjunction theory entirely. As Thorndike makes clear, he worked so hard to articulate the arguments he hoped to refute that "he almost seems to have convinced himself" of a great flood to come. Watering down the prediction, he foresaw torrential rains and much local flooding, but no universal inundation. Nifo strongly implied that the most destructive floods would come in Germany, and it appears that his work, like Pigghe's, was directed largely at the Empire, where a new edition came out in 1520. While the fears were mainly the product of popular opinion, he argued, needless panic had spread to all classes. But Nifo's work could hardly have done much to calm public fears, since he expressed the belief that human sin had reached heights unknown even in the time of Noah.[44]

Both Nifo and Pigghe witnessed explicitly to a state of alarm that was already widespread, and both at least implicitly placed the epicenter of the uproar in Germany. It was after all the German scholars Stöffler and Pflaum who had provided the crucial calculation, and signs of public discussion of the predictions had been most pronounced in the Empire. It may well be that Nifo, by articulating so fully the fears and the reasoning behind them, helped spark attention to the matter. Yet before his book had drawn much notice—perhaps even before a single copy had made it north of the Alps—the whole issue took a sudden and more direct charge from within the Empire. In early January of 1520 came a shocking array of celestial signs over Vienna, reportedly witnessed by thousands. Although they were only the latest phenomena of this kind to draw attention, they soon evoked especially sensational illustrated reports, which quickly drove discussions of the flood forecasts to new levels of intensity, for the portents seemed inevitably linked to the coming 1524 conjunctions. They included an enormous halo around the sun, churches with burning torches, crosses in the sun and moon, and a great rainbow.[45]

Among the first published responses was that of the prolific Pamphilus Gengenbach, who did not dismiss the prevalent astrologically based expectancy, but stressed that these occurrences were direct communications from God. His pamphlet *King Charles* exhorted all men to take the signs to heart, as they surely threatened coming divine punishment. Gengenbach predicted that under Charles's rule all the estates of the Empire would come into open conflict, bringing massive bloodshed. King Charles, however, might head off much of this suffering by supporting the causes of Luther and the common man, which were closely related. Gengenbach drew support for his predictions by looking back to the signs over Urach in 1514 along with manifold recent crises both natural and man-made. Even greater trials could now be expected to culminate in 1524 with the anticipated conjunctions, but all this would be preparatory to a great purification of the Church. The heavenly torches spoke of the common man's burning zeal for a reformation properly led, meaning by the soon-to-be Emperor Charles. Here general prophetic apprehension evoked an uncommon combination of traditional reform advocacy, support for Luther, fears of popular rebellion, and hopes for a heroic emperor.[46]

Johann Virdung, on the other hand, analyzed the signs astrologically as natural appearances with a supernatural meaning. His predictions were vague but dark. Although he did not believe a universal flood or the end of the world was coming, he did think the terrible changes in store included great storms, earthquakes, political and social upheaval, scarcity, plague, and general bloodshed. Since the signs had special import for the lands in which they occurred, the people of Vienna and Austria were to take heed above all others. But the clergy too came in for severe criticism and warning. Echoing once again the sort of late medieval hopes that looked to a great transformation to follow a time of terrible suffering, Virdung thought the signs promised the final restoration of an ideal earthly order. Yet this palliative hope by no means stood out sharply as the work's central message. For "indeed I truly fear," he wrote, "that the signs are portents of the things that are indicated by the stellar aspects of 1524, which according to the teaching of astronomers indicate much evil from wars, mortality, and flood." Numerous large woodcuts depicting the signs and their beholders brought these warnings to life for Virdung's thousands of readers.[47]

The Vienna wonders also triggered the German vernacular publication that probably did more than any other work to whip up the excitement and evoke arguments about what was to be expected from the 1524 conjunctions. This was the bombshell of Alexander Seitz, *Ain Warnung des Sundtfluss*, first published anonymously at Augsburg in 1520 or very early 1521. Seitz was a medical doctor who would soon become involved in the early Reformation tumult of several South German and Swiss cities; at the time of this writing he was a city physician at Munich. He found unequivocal meaning in the anticipated conjunctions. As the knowledge and experience of experts showed, they signified truly enormous changes. But since the scientific evidence derived from the planetary aspects was hard for the common man to grasp, Seitz confined himself mainly to the astounding phenomena at Vienna. God in his mercy had sent these signs as an urgent and general warning to repentance in the face of catastrophe; drawing heavily on passages from the Book of Revelation, Seitz left no doubt that this harrowing would be of apocalyptic scope. The message was therefore for all, but it had special import for some: "Take care you mighty ones, and above all you clerics; the piper has played and God is sending his holy spirit, by which the faith will be well and purely expounded." A divinely ordained purging of a diseased world was imminent. Only sincere prayer and repentance could in any way mitigate the coming disasters. Seitz's pamphlet, appearing on the heels of Luther's famous treatises of 1520, went through at least five editions in rapid succession.[48]

General anger and resentment toward the clergy marked all these writings on the Vienna wonders, which conveyed a profound sense of imminent, dramatic, and calamitous changes. In 1520, a few months before his death, Sebastian Brant issued a poem that spoke of the flood forecasts, expressing the deepest fears for the clergy and for all Christendom. Years earlier, in his *Ship of Fools* and other works, Brant had harbored hopes for a reform of both Church and Empire. Now, however, he seemed to feel little except resignation. Only God, it appeared, could punish the guilty and root out corruption; worldly efforts and aspirations no longer looked to be of any use. The Empire was irreversibly falling apart, and nothing could be done. Brant did not foresee a literal flood, but his verses were fully in line with the perception that an ultimate catastrophe was not far off.[49]

Just as these various publications were greatly accelerating the circulation of the flood forecasts, Martin Luther's anti-Papal, scripturally based, and spiritually egalitarian message reached the broad vernacular-reading public in Germany through the famous Reformation manifestos of 1520. If the astrological predictions together with growing political and social uncertainty had done much to foster an atmosphere in which this message gained instant attention, the Luther affair in turn suddenly and massively escalated the general apprehension, and soon became the main matter of public discourse. Luther was certainly well acquainted with the flood predictions, and may have employed the associated images at least half-consciously. In *The Freedom of a Christian*, for instance, he referred to the devastation that had flowed from Rome "like a flood covering the world," a laying waste of men's bodies, souls, and possessions. In a sermon from the same period he lamented that "at the present moment, the world is so full of wickedness that it overflows. It also lies under a terrible judgment, a punishment that God threatens to inflict."[50]

In January of 1521, shortly before the Diet of Worms opened, Luther noted the 1524 predictions, and wondered whether they were already coming true in the agitation that was swirling around him. That spring the Diet itself became, even more than other recent Imperial assemblies, a forum for the exchange of literature, news, rumors, hopes, and fears. The scene became one of almost feverish discussion, both of the Luther affair and of the flood forecasts. Alexander Seitz attended the meeting to distribute pro-Luther propaganda in an apocalyptic mode.[51] Over the following months, with the Wittenberg professor hidden away at the Wartburg, the evangelical movement began its first serious surge in many German cities. The mushrooming publicity that drove it was accompanied by a powerful sense of urgency, fueled by the conviction that some great worldwide reckoning—a second Flood, some other incalculable disaster, or the Last Judgment itself—was imminent.

Signs of this tremendous flood-related expectancy are found almost anywhere we look during the next two or three years. Luther's early ally Thomas Müntzer, soon to depart on his own radical path, wrote in 1521 that "it would not be surprising if God were to destroy us all, the elect with the damned, in a much more severe deluge than in former times." Another early adherent who would prove more loyal, Michael Stifel, pointed out that "the astrologers speak of dreadful things, and of how the heavens will soon stand in the same order as they did at the time of Noah." Around the same time, Stifel wrote a popular work identifying Luther as the angel of Revelation 14:6, announcer of God's final judgment. To be sure, the flood imagery often became a metaphor for general dread. Facing the growing religious and social upheaval at Wittenberg, Philipp Melanchthon felt overwhelmed: "I cannot hold back the water! It is time to turn in earnest to things that bear on the salvation of souls."[52] Yet it is hard to draw a sharp line between literal and metaphorical uses of the theme, and the two were by no means mutually exclusive.

Nowhere did the predictions evoke more heated discussion and upset than in the German towns. In the early 1520s Zeno Rychard, son of the Ulm city physician Wolfgang Rychard, qualified his new year's greetings by citing widely shared and terrifying expectations for the next few years; according to the astrologers 1524 in particular was to be "most dangerous." The chronicle of the Counts of Zimmern described in no uncertain terms the growing fears of a "Sintflut" (a flood of biblical proportions) in Swabia during 1522 and 1523. In Regensburg, the city chronicler stated that many respected and well-established burghers took steps to protect themselves against the waters. Another writer noted that the city government undertook several extraordinary measures, including major reinforcements to the city walls; similar accounts survive from many other towns.[53] Well known is Martin Luther's report that the Burgermeister of Wittenberg hoped to find some sort of refuge, physical or spiritual, in the reformer's home, and sent a generous supply of beer in anticipation of his stay; apparently he retreated to his own attic instead, nonetheless well supplied. Years later the scholar Johannes Kessler recalled that in his youth Austria had witnessed an extreme wave of panic, with people disposing of their homes and belongings, and many fleeing to the mountains; reportedly even the Emperor Charles had been seriously alarmed.[54]

Nearly all the authors of the major flood tracts, especially those by the humanist astrologers, described an atmosphere of genuine anguish. Actual flooding in many parts of southern Germany early in 1524 pumped up the panic yet more; in January the Danube and its tributaries inundated many towns, causing near-chaos. But actual high water was not the main agent of apprehension, which had been spreading both through the popular literature and by word of mouth for at least a generation. Inevitably mockers turned out as well, especially among members of the humanist elite. In a 1522 missive to Erasmus, for example, the scholar Kaspar Ursinus Velius made fun of the prophecy by facetiously expressing horror over the anticipations of disaster.[55] But far more common were ventings of sober dread. Fears of a great flood were after all intimately bound up with religious anxiety, the terrors of divine punishment, and hopes for deliverance.

The Uses of Fear

The Italian scholar Paola Zambelli established the basic parameters of the modern scholarly debate on the flood panic, and her central arguments continue to shape the prevailing view. Zambelli holds that the flood debate became more intense and more public in the Empire than anywhere else, and that here, "while not all the participants . . . were outspokenly Evangelical, there were fewer and less incisive Catholic elements." Moreover, the most alarming flood predictions came mainly from astrological writers who favored the early evangelical cause, while the more consolatory works tended to come from writers who remained loyal to Rome. Zambelli recognizes that the situation was highly complex, and that there were certainly exceptions to this broad pattern. Many competing and contradictory views have surfaced, but her core interpretation retains a basic resonance.[56]

One needed qualification is that especially through the early 1520s, concepts of reform remained extremely varied, tentative, even fluid. Terms such as Protestant, Catholic, and Lutheran are clearly anachronistic for the years prior to 1525; alternatives such as "evangelical," "old believer," or "radical" can be seriously misleading as well. Mark Edwards has argued that the one positive principle that was shared among Luther's early supporters was that of "scripture alone," yet that concept was and is deceptive in its apparent simplicity.[57] Can the German flood writings issued between the Diet of Worms and 1524 help clarify this murky picture? Acknowledging the inevitable oversimplifications involved, we can identify three main orientations in the literature, three responses to the fears that climaxed at that time. For convenience we can use the labels "humanist astrology," "evangelical astrology," and "evangelical biblicism." These orientations reflected differences that were partly political, partly generational, and partly a function of personal religious experience.

A mainly older generation of German humanist astrologers, including figures such as Georg Tannstetter, Joseph Grünpeck, Johann Virdung, and Johann Stöffler, showed the influence of the Lichtenberger tradition of deeply threatening forecasts for the immediate future together with hopeful scenarios of a return to peace and harmony in a reformed Empire and Church. These figures tended to hold connections with princely courts and with universities. In general, they sought to deny predictions of a universal flood as sensationalistic and misleading; often they cited God's promise in Genesis 9 not to repeat the deluge. Several stated openly that their goal was to console the overly anxious. In many cases they backed away from starkly apocalyptic visions of the imminent Last Judgment. Most of these humanist astrologers, influenced by pro-Habsburg politics, inherited prophetic hopes, and fears of social upset, were inclined to remain with the traditional Church. Yet we cannot discount the effects of their deep pessimism, their evident disgust with the traditional clergy, and their highly ambivalent prophetic scenarios.

Johann Virdung's predictions typified this orientation, for he thought that the disasters to come would be followed by the final triumph of the Ship of St. Peter. Virdung took a common line in denying a universal flood or the imminent end of the world, especially since the Bible made it clear that the end would be brought about not by water but by fire. Neither the astrological nor the biblical evidence supported the extreme scenarios. Virdung's 1521 *Practica Teutsch*, while addressing the outlook for 1524, actually presented forecasts for another forty years, leaving time for coming terrors but also for a final happy outcome. Here as elsewhere he supplemented his astrological calculations with insights from the scriptures, Joachimist texts, the Sibylline Oracles, and other sources.[58] The young Johann Carion, a student of Stöffler who became the Brandenburg court astrologer in 1519, was also among the heirs of Lichtenberger. In his *Prognosticatio und Erklerung der grossen Wesserung*, first published at

Leipzig in 1521, Carion attacked the feverish predictions of Alexander Seitz, and looked forward to a time of triumph. The tide of German suffering would begin its reversal with a victory over the invading Turks at Cologne; then a great emperor would extend his unifying power worldwide. Carion joined other humanistic writers in lamenting the anguish that was leading people to drop constructive activity and live with abandon. Neither nature nor the Bible, he declared, justified the flood predictions or the associated fears of an imminent cataclysmic end.[59]

The most explicit efforts to damp down public panic came from the Viennese professor Georg Tannstetter, whose *Trostbüchlein* appeared in 1523. Tannstetter, now Imperial physician and astronomer, denounced as charlatans those who hawked fears of a worldwide flood; very heavy rains posed the worst meteorological peril. He pointed out the dangers of broadcasting too-specific predictions among the masses, revealing his own mounting worries about the threat of social upheaval. Although very real troubles and pain were no doubt coming, including a major peasant rebellion, the end of the world was not close. All the upheavals would be caused not by stellar influence, but by God's punishing will. A few months later Tannstetter issued a simpler and clearer *Practica*, repeating his forecasts of a popular rising, horrible suffering for the priests, and other calamities, but finally a great victory for the Habsburg cause and a restoration of honor to the Church.[60] Along with other Vienna astrologers such as Andreas Perlach and Johannes Stabius, Tannstetter clearly aimed to allay the deep agitation that seemed to threaten the very foundations of Christendom. By acknowledging the likelihood of near term troubles while offering assurances of eventual peace, these authors hoped to shore up crumbling confidence in a traditional order.

Most of the humanist astrologers acknowledged the probability of massively abundant moisture in 1524, but their typical response followed Tannstetter's: only unusual downpours and partial flooding were likely. This was the position of Peter Apian, for example, another scholar who had studied at Vienna; in 1527 he would join the faculty at Ingolstadt. Apian proffered detailed reckonings that displayed his mathematical learning but probably also limited the popular appeal of his flood tract.[61] Such forecasts of high water did allow for more practical sorts of reassurance, such as Joseph Grünpeck offered in a very brief *Warning* (1523), describing the expected dangers and offering specific advice on how readers might prepare. If one took prudent steps and called on God's grace, one had very little to fear.[62] Yet humanist astrologers were far less concerned with this sort of counsel than with countering predictions that threatened the social order. On the eve of the 1524 conjunctions the Strasbourg scholar Ottmar Nachtigall published a German translation of an antiflood writing by Paul of Middleburg, who now held an Italian bishopric. The translation was commissioned by the Augsburg banker Anton Fugger, who had no investment in social instability of any kind. Middelburg opposed the flood predictions on purely natural and historical grounds, but Nachtigall's preface bitterly attacked the "ignorant scribblers" of popular forecasts for leading the common folk into error and fear.[63]

Yet if a cautious humanism voiced calls for calm, those calls often rang hollow, revealing an underlying dread. While Carion, for instance, scolded Seitz for his awful vision of a doused world, his own picture of flood and chaos was scarcely more reassuring, for he wrote of unprecedented death and destruction. Virdung's 1521 *Practica Teutsch* presented the outlook for 1524 in equally chilling terms. Both his text and the accompanying woodcuts anticipated drownings, bloodshed, and general chaos. If God had not sent the rainbow (Genesis 9:11–16) as a sign of mercy, one would certainly have to expect the end of the world. Renewing a warning he had made twenty years earlier, he explained that the biblical flood itself had arisen out of a conjunction of only two planets, while February of 1524 would see all the planets coming together. The signs threatened all social classes, but the clergy were in for especially horrific suffering.[64] In a separate 1524 work on the Antichrist, Virdung denied that the advent of this feared enemy was imminent, implicitly contradicting Luther's supposed unveiling of the evil in the Papacy. Yet he insisted that these matters were finally known only to God, and his conclusion seemed to come from the other side of his mouth: the current attacks on the Church were a true sign "that the Last Times and the advent of the Antichrist are drawing near."[65] This sort of inconsistency was unlikely to put minds at rest.

Deep apprehension and pessimism were similarly manifest in Tannstetter's *Trostbüchlein*, despite its author's stated goals. Not only the conjunctions but numerous eclipses boded ill; crop failures, social breakdown, war with the Turks, civil unrest, conspiracy, and revolt were probably inevitable. Already, all legitimate authority was breaking down. The current religious upheaval, destroying all established order, was a punishment on a sinful world. Peter Apian's general outlook for 1524 was full of terrors as well. And since Apian showed greater concern than most vernacular writers with precise analysis of the celestial movements and influences, his unsettling forecasts were likely to have appeared especially objective and authoritative. Leonhard Reynmann's prognostication for 1524, best known for its sensational title page, presented forecasts of anarchy and tremendous bloodshed along with floods and every other conceivable misfortune, natural and human, including a rising of the common people against their lords. In the coming year this earthslide of troubles would only begin; in fact the dolorous effects of the conjunctions would extend to 1543. Reynman clung tenuously to the old vision of a reforming emperor, which he tied to hopes for a great Council, but he gave only vague hints about better times to come. While the humanist and physician Lorenz Fries began his main flood writing by reassuring his readers that 1524 would be a fairly good and fruitful year, he ended up expressing horror of the violence he expected among Christians. Though no general deluge was to be feared, war and uproar were probably inescapable.[66]

Thus wishful thoughts tended to pale before the more immediate and frightening prospects. Even writers who aimed explicitly to console often left scant room for hope in anything short of deliverance through a merciful act of God. In a 1522 *Dialog* dedicated to Charles V, Grünpeck spent far less time analyzing the 1524 conjunctions than in issuing bitterly severe moral condemnations of his age. The ruling classes were in for scarcely conceivable trials; the signs all pointed to terrible punishment, and probably to the Last Judgment. The coming floods would be followed by plague, hunger, and suffering, then the long-feared invasion by the Turks, a final scourge of God. In the course of this jeremiad the hope for a savior-emperor nearly faded away to nothing; even this inveterate Imperial propagandist was feeling the thickening pall of disillusionment and fear.[67] Aside from his denial of a universal flood, it is hard to find much that could have been taken as genuinely calming in Grünpeck's major writings from these years.

The commercial interests of authors and printers certainly helped insure that these writings conveyed mixed messages. Except for a few such as Tannstetter's *Trostbüchlein*, they were fronted with illustrations that were at least highly unsettling, while many included rankly sensational depictions of flooding and general catastrophe. As Talkenberger's careful study makes clear, in most cases we do not know whether the author or the printer commissioned these images, but in either case they were hardly calculated to allay personal or public forebodings. Virdung's several flood writings showed drownings, slaughter by pike and sword, and people kneeling in prayer amidst earthly chaos (see Figure 3.2). A woodcut depicting an explosive, all-destructive downpour introduced Grünpeck's

FIGURE 3.2 Title page woodcut from Johann Virdung's practica for 1524. Reproduced from Heinz Artur Strauss, *Der astrologische Gedanke in der deutschen Vergangenheit* (Munich, 1926).

Warning. Carion's *Prognosticatio vnd Erklerung* went through four early editions with three different title pages; at least two included scenes of devastating deluge. Similarly terrifying advertisements abounded.[68]

Sensationalism aside, the humanist flood works continued in the critical attitudes that had grown continually more open in the earlier practicas. Clerical corruption was regularly presented as a prime cause of Christendom's moral decline and the current state of crisis. In the writings of figures such as Grünpeck and Tannstetter, the most severe words of threat and warning were reserved for the clergy. In an updated version of his 1508 *Spiegel* published in 1522, Grünpeck suggested that the heresy that had arisen in the heart of Germany was a punishment for the sins of the clergy above all, though his jeremiads spared no one. Virdung's 1521 *Practica Teutsch* was full of harsh indictments of and warnings to the priests. Virdung expressed the hopes shared by many humanists and political leaders for a German national council that might heal religious divides and sanction a thorough reform of the Church, but this did not mean that priests, monks, and prelates would escape great trials and humiliations. Peter Apian predicted that the clerics would suffer greatly at the hands of rulers, and would have a whole new order imposed on them.[69]

Even if no second biblical flood were coming, in the eyes of humanist stargazers the world still stood in crisis, under the threat of judgment. And just as the authors of the practicas from preceding decades had insisted, God alone ultimately had the power to alter the influence of the stars. Complementing this continuing stress on divine sovereignty was the notion of human dependence, of the need to call directly upon God's grace. In fact the humanist tracts often read like evangelical sermons, appealing to a personal saving faith. Here there were no appeals for saintly intercession, no calls for the ministrations of Holy Mother Church, no clear vision of clerical leadership. In the face of moral collapse, wrote Grünpeck, in a world where one searched in vain for a single righteous man, what was left but to throw oneself on God's mercy? Virdung stated plainly that the 1520 signs were sent so that people might be saved. And because of the 1524 conjunctions, he wrote, "we should now be the more disposed to make our prayers to God the almighty, that he will divert this watery uproar from us." Johann Stöffler, while insisting that he had never predicted a second flood or the end of the world, still had no doubt that 1524 and the following years would bring harrowing troubles. Warning against all complacency, he expounded on Christ's announcement of the signs of the end in Luke 21, and called on Christians always to be ready for the Last Day.[70]

Yet despite their frequent harsh criticisms and dire predictions regarding the clergy, most of these humanist figures would remain at least outwardly loyal to Rome. Tannstetter, for instance, showed bitter hostility to all who rejected Papal authority. Calling the anti-Romanists hypocrites, frauds, and rabble-rousers, he predicted that all evildoers would be rightly punished by the worldly authorities. Peter Apian remained staunchly attached to the old faith, gaining renown at the University of Ingolstadt.

Johann Stöffler despite his connections with former students such as Philipp Melanchthon, continued in the Roman Church until his death in 1531. Johann Virdung maintained his attachment to his patron, the Palatine elector, and to the University of Heidelberg. Lorenz Fries may have flirted with evangelical ideas at Strasbourg, but ultimately disavowed them. It appears unlikely that Joseph Grünpeck adopted Luther's teachings before his death in 1532, although his major prophetic works would later be placed on the *Index of Prohibited Books*, as were those of several other humanist astrologers. Johann Carion, who was a good deal younger than most of these figures, became quietly attached to the Wittenberg movement by the late 1520s, as his close connections to Melanchthon help to confirm; only his position at the Brandenburg court prevented open acknowledgment of the fact.[71]

Before we discuss the other two general orientations in the flood scare, it will be helpful to recognize the emergence in popular print, during these same critical years around 1520, of an important conflict between scholastically inclined astrology and a revived Augustinian and biblical perspective that was deeply skeptical about all philosophical understanding. These tensions had remained largely latent in the pre-Reformation decades; they became visible most notably in exchanges involving the Basel humanist Pamphilus Gengenbach, the Strasbourg physician Lorenz Fries, and Martin Luther himself. We noted that in 1515, Gengenbach had satirized the skyrocketing public obsession with stellar predictions in his *Practica zu Teutsch*. His doubts seem to have grown more severe in 1518, when Luther published a sermon on the Ten Commandments denouncing the stellar science as a form of idolatrous superstition. Luther found particularly offensive the doctrine of elections, which he associated with the popular tradition of "Egyptian days." He called the choosing of days or times a reprehensible, unchristian practice, whether for medical purposes or any other. Luther never issued a more radical, unqualified dismissal of the stargazer's art than he did here. Around this time Gengenbach's play *Die Gouchmatt* appeared, which included a scathing assault on specific predictions by Lorenz Fries. He echoed Luther's indictment of elections, excoriating the physician's employment of them.[72]

Fries responded to these assaults in his 1520 *Schirmrede*, a staunch defense of natural philosophy, and especially of astrology. Most opposition to the art, he asserted, was grounded in ignorance. While Luther, whom he addressed directly, was in other respects "highly learned," in this case he was dealing with matters of which he had no understanding. In his thrust against Egyptian days, for example, Luther showed that he did not know the difference between an unscientific folk tradition and the astrologer's careful discriminations on the basis of planetary aspects and lunar phases. Medicine, among other necessary human pursuits, could not be pursued at all without such learning. Fries insisted that astrology was a Christian art that looked to the true God alone, not to spiritual intermediaries of any kind, and here he recognized a key point of common ground with the Wittenberg reformer. If the stargazers could point to no saint who upheld their art, as Luther had asserted, "that should be no departure for you [Luther], [since] you also cannot rightly judge who is saintly or [who is] not." Beyond revering the Almighty, astrology looked to the stars alone, which lay between God and the terrestrial elements "just like the axe between the carpenter and the wood." To support his arguments he cited not only scripture, the Patriarchs, and classical authorities, but also Philipp Melanchthon, who as he knew stood closer to his own views than to Luther's on these points.[73]

Fries again responded to the arguments of the biblicists in his *Urteil* of 1523, which was also his main attempt to calm the mounting flood fears. In the typical humanist fashion, he predicted worldly trials in years to come but an eventual victory for the traditional order. He also took the opportunity to return Gengenbach's missiles, calling him an ignorant ass, accusing him of utter ignorance and of worsening the flood panic through pressing calls for repentance. Fries then sought to separate astrology, especially as used in medicine, from any form of spiritual prophecy, presenting the stars as an independent source of natural knowledge. As a physician, wrote Fries, his only prophets were Ptolemy, Albumasar, and Aristotle. In fact, he went so far as to assert that in the earthly realm God operated only through the stars, and not by direct intervention. This was to move into extreme and dangerous territory; few if any other astrologers would have publicly sanctioned anything like Fries's insistence that natural scientific knowledge should fully displace the Bible and faith in matters such as medical practice.[74]

Gengenbach's reply, *Ein Christliche vnd ware Practica*, was no less harsh. In this work he was far less concerned with particular predictions than about what he saw as Fries's blasphemies against Holy Scripture. Was the physician to pay attention to the stars rather than to the Bible? Gengenbach retorted that no true science was possible without the word of God. The Christian physician understood that a strong faith was more important than Aristotle and Avicenna to the health of body and soul.

Since health and illness depended on God's will, so finally did the art of healing. Thus too the truest way to prepare for the future was through repentance and faith. Fries had warned against future natural disasters, but "were you a proper astrologer you would warn the people to genuine penitence, which is a true preventative against the wrath of God." Gengenbach's overall judgment thus remained ambiguous. He did not reject the art entirely; in fact at some points he drew on his own knowledge of it in order to refute Fries. But he left no doubt that the God-fearing astrologer would give more heed to biblical truth than to the stars.[75]

The most directly opposed positions in this exchange were apparently those of the astrological physician Fries and the biblical theologian Luther. Although Gengenbach ultimately gave more credence to Luther's assertions, his continuing acknowledgment of astrology's legitimacy meant that he could not fully accept either position. The view of Fries was simply beyond the pale, both for him and for virtually everyone else. Gengenbach stood somewhere between the two orientations to which we now turn, "evangelical astrology" and "evangelical biblicism." In greatly oversimplified terms, the question at issue between these outlooks was this: to what extent, if at all, could the science of the stars serve as a handmaiden to evangelical faith?

The orientation we are calling evangelical astrology, far from any effort to play down astrological predictions of a deluge, accepted them and built upon them. In fact, its representatives positively encouraged a sense of urgency in the face of the universal reckoning. They also proved resistant to currents of medieval thought, such as Joachimism, that looked forward to some sort of breakthrough to peace and unity before the end. In the face of earthly disaster and universal judgment, their message was one of immediate personal repentance and acceptance of gospel faith. Unlike the humanists, the evangelical astrologers did not typically serve at courts or in university posts, and thus usually had less at stake in the way of princely patronage. They were most often city physicians or educated burghers, younger on average than those we have discussed as humanists, and arguably more attuned to urban popular opinion. Hotly anti-Romanist and anticlerical, and harboring no hope for any renewal of the traditional Church, most writers of this orientation were early supporters of Luther, though their understandings of his cause might vary considerably.

We saw that the work of a city physician, Alexander Seitz, was a chief spark to the debate in the vernacular press. His pamphlet on the 1520 signs became a main target for publicists whose stated goal was to allay panic.

The title page woodcut presented its main themes in sensational fashion, showing a flood scene with drowning people and an ark; the call to repentance was clear. Above were the Vienna signs, along with an image from Revelation 12:3, a seven-headed dragon, which underlined the apocalyptic implications. No other writer presented more hair-raising prospects, yet Seitz did not dwell long on images of flood or other natural disasters. The whole work was couched in heavily eschatological terms, and the overall focus was on a final world cataclysm and judgment. Here too the rejection of Rome was unequivocal. Seitz's sympathies were clearly with the common man, for whose sake he skipped a technical reading of the 1524 conjunctions. But it is far from clear that Seitz was calling for a revolution to be led by the commoners. His apocalyptic message may have included the possibility of radical social action, but it was also a call to transcendent gospel faith in the face of existential emergency.[76]

Similarly urgent was a practica by Johann Copp, a city physician and regular producer of annual forecasts. Since 1520 Copp had been a zealous follower of Luther, as his *Judicium* for 1521 showed, asserting that the stars announced the nearing destruction of the "Babylonian" Church, and that the vineyard of God would soon be given over to worthier users. In his *Practica Deutsch* for 1522, he predicted from the heavenly signs that the pope would see his rule "wholly destroyed," which would mean disaster for the entire Roman clergy.[77] These yearly forecasts, full of sobering visions of suffering, were largely unexceptional apart from their unequivocal predictions of doom for the clerical establishment. Copp's next publication, however, which looked ahead to 1523 and 1524, was a more explicitly apocalyptic work that saw no hope but in the purified gospel. Here he foresaw massive upheavals and terrors for the next two years; many people would not live through these trials. He warned against a feared bloody rising of the common man against both earthly and spiritual rulers, which would bring disastrous results all around. Again he predicted an especially horrible punishment and downfall of the Catholic clergy after their centuries-long rule as false teachers. He broadly attacked practices such as pilgrimages and shrine veneration, stressing the need for an immediate relationship to God. For Copp, the evangelical movement meant simply the fulfillment of biblical prophecy; its enemies were those predicted to appear in the Last Times.[78]

Like Seitz, but also like several of the humanist astrologers, Copp directed his vernacular works especially at the common man. He thus kept astrological terminology to a minimum; he thought it "unnecessary for me to say much to the common German man about the [celestial] revolutions, since such matter is beyond his grasp."[79] He showed more concern with the prophetic punishments and promises of God than with particular natural forecasts; indeed, as with Seitz, the flood image itself became secondary for Copp. This astrologer was convinced that the entire creation pointed to God's universal judgment, and harped on the immediate necessity of spiritually inspired reform at every level of society. He called on all rulers, including the princes, bishops, and even the pope himself, to help establish the true gospel teaching. When he wrote this *Urteil* the Roman See was occupied by the Dutchman Adrian VI, on whom hung many humanist hopes for a cleansing of the Church; that Copp could mention the pope in this context reminds us again just how tentative and flexible the concept of reformation was during the years of the flood panic. In any case, the Kingdom of God was dawning; the faithful would triumph with it, and whoever tried to stop it would be swept away. Celebrating Luther's publication of the *Septembertestament* in 1522, the title page woodcut pictured Christ and his army shooting a Bible out of a cannon against their enemies, including fleeing clerics. The apocalyptic cry "we we we" sounded over the town, as flames fell from heaven.[80]

Possibly in response to accusations of dangerous radicalism, Copp worked to clarify his stance in another *Practica Teutsch* published in the following year. Here he carefully recognized that obedience to worldly superiors was a godly commandment. Not the people but the Lord himself would punish the enemies of truth. He again left open the possibility that the Roman clergy might yet accept pure biblical teachings before the Last Day. Ardently promoting astrology as not only Christian but as positively evangelical, he made it clear that huge storms and floods were coming on an apocalyptic scale. Although he emphasized that no man knew the time of the end, he declared its imminence evident both in the horrors of his time and in the spread of the pure gospel.[81]

For physician-astrologers such as Seitz and Copp, the forces of nature were merely proof of God's power and plan, which reduced to naught all human pretensions. Although their style of intense anti-Romanism and apocalypticism was certainly not shared by all urban physicians, it does appear that these views owed something to their medical thinking and concerns. Their profession of healing in the light of the stars had helped inculcate in them a strong belief in divine sovereignty over the created world, as well as a conviction of human weakness and worldly corruption. These polar perceptions allowed for personal prayer directed

to heaven and for practical physic here below, but left little room for mediate contact or exchange between heaven and earth. This in turn meant
that the chasm between heaven and earth could be closed only through a
divine resolution, a prospect that was bound to intensify future-directed
hopes and fears. Seitz, Copp, and many other city physicians belonged to
a flourishing astro-medical culture that had grown up at the intersection
of humanistic learning and the everyday concerns of German townsfolk.
We have good reasons to see their engagement with that culture as more
than coincidentally related to their intense commitment to the general
reform movement of the 1520s. In combining astrological prediction and
evangelical faith, these figures were not departing dramatically from an
outlook that had been in formation for decades.[82]

Conrad Gallianus, "mathematician and licentiate in Holy Scripture,"
similarly combined stellar forecasts with preaching deliverance through
Christ. In a practica for three years issued at Strasbourg in 1522, this writer
stressed the general subjection of terrestrial life to the stars. Although the
wise man could escape their influence, "yet they are not without extraordinary power." He gave horoscopic charts for 1522 through 1524, along
with calendrical data, weather forecasts, and the outlook for each group
of planetary children. Like many other writers on the flood, he adopted
common themes from the earlier practicas. The Pope and the priests,
together with others subject to Jupiter, would suffer "resistance in matters
of faith" as well as violence and disease, while the Emperor and princes
enjoyed a happy outlook. The common folk should ban all thoughts of rising against their rulers and the nobility, for any such eruption was bound
to fail.[83]

The predictions for the first two years were unsettling enough, but the
approaching conjunctions of 1523 to 1524, together with an eclipse of the
moon months earlier, threatened "horrible changes to all creatures, structures, lands and peoples in the whole world." Gallianus pointed out God's
promise in Genesis not to repeat a universal deluge, and also calculated
from the stars that the flooding would be only partial. But these points
were cold comfort in light of his overall outlook. The winter of 1523 to 1524
would see "enormous downpours," massive storms making for "gush-
ing" and "overflowing" that would be especially bad in the lands "toward
midnight," including much or all of Germany.[84] And then it would get
worse: the tempests would destroy castles and buildings, one could expect
paralyzing cold, extreme heat and drought, failed crops and dearth, pestilence, domestic bloodshed, war among Christians as well as with the

Turks. Not all these afflictions would necessarily come in 1524; Gallianus cited Albumasar and other authorities on the delayed effects of conjunctions. But if the timing was uncertain, the terrors themselves were not.

The scriptures complemented the astrological data. "The just shall live by faith" meant that even now the faithful had nothing to fear. The one and only right response to the stellar forecasts was to pray for Christ's grace and mercy. Like almost all other flood writers Gallianus exhorted his audience to better their lives and turn like the Ninivites to God, who could always cancel the disasters. Pious hearts had no cause for terror; unbelievers, on the other hand, had much to fear. The woodcuts accompanying this text expressed the lesson as well. The title page image deliberately conjured up angst in the face of chaos and destruction whose ultimate cause lay in God, not the planets. Additional images at the end of the work taught the way of salvation. One depicted three believers in a ship, praying to Christ and the Virgin; these faithful would be saved from the roiling waters. Another pictured Christ pointing to the signs in the heavens, with words from Luke 21: "And there will be signs in the sun, the moon, and the stars."[85]

Not every evangelical astrologer became permanently alienated from Rome; such cases show again what a fluid scene obtained in the early 1520s. Veit Bild, a Benedictine monk at Augsburg, grew favorably inclined to Luther's teachings during the early 1520s, but he never broke openly with the Papal church, and in the wake of the Peasants' War he reaffirmed his loyalty. His interests were broad, encompassing both astronomy and theology; as an astrologer he had composed annual calendars. Written under the pseudonym Johann Gereon, his practica for 1524 denied like many others that a second flood of biblical proportions was to be expected. Comparing the conjunction of 1524 with one that had occurred in the year 670, he concluded that since no universal flood had happened at the earlier date, none would come now. Sharing the nearly universal fear of popular rebellion, he predicted a fairly happy year for the common people, "so long as they keep themselves from a rising against their lords and the nobles," which would pose enormous dangers for them.[86] Yet the signs most definitely indicated serious troubles, including devastating rains, ruinous wars, and pandemic disease, as well as a brutal persecution of the clergy at the hands of the lay powers. It was up to Christians to pray for God's grace; only in this way could the worst threats of the conjunction be turned to naught. Yet no hope for meaningful worldly reform entered this outlook. Most important in Bild's view was the likelihood that the great conjunction was a sign of the coming Last Judgment. And since the Lord would come "like a thief in the night, and unforeseen," believers were to be ready for his return at any moment. Bild's heavy stress on Christ-centered faith, prayer, and wakeful watching revealed Luther's strong influence. At the same time, he did not cease to value the science of the stars. He concluded his practica with the weather forecasts for the coming year in a standard month-by-month format.[87]

Slightly less explicit forms of evangelical astrology are evident in many other writings that directly or indirectly addressed the flood expectations. Sebastian Ranssmar's *Anzeigung* of 1523, for example, presented urgent warnings on the basis of the 1524 conjunctions, foreseeing a host of horrific evils as shocking as any the imagination could handle. Ranssmar then offered an evangelical sermon, urging faith in divine grace and fervent prayer. Although this author did not make specific references to contemporary conditions, his work nonetheless directly exploited the flood fears in order to focus hopes on the purified gospel. The title page woodcut presented a deliberately shocking scene of storm, flood, and drownings, along with a prayer for God's mercy.[88] More reserved and indirect was the *Practica Wittenbergensis* for 1524 by Johannes Volmar, a professor of mathematics at the very home of Luther's movement. A regular producer of annual practicas, Volmar offered a now familiar array of grisly forecasts about the near future: divisions, upheaval, war, plague, and especially heavy suffering among the priests, monks, and nuns. Showing the influence of astrological reform currents, he based his unhappy projections mostly on a 1523 eclipse of the moon rather than on the upcoming conjunctions. He did, however, refer to the coming great conjunction in 1524, and pointed to the appearance of similar heavenly events before the biblical flood. Volmar felt compelled to keep his forecasts restrained and to avoid explicit preaching, but no modestly informed consumer could have missed the implications.[89]

Finally we have an orientation in the flood discourse that we can term evangelical biblicism. Those who adopted this perspective largely embraced Luther's central teachings and took to preaching them as a vocation, while expressing disinterest, skepticism, or even outright hostility toward scientific astrology, especially in regard to matters of spiritual prophecy. The religious authority of scripture alone was central to this perspective, which also insisted that God alone knew the future. But these views did not imply that one could or should ignore nature. Indeed most evangelical biblicists were intensely awake to heavenly signs and natural wonders sent directly by God as warnings to a world unredeemable short of the final and eternal renewal. Like evangelical astrology, then, evangelical biblicism generally assumed an apocalyptic expectancy that held out little hope for future peace and unity. Similarly shared between these two outlooks was a searing hatred of the Roman clergy and all it stood for. Luther himself was the main representative of evangelical biblicism, which became an explosive movement partly on account of the swelling anxiety evoked by the flood forecasts. His attitude toward the astrological flood predictions was by no means as simple as his 1518 work on the Ten Commandments might suggest.

The reformer's Advent sermon of 1522 on the signs of the end (Luke 21: 25–36) was intimately related to the surge of publications and debate on the threat of a great deluge. This pamphlet-length work saw dozens of editions, many unauthorized; no fewer than eleven separate reprintings came out within the first two years.[90] The preacher made direct parallels between the state of the world just before the biblical flood and the situation in his own day. God was sending more and more signs in the heavens and on earth, but hardly anyone recognized them for what they were. To understand them in merely natural terms was to miss the point; worse, it could lead to complacency. Luther agreed with the astrologers that the expected planetary meetings of 1524 would be truly extraordinary. He mentioned the current flood predictions, not rejecting them explicitly but making nothing of them. What was certain was that the conjunctions, along with the many other wonders and worldly disasters that God was sending, pointed directly to the Last Day. Christians should not regard such signs with fear, but instead rejoice in the nearness of deliverance. The title page woodcut of the original 1522 edition of this tract played potently on the flood theme. It showed Christ pointing to the signs in the sun, moon, and stars. Beneath were words from Matthew 8:25, the desperate cry of the disciples in the storm-rocked ship: "Lord save us, we perish." The message was clear. As Christ had once saved his followers from the stormy waters, so now he gave hope to the faithful as they stood helpless in the face of impending annihilation.[91]

Luther did not simply dismiss fear; rather he stressed its proper use. To this end he often focused on the terrors of the Last Day, the distillate of all anxiety: "Indeed he who feels such fear [of the Last Day] in himself should not give up, but use this fear wisely. For he who does use it wisely allows this fear to hit home and to admonish him to pray for grace, which takes the fear away and gives him joy and longing for this day . . . Therefore such

fearful people are closer to their salvation than those thoughtless, obsti-
nate ones who neither fear nor take comfort in that day [of the Lord]."[92]
Here was an implicit acknowledgment of the way he made use of the flood
scare. Luther first worked to draw attention away from the heavenly phenomena as causes, and to emphasize instead their significance as divinely
sent announcements of the End. Then, to the extent that they evoked
shock in the "old" or natural man, they might turn him to the opposite
point of the existential compass, opening him to the gospel promise. In
short, while Luther did not put the matter this way, the stars served the
message of the law, the necessary prerequisite to the gospel. Thus while
he could occasionally associate the flood predictions with Papal perversions, to make this the sum of the analysis is misleading.

Nor did Luther's colleagues hesitate to exploit the flood fears in their
preaching. In his Advent sermons for 1524, for example, Johannes Brenz
described the widespread terror that had arisen in the face of the conjunctions and of recent flooding. Like scores of other commentators on the
predictions, he made direct parallels between the days of Noah and his
own time, citing Luke 17:26: "And as it was in the days of Noah, so shall
it be also in the days of the son of man." But in essence Brenz adopted
Luther's position, asserting on the basis of the rainbow in Genesis 9 that
no universal flood was coming, and that the conjunctions were likely a
sign of the Last Judgment itself.[93] He shared with Luther and with many
others the perception that eclipses were occurring more frequently than
in earlier generations, a perception no doubt largely owing to the broad
dissemination of the popular astrological works, rife with illustrations
and comments on such phenomena. He agreed that although these darkenings might be explained naturally, and might even have natural effects
on earth, their recent multiplication had another meaning.

The pattern Luther set in his 1522 Advent sermon influenced not only
other prominent reformers such as Brenz but many popular publicists as
well. These writers developed the genre commonly known as the "antipractica" which used the basic practica format to present a biblical message that mainly bypassed astrological science, much as Gengenbach had
done earlier in his 1516 *Practica zu teutsch*, or else opposed it outright.
The term "antipractica" is misleading, for not all these works were written in express opposition to the stellar art; a better label is "Christian
practica." These pamphlets took over much of the outward form and even
the terminology of the annual prognostications, but replaced the astrological content with biblical preaching. Like the evangelical astrologers, their

authors rejected all hopes for genuine worldly reform, adopting instead an apocalyptic vision of an imminent end and stressing the biblical promise of deliverance.

A series of popular works by Heinrich von Kettenbach, a zealous evangelical preacher at Ulm, sounded an urgent note as the panic rose, dwelling repeatedly on the imminence of the Last Day and the believer's utter dependence on God; nothing but the gospel could help. The Lord, he preached, held out his mercy to poor, sick, and suffering souls; wishing "to help them in their sickness, so that they do not perish in water or fire." On the title page of his 1523 *Practica from the Holy Bible for many future years*, Kettenbach declared that "the time has arrived when one should pay more heed to such practicas [as this], than to astronomy," for God now ruled directly over his people. This pamphlet made no direct references to the flood predictions, but the threats it mentioned were just as frightening. Kettenbach described a world riddled with vicious sin, plagued by the Papal Antichrist, as blind and corrupt as any the stellar doomsayers had lamented. "Repent as the Ninivites," he preached, or incalculable woe was coming. No help could be expected from the emperor, but if the Imperial cities would listen to the Word as preached by Luther, they would serve truth and the salvation of many. The "many future years" of the title may have been an invention of the printer, for Kettenbach's work ended on an intensely apocalyptic note, even referring to Luther as a new Christ figure before the end.[94]

Ready to employ the natural signs more openly was the preacher Heinrich Pastoris, whose 1523 *Practica Teutsch* was an equally strident announcement of the coming Day of the Lord. The great conjunction to come in Pisces, wrote Pastoris, "means that God announces to us that he summons everyone—all nations—to his comforting word, by which the world will be judged, as John says in Chapter 9." The time of decision was now at hand. The imminent judgment would bring deliverance for believers; eternal damnation to the faithless. Pastoris did not reject the flood predictions, or the principles of astrology as such. His main whipping-boy was the "Anonymous Practica" first published at Augsburg in 1516, which we noted above as a grab-bag of medieval prophecies drawing on traditions such as Joachimism. Pastoris thought the unnamed editor of this work might be Lichtenberger, and he denounced the collection for its aura of secrecy and obscurity, reminiscent of the *Pronosticatio* itself. He was offended mainly by the blood-curdling and unscriptural forecasts of earthly trials, by which the issuer sought to frighten people in a way that would make them obedient and thus lead to an eventual time of earthly fulfillment. In concluding verses, Pastoris offered his practica as the true and proper response to fears of a deluge or the end of the world, preaching salvation through Christ alone. Again, the goal was to turn the widespread panic to a truly redemptive purpose.[95]

A few Christian practicas did take the further step of explicitly disavowing the science of the stars. One such work was by Stefan Wacker (Vigilius), issued in early 1524. *Das kain Sundfluss* was a sort of sermon against astrology, condemning the art as unchristian and harmful, the epitome of an excessive desire for knowledge. Wacker dismissed the visible evidence of the stars entirely in favor of the Word. The coming conjunction had no significance for Christians; the heavens merely confirmed God's omnipotence. The faithful had not only God's assurance against a second flood; they had the promise of salvation in Christ. Wacker's work conveyed far less apocalyptic urgency than most other Christian practicas, a characteristic we can reasonably see as connected to its exceptionally aggressive antiastrological stance.[96] Closer to the evangelical mainstream in this regard was an anonymous work of 1525 written "against all practica writers and stargazers." Denouncing all systematic stellar science as unchristian, this author used astrological terms as metaphors for Christ and the saving truths of the gospel. While conjunctions and other celestial events were no doubt divine signs of warning and promise, it was foolish to be driven to terror by forecasts of disaster when one could take joy in knowing that God ruled all things. The common people were accepting this good news, but a recalcitrant clergy faced profound threats, as did worldly rulers who failed to change their shameful ways. The work concluded with an apocalyptic use of biblical flood imagery: "And the great rising of the waters harms me not, for that [my] house stands upon the secure rock of Jesus Christ."[97]

Most of the Christian practicas that actively denounced astrology were published after the high point of the flood fears in 1524. Disillusionment with the stellar forecasts may have helped motivate the 1526 *Almanach ewig werend* by the physician, botanist, and popular theologian Otto Brunfels, written for all years "till the end of the world of all worlds." Again using the basic practica form to issue biblical, Christ-centered teaching, Brunfels indicted astrology as a form of heathen blindness. All illnesses and sufferings came not from the stars, but were God's punishments for sin. Brunfels called on the princes to rule with humility, and on the cities to further the common good along with the gospel; he also attacked clerical pride, corruption, and pretentions to power. Since authority was of God, Brunfels denounced all rebellion against worldly rulers. This entire text was laced with intense eschatological expectancy; all signs indicated the closeness of the end.[98] Balthasar Wilhelm's *Practica Deutsch*, published at Zwickau most likely in the late 1520s, was similarly based on scripture exclusively. Wilhelm used terms such as "conjunction" to refer not to the stars but to biblical passages and lessons, and expressed scorn for any effort to read the heavens systematically. He saw the Peasants' War as a quasi-fulfillment of the flood fears, although it was but one sign of a world in its final throes; indeed he saw evidence of the coming end everywhere. The evangelical movement was a saving ark in this chaos, which would soon be resolved at the Last Day.[99] All these biblicists sought to divorce the apocalyptic message of scripture from the astrological forms to which it had so often been bound. In their view, only the pure preaching of the Word could offer a true antidote to anxiety.

What general conclusions might we draw from our effort to sketch out three main orientations in the flood debate? First, it appears that to distinguish clearly between "consoling" and "alarming" flood writings is difficult at best. Green rightly observes that the general strategy of those who engaged in the controversy was "to fight fear with fear"; indeed despite their stated intentions, even the humanist astrologers surely did as much to stir up the flood fears as to calm them.[100] Their popular publications not only betrayed their own underlying anxieties, but also contributed directly to common public perceptions of a world in crisis; these works can be called consoling only in the sense that they included compensatory visions of an eventual restoration of earthly order. But neither could the pervasive sense of crisis have been eased by the more starkly apocalyptic tone of both the evangelical astrologers and biblicists, emphasizing the corruption of this world and the need for transcendent hope; indeed in one real sense their message depended on the perception of worldly breakdown. Here, consolation depended entirely on a transcendent faith.

Virtually all the flood writings involved some sort of call for repentance in the face of current or coming crisis; so for example we encounter references to the biblical lesson of the Ninivites in each of our three groups. Moreover, among this whole array of German authors readers found no appeals to the saints as models or intercessors, no calls for priestly ministrations, no visions of deliverance by an angelic Pope. They discovered instead a heavy dwelling on clerical failings, bitter laments over the shared sins of the world, countless biblical references, calls for prayer and

repentance in the face of a great reckoning, general fears of peasant violence, and the recognition that everything lay finally in God's hands.

On the other hand, the differences among our three groups were far
from insignificant. The writers whose use of astrology was most closely
tied to humanistic visions of reform could express deep anxiety, but tended
to perpetuate inherited medieval hopes of final unity and triumph within
history. Most of these figures had ties to the princely courts and to the
older, well-established universities. They would also prove mostly unwilling to renounce the traditional Church. Those whom we have labeled
evangelical astrologers and evangelical biblicists, on the other hand, were
both more radically apocalyptic in outlook, foreseeing only divine wrath
or final deliverance. These publicists came more often from the ranks of
urban physicians and preachers, and were also generally united in their
support of anti-Roman reform. The biblicists worked to divorce scriptural
prophecy from the astrological forms with which it had become bound
up in the popular literature over the preceding decades. In their view, not
the science of nature but only the preaching of the word could offer what
was truly needed, an antidote to anxiety. But it was the evangelical astrologers who continued the main trajectory of the popular astrological culture
that had spread above all through the calendars and practicas. For them
nature and scripture carried urgent and mutually reinforcing messages
that sanctioned no delusions about earthly deliverance. This idea, that the
Bible and the heavens were two books that taught crucial and complementary lessons, would prevail among the majority of Luther's heirs throughout the sixteenth century.

The late Robert Scribner stressed the ways in which the early
Reformation created a new structure of meanings "by taking over the
experience of the past and supplying it with a new context." Evangelical
propaganda depended on "codes drawn from common experience" that
were invested with new significance.[101] Our analysis of the flood works
complements this insight. Implicitly, Luther and other early evangelicals
realized that the astrologically inspired flood imagery had evoked a more
focused and indeed a purer form of anxiety than medieval prophetic traditions had allowed. This was an anxiety that could not be fully assuaged
by carnivalesque renewals, by hopes for a new age, by dreams of deliverance through a messianic emperor, or even through individual acts of
repentance. The deluge represented the ultimate disaster, but also a great
purging, the final purification of a sinful world. It was a climax to be
both feared and longed for, a terrible but perhaps unconsciously desired

outcome. For many evangelicals, this cleansing and deliverance had to be understood in biblical terms, as purely an act of God. In their preaching, faith was conceived as an attitude of trust and positive longing that would drive out paralyzing fear. In one sense they had triumphed over a naive cosmological expression of existential apprehension. In another, they had appropriated and reformulated the anticlerical and apocalyptic sensibility that had grown up under the influence of popular astrology.

Aftermath

The winter and spring of 1524 did in fact bring some heavy downpours and regional flooding, but as it happened no one needed an ark. Still, the astrologers made it clear that major conjunctions could take years to work their effects, and the signs are few that fears waned in a major way once the February conjunctions were a matter of memory rather than expectancy. A popular saying of the time gave reasons for ongoing worry: "Whoever survives in 23, is not drowned in 24, and remains unslain in 25 may speak of wondrous things indeed."[102] Given the shrill warnings of the astrologers about social upheaval, and woodcuts in the popular tracts showing scenes of peasant violence, few observers could have been surprised at reports of spreading rural unrest in upper Germany during the summer and fall of 1524. The great convulsions of the Peasants' War, peaking in the following spring, were widely and inevitably regarded as at least partial fulfillments of many forecasts for general disaster.

Since even an author as generally conservative as Georg Tannstetter could predict "disunity and upheaval" between the common man and the clergy, and because dozens of popular works included prophetic scenes of humble folk attacking lords and prelates, it is possible that some peasants felt emboldened by the sense that a popular rising was part of a predetermined world drama. But we need to be extremely cautious about any temptation to expand the arguments presented here in order to help explain the outbreak of peasant violence. We know almost nothing about the extent to which the systematic astrology of the calendars and prognostications affected the world of rural commoners. And even if we could find evidence that peasant outlooks were significantly influenced by the new astrological culture, we could hardly hope to establish anything more than a highly indirect relationship between that culture and the great civil conflict of 1524 to 1525. The argument of

Denis Crouzet that the spread of popular astrology cultivated a habit of "mental violence" leading to the actual violence of the Peasants' War is too abstract and speculative to carry any real weight. The most we could plausibly say about the role of the stargazers in that upheaval is that widespread rumors of impending disaster and judgment likely heightened social tensions and therefore contributed to the conditions for a general uprising.[103]

Reactions to the events and nonevents of 1524 to 1525 varied greatly. Had the predictions for massive flooding been simply wrong, or had God averted this terrible punishment? Had the Peasants' War been a full or partial fulfillment of the astrologers' calculations? Had those who had denied a universal flood been vindicated? Already in 1524 Peter Apian thought of issuing no practica for the following year, since so many of his fellow stargazers had made themselves and their art look foolish. With the spread of the violent uprisings he changed his mind, concluding that the forecasts had not all been mistaken. Johann Virdung defended himself with especial vigor, holding that much of what he had written had in fact proved correct. Caritas Pirckheimer, prominent abbess of a Nuremberg convent and sister of the humanist Willibald Pirckheimer, saw the anticipations of devastation fulfilled in Luther's movement, which in her eyes had brought paralyzing divisions, strife, destruction, harm to the clergy and to the faith. For no one, among either the astrologers or other observers, was the absence of a worldwide flood in 1524 evidence of the bankruptcy of astrology itself; the upheavals that actually unfolded were proof enough that the stars had not lied.[104]

Several oft-cited incidents attest to the continuing psychological impact of the flood panic. Probably best known of all is the nightmare reported by the artist Albrecht Dürer around Pentecost in 1525, so vivid that he drew a breathtaking watercolor image to accompany his description. Looking out over the landscape, he saw some four miles away an enormous column of water descending from an angry sky toward the earth, splashing down with a thunderous roar and churning explosively outward, the inverted sixteenth-century version of an atomic mushroom cloud. As more torrents began to pour down, and just as the surging storm from the first was already about to reach him, he awoke terrified and trembling.[105] Johann Carion, the Brandenburg court astrologer, had meanwhile recalculated the likely date for a great flood as July 15, 1525, at which time the Elector and his family reportedly took refuge on a mountaintop. Peter Creutzer, who billed himself Lichtenberger's "disciple," argued that a strange heavenly appearance of 1527—which he called a comet—had resulted from the 1524 conjunctions, and would yet magnify their ill effects.[106]

It does appear, however, that after 1525 and the end of the Peasants' War the most immediate and extreme fears that spurred and were spurred by the flood tracts began to wane. For some publicists, older traditions thus seemed once again potentially relevant. Despite all its fame, Lichtenberger's *Pronosticatio* had played virtually no role at all in the flood forecasts and debate; in fact only a single edition had been produced in Germany since before 1500. But suddenly in 1526 several new printings appeared, including one from Cologne, a traditional bastion of Roman orthodoxy.[107] Once the tremendous peasant uprisings had been suppressed and nightmares of a literal deluge had begun to fade, newly encouraged defenders of the traditional order took the opportunity to refocus their hopes through Lichtenberger's vision of recovery before the end. The *Pronosticatio* now offered a welcome scenario for Roman clerics especially, who believed the peasants had been misled by the false prophet of Wittenberg.

Luther himself, recognizing the danger and looking to head off notions that the crisis for Rome and the clergy might be passing, sanctioned a new edition of Lichtenberger in the spring of 1527. This version, edited by Luther's friend Stephan Roth, included numerous wording changes, marginal glosses, and altered woodcuts suggesting readings that favored the evangelical cause. But with this redaction Luther sought above all to counter what he saw as vain hopes for any genuine reformation of the Papal church. At the same time, in his preface to this work Luther made known his views about astrological prophecy. His outlook was by no means a simple rejection of pagan superstition. Lichtenberger's prophecies, he wrote, were neither of the truly inspired kind that could come only from the Holy Spirit, nor of the false sort that came from the Devil. Rather they were simply natural predictions from the movements of the heavens. This sort of forecast had nothing to do with faith; it was an old heathen art, a human invention, and thus necessarily uncertain. Here Luther simply ignored the powerful traditions of Christian prophecy on which Lichtenberger drew, not to mention his many references to the scriptures. It was simpler, and better served his purposes in this case, to portray this famous writer as practicing a highly fallible human art by which he had happened to hit some things right, but which had misled him on other points. Luther did think many of the *Pronosticatio*'s illustrations had value, especially those that depicted approaching disasters for a corrupt clergy. Yet when the astrologer had hit the mark it was not because his science was correct, but merely because his readings happened to agree with the actual meaning of the warning signs God had sent. The faithful, Luther argued, had nothing to fear from such signs, and thus had no need to be concerned with prophecies such as Lichtenberger's. The godless, on the other hand, had much to fear, not on the basis of the astrologer's art, but because of true divine warnings.[108]

We saw in his 1522 sermon on the signs of the end that Luther implicitly allowed attention to the celestial signs as law. He retained this view in his preface to Lichtenberger. He did not denounce the natural science of reading the stars as a violation of the First Commandment, as he had done in a sermon of 1518. He could hardly have pushed this principle consistently without destroying the very possibility of rational, scientific knowledge.[109] In his eyes, the excesses and follies of the stargazers posed but a minor threat to faith in comparison with the satanic perversions of Roman theology and practice. Otherwise he would never have been able to tolerate the astrological culture that continued to surround him for his whole life. The worst charge he could make consistently against the stellar art was that it drew attention away from the crucial deeper meaning of the signs in the heavens.

We do find some evidence of a heightened reserve and defensiveness among German star-trackers after the widespread panic and bloodshed of the mid-decade. In the late 1520s only the Christian practicas retained a strongly apocalyptic character, looking almost entirely to the Bible and to direct divine signs to confirm that the Day of the Lord drew near. The astrological practicas, on the other hand, grew notably more restrained. In many annual forecasts from the latter part of the decade, hardly a word appeared but for purely natural and practical forecasting. Some writers tried, in most cases quite disingenuously, to fend off critics by asserting that their prognostications were by no means intended for the common people.[110] A similar defensiveness may also have promoted a move to longer-range forecasts in which relatively vague scenarios could be safely proposed. In the late 1520s annual practicas fell out of fashion most notably among the Vienna writers, whose connections with Imperial interests made them especially eager to distance themselves from a prophetic culture that seemed to foster heresy and disorder. Georg Tannstetter never published another annual calendar after 1527, preferring to focus on medical texts instead. Yet another expression of caution that now began appearing was the phrase "Teneo medium" ("I hold to the middle"), a usefully ambiguous suggestion of moderation printed for instance at the end of Matthias Brotbeyhel's annual forecast for 1527.[111]

In cities where the evangelical reform was in motion or already realized, the most significant immediate shift in the popular forecasts involved the persons or groups who sanctioned them and to whom they were formally addressed. Here, while a larger percentage of earlier predictive works were dedicated to nobles, princes, bishops, or other traditional holders of power, surviving practicas from the late 1520s were now usually dedicated to local city councils or mayors. This shift was an implicit acknowledgment that anti-Roman reform was a powerful reality, and that the cities were taking matters into their own hands. Councils sought closer supervision of calendar and practica production, and while efforts at actual censorship remained sporadic and generally weak, local authorities did sometimes confiscate unauthorized printings, or otherwise punish authors or printers. A note of political caution became more prominent in the practicas; submission to worldly authority was absolutely necessary, they advised, and all rebels deserved the harshest sorts of punishment. Predictions of disaster for the clergy now appeared less often; in their place came calls for stability and the consolidation of authority in the hands of godly magistrates. The main claim of astrologers to social utility had long come from their role as physicians, and the city physician took on a yet higher and more central profile in the reformed civic order. In the late 1520s numerous church ordinances and other new regulations gave greater formal recognition to the integral nature of this office in the life of the towns, and to the role of other public health personnel such as barbers, surgeons, and midwives. Brotbeyhel introduced his 1527 practica by referring to astrology as "a calling of God" that redounded to the honor and glory of the Creator; here he appealed implicitly to Luther's doctrine of vocation, stressing more forcefully than ever the utility of the art in a civic setting.[112]

As later chapters will show, the modest retreat of the practica writers in the late 1520s did not last long. Indeed what stands out is the continued flourishing of the common astrological culture of the towns. Arguments for the social usefulness of the art continued unabated, and positive, confident claims show a profession unfazed. Anton Brelochs of Schwäbisch Hall was echoing generations of practica writers when he wrote in his forecast for 1528 that "the almighty eternal God in truth created the heavens, the sun and moon together with the other stars, for the especial use of mankind and the lower world; in them will be found written the future of this world's mortal creatures."[113] Several of the pre-Reformation authors of almanacs and practicas remained active, even as a generation of new names began to emerge. This overall continuity stands in stark contrast to what scholars have found in Italy, for example, where by 1530 the culture of popular astrology was in rapid decline.[114] Despite the efforts of some early Reformation preachers and writers to foster a purely biblical culture that would eclipse astrological imagery and other forms of popular belief, what soon emerged was in fact a new civic, philosophical, and religious appropriation of astrology that would both complement and shape the outlook of evangelical burghers.[115] Both within and without the Empire, Catholic observers commonly saw close links between astrological publicity and Lutheran heresy, and with good reason this perception would only grow stronger as the century of the Reformation progressed.

The Campaign Against Superstition

A New Offensive

A hoary conventional wisdom among students of the early modern age is that even as Renaissance astrology saw its greatest popular flowering in the sixteenth century, its theorists and practitioners were coming under mounting attack from several directions at once, thrown more and more on the defensive. On this view, Pico's famous work of 1494 helped inspire a growing army of critics, who employed an array of religious, philosophical, and natural-scientific weapons to mount a sustained siege against the ancient fortress of the stargazers. The defenders fought more and more desperately to protect their sprawling domain, and while they were able to make certain tactical shifts that prolonged the intellectual battle until at least the late seventeenth century, they achieved few if any real victories. Throughout the period they were in overall retreat as the science of the stars grew more and more controversial. Not only the expert mathematicians but even the popularizers felt ever mounting pressure to justify themselves.[1]

While this general perspective cannot be dismissed entirely, it hardly takes into account the outlook of countless early modern theorists and practitioners, including a great many sophisticated thinkers, who saw matters in dramatically different terms. In particular, it fails as a context for understanding the sustained program of astrological study, teaching, publicity, and practice that took shape among German evangelicals during the middle decades of the sixteenth century, from the 1530s through at least the 1560s. This program, centrally though by no means exclusively associated with Philipp Melanchthon (Figure 4.1) and the University of Wittenberg, was far from merely a defensive effort to shore up the

FIGURE 4.1 Philipp Melanchthon, 1540. Portrait engraving by Heinrich Aldegrever.

crumbling citadels of a threatened discipline. For the evangelical espousers of the art saw themselves as participants in an enlightened offensive, a campaign against superstition, in which a purified astrology was the natural ally of a purified gospel. In their eyes, indeed, the art was necessary as the practical philosophical complement to Reformation theology.

Like Christian teaching, the pure ancient science had been obscured or perverted over the centuries by various superstitious accretions. For Melanchthon, his colleagues, and a great many of their educated contemporaries in the cities of the Empire, the reform of astrology symbolized by Peurbach and Regiomontanus was providentially related to Luther's revival of the gospel.[2] Evangelical humanists typically made similar arguments about the revival of letters and learning in general; Luther's movement was the heart of a great enlightenment in both faith and learning. But for many if not most of these thinkers, the art of the stars, as the very framework of philosophical knowledge, stood in especially close alliance with the restored Word.

This campaign was by no means the product of an astrological "fever" or "spell" that gripped a handful of German Protestant academics.[3] On the contrary, we find a quickly growing network of evangelical scholars, physicians, and publicists whose labors showed basic continuities with the earlier scholastic and humanistic trends in the universities, and with the growth of an astrological culture in the pre-Reformation German towns. The persisting ideal was a natural astrology that not only served everyday human needs, but also provided a basic orientation in the world at large. In addition, Melanchthonian teachings now gave the art a theological dynamic that was lacking among pre-Reformation astrologers, providing even greater legitimacy to the astrological world-picture that had grown so pervasive over the prior decades. Melanchthon himself greatly energized evangelical humanists in the common goals of promoting the academic institutionalization of celestial science, encouraging the ongoing refinement of the discipline, and articulating its benefits in the realms of both public and personal life. From the 1530s on these ideals were adopted and publicized by new generations of evangelical astrological writers who saw themselves engaged in a positive program of religious and intellectual edification uniting a purified science with a purified faith. As these promoters conceived it, the renewed art was antimagical, shorn of all human delusions, and quite the opposite of those dark pursuits that were rightly condemned as viciously sinful. In this sense, evangelical astrology became an integral part of what historians have often called the Reformation "offensive against superstition."[4]

To be sure, their science did not lack for adversaries, both within and without evangelical ranks. The voices of Pico and those who echoed his criticisms were now followed by more radically skeptical views such as those of Agrippa of Nettesheim, whose famous treatise *De Incertitudine* appeared in 1531.[5] As we saw earlier, the general revival of Augustinianism had fostered a doubtful if not hostile attitude in some quarters. Among evangelicals there would always be a scattering of radical biblicists whose extreme distrust of any and all philosophy made them knee-jerk antagonists of the stellar science, although we will see that even the strict "Gnesio-Lutherans," theologians who became outspoken critics of Melanchthon after the death of Luther in 1546, developed no sustained program of opposition. The genre of the Christian practica (or "antiprac-tica") continued to evolve, using astrological terms and formats to convey biblical teachings in ways that were more or less openly hostile to the art.[6] But such critics were often themselves forced into more of a defensive than an offensive stance; as in the pre-Reformation era, the skeptics and the mockers remained well outside the main cultural currents of the time. Few if any of the critical arguments adduced in the sixteenth century were new; in fact the only really novel points came from Melanchthon and his allies. Those who stood as apologists for astrology could and did adopt this posture as a useful rhetorical pose in order to propagate their teachings. They did not feel any great pressure to save the art from "the furnace of antipagan polemic," or to silence lurking doubts of their own.[7] Overall, the evangelical humanists promoted stellar science with positive confidence, and with few worries about the arguments of critics.

Among the evangelical detractors, Luther himself has naturally been cited far more often than any other. The typical depiction of Luther as a critic of Melanchthon's astrological obsessions is not without basis, but it is usually part of a highly oversimplified larger picture in which committed biblical evangelicals were inherently at odds with the advocates of stellar prediction. Luther's more or less scoffing attitude, reflexively over-emphasized by generations of historians, never came close to a program of opposition. True, he was frequently dismissive of the art in conversations with students and colleagues, comparing it to the vain rituals and ceremonies of the Papists. He could openly defend "astronomy" as a science separate from the presumed nonsense of astrology.[8] Yet his position was far less one of principled opposition than a mixture of disinclination, ridicule, and bemused tolerance; he never made the matter one of serious open debate. Even on matters we might think likely to have aroused his strongest ire, such as the famous efforts by several astrologers to reckon his nativity and to connect it with prophecies bearing on him and on the evangelical movement, Luther refrained from the sort of violent public blasts he often fired at those whom he saw as his true enemies.[9]

Despite his passionate opposition to all uses of reason as an arbiter of faith, Luther had nothing at all against natural philosophy properly pursued within its own sphere.[10] He accepted the systematic investigation of nature as a valid and useful enterprise, and had no problem with the possibility of natural predictions bearing on external, physical things. His main concern was not the same as John Calvin's, namely that astrological predictions regarding human life amounted to a sinful effort to comprehend divine providence. Instead he was simply unconvinced that any science based on natural law could dependably predict human events. For the faithful Christian the future was essentially a matter of God's will and grace, not of natural causation. Beyond this, especially in his later sermons and writings, Luther dwelled so often and so heavily on the signs of future disaster and the Second Advent that he seemed to endorse the threatening forecasts of the prognosticators. And as we have seen in connection with the flood fears and the prophecies of Lichtenberger, he was ready to exploit popular astrological notions when they could serve his cause. His firm belief in the spiritual meaning of the sidereal signs was of far greater consequence for his sixteenth-century heirs than his more negative and mostly private judgments on the stargazers' art.[11]

The dismissive comments Luther did make, so often cited by modern scholars, would hardly weigh at all in the balance against the influence of Melanchthon. The divergence between the two men is sometimes reduced to a simple difference between law and gospel, or between philosophy and theology. As a practical matter, however, evangelical thinkers could not entirely escape the need to philosophize, and the philosophy they mainly adopted was based on the framework articulated at Wittenberg in the 1530s. We have few reasons to think that students felt torn by a choice between the positions of their two most influential mentors. On the contrary, what we know of those who trained here in the 1530s, 1540s, and 1550s suggests that most learned to take for granted the general complementarity of nature and scripture, and thus to assume that astrology properly conceived and applied was a necessary instrument for the Christian life.[12]

Melanchthonian teachings were crucial in inspiring and shaping the far-reaching program of astrological education and discipline that his evangelical colleagues and students worked to establish. This campaign's many agents shared the conviction of the city physician Christoph Stathmion that the science of the stars was "an excellent gift of God, and a mirror of his divine will."[13] Stathmion and a new generation of emerging advocates sought to promote the personal and social benefits of the art, which they viewed as the practical philosophical complement to biblical faith. Their interrelated tasks included celebrating God's power and glory as revealed in the heavens, showing people their utter weakness and dependence on the divine will, warning all against disobedience and derangement, and supplying the knowledge necessary for effective adaptation to the divinely instituted natural order. Employing channels that reached all the way from learned humanistic treatises down to the cheap annual predictive works, the expanding network of evangelical stargazers undertook to disseminate the ideal of a revived stellar science as part of a general enlightenment, a war on superstition of any kind.

Neither the renowned university scholars nor the publicists who followed their lead could altogether avoid the use of conventionally defensive language. After all, nothing was easier for critics than to mock and sneer at the countless disagreements and the apparent theoretical chaos that reigned among the yearly forecasts. Even with the new and improved data available in published ephemerides by recognized experts, agreement among the prognosticators was scarce. On such basic points as the ruling planets for a given year, the annual practicas continued to contradict one another.[14] Weather forecasts remained vague and conflicting. Arguments over the proper timing of bloodletting and other medical treatments were as angry as ever, and in general the mass publicists remained energetic in criticizing one another.[15] But the growing ranks of astrological publicists remained remarkably unfazed by such contradictions and controversy. For one thing, as Stephen Vanden Broecke has pointed out, these disputes themselves helped to hasten the push for reform at the learned level. And since both the disagreements and the reform efforts quickly became known among those who advocated and practiced the stellar art, even the lowliest calendar maker could thus sense that he was somehow participating in an ongoing process of recovery and refinement.[16] Moreover, such unassailable defenses were at hand that it was only too easy to make the critics themselves look foolish. Most ostensible apologies barely disguised an essentially peremptory outlook.

For many writers, defensive comments simply provided an excuse for popular instruction. The Schweinfurth physician Gregor Fabricius followed this common path, moving quickly beyond words against presumed detractors into a primer on the art's basic principles, and then to a lesson on the value of astrology to true piety.[17] Often, though, a dismissive attitude was hardly disguised at all. Johann Schöner of Nuremberg showed near incredulity toward the charges of the presumed critics. In justifying his calling he laid out his points as painfully obvious, conveying more than a hint of condescension: these were matters even a child should be able to understand. Astrology's enemies were like dogs who charged at strangers; they did not even know whom or what they were attacking. Such woeful ignorance, wrote Schöner, was manifest in the anonymous author of *Die getrew Eckart*, the most widely circulated Christian practica of the 1530s and 1540s, who abused the scriptures with his "crazy understanding," and was rightly afraid to reveal himself. The complaint that the astrologers contradicted one another carried no weight at all; interpreters of the scriptures differed seriously among themselves as well; was one to throw out the Bible on that account? Indeed to negate the art of the stars one would have to disavow scripture, for the Lord had instructed the faithful not to fear the heavenly signs, but to watch for them; in fact the stars gave testimony to his birth and death. Pushing the limits of offense in the guise of defense, Schöner even reminded his readers of Christ's warning that the truth must suffer persecution. Thus the allegedly persecuted stargazers became virtual Christian martyrs.[18]

The astrologers' bearing of incredulity, condescension, and dismissal toward critics continued despite a surge of attacks against them, mainly though not exclusively from outside evangelical circles, in the decades following Luther's death in 1546. We will discuss these hostile works mainly in Chapter 5; here we need only take note of their very limited effects on the overall Melanchthonian campaign. In a few cases, to be sure, practica writers felt forced to give a bit of ground. In 1555, for example, Christoph Stathmion felt compelled to admit that scripture said nothing specific about the art of astrology. But this point was insignificant, he insisted, since the Bible was not essentially concerned with natural things at all. Christians were certainly not forbidden to investigate the material creation, present or future; indeed the scriptures exhorted believers to study the wonderful works of God. Again in his practica for 1563 Stathmion answered those who held that whoever heard the promise of God's Word required no further knowledge of the past or future. He conceded that natural knowledge was not needed for the spiritual life, but it was clearly necessary for the life of the body in this world; in this sense it had broad scriptural sanction.[19] Other writers were moved to acknowledge the inherent uncertainty of their art. In his forecast for 1562, for example, Gregor Fabricius made extensive references to Aristotle to show why his weather forecasts were necessarily conjectural, and cited a scriptural mystery: "The wind bloweth where it listeth, and thou hearest the sound thereof, but canst not tell whence it cometh, and whither it goeth" (John 3:8). Johann Klain introduced his forecasts with more than a hint of humility. Naturally we do not hit all things right, but we astrologers are only human, and have lots to learn. Despite our errors, he wrote, the art itself is noble and Christian.[20]

The majority of evangelical practitioners, however, conceded nothing. Fiercely turning the tables on those who questioned their art as unchristian, deluded, or superstitious, many publicists launched punishing verbal counter-bombardments. In 1558 Johann Hebenstreit expressed astonishment that anyone could be so afflicted with "a cerebral vacuum, and openly display their crude, coarse, epicurean asses' pates." Supposedly learned people had argued that one could not predict anything from eclipses, since they occurred frequently in all lands. But "since Moses, yea Christ himself calls them signs, thus they must mean something. And if they mean something, why should one then not [use them to] warn and prod the people to repentance?" It was not superstitious but Godly and necessary to seek the divine order in nature. On the proper basis of this art, "the most able philosophers and natural astrologers have founded their prognostications from the beginning of the world."[21]

The scholar and evangelical polemicist Joachim Heller showed equal aggressiveness, declaring that opposition to the astrologers amounted to "rank impiety." Johannes Paceus maintained that those who spouted such evil nonsense were ultimately mouthpieces of the devil, who were trying to deny the great benefits of the art to individuals, to the common good, and to the Church. The Marburg medical professor Victorin Schönfelt borrowed an image from Melanchthon, that of the Cyclops, depicting as brutish and half blind those who showed no respect for the arts and philosophy, by which he meant above all the study of the heavens. In 1574 the Danish Lutheran Tycho Brahe struck a solid Melanchthonian note, claiming that to deny the art was not only patently to contradict experience, but also to doubt the wisdom and providence of God.[22] These were not the expressions of beleaguered defenders, but mainly the annoyed asides of dedicated writers and practitioners, men who saw themselves as participants in a great and general reform, and who found only ignorance and dark delusions in those who denied the value of natural understanding.

One prime example of this Melanchthonian offensive to promote the science of the stars and to bury superstition was also among the best known of all sixteenth-century treatments of astrology and divination. This was Caspar Peucer's often-cited *Commentarius de praecipuis divinationum generibus*, first published at Wittenberg in 1553.[23] Peucer's aim was straightforward: to distinguish clearly between legitimate and illegitimate forms of divination. His criteria were no less explicit: he accepted those arts that he believed were based on the analysis of physical causes and effects, and rejected all others. He thus drew the sharpest possible line between astrology, the chief and most noble branch of natural divination, and a broad range of ancient "mancies"—geomancy, hydromancy, pyromancy, and so on—as well as all methods that looked in any way to the occult operation of spirits. All these unnatural forms were ultimately of the devil. But to discard the legitimate natural methods along with them was in fact to deny God's providence, and to ignore the Bible's witness to nature as an avenue of divine instruction and warning.

Peucer's insistence that natural divination was a scripturally sanctioned path to knowledge of the Creator has been construed as a way of carving out space to protect stellar science from the attacks of theologians.[24] But this view fails to recognize the positive conviction of Melanchthonian thinkers that God revealed and exercised his sovereignty through the stars, a confidence now flourishing among evangelical humanists with fresh sources of theological and civic support. Again, these evangelical advocates saw the revived study of the heavens as closely related to the renewal of true gospel teaching, while all illegitimate heathen arts were directly analogous to the perversions of the Romanists. Peucer himself made this connection, peppering his discussion with anti-Catholic passages.[25] We should regard his work far less as a defensive measure than as the product of a concerted, aggressive push to establish a close alliance between celestial science and biblical faith.

The Teacher

The spearhead of the new offensive came in Melanchthon's curricular initiatives at Wittenberg, which began to take shape in the late 1520s. These changes insured that astrology took on a broadened role as a fundamental part of three disciplines: mathematics, natural philosophy, and medicine. Melanchthon himself took the lead in lecturing, presiding over disputations, and encouraging study and publication. His influence was reinforced by the prolific labors of colleagues such as Erasmus Reinhold, George Joachim Rheticus, Caspar Peucer, and Johann Garcaeus. As recent studies have shown, however, the notion of a "Melanchthon circle" of star-struck scholars at Wittenberg is misleading, for it suggests a distinct group set apart from the larger academic and humanistic world of evangelical thought.[26] The *Praeceptor Germaniae* and his faculty colleagues were merely the most active and prominent agents of the push for a renewed and reformed science of the stars, which evolved into a pervasive movement of education, publicity, and propaganda.

Melanchthon himself was profoundly shaped by the astrological culture of the late-medieval universities and towns. His father had asked no less a figure than Johann Virdung to cast his horoscope at his birth, and Melanchthon would later request similar readings for his two daughters. Studying at Tübingen under Johann Stöffler, for whom the study of the eternal laws by which God governed the world was virtually an obligatory form of worship, he absorbed the same atmosphere of nature piety that had produced the annual calendars and practicas. He had helped with the publication of Stöffler's 1514 astronomical tables, an important reference work for practicing physicians and forecasters.[27] Although we know almost nothing about his reaction to the great flood debate while it raged, he later sought to justify the predictions that gave rise to it, arguing that in fact 1524 had been an extremely moist year. His letters and other writings reveal a deep and lifelong preoccupation with issues of celestial prediction. He never tired of reading or commenting on the annual almanacs, on reports of portents, and on a broad range of forecasts both popular and learned; he was also known to plan, delay, or refuse particular voyages on the basis of the stars.[28] We cannot write off Melanchthon's interest in astrology as a private and marginal diversion, or as in any way truly anomalous in the context of the early German Reformation. Indeed it is now well established that this interest was intimately tied to his overall philosophy of nature and to his broad pedagogical project.

While Melanchthon's efforts to promote astronomical and astrological study had already begun with the cooperation of the Wittenberg mathematician Volmar in the 1520s, in the early 1530s this push became more open and consistent. Around this time his correspondence and publications show a growing preoccupation with all aspects of stellar science. He became caught up, for instance, in an intense discussion of birth horoscopes and their meaning for contemporary circumstances. Notoriously, this exchange included a debate over Luther's nativity that became bound up with the early propaganda wars between the reformer's enemies and supporters. The famous Italian stargazer Luca Gaurico, for whom Melanchthon had great respect and who even visited him at Wittenberg in 1532, worked to connect Luther's birth with the great conjunction of 1484, which Lichtenberger and others had associated with the birth of a prophet-figure. Melanchthon denied the supposition that a false prophet was indicated, but along with prominent interpreters such as Johann Carion and Erasmus Reinhold he thought the astrological evidence too significant to be discounted; he thus upheld 1484—rather than 1483 as Luther and others had assumed—as the true year of the reformer's birth. The controversy flared for some time and was never really resolved.[29]

Of greater long-term significance than this affair, both for Melanchthon and for the burgeoning world of astrological publicity, was the shocking appearance of an unusually large and bright comet late in 1531, later to be named for the English astronomer Halley. The phenomenon offered a new focus for the discussion of common fears, and as so often in the past, these fears were bound up with religious and political circumstances in the Empire. In the wake of the 1530 Diet of Augsburg and the adoption of the Augsburg Confession by evangelical cities and princes, tensions were soaring. Nearly every German astrologer with any claim to expertise or renown published a description and reading of the comet, and despite countless variations on particular details virtually all detected a divine warning of greatest severity. Melanchthon shared fully in the widespread alarm, and anxiously inquired of Carion and other professionals about the meaning of this "hairy star." From this point on especially, his convictions about the need for astrological study at all levels would remain consistently strong and explicit.[30]

Melanchthon issued what amounted to a manifesto of his astrological program in a famous letter to his former student Simon Grynaeus, which first appeared in print as the preface to a new edition of Sacrobosco's *Sphaera* in 1531 and went through many later editions. Indeed, the epistle had a remarkable public career; it was reissued in conjunction with a variety of other texts, and found a printer as late as 1629. Almost all the points he raised here would crop up repeatedly in Melanchthon's lectures, orations, sermons, and writings over the following three decades. While the letter did include a couple of references to the opponents of celestial prediction, it was in no sense a defensive work, and shows no signs of having been written as a contribution to an ongoing debate over the stellar art. Far from writing to parry earlier attacks, Melanchthon looked to the positive goal of enhancing astrology's academic and institutional status. His widely read epistle was a kickoff in this broad campaign.[31]

The professor began with praise of Sacrobosco himself, who had achieved great things in this science. Men of learning and wisdom had long regarded the *Sphaera* as a book that should be taught in all schools, and made available to all students. Who, after all, was so utterly without sense and feeling that he had never looked upon the heavens and their movements with wonder and admiration? Plato had stated clearly that humans were given eyes for the study of astronomy. Here Melanchthon gave a half nod to the notion of man as microcosm, citing though not positively endorsing the belief that each person had within himself a nature corresponding to the heavenly firmament. In any case, those who paid no heed to the stars were ignoring the ends for which they were created, meaning first of all to make us aware of God and our own immortality. The study of the heavens simply compelled one to acknowledge that an all-powerful spirit guided the universe. Scripture gave the clearest possible sanction to this discipline, for in Genesis 1:14 God himself declared that the lights in the firmament were "for signs and for seasons, and for days and years." They were therefore the basic measure of time itself, a knowledge of which was the very foundation of both religion and civic life. Without such understanding, humans would sink into utter barbarism.

Melanchthon then linked the recent revival of the art with the glory of the fatherland: "For this teaching, after languishing in neglect for several centuries, has experienced a new flowering in Germany." It had been called back to life by Peurbach and Regiomontanus, who were driven by a virtually divine inspiration. When since ancient times had this study shown such illuminating power as now? The Egyptians had all but extinguished its brilliance. The Arabs, to be sure, had carried the art to Spain and thus to the Christian West. But their writings were informed by mere curiosity, with the crude goal of making specific predictions. They strayed far from the teachings of Ptolemy, pursuing oracles and other baseless forms of divination. The German heroes of recent memory had revived the essential principles of the great theorist, spreading the seeds of a genuinely useful astrological science in the only land where this learning was rightly valued. Melanchthon left implicit the connection between this new German blossoming and the recovery of the gospel, but the association was unmistakable.

The "epicurean" theologians who wished to deny credibility to the science not only mocked future forecasts, but went so far as to ridicule all study of the heavenly motions as if it were useless, or worse. Yet neither Pico nor anyone else, declared Melanchthon, could reasonably maintain that this art was without tremendous benefit. Experience alone showed that conjunctions of the "glowing" stars caused burning and dryness, while meetings of the "moist" stars increased wetness. It was true that the planetary forces became mixed up in complex ways with terrestrial nature. But Aristotle was certainly right in saying that the celestial bodies were the basic determinants of earthly movement; his words should be impressed permanently upon the minds of students. While physicians tended to look for causes in terrestrial matter rather than in the stars, properly they had to refer to the celestial movements and their effects as well. These teachings were perfectly consistent with Christian doctrine, which held that everything was ruled by God yet readily acknowledged his natural instruments. Indeed the ability to distinguish between the actions of God through natural law and those he performed directly was wisdom worthy of a Christian.

Broadening his scope, the professor next discussed three sources of influence upon human beings. The effects of nature were the most clearly manifest to reason and sense. They included not only celestial and terrestrial causes, but also the secondary results of nurture: parental example, discipline and habits, education and the laws. The second influence was grace, that which God gave to man above and beyond his elemental composition and reason. Grace was at work whenever God chose to overrule nature in any way, to alter or correct the natural course of things. By this gift one could overcome the inherent saddening influences in nature, the thoughts that come through reason and experience to humans in their weakness. Here Melanchthon turned on its head the usual interpretation of the biblical passage most often used against the astrologers, "fear not the signs in the heavens" (Jeremiah 10:2). Far from admonishing against astrology, these words meant that the stars pointed to a fearsome reality for unbelievers, while the faithful were freed from this burden and could behold the heavens with joy. In just the same way, Christ forbade the fear of death, not because the reality was anything other than bitter, but to lead people to understand that he could save them even from the grave.

A third influence on human life lay in the workings of the Devil, who was always exploiting inherent human weakness and leading people astray. By confusing and confounding earthly nature, Satan perverted natural influences and evoked evil. Here Melanchthon followed a long tradition in limiting the effects of evil to the terrestrial realm. This lower world was indeed corrupt, hence constantly and dangerously subject to the machinations of the Devil. The heavens, however, remained pure, both an announcement and an instrument of divine justice. To be sure, this approach did not resolve basic, intractable questions about the relationship between God's rule over nature on one hand and sin and evil on the other. How, for example, could the stars enforce God's justice in a realm of permanently broken law? Avoiding such conceptual wasps' nests, the teacher simply sought to show that nature, grace, and sin all had a basic role in shaping human life.

Ignorant mockers, wrote Melanchthon, must not be allowed to lead young people to condemn the study of the stars, which in fact brought the most worthy sort of human knowledge. The predictive aspect of the art was precisely analogous to the role of diagnosis and prognosis in medicine, which looked to human health and well-being. A knowledge of the heavenly influences was indeed basic for the physician, and indeed the regularities of the heavens were essential tools for human civilization. So closely were these patterns linked to the highest forms of reason that one could find in the stars a symbolic expression of natural political order and authority: the Sun reigned in the center of the heavens with his general, his senators, orators, and co-regents. Such analogies could help one appreciate the divine reason that governed the universe. But if they fell short, Genesis 1:14 stated plainly that the stars were not only the causes of day and night, seasons and years, but also signs with a further meaning. And so for instance a unanimous opinion down through the centuries was that eclipses were indicators of things to come. For all these reasons the preceptor exhorted all, and especially the young, to undertake the study of the heavens with reverence.

This letter did not cover all aspects of its author's thinking about the value of astrology. In particular, Melanchthon did not say much here about the role of the stars in regard to the Last Things. Especially at this early stage in his campaign to promote the stellar art, he was most concerned to emphasize its positive benefits for piety and civic order, for both personal and public welfare. The same assertive and confident tone characterized his 1535 preface to a new edition of Peurbach's *Theoreticae Novae Planetarum*, where he emphasized that research in the heavens was a form of obedience to God, who wanted humans to understand his workings through nature.[32] The same year brought his *Oration on the Dignity of Astrology*, delivered by his student Jacob Milich at the celebration of the latter's doctoral degree; here the teacher professed straightforwardly that "the science of heavenly influences is true and that it brings great benefits for life." His famous lectures on physical science, published in 1549 as the *Initia doctrinae physicae*, were grounded on the premise that the whole physical cosmos was a direct result of God's providential design, and that therefore the study of astronomy and astrology—which could not be separated—were essential both to education and to the Christian life. Here was no defensive apology for the stellar art, but an unproblematic assertion of its necessity on the basis of ancient authority: "according to the usual teaching of Ptolemy." As Robert Westman states convincingly, "he took for granted that there was a consensus among the astronomers."[33]

Integral to this emphasis on the positive benefits of the art to piety and the practical business of life was the recognition that astrology was first and foremost a natural science. Melanchthon repeatedly harped on the need to distinguish astrology from "the superstitious divinations" that Ptolemy dismissed because they did not deal with causes. Astrology was "a part of natural philosophy, which teaches what effects the light of the stars has on the elements and on mixed bodies, and which temperaments, alterations or inclinations it contrives." Again and again the teacher returned to the parallels with medicine, to which Galen himself had attested. Like medicine it was a practical, a posteriori art, which inevitably worked with probabilities rather than certainties. It depended in no small measure on experience, and while astrologers were often wrong, this did not undermine the usefulness of their work as a means of insight into the future and for choosing a course of action.[34] A sober natural science had little need for speculations that went beyond physical causes.

Although scholars have noted certain Neoplatonic affinities in Melanchthon and his associates, these thinkers remained committed to an essentially Aristotelian framework.[35] In line with prevailing German trends since the fifteenth century, the Wittenbergers showed a general resistance to Neoplatonic concepts of universal hierarchy and cosmic correspondence. Thus Melanchthonian astrology was opposed to the sort of thinking represented by the famous Swiss-German physician Paracelsus, whose highly unorthodox medical and astrological teachings—which included astral magic—would be slow to gain ground until later in the century. The study of the stars meant in practical terms not the active use of heavenly powers, but simply understanding and adjusting to the stellar forces. These forces were "occult" or imperceptible in the same way that gravity cannot be perceived; they were measured by their effects. Thus too, just as in the scholastic strains that had reigned in the early printed almanacs and practicas, ideas about planetary intelligences played no role.

God could act either indirectly, through secondary causes, or directly by acts of will; in neither case were any intermediate intelligences at work. Interpretations that find a revival of ancient demonic beliefs in Renaissance astrology simply do not apply to the art as conceived by Melanchthon and his heirs, who resolutely opposed anything resembling demonic magic.

Ultimately, however, the science of nature was for Melanchthon part of a larger program of theological teaching. All study of nature began with God and the creation, and thus astrology became the handmaid of theology, a means of insight into the divine order and will. Above every other benefit of this and related arts, it was delightful to contemplate "the marvelous agreement of the heavenly bodies with those below," for "that very order and harmony remind me that the world is not driven by chance, but guided by divine providence."[36] In this conception, physical causes were in fact "ordinances of God"; natural predictions were based on and justified by the assumption of a divine order. Moreover, since all of history and creation stood under the providence of God, Melanchthon did not make any final distinction between celestial signs and causes. He felt justified in moving indifferently between causality and signification since they were but two aspects of a single divinely instituted order of nature. As Stefano Caroti explains, Melanchthon held "that natural and historical events have, besides their immediate natural and historical significance, a hidden symbolism relating them to God's providential design for man's salvation."[37] In his eyes, the stellar art could and should strengthen and console the faithful by manifesting divine glory and governance.

His resistance to any sharp distinction between signs and causes was connected with Melanchthon's acceptance of the common belief that the stargazer's purview included irregular and potentially disturbing celestial phenomena such as the 1531 comet. If according to some contemporaries a presumed biblical and patristic approach to wondrous signs had to be vindicated over against the supposed science of stellar patterns, for the Wittenberg professor and the vast majority of his fellow evangelicals these were scarcely distinguishable aspects of a single art. Both predictable and unpredictable natural events were ultimately manifestations of law in the largest sense, of God's providential actions through nature. With Melanchthon's concept of divine law we are therefore ironically never very far from the Augustinian notion that all of nature is miraculous when regarded through the eyes of faith.

Philosophy, as Melanchthon conceived it, was nothing other than the study of law, both natural and moral. God commanded humankind to recognize and learn to obey him through the knowledge of law.[38] Thus again careful observation of the heavens was itself divinely mandated, for the stars, far more fully than any aspect of the sublunary world, revealed the truths of natural law. A crucial corollary was that the stars exercised their influence without being thereby responsible for the negative effects. Stellar influence, coming as it did through light and motion from the heavenly spheres, was naturally good; it was corrupted by fallen nature, especially by sinful human nature. If nature had remained unfallen, the stars would have worked very differently in a still-pure material, and their godly light would have directed all human drives to the good. But in this world their proper effects were distorted.[39] As we noted, Melanchthon and his colleagues never resolved the paradoxical matter of how natural law—the very law of God—could remain law in a fallen world, how a science of the stars could discern patterns where brokenness and irregularity reigned. But neither Melanchthon himself, nor even his yet more systematically minded associate Peucer, was a philosopher in the sense of a thinker who looked for a thoroughly logical understanding of reality. They were finally Christian theologians whose approach to nature was rooted in awe at the infinite power of a sovereign God.

While the art of reading the heavens could and should teach of divine power and glory, this lesson actually depended on turning one's eyes upward in faith, which no follower of Luther could take for granted. Indeed the natural law of the stars applied first of all to the natural man, who was fallen and in need of grace; this law revealed human weakness and helplessness. A basic theme in Melanchthonian teaching was the subjection of the whole natural man, the "old" man of the flesh, to the power of the stars. This notion was implicit in the 1531 letter to Grynaeus, which spoke of no influences beyond nature, God, and the devil. Since humans were ultimately helpless as natural creatures, the only true freedom lay in God's grace, his power to change or cancel the effects of natural law at any time or place. What astrology could not actually teach, what no philosophy at all could teach, was the liberating gift of the gospel, for which the law merely prepared the way. To be sure, evangelical astrologers continued to cite the traditional dictum "the stars incline, but they do not compel." To medieval schoolmen these words had meant that the human intellect and will stood apart from the forces of nature, and could freely resist them. But now the freedom implied in the phrase shifted away from the human will to God's will, which was sovereign over all. This change marked a fundamental departure from the accepted scholastic doctrine.[40] It brought

a sober acceptance of natural necessity, yet at the same time a Christian
rejection of Stoic fatalism: "Great is the power of the stars, but they are
subject to Christ, as are all other creatures."[41]

This perspective assumed a dialectical relationship between law and
gospel. The Christian encountered the law not simply through reason;
rather law and gospel illuminated one another. Thus as Ralph Keen
remarks, for Melanchthon the truest understanding of the divine through
nature was the knowledge of God's goodness, a pious awareness rather
than a merely rational apprehension.[42] In this sense, the observations of
the astrologer might be not only a warning to the godless, but also a source
of consolation to the faithful—the consolation found in the confidence
that God's Providence reigned supreme, and in the implicit promise of
grace to the faithful. But this assumption also meant that a full apprecia-
tion of physical doctrine was impossible except in the light of gospel faith,
was open only to those who had heard the biblical word. In the eyes of
evangelical stargazers, this teaching amounted to a quite straightforward
Augustinianism: faith ultimately preceded understanding.

None of this was to deny that human beings possessed a certain
lower-order freedom of the sort that Luther himself fully acknowledged.
Melanchthon and his colleagues often spoke of free will in the sense of a
limited liberty of human reason and will to adapt to natural changes and
conditions. This sort of practical, lower-order freedom had an important
place in Christian life, even if God might choose at any moment to over-
whelm it and reduce it to naught. It was not to be confused with Christian
liberty, the freedom of the gospel. While the only hope of actually escaping natural law came from trust in the Lord's mercy, humans did retain a
rational capacity to adapt within the bounds of the law. In the sense that it
supplied certain principles and practical tools for earthly survival, benefit,
and comfort, astrology offered a strictly limited form of empowerment,
but one with enormous consequences for life in this world. Melanchthon
stressed the great need for turning one's mind toward all the signs in the
heavens, for this study brought "the greatest power and varied benefit for
life."[43] In fact such knowledge was basic for the maintenance of the essential human institutions: family, economy, and civil community. The right
ordering of human relationships through these institutions according to
natural law was the essence of moral philosophy.

While he often referred to astrology as a practical art closely analogous
to others such as medicine and meteorology, in a broader sense it was
an umbrella science, the principles of which were basic to these and all

other fields of natural and philosophical knowledge. It was obvious, he wrote in the *Oration*, that observation of the stars was necessary in medicine: "But how much greater is the usefulness ... for the state, of considering the causes or meanings of the greatest changes, so that we can adapt our decisions to them, and mitigate misfortunes by art. For Plato says truthfully that the revolutions of the stars cause various vicissitudes, not only for animated bodies, but also for the entire nature of things, the life of men, empires, and states."[44] Indeed it was universally "profitable in the administration of things" to consider the signs and causes that God had established in nature. In a 1542 address on natural philosophy, the *praeceptor* again emphasized that astrology was not only useful but necessary to every aspect of worldly life. While not all persons could be prepared to practice the full arts of healing, "all who do not live like barbarians need some kind of general knowledge of . . . the elements, of the temperaments, of the function and nature of the limbs and organs in humans, of the causes of diseases, and further of the movements of the heavens and of the various effects that accompany these motions." Similar benefits of the stellar art applied "in choosing a way of life or type of studies, and in undertaking business that is either fitting or unfit for one's intellect." He could assert that this knowledge was useful for "the mothers of families," since it was crucial to proper health and education. A sort of household science, inseparable from astrological principles, was indeed necessary for everyone, and one could point to a raft of broader "economic" benefits: "In civil affairs, too, there are benefits to be gained from the science of natural philosophy." And likewise with the moral life of the individual: "If someone understands the tendencies of his nature, he is able to nourish and strengthen what is good, and to avoid vices by diligence and reason."[45]

When he discussed the concept of law in theological terms, Melanchthon adopted Luther's understanding of two primary functions: maintaining outward worldly order, and bringing humans to recognize their sinful and utterly helpless state. In addition, however, and in some eyes controversially, he taught that law could and should serve to instruct believers in living the Christian life. This so-called third use of the law corresponded precisely to the mundane goal of the stellar science in Melanchthon's teaching. His evangelical astrology emerged as a form of worldly discipline for the faithful, a rediscovered basis for personal and social order, grounded in nature itself, which together with a purified faith could overcome the confused human imaginings that had overtaken Christendom. Moreover, the sorts of astrological knowledge and practice he thought useful were not merely of the bland sort, often called "natural" astrology, that even a general enemy of sidereal prediction such as John Calvin could acknowledge.[46] His preoccupation with horoscopic analysis reflected Melanchthon's conviction that the benefits of stellar diagnosis and prognosis applied to the entire range of human affairs both private and public, including the effects on individual human temperaments and natural behavior.

In the last analysis, however, the human capacity for effective adaptation was severely limited. One might well gain some understanding of fate, either universal or personal, but one had no independent power to change the dictates of nature. There could be no mistake about the great gulf between heavenly power and human capacities. Although Melanchthon very often expressed confidence in astrology as a tool for worldly betterment, this element was always qualified and kept in its place by his underlying awareness of the final contingency of all created orders, and his conviction that God's plan for history was coming rapidly to fulfillment. As Claudia Brosseder rightly points out, Melanchthon feared not demons, but God's will and the threat of divine wrath.[47] The preceptor's letters frequently reflected premonitions of approaching disaster, and in many cases these thoughts were directly related both to astrological predictions and to apocalyptic prophecy. Indeed God's rule through nature ultimately pointed to the certain coming of the Last Judgment. Thus in a 1553 oration, for instance, he celebrated the order and reliability of the heavens, and made parallels between that dependability and divinely inspired prophecies about the end of the world. The apprehension of a universal providence through nature should confirm the trust of the faithful that God would keep his promises, and that his plan would be unfailingly fulfilled.[48]

At the same time, Melanchthon was strongly affected by the late-medieval assumption that the world was sinking into weakness and old age. Undoubtedly Luther's influence played a role here; the reformer repeatedly referred to the entire creation, the heavens and the earth, as an old house that was cracking up and preparing to collapse. But Melanchthon characteristically applied the notion in a more systematic way, introducing his famous *Initia Doctrinae Physicae* lectures in 1549 with the idea that the creation was in its "extreme dotage." He had learned that Copernicus's reckonings reduced of the scale of the planetary system, and thus concluded along with other learned contemporaries that the sun had come nearly ten thousand miles closer to earth since the time of Ptolemy.[49] It appeared, in other words, that the celestial spheres themselves were show-ing signs of breakdown. In these lectures as well as in his preaching, he interpreted the phenomenon as one among many signs of the approach-ing Last Judgment. Here too was a manifestation of divine law, for any such decline had to be part of God's plan. The glaring contradiction between his repeated stress on nature's beautiful order on one hand and its apparent contraction on the other merely expressed in stark terms the inescapable Christian paradox of a creation that was at once inherently good and inherently fallen. For Melanchthon, the signs of impending cos-mic dissolution held out terror to the faithless, but could offer consolation to the faithful by showing that deliverance was near.

In several basic ways Melanchthon's program was a continuation and synthesis of ideals that had emerged in literature of the pre-Reformation decades. Indeed his labors reflected and strongly reinforced mental habits that had been cultivated since well before he was born by the authors of the popular calendars and practicas. In his lectures on physical science he echoed, perhaps unwittingly, the very sorts of basic astrological instruc-tion that had already been common in vernacular literature many decades earlier: "The moon is the lowest luminary in the heavens, which traverses the entire Zodiac in 27 days, 7 hours, 43 minutes and 7 seconds." He laid it heavily on his students: "How great a madness it is," he declared in another lecture, "to undervalue the uses of calendars! It is a great benefaction of God that every person can have an almanac on the wall."[50] Such instruc-tion and advice might just as well have come from an annual broadsheet from the 1490s, or from his teacher Stöffler at Tübingen, or from one of the countless popular astrological handbooks found in the homes of his contemporaries. The "teacher of Germany" saw himself and his colleagues as carrying on the humanistic reform movement begun by Peurbach and Regiomontanus; at the same time, he reinforced the late-medieval tradi-tions of astrological medicine and meteorology, traditions that had already penetrated deep into the burgher outlook. Conforming to central aspects of the pre-Reformation trends we have surveyed, his teaching made it clear that the stars revealed God's omnipotence and his gifts, as well as warnings to a sinful world.

Yet while he owed much to this synthetic inheritance, Melanchthon gave a forceful new impetus to the star-stirred culture of the German towns, particularly those in which the religious reform was taking hold. As the leading exponent of evangelical humanism and the famed teacher of Germany, he gave unprecedented sanction to the study of the physical heavens, encouraging this learning at all the newly Protestant universities. Although he could not accept the heliocentrism of Copernicus as a physical model, he was open to its use as a basis for astronomical calculations; on balance he did far more to stimulate than to dampen cosmological speculation. Above all by establishing a new understanding of the relationship between natural philosophy and theology, Melanchthon did more than any other single figure to insure the continuing massive spread of astrology at all levels among Luther's sixteenth-century heirs.[51] We will find the main elements of his vision establishing themselves in evangelical culture through a vast publicity machine as the sixteenth century progressed.

Works and Networks

Hundreds of students from Wittenberg and other Lutheran schools carried Melanchthonian doctrines to a broader public in the Protestant towns of the Empire, further magnifying the main trends we have traced through the pre-Reformation era and into the 1520s. The extended and interrelated networks that emerged included academics, humanist scholars, printers, court physicians and consultants, princely bureaucrats, the whole range of urban medical practitioners, pastors, schoolmasters, nobles, and significant numbers of literate and semi-literate burghers. The engagement of all these groups with astrological assumptions, teachings, and practices helped cultivate a distinctive evangelical culture.

The dizzying political confusion of the early Reformation era certainly contributed to the increasingly common employment of astrologers at courts throughout the Empire. Although it does not appear that in the mid-sixteenth century evangelical princes were any more or less likely than Catholic rulers to consult professional forecasters, it is also true, as Brosseder has shown, that an extensive network of consultation developed between evangelical princes on one hand, and astrologers trained at or associated with Wittenberg on the other. Such ongoing contacts were encouraged by princely agents such as Georg Spalatin (d. 1545), secretary to the electors of Saxony, who frequently included discussion of astrological predictions in his correspondence. Relationships between rulers and stargazers were highly varied and complex; it is difficult to generalize about the role of patronage, the frequency of consultations, or the sorts of advice sought or given. Some rulers, particularly those with the most resources, retained several astrologers at once so as to be able to compare their advice. Others appear to have called only occasionally on the expertise of a university physician or mathematician, and then mainly in non-political matters.[52]

Astrological predictions bearing on princely politics had always been the most dangerous sort, and any stargazer who engaged in speculations touching directly on the fate of his ruler inevitably stood in great peril. In principle Melanchthon and his colleagues insisted that the public and private uses of astrology could not be divorced; nonetheless a marked separation of private political counsel from public astrology did become evident in the evangelical sphere. While this development was very much in line with the overall political conservatism of the Wittenbergers, it also reflected a broader sixteenth-century trend emphasized by Stephen Vanden Broecke, whereby the confidential counsels given powerful persons gradually became an almost wholly separate dimension of astrological practice.[53] One prominent German stargazer who continued to publish more or less obscure political forecasts was Johann Carion, who served the last Catholic ruler of Brandenburg, Joachim I. As a friend and correspondent of Melanchthon who had also studied under Stöffler at Tübingen, Carion had by the early 1530s become a closet evangelical, but he was not about to give up the benefits and prestige of his position at the Brandenburg court. He felt safe enough to issue predictions that painted a dark picture for the House of Austria, which brought him under attack from the Viennese mathematician Perlach. In 1538 he reputedly drank himself into his grave, but the cryptic nature of his multi-year forecasts helped insure that his reputation long outlived him.[54]

The trend to more private political consultations is evidenced in a figure such as Petrus Cnemiander (Hosmann), who studied at Wittenberg, later became city physician at Cottbus, and served the Protestant Margrave of Brandenburg Joachim II for fourteen years (1552–1566). During this latter period, during which the Margrave followed his stargazer's predictions often virtually day by day, Cnemiander composed his forecasts entirely for the personal use of his patron, and they remained in manuscript form.[55] His name thus remained mainly unknown in the world of astrological publication. For all the patronage and status he and numerous others gained from their association with princes, then, in general the work of astrologers at the courts had a limited role in shaping the common astrological atmosphere of the day. Too much emphasis on the relationships between astrologers and princes can easily obscure the far more broadly consequential role of astrology as a form of mass-publicity with the potential to shape a confessional culture.

The alliance between university and town, on the other hand, remained crucial in this connection. The most notable example of this sort of interaction developed between Melanchthon and his colleagues at Wittenberg and the scholars, printers, and publicists of Nuremberg. What has sometimes been unhappily dubbed the Wittenberg-Nuremberg "axis" represented the main intellectual and commercial forces that shaped the German evangelical realm. Melanchthon's connections in the leading Franconian city were many and strong. They included elite humanists such as Joachim Camerarius, prominent mathematicians such as Johann Schöner (another onetime Stöffler student) and astrologically engaged church leaders such as Andreas Osiander, who guided the *De Revolutionibus* of Copernicus into print.[56] As Melanchthon well knew, the heritage of Regiomontanus weighed enormously at Nuremberg, and the city had emerged as the preeminent printing center of the Empire, especially for natural scientific works. Needless to say, other universities and other towns were also closely tied into the production and consumption of astrological materials. Yet the turmoil of the early Reformation had thrown so many of the German universities into disarray that few of them would match Wittenberg's influence for some time to come. And while widening streams of calendars, practicas, astro-medical tracts, lay handbooks, and related materials flowed from such centers as Augsburg, Strasbourg, Leipzig, and Wittenberg itself, the Nuremberg printers only heightened their overall dominance as the century progressed [57] (Figure 4.2).

The emerging network of astrological learning and publicity produced a huge outpouring of printed texts by ancient, medieval, and contemporary authorities. Scholars and printers in the evangelical towns found themselves in an especially advantageous position to carry forward the sorts of textual editing and publishing that had begun well before 1500. The market had room for many texts that did not fit easily together with the humanist reform ideal of a return to the supposed purity of the Greeks. The ardently evangelical Joachim Heller, for example, a protégé of Melanchthon who became rector of the Nuremberg Gymnasium, edited and published in 1548 the *Epitome* of Johannes Hispalensis, a key source of Arabic astrological learning; here he promoted astrology as not only useful, but necessary to true piety. In addition he edited works by the Arab writer Haly Abenragel and the Jewish stargazer Messahala,

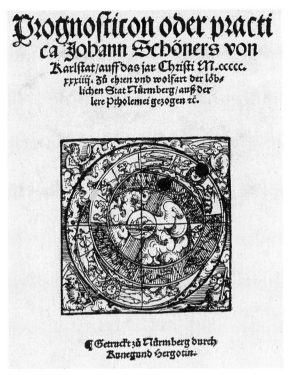

FIGURE 4.2 Title page from Johann Schöner's *Prognosticon oder practica* for 1534. Courtesy of the Herzog August Bibliothek Wolfenbüttel, 240.60.11 Quod.

citing these and a wide range of other sources in his immensely popular calendars and practicas. Always enterprising, Heller (Figure 4.3) published many of his editions through his own printing shop.[58] Already by midcentury the number of classical and Arabic texts available to scholars had risen manyfold, even as old standby volumes by Sacrobosco, Guido Bonatti, and Peurbach were reissued. Standard data collections such as the *Alfonsine Tables* and the updated calendar of Stöffler and Pflaum went through frequent printings, though they were now joined by highly touted improvements such as the *Prutenic Tables*, Erasmus Reinhold's 1551 compilation drawn from the work of Copernicus, which quickly became a stock source for evangelical physicians, almanac makers, practica writers, and others.[59] No printer did more to fuel the still-exploding interest in the stars than Johann Petreius of Nuremberg, who in the 1530s undertook an ambitious program of publication that included astrological works both old and new, Latin and vernacular; indeed his productions ran the gamut, from Greek and Arabic texts to major tracts by leading

IOACHIMVS   HELLER,
Weiſſenfelſenſis;
Mathematum et Aſtronomiae Profeſſor Publicus
Noriberg. et Typographiae publicae praefectus ab
A. 1544. ad A. 1556.
Natus A.   *Donatus A.*

FIGURE 4.3 Joachim Heller, Nuremberg's official calendar writer in the 1550s.
Courtesy of the Germanisches Nationalmuseum, Nürnberg, Kupferstichkabinett.

Italian figures such as Gaurico and Cardano, to annual practicas by an
assortment of evangelical authors.

The market was increasingly awash as well in handbooks for the practical application of the art. Johann Schöner gave this trend a major push
with his *Opusculum Astrologicum,* published by Petreius in 1539. This was
a no-nonsense introductory textbook covering essential principles as well
as their application in the reckoning of elections and nativities. It was at
the same time a powerful promotional tract, in which Schöner explained
the centrality of this knowledge to the liberal arts and made clear his
deep admiration for and debt to Melanchthon as a great motivator of astrological study. He appended several other writings, perhaps most notably
the *Assertio,* a lively stellar manifesto by Eberhard Schlei nger, a physician and almanac-writer active at Zurich in the late fift nth century.
Part of Schöner's purpose, in which he received Melanchthon's warm
encouragement, was to make sense of the increasingly dizzying array of

published sources. He pursued a similar aim in his 1545 work *De iudiciis nativitatum libri tres*; here he also covered basic points about the nature of the planets, signs, and houses, but devoted his main attention to the construction and reading of birth horoscopes.[60] The idea of gathering and publishing key works in order to advertise the value of stellar science was adopted by others such as the Lutheran Gervasius Marstaller, who issued in Paris a collection of writings all of which had been published earlier in Germany; here the words of Melanchthon and of Nuremberg associates such as Schöner and Heller took the spotlight.[61] Marstaller's choice to publish this collection in the French capital seems to have been calculated at least partly as a way of trumpeting abroad the leadership of the Germans, and especially the Lutherans, in this field.

Along with the rapid uptick in learned publication on astrology came an unstoppable torrent of popular German instructional texts. Most common were reinvented versions of the fifteenth- and early sixteenth-century planet books such as the 1512 *Teutsch Kalender* that had appeared under the name of Regiomontanus. These works were presented as comprehensive astronomical and astrological handbooks for the literate burgher. Typically regarded along with the annual predictive genres as beneath the notice of modern historians of science, their tremendous popularity speaks at least to their widespread appeal. Dozens of editions sprang off the presses at Frankfurt, Strasbourg, Nuremberg, Augsburg, Oppenheim, and other cities from the 1530s on. Fairly typical was the *Teutsch Astronomei*, an ample compendium of knowledge about the cosmos along with practical applications. Nearly every basic aspect of such learning was explained here in highly simplified terms, including the structure of the cosmos, the zodiac, the houses; the size, distance, and nature of each planet; the aspects, eclipses, epicycles, and comets; the terrestrial climatic zones; and calendrical reckoning. Many of these compendia, such as Eucharius Roesslin's highly popular *Kalender mit allen Astronomischen haltungen*, included instruction in the fundamentals of astrological medicine (Figure 4.4). Some offered sections on forms of divination such as chiromancy and physiognomy. Almost all were generously illustrated, although in many versions the images were no more than borrowed stereotypes. Yet another similar production, titled *Planeten Buechlin,* was issued in multiple editions under the name of Peter Creutzer, the self-styled disciple of Lichtenberger. Further variations would continue to compete with one another until well into the following century.[62]

FIGURE 4.4 Title page from Eucharius Rösslin's work of popular astrological instruction, *Kalender mit allen Asstronomischen haltungen* (Frankfurt am Main, 1534). Courtesy of the Bayerische Staatsbibliothek München, Res/Astr.p. 208 a.

Despite their frequent inclusion of precisely the sorts of material that leading mathematical reformers hoped to discredit, these popular planet books had more in common with learned writings than is generally recognized; in fact their authors often showed familiarity with sophisticated aspects of the stellar art. Several versions, for instance, gave quite detailed instructions for the use of the astrolabe and other instruments. Estimates of the distances from the earth of the various planets often followed the calculations of recognized experts. In some cases these popular works demanded considerable mathematical sophistication from their readers; a few even spoke in simplified terms about the precession of the equinoxes. Their compilers invoked a full stall of Greek and Arab masters, quoting freely from newly available editions. They were also careful to point out that the science had its limits, for God could alter the heavenly forces at any moment. Thus "we should give God the honor, who can turn cold to hot, hot to cold, moist to dry, and evil to good."[63]

These astrological handbooks were part of a broader upwelling of vernacular natural-scientific publications, most of which were produced in
cities that had joined the reform movement. This huge stock of new literature, aimed explicitly at the common man, was closely related to the rapid
expansion of lay schooling in these towns during the 1530s and 1540s.
A mushroom crop of popular medical works arose, including dozens on
hygiene and "regimen," many of which included references to astrological timing. Allied genres included herbals such as those of the prolific
botanist and physician Leonhard Fuchs, or the highly successful version
issued by Eucharius Roesslin.[64] This same era witnessed a tremendous
proliferation of pamphlets and broadsheets on meteorological events,
most of which included astrological description and analysis. The interest
in weather observations and forecasting that we found on the rise around
1500 had not abated; we know that members of the academic community around Melanchthon, as well as proponents of astrological reform in
Nuremberg and other towns, kept careful weather records.[65]

Just as in the late fifteenth century, respected humanists and professors were among the eager conveyors of stellar teachings and forecasts
to a much broader lay world. Although the network of German evangelical astrologers was stratified much like the rest of society, it did create
links among several layers of culture that would otherwise have experienced very little interaction. Thanks to Jonathan Green, we now know
that the very first German-language reference to the work of Copernicus
came in an annual practica for 1541 by Andreas Aurifaber (Goldschmid),
a Melanchthon student and associate who had taken a teaching post at
Danzig. Like others who had studied alongside him, Aurifaber praised
the art of computing and interpreting the stellar motions for each year
in highly positive terms; he issued his practica "so that such art may be
maintained for the praise of Almighty God, who gave mankind such
understanding of the signs of the heavens, and for the manifold utility
that people might obtain from it."[66] To be sure, a few evangelical humanists such as Joachim Camerarius engaged with the celestial art more or
less exclusively on an elite, learned level. More typical, however, was the
renowned Schöner, not only a leading elite mathematician but also an
eager and dedicated producer of annual German calendars and practicas,
along with other vernacular works aimed at the common man. These
included an instructional *Arzneibüchlein* of 1528 that he issued explicitly for the use of laymen with little or no access to professional medical
care. Here Schöner sought to provide basic rules for treatments scheduled

according to the moon's position in the Zodiac, and referred readers to "the common annual medical calendars" to obtain the necessary data.[67]

The same tendency to navigate freely between learned and lay cultures is evident in many other evangelical humanists. The learned Hebraist and cosmographer Sebastian Münster tried his hand at least once in the market for popular practicas, issuing predictions for 1533. Georg Joachim Rheticus, one of Melanchthon's closest colleagues and the most important announcer of the Copernicus's work through his *Narratio prima* of 1540, also wrote annual ephemera for the common man. The physician Nicholas Pruckner was similarly among the many who wrote in both Latin and German; the yearly practicas he issued at Strasbourg, though clearly aimed at a humble readership, also showed off his considerable erudition. Johann Garcaeus, a learned pastor and scholar much concerned with astrological reform, eagerly took the offensive against the blind and shameless opponents of stellar science, and wrote vernacular texts instructing layfolk on the proper use of the stars in ordering daily life. The scholarly physician Christoph Stathmion produced Latin works in aggressive response to Pico and other critics; he was also among the most prolific of all the common forecasters. These and many parallel cases lead us reasonably to question slapdash characterizations of popular astrology as the realm of "market scribblers."[68]

If the new and quickly expanding army of almanac writers that emerged between 1530 and the 1560s was dominated by any sort, they were city physicians, schoolmasters, and other middle-class professionals. These men remained in contact with their university teachers and former fellow students, many of whom became Lutheran pastors. In this way they became part of a loose fraternity whose members were in frequent contact with one another but who also tended to have close ties to the communities in which they worked. This network of "cultural brokers," as they have been called, assumed a central role in the dissemination of a world-picture in which the stars were guides for the proper ordering of life, and for a full understanding of nature, history, and the divine.[69] In addition to figures such as Heller, Pruckner, and Stathmion, they included prolific popular writers with close ties to Melanchthon such as Achilles Pirmin Gasser (d. 1577), city physician at Feldkirch and after 1546 at Augsburg. A fervent Lutheran from 1522, Gasser clearly saw his role as that of a mediator between learned and lay cultures. Among many other vernacular works he produced a series of comet-books and annual practicas, all clearly written for the common man, and full of sober warnings and references to man's dependence on grace. His practica for 1546 was the first popular work to discuss the heliocentric model of Copernicus. Similarly situated was the Marburg professor and Calenburg court physician Burkhard Mithob (d. 1564), for whom evangelical theology and medical teaching were intimately connected. Mithob had studied at Rostock, Erfurt, and Marburg, but his medical works and annual practicas reflect a wholesale adoption of the Wittenberg program, and a commitment to its dissemination.[70]

In the writings of these and other astrological publicists who rode the Melanchthonian wave, the emphases on lay education and civic welfare that had emerged in the vernacular works of the pre-Reformation decades grew more consistent and pronounced. The popularizers of stellar science repeatedly stressed that their works were "for the use and benefit of the common man," as the physician Bartholomew Mangolt announced on the title page of his practica for 1532. Gregor Saltzmann of Ulm was among many who clearly sought to reach beyond the bounds of literacy, addressing the "beloved readers and hearers" of his works. In the 1550s Christoph Stathmion exemplified this trend, advertising his practicas as written "plainly and without obscurity, so as to be understandable to everyone." Very few hints of high secrets or hidden wisdom emerged; instead the typical annual guide echoed Victorin Schönfelt's declaration that his labors were for the use and benefit of "the whole community and citizenry." The Saxon pastor Johann Paceus wrote his practicas to serve "the common good and the Christian church."[71] As in prior decades, this sort of emphasis was partly a function of princes' and local governments' concerns with both public health and social order; many practicas and calendars were after all still sanctioned by city councils or other authorities. Yet these works were by no means merely elite tools for enforcing order and discipline. They were vehicles for the assertion of lay interests and attitudes that had been on the rise for generations.

Practical Philosophy and Piety

Over the middle decades of the sixteenth century the great majority of German calendar and practica writers adopted Melanchthonian teachings, and self-consciously advertised their subscription to the humanist ideal of a reformed natural science of the stars. Nearly all writers cited Ptolemy as the outstanding formulator of essential principles. Sophisticated figures such as Schöner touted especially strongly their preference for this supreme authority; the Nuremberg scholar prominently advertised several of his practicas as "drawn from the teaching of Ptolemy." Introducing his predictions for 1540, he explained that on the basic matter of determining the ruling planets for the year, the methods of the Greek and the Arab teachers produced great discrepancies. His choice was clear: "I will stay with Ptolemy."[72] Other practica writers frequently paid lip service, if nothing more, to the idea that the art had been obscured and corrupted by the Arabs among others. Thus too the popular forecasters often associated themselves with the latter-day humanist restorers and reformers of the art. According to Burkhard Mithob, the Almighty had created men of great understanding to make discoveries in astronomy and astrology that would otherwise remain beyond most people. These were "high and subtle arts that are not only necessary and useful to humans for their daily and physical welfare, but also extend to the honor of God." The name of Regiomontanus remained atop the list of heroes; the many editions of his calendar had already made him famous in the German lands, and the popular writers more than redoubled the effect.[73] From midcentury on, references to Copernicus and to the *Prutenic Tables* (1551) multiplied, showing writers' awareness of the need to keep up with astronomical advances.[74] In somewhat cruder displays of their humanist learning, the authors of the annual ephemera often sprinkled their works with Latin epigrams, terms, and phrases.

While in theory the astrological publicists promoted a pure Greek science, most were far more eclectic in practice. In fact a majority of the practicas continued to list masters such as Albumasar, Haly Eben Rodan, and Messahala among their authorities. Occasionally such references came with qualifications. Erhard Hoffman told his readers that were he to follow the Arab teachings strictly, he would have to foresee serious shortages of corn and wine in the coming year. But those doctrines, he suggested, were by themselves too limited: since astral causes worked together with atmospheric conditions and other variables, the prospects might in fact be somewhat better. Along with classical and Arabic authorities and expert mathematicians such as Peurbach, Regiomontanus, and Copernicus, the practicas often invoked recent or contemporary Italian figures such as Guido Bonatti, Gaurico, and Cardano; here again they were echoing Melanchthon, who thought highly of the Italians and did not hesitate to refer to them. In some cases writers reached farther afield in order to highlight the art's origins in the oldest fonts of wisdom. Gregor

Saltzmann's practica for 1539 included references not only to Aristotle, Albertus Magnus, and the main Arab writers, but also to the Egyptians and Chaldeans. According to Johannes Reinstein, a pastor-astrologer near Erfurt, Moses himself had been learned in all the wisdom of the Egyptians. In his practica for 1548 Anton Brelochs could refer not only to Ptolemy, Albumasar, and Haly Abenragel, but even to "Zoroaster, a very ancient teacher of the celestial art."[75]

Notably absent from the great majority of midcentury practicas were references to figures of recent fame such as Lichtenberger or Grünpeck. In the eyes of evangelical writers these figures were too closely associated with pro-Imperial propaganda and with visions of an eventual return to Roman unity. Not that this tradition died out altogether. Peter Creutzer, who continued to issue practicas in the 1530s and 1540s, called himself Lichtenberger's disciple, although he tended to steer away from politically dangerous forecasts. More generally, the Lichtenberger tradition included deliberately obscure references and cryptic images that did not sit well with the ideal of pure natural philosophy among the evangelical astrologers. A related sign of the spreading ideal of a self-consciously reformed astrology was that various echoes of folk culture that had persisted through the pre-Reformation era were fading from the popular literature. Thus for instance fewer and fewer works included the time-worn weather-forecasting customs from the old "Bauernpraktik," traditions that failed to square with the notion of a pure Ptolemaic science. In his practica "on the true knowledge of the weather" of around 1540, Matthias Brotbeihel could still include these and other similar folk rules without comment, but other authors now more commonly omitted them.[76]

In Melanchthon's philosophy the natural man, the old man of the flesh in Lutheran teaching, was entirely subject to the celestial influences as received by the fallen nature of the sublunary realm. This principle did not work its way into the popular literature all at once; in his 1532 forecast, for example, Bartholomew Mangolt resorted to the crude explanation that the stars affected only the body, not the soul, which resided in the body "as in a sack." Yet publicists increasingly expressed an evangelical understanding of the dictum that "the stars incline, but they do not force." Schöner had patently incorporated Luther's teaching by 1533: the stars, he wrote, "merely incline us and do not force us, for only the fleshly man is subject to their influence, and not the spiritual [man]." Other writers soon showed their agreement that the only true freedom was God's; apart from grace, man had but a weak and subordinate form of agency. As Jerome

Brotbeihel explained straightforwardly in his practica for 1549, man had a dual nature, one of flesh and blood, the other created in God's image through the word. But God's image in man had been so perverted by the fall that the whole person, body and soul, had become the child of sin; hence it was not in vain that learned masters undertook to predict future human events.[77]

No reader of the practicas could miss the repeated emphases on divine power and corresponding human helplessness. The stars revealed a divinely instituted natural order to which humans could merely adapt unless God intervened to answer their prayers. Joachim Heller, who followed Schöner as Nuremburg's leading stargazer, made the point bluntly in a dedicatory distich to his predecessor's predictions for 1547: "Learn, O Reader, to fear God, and know that only faith can counteract stellar fate."[78] Authors repeatedly emphasized that the normal course of things was according to unchanging, strictly natural laws. "While it is certain that the Creator is not bound to the stars in such a way that he must always do what they threaten," wrote Stathmion in 1550, "it is also true that he has set the course of the stars along with all other natural processes and properties for as long as this world will last." Just as he remained constant in his Word, so for the sake of humankind he did not interrupt or change these processes, except when he chose to punish or reward directly. In light of the grim outlook afforded by the stars, Stathmion expressed the fervent hope that faithful Christians would make a liar of him through their prayers. In his practica for 1563 he made the point yet more starkly. We must address those who know nothing of God and His Word, he wrote, as if God and nature are one thing, a single fate, "as the Stoics speak of it."[79] The man of flesh, in other words, should be brought to see that he was essentially powerless in the face of forces that were natural, but also divinely ordained. The title page of Victorin Schönfelt's predictions for 1562 shouted out this sort of natural fatalism: "The Heavens, Indicators of Fate."[80]

If humans were naturally helpless, the ruler of all was both free and active, in no sense bound by the natural laws he had established. "Our God," wrote the pastor-astrologer Hieronymus Wilhelm in 1570, "is not some Stoic principle, but a fully free agent. He does not sit in idle majesty, allowing the world to run on as it will. Rather he cares for his creation; he watches over his handiwork, and exercises his wonderful rule especially over his elect." Another stargazing preacher, Johannes Rhau, similarly averred that Ptolemy, though an "unbelieving heathen," knew well that "Astrorum decreta non sunt praetoria." Prayer, repentance, and God's power could work to overrule the fate threatened by the stars. The Salzwedel physician Christopher Germanus thought it obvious to reasonable people that astrological conjectures were neither articles of faith, nor "praetorian edicts." Introducing his predictions for 1583, the prolific George Caesius made a complementary point: "I know and believe in my heart that God almighty can change the order of nature and hear the prayers of the just."[81] Here was an application of the basic Melanchthonian principle: stellar fate applied to the old man; gospel faith was the great gift possessed of the new.

Authors did continue to fall back occasionally into formulations that did not altogether fit with a natural determinism that reserved all real freedom to God. Gregor Fabricius, for instance, insisted that the science of the stars warned and exhorted us "to employ our reason, circumspection, and wits, since a wise man is not subject to the stars but rules over them, as Ptolemy shows." Yet far more often it was made plain that neither reason nor wits, which were things of the flesh and not of the spirit, could overcome the dictates of nature. Anton Brelochs explained the saying attributed to Ptolemy as conveying no sense of human liberty, but rather the lesson that "in our troubles and adversities we are to call to the creator of the stars alone." For just as he had created the heavens and their influence out of his good will for our benefit, so too he could out of his grace and mercy turn that influence to the good. As he made the sun stand still at the time of Joshua, so he could change or cancel the force of the stars at any moment. Prayer and repentance might lead God to alter or cancel the effects of natural law, but such action represented divine power, not human freedom of the will.[82]

Over and again the publicists pointed out that what the stars revealed was a middle ground between necessity and possibility. As Ptolemy taught, this was the realm of probability, about which humans could make reasonable and useful conjectures. But it was crucial to recognize that the element of uncertainty came not from failings inherent in the stellar art per se but rather from human errors in application, and above all from God's liberty to intervene at any moment. Burkhard Mithob put the matter succinctly in 1539. His predictions were necessarily conjectural, he acknowledged, for while the stars gave definite indications, "God can indeed take it all in hand and turn it to nothing, for he is the first cause of all things without any secondary causes whatever." Therefore readers were exhorted to give themselves entirely to God, to learn to recognize him through his heavenly seat and instruments, and to place their purposes and hopes in him; thereby they might escape all danger. The effects of the heavens, wrote Brelochs in 1558, "hold the mean between necessity and possibility. For they incline us and do not force us, as the great Ptolemy shows. Thus too we are to call only upon the maker of the stars in our afflictions and adversities. For just as he has created them out of his good will, so too may he change their influence to the good through his grace and mercy."[83]

Yet along with the polar emphases on God's sovereign rule and human weakness, the practicas built solidly on the Melanchthonian assumption of a lower-order freedom that allowed human beings to adapt to the regular natural order. This was the entire worldly, practical purpose of the stellar science. Christoph Stathmion acknowledged that in theological terms one who held to God's Word no longer needed natural knowledge or any natural means at all. Yet, he explained, we must also recognize that "man is established and ordained by God here in nature and the world in such a way that without natural means and without natural knowledge of the Creation he cannot and may not live long according to the divine order; and thus this science or observation of nature, whether future or present, is most highly necessary to the maintenance of his temporal life."[84] The annual forecasters preached with remarkable consistency this ideal of the stellar art as God's great practical gift and instrument for daily existence, a doctrine of nature that bypassed all deluded, humanly invented beliefs and rites.

In general conformity with the ideals broadcast from Wittenberg, the calendar and practica writers put the proper ordering of time at the very center of their concerns. Could there be anything more necessary in life, asked Johann Reinstein, than to study the heavens as the astrologer does in order to mark out the year, and "to divide time in an orderly way, so that one has cause to orient himself properly?" Without such reckoning this life would be "beastly, barbaric, and cyclopic, rather than human." Likewise according to Victorin Schönfelt, without a proper awareness of time men would live like beasts. Demonstrating his own commitment to a revived science, he drew the data for his own annual works primarily from Reinhold's *Prutenic Tables*. Schönfelt argued that all social order depended upon the proper work of the astrologer, especially on the correct determination of the calendar. Not only were affairs of the Church and matters of faith at stake, but also worldly justice, agriculture, commerce, and daily household economy. Without a proper understanding of time, there could be no understanding at all; everything from personal health and medical treatments to the proper observance of public holidays hung finally on attention to celestial mathematics as enjoined by Holy Scripture. Where we see problems and breakdowns in daily life, he wrote, we find a failure to use, or defects in, the annual astrological calendar. The art of chronology, inseparable from study of the heavens, had recently led to better, more orderly lives, but it was deeply frustrating that "because of venomous quarreling the work remains undone, the feast days are still listed, and so on."[85]

Indeed on the matter of time and its uses, the goals of the astrologers stood in direct and explicit alliance with the evangelical reform. Their aversion toward the irregular medieval cycles of feast and fast, holy and secular days revealed openly and insistently the tendencies that had already marked the pre-Reformation calendars and practicas. In simple and straightforward German prose, Christoph Stathmion explained that neither scripture nor the stars allowed for any distinction between sacred and profane time, but demanded reverence to God at all times without exception. A continuing move away from the use of saints' days is evident in the annual works, with some authors moving more quickly than others. In the 1530s and 1540s astronomers such as Schöner and physicians such as Achilles Pirmin Gasser of Feldkirch led the way, often avoiding almost any mention of the saints' days at all.[86] Among other evangelical authors, the practice of including them waned gradually over the middle decades of the century, giving way more and more to the exclusive use of numbered days. Especially in the presentation of weather forecasts, the saints' days appears to have hung on somewhat longer than in other contexts, but even here they were employed purely for chronological purposes, with little hint of any larger significance.

More immediately objectionable was the medieval belief in unfortunate Egyptian days, which lacked even such marginal calendrical usefulness. At least in the annual publications, the Reformation era saw the rapid waning of this tradition; the name itself was probably enough to disqualify it. More persistent was the general practice, presumably though not always clearly grounded in astrological reckoning, of listing lucky and unlucky days for the coming year. The expert Schöner continued to list such days in his annual forecasts; Joachim Heller was one among several writers who continued the practice a generation later. Various refinements of the idea surfaced. In 1544 Anton Brelochs specified different good and bad days for persons born under each sign of the Zodiac. In his calendar for 1547 Achilles Gasser offered a list of the most propitious days for undertaking specific tasks, but mentioned no dangerous days, and offered the assurance that his procedure was "well-grounded, without any superstition."[87] For these men, preoccupied with the measure of the heavens, days were to be distinguished not by a humanly conceived flux of sacred and profane, and not on some arbitrary or occult scheme, but on the basis of the natural forces that bore on particular times and places. The variable of place was less central than that of time. Yet since most predictions depended in part upon the geographical coordinates of particular locations, or on the groupings of lands and cities under Zodiacal quadrangles, it retained great importance. And calculations that took these geographical factors into account inevitably worked to pre-empt the notion that some places were more sacred than others.

The insistence on a proper awareness and ordering of time and space was one aspect of the heavy moral didacticism inherent in the Melanchthonian program. In the eyes of the practica writers, the art of the stars was a necessary foundation for Christian discipline; indeed in a world of such frightening instability it appeared as one of the precious few instruments of order. Scholars have often pointed to a strongly antinomian impulse in the early Reformation movement, a push for emancipation from all artificial restraints.[88] But evangelical stargazers quickly compensated by dwelling on the divinely sanctioned natural order revealed in the heavens. Sachiko Kusukawa argues that the distinctive Lutheran astrological tradition encouraged by Melanchthon "served political and moral purposes."[89] Yet here was no hidden agenda; in fact a patent obsession with both personal and social discipline increasingly marked the practicas over the middle decades of the century. Victorin Schönfelt declared that only those who lived ordered, disciplined lives, which included use of the proper astrological medicine, could maintain their natural bodily strength, balance, and health. Along with dozens of other writers who absorbed key aspects of Melanchthonian teaching, he argued that by providing a fundamental structure for individual and social existence, the science of the stars raised human beings above the level of the beasts. Neglect of this knowledge brought disease not only through breakdowns in nature, but also as a direct expression of God's wrath. According to Jerome Brotbeihel, a series of devastating plagues were to bring divine punishment upon "stiff-necked or disobedient persons, for God always punishes the stubborn and unruly people, as we see in Holy Scripture." In a practica for 1564 Wolff Geuss warned and exhorted rulers to a timely suppression of dangerous sects and uprisings, always to "extinguish the fire in time, before it gains the upper hand."[90]

Once again, however, we encounter the paradox: the Melanchthonian understanding of natural law reinforced the traditional tendency of astrologers to focus on future threats, to issue dark warnings of disaster and wrath. In turn, such sobering observations complemented and supported evangelical preaching on the law; as Volker Leppin has pointed out, theologians regularly emphasized that all natural disasters and sufferings were nothing but an expression of God's use of the law to make us aware of our sinfulness.[91] In his forecast for 1540 Schöner affirmed that God ruled the world absolutely. "But when he sees the wickedness of men increase from day to day, although he wants to console rather than chastise us, he first threatens his sons like an all-loving father," and he did this through the heavens. Thus too for Christoph Stathmion, while astrology was "an excellent gift of God and a mirror of the divine will," it was essentially "nothing other than a gracious warning of God given to man for his betterment." He insisted, moreover, that his general forecasts of disaster would remain valid until "prayer is universal and the devil is no longer prince of this world"; in other words, until God brought it all to an end. The Königsberg professor and physician Simon Titius joined the chorus of practica writers who combined detailed stellar reckonings of coming disasters with prayers that "God Almighty will turn his wrath from us, and graciously soften such severe punishment."[92]

Because the proper task of astrologers was to warn, no one could accuse them of impiety or superstition. Proper forecasters, wrote Jerome Brotbeihel, did not assert that anything was inevitable, and thus gave no reason for paralyzing fear. Instead they warned of future misfortune and punishment that people might change their lives and repent. Brotbeihel echoed Melanchthon's reading of Jeremiah's "be not dismayed at the signs in the heavens." Anyone who hurled these words at the astrologers in blame was simply wrong, for the prophet clearly went on to explain the right use of the stars: when we see the signs, we should lift up our heads and cry out to God that he might turn away the indicated affliction. Hieronymus Wilhelm composed his practica for 1571 "simply, for the good of simple folk and for their warning, that they may learn not to be arrogantly secure, but to keep God before their eyes and to pray devoutly for their daily bread."[93]

Through the midcentury decades most practica writers made few explicit or sustained references to the New Testament and to Christ. Yet most clearly did intend their warnings finally to point in this direction. Freedom from earthly suffering under the law, as from the horror of eternal perdition itself, came only through God's gracious choice to intervene directly. Therefore in the end the only answer was to repent and to pray for God's gift of grace. In some cases the gospel message came openly to the fore. Gregor Salzman's practica for 1539, for example, followed the usual barrage of deeply sober warnings with earnest and positive preaching about Christ as the one and only savior. Similarly G. J. Rheticus, though stressing that the central lesson of the stars was repentance in a sinful world, called on his readers to "turn to the lord, creator, and ruler of nature and all things, with true faith in Jesus Christ our sole deliverer and savior"; he also conveyed hope in "the dissemination of his holy Word." Stathmion too could speak of the heavens as a source of direct consolation as well as warning. Nothing on earth after scripture itself, he argued, was of more use than astrology, "which daily presents to the eyes of man both the favorable and the unfavorable will of God. For mankind needs such reminders every day, like a forgetful student." Thus, he added, "as I have written and shown clearly elsewhere, not only is astrology a true art; it is also useful and necessary to the Christian."[94]

When in 1557 Thomas Erastus expressed his amazement and despair at the utter pervasiveness of astrology in Protestant Germany, he was inadvertently attesting to the success of the broad Melanchthon-inspired campaign we have explored, a campaign that was then already at least a quarter-century old. In several basic ways, Melanchthonian teachings helped bring about a systematization and articulation of assumptions about the stars and human life that had already grown widespread in the German towns over the half-century before the Luther affair exploded. But if up to the 1520s the spread of popular astrology had worked mainly to undermine a traditional religious order, from the 1530s on its new purveyors worked to help build a new one. To be sure, it was and is easy to find contradictions and confusion in the practicas, almanacs, and other popular literature. In the Melanchthonian teachings, and even more in the popular literature, there remained countless theoretical and practical uncertainties.[95] Still, the main outlines of a common and self-conscious program are clearly discernible.

Denying fatalism on one hand and delusions of human capacity on the other, Lutheran astrologers were in effect engaged in an effort to establish a natural science that remained conscious of its own limits even as it reinforced basic biblical truths. These men saw themselves essentially as natural philosophers, yet their insistence on the inherent dependence of humankind upon the divine will inevitably lent their work a prophetic dimension. Their aggressive program is difficult to reconcile with the persistent assumption that during the Reformation era astrologers were increasingly embattled and on the defensive. As the heirs of both Luther and Melanchthon, evangelical stargazers saw themselves as proponents of a broad Christian offensive against false teaching and superstition. Not only university professors and humanist scholars but also local physicians, teachers, and pastors conceived the stellar art as the indispensable natural philosophical complement to the purified gospel; in their eyes the evangelical movement was an enlightenment on all fronts.

5

Confessional Constellations

BY FAR THE most prominent of Renaissance divinatory arts, astrology reached a high point of pervasiveness and influence in many parts of Europe in the late sixteenth and early seventeenth centuries, the very same time when confessional lines hardened and came to divide mutually hostile camps. The prevailing traditional picture has the art growing both more popular and more controversial nearly everywhere, increasingly subject to learned debate and the opposition—actual or supposed—of religious leaders including Martin Luther, John Calvin, and the post-Tridentine popes. This perspective fails to take into account striking regional and confessional variations in teaching, preaching, propaganda, and practice. Only recently have scholars begun to recognize "the especially free development of astrology in the Lutheran realm," and the broader implications of this exceptional pattern have received very sparse attention.[1]

Over the second half of the sixteenth century and into the early seventeenth, printers in the cities of the Empire took advantage of a nearly insatiable demand for vernacular astrological works. Looking solely at the genre of the annual practica, we find over sixteen hundred known editions from the period c. 1530 to 1630. Tracing the statistics can help illuminate our picture (see Graph 5.1). From the 1530s through the 1550s production fluctuated at levels that did not depart greatly from the averages of the prior half-century. In the early 1560s the numbers mounted dramatically, continuing a steady climb through the 1570s. Another large leap followed in the early 1580s, and for at least three decades thereafter some twenty editions were marketed nearly every year. The rate slackened only after 1610; by the 1620s a more rapid if uneven decline had set in.[2] The annual astrological literature was central to what Thomas Kaufmann

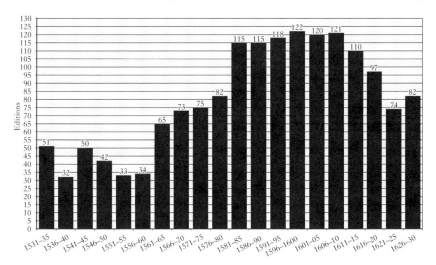

GRAPH 5.1 German annual practicas, 1531–1630.

has characterized as an accelerating "media revolution" in Germany during the period around 1600, closely linked to the ongoing expansion of the public sphere and to an atmosphere of continuing apocalyptic expectancy.[3]

Without doubt we are looking at a major channel of publicity among German townsfolk, above all in the evangelical cities and towns. While it is often impossible to establish a definite confessional connection for particular calendar-makers or printers, we can hardly overlook the fact that of the works with a known place of publication issued between 1550 and 1620, some 90 percent came from towns that had accepted the evangelical movement either wholly or—as at Augsburg—in a biconfessional compromise.[4] But beyond the numbers we have rich evidence to show that of the three main confessional groups within the Empire, Lutheranism proved by far the most hospitable to the perpetuation and intensification of a popular astrological worldview. While in the generations after Luther's death (1546) not all his followers positively welcomed the astrologers' burgeoning role in public preaching and discourse, attention to the heavens became so deeply ingrained in the culture of evangelical townsfolk that by the 1570s scoffers within the ranks were marginalized, if not silenced almost entirely. The popular astrological literature, pouring unceasingly from the presses of Nuremberg, Augsburg, Strasbourg, Erfurt, Leipzig, and many other cities, both reflected and reinforced prevailing outlooks among German Lutherans.

Roman Reactions

Despite the Wittenberg-led push to promote astrology in service to the evangelical cause, we can hardly point to a significant "confessionalization" of the stellar art in the Empire before the middle decades of the sixteenth century. In the 1530s and 1540s numerous Catholic and evangelical humanists remained in contact and kept up relationships of mutual respect. So for instance the renowned Ingolstadt professor Peter Apian and the equally prominent Nuremberg scholar Johann Schöner continued to express admiration for one another across the religious divide. Anton Brelochs, city physician at the Lutheran stronghold of Schwäbisch-Hall and a phenomenally successful writer of calendars and practicas, was still issuing editions tailored to sell in the Bishopric of Bamberg as late as 1546.[5] But the scene was shifting; in the realm of astrological publicity as in so many others, confessional differences would become increasingly evident.

The last phase of the older Catholic humanist astrology saw the continuation of a strong pro-Habsburg strain, especially since Vienna, with the Imperial court, was one of the few major centers of stellar science that remained wedded to the inherited faith. Yet writers in this tradition were in an increasingly difficult position, caught between the pressure to produce pro-Imperial political propaganda on one hand and a rising Catholic distrust of public predictions on the other. As noted earlier, Georg Tannstetter gave up on popular practicas altogether after 1527; in fact by this time the annual forecast was already falling out of general favor at Vienna. Around the same time Tannstetter's student Andreas Perlach took up an explicitly pro-Habsburg stance in his almanacs, foretelling for instance Ferdinand of Austria's 1531 election as King of the Romans. Perlach sought to refute the widely known and dire predictions that Johann Carion had issued for Austria. He attacked Carion for unnatural methods as well as for erroneous forecasts, working at the same time to calm fears and rally support for Ferdinand. But as a publicist Perlach placed himself under a crushing disadvantage, for he wrote only in Latin.[6]

Peter Apian took a different tack, publishing vernacular practicas that were less openly political, and placing the ideal of a truly scientific astrology closer to the center of attention. This highly respected Ingolstadt professor fully shared Melanchthon's goal of reviving the pure Ptolemaic science, although he was far more reserved than the Wittenbergers in discussing the art as a source of insight into God's providence. In his earlier and more popular works Apian could still issue warnings not unlike those found in the Protestant literature; the title page for his practica for 1532 even included verses warning Rome against the evils portended by the comet of 1531. Yet he more and more emphatically lamented the decline of the noble ancient art, and came to ridicule the popular writers who bragged about composing both an almanac and a practica in fourteen days. His elaborate, sophisticated, and expensive *Astronomicum Caesareum* of 1540, designed to facilitate both astronomical calculation and natural astrological reckoning, helped earn him the post of Imperial court mathematician.[7] Ultimately his renown as an expert in the stargazer's art went far to inspire and encourage a host of humbler practitioners, most of whom simply ignored his adherence to the old faith.

Johann Virdung enjoyed popular renown far exceeding that of Apian, but he too remained in communication with numerous evangelical stargazers and clients. Having taken the medical doctorate at Heidelberg around 1530, he seems to have become especially concerned with the healing art in the years before his death in 1538. Although he remained formally loyal to Rome and to a vision of ultimate Imperial triumph, his predictions in the 1530s were vague enough to allow for a variety of readings, and he continued energetically to announce God's wrath over the failure of people to amend their sinful lives. His death in 1538 brought the end of a career that spanned a half-century, and stilled the last voice of the generation of stargazers that had gained prominence by 1500.[8]

Meanwhile in towns that remained in the old faith or where the evangelical movement was officially suppressed, we find a number of forecasters who were likely closet supporters of the reform. Matthias Brotbeihel, for example, a Latin schoolmaster from Kaufbeuren who taught at Munich in the 1530s, hinted more and more at Lutheran sympathies in his practicas, which he published with Protestant-leaning firms in Nuremberg and Augsburg. He dedicated his practica for 1539 to the Palatine ruler Ottheinrich just as this prince was embracing Luther's teachings; soon thereafter he left Munich for Württemberg, and his dedicatee for 1542 was the evangelical Duke Christoph. Jerome Brotbeihel, possibly a brother or cousin to Matthias, was most active in Mainz, where a strong evangelical movement had arisen, and where the citizenry had remained hotly divided after the bishop's authority was restored in the 1550s. This Brotbeihel dedicated several of his practicas to Lutheran princes, and all his annual works presented a typically Melanchthonian line. In the preface to his forecast for 1560 he drew on Luther's preface to Micah, using Luther's words about the present need to do as Micah did—that is, "rebuke, denounce, encourage, and preach"; he also emphasized Christ's impending deliverance from all troubles at the Last Day.[9]

As the lines between the religious camps hardened, the Roman Church grew markedly unfriendlier to astrological theory and practice, especially as an element of lay culture. R. J. W. Evans has suggested that "Catholics mistrusted prediction from the start, and the more Protestants stressed it, the more they could assail it with an easy conscience." Evans finds evidence of a serious Catholic campaign in central Europe, beginning around midcentury, to rein in all forms of popular divination.[10] By this time the older generation of German humanists was mostly gone, and with new strictures imposed by the Council of Trent and a generally more cautious atmosphere, few notable successors appeared to fill their shoes. While learned engagement with the stars retreated gradually into the privacy of elite circles, the popular art slid steadily into disfavor. Over the second half of the century the signs of an ongoing tightening were everywhere.[11]

Already as the older generation was passing, German bishops had begun to rein in the almanac and practica writers, to restrict the scope of their predictions, to guard against questionable forecasts, and to tighten control over the market for calendars and practicas. In Würzburg the bishop had exercised close oversight of all publications from an early date; by the 1520s the arms of the cathedral chapter appeared on all approved calendars. Here, as in other cities where episcopal authority remained strong, the genre of the annual practica never became well established, and in the early Reformation era it appears to have died out almost completely. As the century progressed the calendars published in centers such as Würzburg and Bamberg came to include less and less medical and astrological content, while those issued in Protestant cities maintained these concerns as central.[12] This difference was no doubt partly a result of episcopal censorship, but the reasons may have gone deeper. Studies on the role of shrines and saintly miracles in the piety of Catholic regions suggest that here the prevailing forms of popular healing remained far less closely linked to astrological teachings than in Protestant towns. In Bavaria and other Catholic territories, clerics developed doctrines of spiritual healing that were designed to gain a monopoly on the whole field of health and healing.[13] In the Catholic cities, publicly appointed astrologer-physicians rarely gained the sort of status they enjoyed in the Lutheran burgs. From a broader perspective, it appears likely that since the Catholic population of the Empire was on the whole less urban and less literate than Protestants, the sorts of astrology conveyed in the popular literature simply could not gain a comparable currency here.

The years around midcentury and later proved increasingly difficult for prominent Catholic astrologers such as the Italians Luca Gaurico and Girolamo Cardano, whose contacts among German Protestants made them all the more suspect in the eyes of the Roman hierarchy. Along with other forms of humanistic learning, the art of the stars was becoming subject to mounting confessional pressures.[14] In 1559 the Congregation of the Index declared a general prohibition on judicial astrology along with a long list of other divinatory arts; the works of prominent astrologers, including the Arab writers, were now declared formally taboo. The Papal Bull issued at the close of the Council of Trent (1563) sought to forbid all predictions not directly related to agriculture, medicine, or navigation. The gradual disappearance of popular astrological publications in Catholic regions of the Empire was furthered by the broader post-Tridentine crackdown on all forms of prophecy and divination. Although the direct effects of the 1563 decrees were at first quite limited, they reinforced trends already in motion.[15]

To be sure, Catholics never entirely abandoned efforts to compete by exploiting the common annual forecasts. We find ongoing if scattered efforts to contend with the Protestants on these increasingly unfavorable grounds. In the early 1550s, for example, the Bishop of Würzburg appears to have sanctioned at least a trial run in the practica market. The physician Georg Schoder, who dedicated his predictions for 1551 to the bishop, offered a quite positive outlook for the clergy, and special good fortune for the Emperor; also the sun in the ninth house indicated a "great change" in matters bearing on religion. The author's hope for an Imperial military triumph and the restoration of unity was clear enough. But this is the only surviving practica we have from Schoder or from Würzburg during this period, which suggests that this printing was probably an experiment that was not renewed.[16]

To the West in the Netherlands, the university of Louvain emerged around midcentury as a center of the Catholic campaign against popular astrology. The humanist mathematicians here felt their whole discipline threatened by the annual works pouring from the presses in Germany. Scholars such as Cornelius Gemma worked hard to reform the yearly prognostication, supplying more careful data, pointedly restricting his forecasts to the weather, and showing increased attention to theoretical underpinnings. Gemma's 1561 *Ephemerides* departed intentionally from the typical format of the compilations on which the mass publications drew; not coincidentally, it was the first astrological work from the Low Countries to gain an official *imprimatur* from Catholic authorities. Numerous Louvain graduates began to show serious hesitation about the common yearly forecasts. They included the physician Levinus Lemnius (1505–1568), who refused requests to compose such works, calling them harmful to piety and morals.[17] This battle against the "urban prognosticators" was intertwined with the perception of an exploding culture of popular astrology closely tied to Wittenberg and the broader network of German evangelical almanac makers. The prominence of Louvain in the Catholic mobilization against popular astrology and evangelical heresy would continue; in the 1580s, that campaign was a key part of the background to perhaps the most famous learned attack on horoscopic astrology of the entire sixteenth century, the 1580 *Astrologiae refutatae liber* of Sixtus Hemminga.[18]

By the 1560s we find German Catholic polemicists more and more often ridiculing and attacking the galloping merger of popular astrology and Lutheran propaganda. Among them was the Franciscan Johann Nas, who both satirized the art and denounced it as the mother—or sometimes the twin sister—of heresy. For Nas, Luther was an exception among the heretics in his supposed scorn for the stargazers, for he had seen affinities between astrological and theological error. Like the heretics, the astrologers denied free will; their perverse teachings implied fatalism, thus spreading feelings of helplessness and fear. Here Nas engaged in an increasingly common tactic among his coreligionists: although learned Catholic theologians well understood that Luther's denial of free will was not to be equated with astrological determinism, associating these teachings proved a convenient polemical weapon. In his *Practica Practicarum* of 1566, written under the Pseudonym Johannes Philognysius, Nas expressed disgust at "the lying pamphlets and practicas of the stargazers," which were mainly a way to steal money from the already poor common man. These authors hawked false certainties among confused and desperate people, "for these days it's all about knowing, knowing, rather than believing or thinking." They spoke shamelessly of divine truth, as if they had themselves just descended from heaven, filled with Godly wisdom. In fact they echoed the Manichaeans, those fraudulent preachers of a secret, higher knowledge. And as if the astrologers themselves had not filled the air with perversity enough, "one now even finds evangelical pastors who pursue and defend this sort of nonsense, and cast nativities."[19]

A handful of learned Catholic astrologers did undertake to employ the art in order to wage battle against the Protestant heretics. One was the Cologne mathematician, publisher, and propagandist Theodor Graminaeus (Gras), who produced a series of works drawing on the evidence of history and the stars in order to discredit the Lutherans in particular. Yet his form of propaganda was mainly a throwback to the traditions of Lichtenberger and of Joachimist prophecy, which had by now lost much of their resonance among German townsfolk. In a work on the amazing new star of 1572 and a comet of the following year Graminaeus drew heavily on these older currents, as well as on figures such as Gaurico and Cardano, in an effort to reverse the tide of evangelical star-preaching. But in the end his arguments depended less on the evidence of the heavens, and more on the grim statements of Luther and his followers about the present and future state of Germany. Like his other publications, this wandering tract of some 176 pages was not optimally designed for broad publicity, and Graminaeus does not appear to have issued annual calendars or prognostications.[20]

A more prolific and tireless polemicist against the evangelical astrologers was Johann Rasch, who worked in a circle of Habsburg supporters and had close connections with the Jesuits. Although a practicing astrologer himself, he saw a general equation between Protestant heresy and the common popular forms of the art. In their "yearly books of lies" the growing army of almanac makers flouted Ptolemaic principles, sowing theological error and vast confusion. "These short practicas," he scoffed, "are every year almost all alike, in that they have little to say about illnesses and fruitfulness, but commonly deal only with war, tumult, the unfaithfulness of the people, dangers to the clergy, upheavals in religion, and the like."[21] Nowadays, he complained, the astrologers drew most of their predictions from the Bible and a supposed "prophetic spirit," and these delusions were all finally spawned by the teachings from Wittenberg. Catholic authorities were fully justified in forbidding the publication and circulation of such pernicious materials. Rasch aimed his weapons especially at the astrological apocalypticism that was stoking fears about the great conjunction to come in 1584 and speculations about the end of the world in 1588. Deriding the scores of practicas and other publications that drew on newly published catalogues of expected eclipses, conjunctions, and comets, he insisted that the astrological configurations had no connection to the signs that Christ had announced would precede the Last Day. The evangelicals were guilty of running a debased astrology together with insane readings of scripture, producing a fabric of rank fallacy.[22]

Not to be denied his own propagandistic use of the stars, Rasch drew on the 1584 great conjunction to speculate about the defeat of the Turks and a great flowering of the true Church. He looked to comfort his audience by promoting typically hopeful strains of late medieval prophecy, including Joachimism and the savior-emperor traditions associated with the pseudo-Methodius. Ultimately, then, his attacks had less to do with astrology than with the doomsday notions that so pervaded the practicas. Still, he left no doubt about the close connection between the omnipresent astrological publicity and Lutheran errors; the heretics and their prognostications were undermining all political and churchly order. In the mid-1590s he was still railing against the astrological apocalypticism of the "priestly practica-writers." To believe them would require one to believe that "the heavens at once cause and punish sin"; here Rasch echoed countless efforts to indict the astrologers for denying free will. The heavens, he insisted once again, had nothing to do with sin and repentance.[23]

Rasch was among the Catholic publicists who wrote in defense of the new Gregorian calendar (1582) against a firestorm of Protestant outrage and vituperation. German Lutherans denounced this innovation as a trick of the Antichrist, designed to confuse and upset Christendom in the Last Times. But for Rasch and other defenders of the change it was the old Julian calendar that had corrupted the order of time, thus helping to ignite the present-day explosion of heresy. It was no wonder the saints' days were under attack; they had fallen out of their natural places. The errors of the common stargazers had been redoubled by false data and inevitably botched reckonings. The proper authority of Pope and Emperor, consistent with natural laws and natural time, might now be restored by bringing the stars and the calendar back into synchronicity. The calendar controversy, erupting just as speculation over the conjunction of 1584 was reaching a peak of intensity, brought the status of astrology yet closer to the center of confessional disputes.[24]

Not coincidentally, in 1586 Pope Sixtus V issued the Bull *Coela et Terra*, which reinforced the Tridentine strictures, severely proscribing judicial astrology along with other forms of divination. "Natural" astrology was of course still necessary and allowable for use in medicine, agriculture, and travel. But this acknowledgment had become by now almost a formality. In fact the bull offered no guidance as to how one might identify legitimate natural predictions, and debate ensued even among Catholic professors about whether its wording was too strict, effectively prohibiting any sort of prediction at all. The main intention was to denounce the spread of vernacular astrological discourse generally in light of its near-complete domination by German Protestants, and in defensive reaction against the cresting waves of astrological and apocalyptic speculation. Since by this time relatively few astrological works were being printed in Catholic towns or territories, the bull was for practical purposes an anti-Lutheran measure.[25]

The Papal decree gave fresh sanction to the ongoing Jesuit battle against the prognosticators and against "judicial" astrology generally. Since at least the 1560s members of the order had been working energetically to exclude the art from university curricula whenever possible. The available evidence suggests that the Jesuit curriculum essentially banned stellar science; hence the differences between Ingolstadt and schools such as Wittenberg and Tübingen were dramatic in regard to the subject. Peter Apian's son Philip, also a mathematician, left Ingolstadt in 1563 because he refused to accept the new Tridentine strictures on his teaching; he was welcomed by the Lutherans at Tübingen.[26] Christopher Clavius, the most famous Jesuit mathematician of the age, worked to distinguish sharply between astronomy and astrology, and denounced in severe terms the vulgar predictive genres. A Latin work by the Spaniard Benedictus Pereira, published at Ingolstadt in 1591 and several times thereafter, became an influential model for later Jesuit works of the same sort. This author rehearsed a host of well-worn arguments, biblical, historical, and scientific, to counter the notion that one could read the future in the heavens. Pereira even rejected the notion that God issued warning signs to mankind through irregular and wondrous celestial phenomena. All such practices were not merely full of lies and errors; they were specifically opposed to the authority of the Roman Church. The fantasies of the astrologers were implanted by demons, inevitably spawning credulity, godlessness, heresy, and social breakdown. Pereira aimed his critique especially at those who claimed that the stars announced imminent upheaval, shocking disasters, and the end of the world.[27]

No contemporary reader could have failed to see in this work an indictment of Lutheran practica writers and evangelical preachers who appealed to the heavens to cultivate both apocalyptic expectancy and hostility against the Roman Church. But other Jesuit critics left nothing implicit. In a 1589 vernacular treatise defending the Bishop of Würzburg and a variety of traditional rites, Georg Scherer deplored the maliciousness with which the Lutheran preachers railed against the Catholics at every opportunity: "And if they know of no other way, they peer at the stars, and thus venture to persuade peaceful princes to join in harness against the Papists." As an example he cited the prominent pastor-astrologer Georg Caesius, who had seen a recent planetary conjunction as confirmation of Luther's warning against the supposedly Satanic origins of the Papacy, and as a sign that "our princes and Christian potentates will the more joyfully and courageously come together to suppress the Pope's power." Scherer ridiculed such tactics as a measure of the desperation as well as the delusions of their authors.[28]

A similar sort of polemic, but one couched in a more creative style, appeared in popular works by Lorenz Albrecht, a former Lutheran preacher who had become disillusioned and converted to the Roman faith in 1567. In an *Evangelisch Prognostic* published at Munich in 1589, Albrecht turned the genre of the popular evangelical practica on itself. The natural influence of the planets, if left unopposed by free will and the Spirit, would lead inevitably to beastly heresy, and such was the origin of the current Lutheran depravity. The good Catholic would therefore resist slavery to the stars, and in so doing would also avoid the way of religious error.[29] Albrecht was also the likely author of a 1592 *New Preacher's Practica,* a blast against the evangelical clergy and their close alliance with the "star-prophets." This writing included drippingly sarcastic uses of astrological terms in order to denounce virtually the whole range of Protestant teachings and practices. Much as in his 1589 tract, Albrecht described the destructive influence of each planet, and showed how these effects were most fully realized among the heretics. Thus for instance Mars was powerfully at work when Luther had called for the merciless slaughter of the peasants in 1525, while Venus had lured the monks and nuns out of their cloisters and provoked general sexual license. Similarly the baleful effects of each zodiacal sign were manifest in various Lutheran vices. To some extent this was all tongue-in-cheek, yet Albrecht allowed readers room to conceive the stellar powers as malignant forces actually spurring the behavior of apostates. He referred to the *Practica Practicarum* of Nas, which clearly served as a partial model for his own approach. Like Nas, he was both mocking the "star-prophets" and vilifying them vehemently as bedfellows of the Lutheran heretics.[30]

Led most prominently by the Jesuits, the Catholic campaign only intensified further in the years after 1600. According to Evans, at this time "a chorus of official theologians denounced the art" in Catholic Central Europe; the prominent Hungarian Jesuit Peter Pazmany was among the writers who condemned it as "a characteristically Lutheran aberration." In 1602 the Jesuit-trained Bavarian polemicist Aegidius Albertinus issued a German adaptation of a work by the Spaniard Francisco de Osuna that lumped all divinatory astrology together with sorcery and a broad range of magical superstitions, but that nonetheless found enough in the true "natural" stellar art to explain Martin Luther's inherent inclination to heresy and evil. The Ingolstadt theologian Adam Tanner published in 1615 a learned *Astrologia Sacra* that was, despite its provocative title, essentially a dismissal of all but the very tamest forms of natural forecasting.[31]

Tanner and his fellow professors at Ingolstadt sanctioned vernacular works that pursued largely parallel goals. These included a fervid popular polemic against all anti-Roman heresy by Hippolytus Guarinonius, a physician at Steyr in the Tyrol, titled *The Abomination of Desolation of the Human Race*. An early chapter of this work assaulted the fables of the astrologers, who along with a certain vicious and shameless table-talking monk had led the poor German people horribly astray. The calendar-making soothsayers taught a false and perverse doctrine of natural knowledge; belief in the forecasts of these would-be prophets oppressed the spirit, stoked anxiety, stole one's strength, and inevitably led to ruin. Associating the lies of the planet watchers with the delusions of alchemists and other fantasy hawkers, Guarinonius saw the science of the stars as inseparable from the evils of heresy and godlessness he believed were infecting Germany.[32]

Again, attempts to compete with the evangelicals in the popular star-market never waned entirely, and in a few cases Catholic writers seem to have gained some success, at least on a local level. Adrianus Romanus (d. 1615), a highly regarded astronomer and professor of medicine at Würzburg, issued a series of annual almanacs and practicas as the city's official calendar-maker starting around 1594; a predecessor, Wilhelm Upilio, had apparently gained the Bishop's permission to revive the printing of practicas in the highly anxious time around 1588. Similarly the Viennese cathedral canon Maximilian Tripet issued yearly prognostications in the 1590s. Probably more prominent, though of a later generation, was the physician and cartographer Johann Gigas (c. 1582–1637), who as a young evangelical had studied at Wittenberg and Helmstedt, but who moved to Münster around 1611 and converted to Catholicism; his annual calendars gained such high regard that his name was retained on title pages long after his death. But most such writers were subject to intensive episcopal oversight, and nearly all avoided the kind of preaching and propaganda that so pervaded the evangelical practicas. In any case they were exceptions to a broad and forceful movement to restrict the role of astrology in the everyday lives of Catholics in the Empire.[33]

Calvinist Strictures

On the grounds just surveyed it is surely an understatement to assert that "judicial astrology found more practitioners among committed Protestants than committed Catholics in this period," especially if we are looking primarily at the vernacular realm in the Empire.[34] Yet in regard to the stellar art as in more basic ways, Protestantism was by no means monolithic. Although German Reformed or Calvinist attitudes are a bit harder to assess than the Jesuit outlook, John Calvin's well-known opposition to divination of any sort does appear to have set the tone among his heirs in central Europe as elsewhere. Calvin's brief and forceful tract of 1549, *A Warning Against Judiciary Astrology,* was far from truly original in any respect. But it did articulate a notably uncompromising position that was widely adopted among Reformed thinkers.

In the eyes of the Genevan reformer stellar forecasting of human events was no mere frivolous vanity, and far worse than simply a debased science deployed for polemical purposes. Rather it was a direct affront to the power and majesty of God, to be condemned as a diabolical superstition on the explicit authority of the Bible. His attitude could hardly have diverged more sharply from that of Melanchthon, and it differed in basic ways from Luther's skeptical forbearance. Assaulting both the casters of horoscopes and the makers of more general forecasts, Calvin saw a radical incompatibility between faith in divine Providence and any subjection of the self to natural law. Like the Roman cult of images, astrology served to bind the conscience rather than to free it. To try to merge this supposed art with Christian faith was like trying to mix fire and water; attempts to justify it on the basis of scripture were thoroughly perverse. Those who worked to gain prophetic insight from the stars were seriously deluded; the heavenly signs that Christ had announced would precede the Last Day would be nothing like normal constellations, but utterly extraordinary events that would shake the entire natural order.[35]

Following countless other critics, Calvin tried to draw a clear line between legitimate and illegitimate forms: "one can distinguish between natural astrology and their bastard astrology which has been manufactured by the magicians."[36] The agents of the bastard art sought to disguise themselves, calling themselves mathematicians, but this was shameful deceit. He regarded as a "subterfuge" the argument that it was one thing to fear dominion of the stars, but another to recognize that they exercised a sort of "subalternate superiority under the control and the guidance of God." That the stars did influence terrestrial nature was perfectly clear, but to imagine a natural science by which one could understand and predict human events was to turn away altogether from trust in the divine plan. It was for good reasons that secular governments had long sought to ban the prognosticators; indeed in Leviticus God had called for them to be put to death: "So let us learn to rest with the promises and threats of God, which have nothing to do with the position of the stars and which teach us that we should not divert our thoughts with star-gazing."[37]

Published originally in French, the *Warning* was aimed at "the simple and non-lettered" folk who were easily seduced by the widespread popular works, and who did not know enough to distinguish between "true astrology" and the superstitions of magicians and sorcerers. The goal was by no means new to him, for well before this booklet appeared Calvin had initiated a lengthy battle to control or suppress altogether the publication of popular almanacs and prognostications. His associates and successors at Geneva joined him in this effort; Theodore Beza, for instance, fulminated against "false and profane judicial astrology."[38] Indeed students of the Reformation are generally agreed that among the major emerging confessional groups, Calvin's heirs made the strictest efforts to reform popular religion, to "de-mythologize" the faith by divorcing it from magical, natural-scientific, or cosmological notions of any sort.[39] Denis Crouzet has depicted the Calvinist movement as a severe enemy of astrology in most of its common forms. Like the Roman cult of images, the stargazer's art offended belief in divine sovereignty, and served to torment the conscience rather than to free it. Crouzet finds some objective grounds for such a judgment, particularly in France, where since the early years of the century the growth of popular astrology had contributed strongly to a "culture of anguish." Mounting eschatological fears, stoked in the gloom of stellar disaster-forecasts, had created an existentially intolerable world for many French townspeople. Calvinist preaching, spreading rapidly by the late 1550s, was the antidote to this rising apprehension, offering a message of calm assurance and serenity based on trust in divine providence; sin, after all, lay in doubt and fear. Although the evidence suggests that

Crouzet's picture of astrology's prevalence in France is greatly exaggerated, his view of early Calvinism's central psychological thrust is certainly in keeping with what we know about the typical relationship between astrologers and Calvinist reformers elsewhere. The best-known case is no doubt that of England, where from the late sixteenth century on, by far the heaviest and most sustained opposition came from the Puritans. In that setting the disaffection was mutual; indeed most almanac makers would emerge as impassioned enemies of both Presbyterianism and Popery.[40]

The Reformed physician and scholar Thomas Erastus, returning home in the late 1540s from an Italian sojourn of several years, was struck by the far greater pervasiveness of astrological beliefs and practices among German Protestants than among his recent hosts. The Italians, he noted, paid little attention to the heavens except for the phases of the moon. "In fact they produce no almanacs of the sort made among us year after year," which specified times for medical and hygienic treatments "right down to the cutting of hair and nails." Erastus complained that this superstition was harmful not only to physical health, but also to piety. He worked hard to discredit contemporary German practitioners along with their art; for him as for many like-minded Reformed thinkers, this false learning was part of the undergrowth of Catholic superstition. In the eyes of the Palatine physician only the most toothless forms of the art were justifiable among Christians, and in stark contrast to the Melanchthonian view, he held that medical practice had no need of astrological theory.[41]

In 1557 Erastus translated, heavily edited, and published an antiastrological tract from the 1490s by the Florentine preacher Savonarola, a work based largely on Pico's famous attack of a few years earlier. His preface to this work, which gave full vent to his criticisms, was clearly aimed at the already massive but still rapidly expanding market for popular calendars, prognostications, and related materials in the Empire. Erastus insisted that God alone knew future contingents, and that one could gain no insight into divine providence by observing nature. He showed general scorn for what he saw as the superstitions of calendrical medicine. The Savonarolan tract sought to oppose the art of the stars on three main grounds: it could not be reconciled with scripture or with fundamental theological truths; it lacked all legitimate natural philosophical foundation; and it was undone by its own internal contradictions. To these arguments Erastus added a summary of what he claimed was an Italian disputation proving the impossibility of predicting any future fortune or misfortune from a birth horoscope, and a brief concluding section discussing the origins of astrology and its inherent appeal, especially to the philosophically and theologically naive. Throughout his remaining career Erastus continued to battle energetically against the astrologers. In 1569 he responded to a point-by-point refutation of his Savonarola edition by the Lutheran Christoph Stathmion, and in 1580 he published a Latin work against nativities. Charles Gunnoe has made the telling observation that Erastus's writings on stellar prediction "found a far more receptive audience in Geneva than in Wittenberg."[42]

As a professor at Heidelberg and physician to the Elector, Erastus supported the introduction of the Reformed faith in the Palatinate during the early 1560s. Heidelberg soon became the main bastion of Calvinism in the Empire. Not coincidentally, the city was notably underrepresented as a place of publication for popular astrological works in later decades. One of the few surviving prognostications issued here appeared in 1563, just as the new Reformed teachings were being officially adopted through the Heidelberg Catechism. The author of this work, Nikolas Gugler, lamented that anyone was free to produce calendars and practicas and to sell them far and wide; he called for measures to limit the enterprise to licensed professionals.[43] But such calls for restrictive measures were soon overshadowed by a broader program to discredit all forms of divination as either deluded or demonic. Calvinist practica writers were few and far between in the Empire. This small handful may have included Wilhelm Misocacus, a refugee physician from Brussels who settled in the Baltic port of Danzig around 1568; here he issued annual practicas from 1571 until 1590. Misocacus's confessional identity remains unclear, but even if he continued in the Reformed faith of his fellow refugees, his freedom to publish his forecasts depended largely on the supportive atmosphere of Danzig, a heavily Lutheran city with a strong tradition of interest in stellar science.[44]

Perhaps even more than their Catholic neighbors, German Calvinists came to fear the popular rumors, speculations, passions, and disorders that they associated with astrological publicity. Reformed preachers and theologians such as Hieronymus Zanchi, Wolfgang Musculus, and Abraham Scultetus took a consistent line, denouncing the annual publications that flowed from the presses in the major evangelical towns. Scultetus, another theologian active in Heidelberg and the Palatinate, issued in 1609 an especially severe *Warning against the Divinations of the Magicians and Stargazers*.[45] The title of this work revealed a tendency among these Reformed critics to lump predictive astrology together with magical beliefs and practices, including other forms of divination as well as alchemy, under a broad concept of superstition. Erastus's campaign against the art, for instance, was closely related to his denunciations of Paracelsianism. In the eyes of such opponents, there was little to distinguish between the Melanchthonian approach to the stars and the newly popular notions introduced by Paracelsus.

By the 1570s, the problem of Crypto-Calvinism was raising its head among Luther's heirs. Some evangelical preachers and writers, many of whom were supporters of the Melanchthonian or Philippist position in the intra-Lutheran disputes of this era, began to gravitate in the direction of Reformed teachings. More than a few of these figures did become openly Calvinist, moving to take up new positions in the Palatinate, in Bremen, or elsewhere. Others, including Melanchthon's close associate Caspar Peucer, would suffer imprisonment or expulsion at the hands of Lutheran rulers. Something of a riddle may arise here, for if we assume that humanistically minded evangelicals in the Melanchthonian mold were the most active promoters of astrology as a handmaid to biblical theology, how are we to explain that these men were also those most likely to favor Calvinism, with its general hostility to celestial prediction? The basic answer to the apparent riddle is that the main theological positions among the evangelical factions did not actually correspond at all closely with pro- or antiastrological positions. As we will see, astrologers were notably at odds on the doctrinal issues that divided Melanchthon's opponents and supporters, while those who opposed Melanchthon's theology were by no means uniformly dismissive of stellar science.

Moreover, Melanchthonian evangelicals who did in fact adopt Reformed teachings most often appear to have either muted or dropped their engagement with the stars. Johannes Crato, a Melanchthon protégé who became city physician at Breslau in the 1550s and later personal physician to the Emperor Maximilian II, drifted by the 1570s toward a crypto-Calvinist stance. While he hesitated to deny basic astrological assumptions, increasingly he preferred to consider medical issues within their own sphere. In 1585 he warned that a fanatical attachment to astrology could easily lead to a denial of "pure religion." Like his fellow Reformed physician Erastus, he also took a hard line against the teachings of Paracelsus.[46] Another Melanchthon student who adopted Reformed teachings in the 1570s was Christoph Pezel (d. 1604), who would become active in the Second Reformation movement at Bremen; we have no evidence that he continued to teach or write about the art of the stars in this later phase of

his life.[47] More dramatic was the case of Peucer, Melanchthon's main associate in the promotion of astrological study throughout the midcentury
decades. Accused of Crypto-Calvinism and imprisoned for twelve years by
the Saxon Elector (1574–1586), Peucer moved upon his release to Anhalt,
and appears to have become for all practical purposes a Calvinist in the
relatively quiet years before his death in 1602. Although he did continue
to practice medicine during this period, his days as an active professor
of the stellar science were over. At the commemorative ceremony held at
Heidelberg a year after his death, not a word was spoken about his long
and influential career as a Wittenberg astrologer.[48]

Perhaps most striking of all in this connection was Hermann Witekind
(1522–1603), a student and close friend of Melanchthon who adopted the
Reformed faith some time around the death of his mentor in 1560 and
spent most of the remainder of his career at Heidelberg. He is best known
for his polemic against magic and witchcraft, the *Christian Thoughts and
Notes on Sorcery,* first published in 1585 under the pseudonym of Augustin
Lercheimer. The work has drawn major attention as a key source for the
original Faust-book, the anonymous *History of Doctor John Faustus* (1587).
Witekind declared that divination from the stars "has no basis, and is
no art." As vain curiosity it always invited the involvement of evil spirits; it was thus the first step down the slippery slope to demonic magic,
witchcraft, and eternal perdition. Admitting that he had studied under
Melanchthon, Witekind made no direct personal attack on his late friend.
But the training supplied at Wittenberg had cultivated wicked folk, "enemies to our religion," who had done incalculable damage through their
countless astrological publications. Indeed the great medium of the press,
a gift of God, had thus been misused for perverse ends. It was "wrong and
regrettable that also our printers can without fear or shame bring out such
books and make them common, so that respectable people are slandered,
while the curious youths who obtain them are vexed and seduced like apes
to wish and see (so that the devil soon gets involved) if they can imitate
the same sort of miracle-working, not thinking or noting the sort of end
Doctor Faustus and his ilk earned."[49]

Despite such strong Calvinist hostility, astrological thinking would
soon become an earnest pursuit among at least a few of the leading
Reformed thinkers in central Europe. As Howard Hotson's work on
J. H. Alsted shows, the main centers for Reformed ventures into astrologi-
cal speculation, as well as into such realms as iatrochemistry, alchemy, and
Hermeticism, lay in Hesse-Kassel, especially at the University of Marburg,

where by the early years of the seventeenth century a quite different atmosphere obtained from that which the young Alsted had found earlier at Herborn or Heidelberg. Hotson points to astrology as the main "Hermetic" influence on the young Alsted, who along with figures such as the physician Rudolph Goclenius became part of a Marburg circle caught up in currents of encyclopedism and magical reformism in the period leading up to the Thirty Years' War. His was a world of dramatic polar tensions, most obviously between Calvinist biblicism and dreams of magical transformation. Alsted's early Calvinist training gave scant sanction to this latter quest, and as a result his intellectual life was marked by ongoing efforts to synthesize powerful but highly disparate ideals.[50]

Unlike the sort of astrology that prevailed in the popular planet books and almanacs, however, the art as conceived by Alsted and Goclenius was not a resource broadly available to a large number of practitioners or to the public at large. It was a high form of magic, rooted far more in Neoplatonic visions of human potential than in the more common framework of Aristotelian, Ptolemaic, and Galenic doctrines. Thus it was directed largely to an intellectual elite, to those who possessed the education, social standing, and wisdom necessary to help lead an ambitious transformation of the world. Since his astrological speculations were extremely difficult to reconcile with Calvinist orthodoxy, Alsted was increasingly forced to live in two separate worlds, one public and orthodox, the other private and Hermetic. Hotson describes the atmosphere that nourished Alsted's astrological ideals as unusual in the Reformed world, calling the intellectual situation at Marburg "unique within the ambit of the second reformation." Far more typical were Reformed principalities such as Nassau, where "endeavors to purify ritual of all traces of impurity and magic were related to a general abhorrence of magic and superstition."[51] The rarified forms of astrology cultivated at Marburg thus had little to do with the emergence of Calvinist confessional identity in the empire; in this respect the Reformed scene appears not dissimilar to the Catholic one. In both cases, an immense gulf came to separate the intellectual world of an elite, where astrological and magical speculations could be discreetly indulged, from the larger public setting in which demands for confessional conformity were building.

The wing of the Reformed tradition that originated in Zurich had never been friendly to stellar prediction, but in its early stages it had been forced to accommodate the same absorption with the art that prevailed in the nearby south-German cities. Ulrich Zwingli's near-total aversion to the art anticipated Calvin's own. His successor as leader of the Zurich movement, Heinrich Bullinger, could only wish that the faithful would read the scriptures with the same zeal they showed for the pronouncements of the stargazers.[52] But these theologians were surrounded by humanists, physicians, and literate layfolk whose natural-scientific interests extended to the study of planetary influences. Since the fifteenth century Zurich had appointed city physicians who issued calendars and promoted astrological medicine; prominent among them was Eberhard Schleusinger, who held this position from 1477 to 1488. His professional heirs included men such as the calendar-writing city physician Christopher Clauser, who through the 1530s and 1540s produced annual works reckoned for Zurich, and who likewise taught that astrology was central to medical practice. Clauser belonged to a circle of Swiss thinkers who shared the ideals of Melanchthon, and who maintained strong connections with the networks extending from Wittenberg.[53]

Even more energetic as a promoter and popularizer of the art was the remarkable Jacob Ruf (d. 1558), a city surgeon, playwright, and zealous anti-Roman polemicist whose varied and voluminous writings included not only calendars and practicas, but also at least two large works celebrating the great astrologers and astrologer-physicians down through the centuries. Very much in the tradition of urban practitioners going back to the pre-Reformation era and holding a great deal in common with contemporary medical popularizers such as Achilles Gasser and Burkhard Mithob, Ruf saw the celestial science as anything but an esoteric discipline; rather it was a natural study of immense civic as well as individual benefit. A zealous Protestant, he warned strongly against the works of Hermes Trismegistus; the true stellar science had almost nothing to do with such confused and pretentious notions.[54]

Yet in Ruf and his fellow Swiss Reformed thinkers and writers we find signs of shifting attitudes by shortly after midcentury, and the growth of a notably less welcoming climate for the stargazers. While calendars and practicas published in Zurich had typically remained quite restrained in their predictions, a new and more severely skeptical position was now in evidence. Ruf's practica for 1558, for instance, was sharply critical of authors who made predictions of deaths, war, scarcity, political conditions, and countless other aspects of life, "just as if they had sat with God in heaven for his divine counsel," and had learned these things directly from Him in order to announce them to the world. This was all godless doing, without any basis at all in scripture; the heavens and the earth were not made to satisfy such vain human curiosity. Blind devotion to the wide-spread popular forecasts had led only to confused sensationalism. As Ruf explained, the basis for his outlook in this practica lay not in the planetary movements but in the Book of Revelation, a truly divine prophecy for the last days of the world; here he showed the likely influence of Bullinger's recently published *One Hundred Sermons on the Apocalypse*. Also worth noting is that Ruf's shift in attitude came hard on the heels of Thomas Erastus's first major assault on stellar science; the Zurich surgeon was likely to have read immediately any work by this prominent physician and compatriot.[55]

Already in 1553 another writer of Zwinglian background, Urban Luginsland, had issued a practica that similarly moved in the direction of an antiastrological sermon. The work showed signs of its author's struggle to define his own position; it presented some apparently straightforward forecasting, but also emphasized the centrality of the Scriptural Word, and even suggested a parallel between astrological delusions and the false rules of the Papists. By 1558, though, Luginsland's outlook was less ambiguous, his hostility more consistent. Through the mid-1570s this Württemberger continued to issue annual works in which biblical preaching left room for only the very simplest, least controversial uses of the stars. Other similar works of likely Swiss Reformed provenance continued to appear; a *Fröliche Practick* for 1588 attacked the widely discussed fears focused on that year, arguing that if they meant anything at all the constellations pointed to a peaceful and prosperous time. An overall decline in popular astrological publication at Zurich from the 1550s on suggests that as the city became gradually more integrated into the broader Reformed movement, the hostile views of Calvin, Zwingli and Bullinger were gaining the upper hand.[56]

Lutheran Factionalism

While students of the late-Reformation era have occasionally noted the exceptional prominence of astrology in the Lutheran sphere, analyses of the matter from a confessional perspective remain sketchy. When scholars have addressed it all, they have often merely echoed the English observer Christopher Heydon, who observed in 1603 that in Germany both Lutherans and Catholics could be found among both the opponents and the defenders of astrology.[57] Heydon was at least partly correct, for the lines of learned debate never conformed closely to confessional boundaries. Yet he failed to recognize major differences in regard to the broader confessional patterns of the day. By all indications the massive and deliberate advocacy of stellar science led through the midcentury by the doctors of Wittenberg had lasting effects. The appropriation they encouraged continued and even deepened through the second half of the century, as the science of the stars gained yet more weight in the schools, the courts, among learned devotees, and above all in the expanding market for popular astrological works. Indeed in contrast to what we find among Catholics and Calvinists in the Empire, the evidence for an ongoing intensification of a vernacular astrological culture among German Lutherans almost jumps out at us.

The full flowering of this culture did not happen without resistance from evangelicals who continued to stress scripture as the essential text for the Christian life. The humanist poet and historian Kaspar Brusch, for example, issued an *Uralte Practica* in 1548 that shared features with the Christian practicas of the prior generation, and with publications such as *Der Getrew Eckhart*. Here he bewailed the annual tide of predictive pamphlets that were full of pious words and preaching but that actually spewed idolatry and superstition. God's word supplied the only practica believers would ever need. The calendar and practica writers were overwhelming the people and utterly perverting the gospel with their demonic superstitions; consciously or not, they were doing the Devil's work. Scripture left no doubt that God alone was the ruler over this coming year and every other. Packed with threatening Old Testament prophecies and apocalyptic preaching on Christ as the only hope, this tract took the now familiar tack of turning readers from astrological to biblical apocalypticism. Such writing was not typical of its author, an Imperial poet laureate, and the circumstances that prompted the publication are obscure. Brusch had spent time studying at Wittenberg earlier in the 1540s and was a close friend of the mathematician Rheticus. Was he reacting against an overwhelming preoccupation that he found genuinely harmful to gospel faith? Or was this work partly a humanist exercise, an opportunity for the literary star to extend his talents in a new direction that could only add to his fame?[58]

Brusch was not clearly aligned with either of the main theological factions that emerged after the death of Luther in 1546, Gnesio-Lutherans and Philippists. But it was the disputes between these groups that formed the main background to the scattered midcentury volley of evangelical attacks on the astrologers. Oversimplifying greatly, we can associate the

former party with resistance to any sort of compromise, however tempo-
rary, with Roman teachings or practices, while the latter group, centering on Melanchthon, took a somewhat more pragmatic stance. Gnesios
insisted on denying any and all value to "works," while Philippists tended
to see good works as integral to the Christian life. Scholars have typically assumed that the theological orientation of the Gnesios made them
natural enemies of astrology, that their principled aversion to the natural philosophy taught by the pedagogues at Wittenberg was what mainly
prompted them to denounce the stargazers. But this view needs qualification. No inevitable conceptual gulf prevented a strict Lutheran from
accepting the art of the stars in its practical or even in limited prophetic
applications. While most of the midcentury Lutheran assaults on stargazing did come from Gnesios, we should not overlook the tactical aspect of
the situation. In the heat of these bitter battles, Melanchthon's theological
enemies were moved to attack nearly anything and everything with which
he was associated, including his advocacy of astrology. All but the most
hard-line Gnesio-Lutheran theologians, those who showed a deep aversion to any sort of philosophy, would have felt far less need to impugn the
astrologers had Melanchthon not been so widely known as the leading
promoter of stellar science.

A direct Lutheran attack on the practica writers was issued at Jena in
1554 by Johann Aurifaber and Johann Stoltz, Gnesio-Lutheran court theologians at Weimar. These critics saw the real takeoff of the preaching practicas as having come around 1540, and since then the pretentions of their
authors had only grown worse. Publicists of this ilk were driving Paul from
the pulpit, and putting Plato and Aristotle in his place. Yet they supported
their fraud with citations from the Bible and the Church Fathers, twisting
the truth beyond all recognition. Learned university professors—a barely
disguised reference to Melanchthon and his Wittenberg colleagues—had
corrupted a younger generation who were now furthering such dangerous inanity; likewise they had promoted the commercial expansion of the
calendars and practicas and the resulting obsessions. Every year more and
more prognosticators drew people into "Egyptian darkness and Chaldean
curiosity," undermining the proper fear of God and Christian discipline.
And to top it all, these writers cast vicious invective and abuse against
anyone who questioned their predictions.[59]

The main target of these Weimar theologians, however, was Johann
Hebenstreit of Erfurt, a physician whose practicas had included rude
fulminations against Matthias Flacius and other critics of Melanchthon.

Hebenstreit had dedicated his predictions for 1554 to the Saxon Elector, to whom Aurifaber and Stoltz now directed their work in turn. Their ostensible goal was to show that the effort to ground the supposed stellar art in scripture, Augustine, or Luther's writings was completely fraudulent. One had to distinguish clearly between the heavenly signs mentioned by Christ or by Luther, signs sent as warnings directly by God, and the fanatical mathematics of this dangerous liar. The authors offered long quotations from Luther in particular, revealing his deep skepticism and distrust of any systematic reading of the heavens. This great man, they concluded, had in fact rejected the entire enterprise as a satanic perversion. At the end of their tract, Aurifaber and Stoltz called on Hebenstreit to do penance and ask divine forgiveness publicly in print, thus restoring honor to the Bible and the other sources he had wrongly adduced.[60]

That this work was addressed directly to the Saxon Elector is one of several circumstances suggesting that its authors were prompted by concerns that went well beyond the legitimacy of sidereal prediction. The antipathy of these Gnesio-Lutherans was directed in the first place at a popular writer who had attacked their theology and who was an open supporter of the Philippists. To denounce Hebenstreit was therefore a means of publicly besmirching the Wittenbergers without having to enter into the complexities of theological debate. To be sure, the antiastrological position of Aurifaber and Stoltz cannot be dismissed as merely tactical. Many practica writers had come to regard the teaching that the heavens represented divine law as naturally implying the astrologer's responsibility to issue prophetic warnings against widespread corruption and sin, and the apparent sanction to denounce human failings in the mode of Old Testament prophets was not one they were slow to seize. For the Weimar theologians, this rapidly waxing tendency to blend the roles of natural forecaster and prophetic preacher threw the human pretensions of the astrologers into bold relief. And now Hebenstreit was attempting to give his predictions divine sanction by adducing even the New Testament and Luther. In the eyes of these Biblicists, the stargazers were corrupting the evangelical cause.

Still, Gnesio-Lutheran theology by no means implied automatic hostility to astrology. Several astrological writers who were grounded in the Wittenberg tradition of natural philosophy would prove violently anti-Philippist and anti-Calvinist. One such was Joachim Heller, another product of Melanchthonian schooling, Johann Schöner's successor as Rector of the Nuremberg Gymnasium, and the city's main calendar writer for at least a decade. Heller had a tumultuous relationship with the city council after accepting this position in 1548. He survived these mainly minor conflicts, but in the course of the 1550s he moved into more perilous territory, becoming an ever more open and energetic advocate of the Flacian position, increasingly critical of the Philippists and of any perceived leanings toward Reformed teaching. The Nuremberg Council, concerned above all to keep a lid on public disputes of this sort, came to regard Heller more and more as a dangerous agitator. In 1562 he accused prominent local clerics of spreading Calvinist errors; as a result of the ensuing uproar he was first imprisoned, then permanently banned from the city. For the rest of his long life he would remain both an ardent evangelical and an active prognosticator.[61]

Despite the signs of caution and modesty we noted in some practicas of the 1550s and 1560s, the aggressive tone that had marked the Melanchthonian campaign from the start certainly did not disappear, and often grew even more strident in the face of challenges. Christoph Stathmion's forceful *Astrologia Asserta* of 1558, written largely in response to Erastus and probably at the instigation of Melanchthon himself, was only one of a series of similarly energetic works in which defense and offense were hard to distinguish. In his effort to use Savonarola to show that astrology was an unnatural, demonic art condemned by scripture, wrote Stathmion, Erastus merely showed that he misunderstood the matter. He could not show that astrology was anything but a form of natural philosophy, which was nowhere outlawed in God's Word. This full-tilt refutation followed a good Melanchthonian line. A key weapon was the medicine-astrology parallel; as a physician, Erastus had to acknowledge that he regularly drew general conclusions from observation and experience. The only important point on which Stathmion had to take a mildly defensive pose was the charge that astrologers were now often presuming to make predictions about matters of faith. He had to acknowledge "errors and abuses" on the parts of some writers, but he quickly insisted that "Christian astrologers" understood supernatural matters to be beyond their reach. Given the prevailing assumptions of the age, especially among German Protestants, Stathmion more than held his own in this debate. His work breathed the righteous conviction that a pious natural philosophy of celestial causation was perfectly complementary to faith (Figure 5.1)[62].

Similarly hard-hitting vindications came not only from the pens of medical men like Stathmion, but also from a growing body of young

ASTROLO-
GIA ASSERTA.

Oder

Ein kurtze vnnd
gründtliche verlegung/der
langen vnnd vngegründten schrifft
D.Thome Erasti/Darinne er sich vn-
terstehet/ die Kunst/ so auß der
Sternen lauff natürlich vrtey-
let/zu vernichten.
Durch

Christophorum Stath-
mionem/der Artzney
Doctorn.

Veritas uinci nequit.

M. D. LVIII.

FIGURE 5.1 Title page from Christoph Stathmion's *Astrologia Asserta* (Nuremberg, 1558). Courtesy of the Bayerische Staatsbibliothek München, Astr.p.166.

pastor-astrologers whose commitment to a Christian use of stellar science was if anything more ardent than that of the evangelical physicians. Along with Melanchthon's student Johann Garcaeus, this group included Johann Paceus, pastor at Weihe in Thuringia, who began to issue annual calendars and practicas around 1560, and who brought out in 1562 a pugnacious *Astrologia Vindicata* against those who called the art unchristian or superstitious. He was responding especially to a fellow pastor, Eucharius Gotthart [or Golthart] of Engelburg, a Flacian or supporter of Matthias Flacius, a leading Gnesio-Lutheran. Echoing Melanchthon, Paceus decried as "Cyclopic" those who could not understand the purposes for which the heavens were created. Such people were ignorant, oblivious to the art's great benefits for public order as well as for the Church. He first showed that scientific astronomy and astrology could not be separated, and indeed depended on one another; he then explained at some length how astrology was perfectly consonant with the principle of divine sovereignty over all nature, and the freedom that remained to human beings.[63] The rest of his tract was given over to showing that both the Old and New Testaments witnessed to the godly status of the art, as well as to exposing the errors of those who used scripture to condemn attention to the stars, and explaining what the Church Fathers had to say on the subject. Paceus had nothing but harsh disdain for those who found fault with Christian astrology.

Eucharius Gotthart and the Flacians came under more abusive attack from Christian Heiden, Heller's successor as the Nuremberg Gymnasium Rector and an ardent supporter of the Philippists. In the mid-1560s Heiden's practicas included impassioned assaults on such critics; here again, as in Heller's case, this sort of involvement led to trouble with the Nuremberg Council, although Heiden's position was precisely the opposite of his predecessor's. In his practicas he did not hesitate to report the threats the stars held for his theological enemies. Thus in his forecast for 1567, along with typically bleak admonitory predictions for fruitfulness, health and sickness, war and peace, and so on, he referred to the "Wendisch Cuckoo," or Flacius, predicting that he would "let his blasphemous song be heard again this year," but that the singing would be stopped after May of 1568 by a stronger bird of the night, meaning Melanchthon, the new "Wittenberg Nightingale." Heiden excoriated all classes for their failings, but included pointed pronouncements about a great weakening of the Roman clergy in upper Germany, and tremendous harm to be done by the Jesuits; he had portentous things to say as well about the Turks, the King of Spain, and other rulers. These blatantly partisan predictions led the Nuremberg authorities to attempt to suppress the work, but with little success. And despite severe warnings, Heiden continued to attack the Flacians, if only slightly less openly, in his subsequent practicas.[64]

Gotthart charged still more deeply into this fray in 1568 with his work *Against the Unchristian Heathen Practica of Christian Heiden.* Roundly attacking both this "Heathen" and Paceus for overstepping their bounds as astrologers, he let loose a barrage of scorn, ridicule, and outrage, denouncing Heiden in particular for his foul divination and star-gawking, entering the realm of theology and religion "like a pig in a beautiful pleasure garden," and finding his prophecies about the future of God's Church "IM ARS" (in the art, or the arse). The hordes of popular writers who followed the likes of Heiden did not stop at inundating the market with almanacs and practicas; they also undertook "to publish their superstitious astrological prophecies as useful and necessary to the maintenance of both worldly and churchly regiments, with shameless audacity, forced interpretations, and perverse readings of passages from Holy Scripture."[65]

True gospel preachers and teachers such as the unjustly maligned Flacius and other upholders of the unsullied Augsburg Confession had to be defended against such corrosive trends. Gotthart also sought to invoke lines from Erasmus, as well as Luther's warnings against worry over the future, to serve his aim of undercutting the supporters of Melanchthon.

Heiden's repeated lobbing of grenades at the Flacians insured that he would become a main target of their counterattacks. Since his assaults came in works of astrological publicity, his status as a stargazer inevitably came under fire. But again, astrology was ultimately not the central issue in these battles. Further evidence for this point appears in the 1568 *Defensio* of Wolfgang Waldner, a volatile participant in the midcentury theological skirmishes who was known for his especially strong apocalyptic convictions. This defense opposed "the heathen (*Heidnischen*) and unchristian slander and defamation of the supernatural stargazer Christian Heiden against the persecuted, innocent servants of Christ." Waldner did devote space to mocking the astrological predictions and pretensions of Heiden and his fellow forecasters. Heiden "puts so much stock in astrology, making a magical fortune-telling out of it such as comes from the Devil (as Luther says in his Table-Talk), that for him the stars must cause, portend, and signify everything that he projects for those whom he is set against in his heart."[66] Like other false prophets, Heiden adopted an erroneous conception, and then read the Bible so as to twist it in favor of his error. Yet for all this, Waldner was far less concerned with Heiden's use of the stars than with his propaganda in favor of the "Adiaphorists," meaning essentially the theological party of Melanchthon. Waldner's main goal was to discredit these false teachers, who were willing to compromise the Word of God for the sake of peace. In the latter parts of his tract he dropped references to astrology almost entirely, and focused on a defense of the pure, besieged Word of God; these pages bristled with snarling charges against Papists, Majorists, Antinomians, Synergists, Sacramentarians, Calvinists, Jews, and Anabaptists.

For the purposes of popular polemic, and because his immediate opponent was a stargazer, Waldner evidently felt it made sense to wrap his attack on Heiden in antiastrological terms, even though the deeper matter was to vindicate his theological position. We can justifiably ask whether, as in the case of Aurifaber and Stoltz, the matter of astrology would have drawn such controversy had such aggressive public attacks on the Flacians not come from well-known practica writers. Waldner could even assert, after all, that if Heiden and his fellow stargazers would remain within the bounds of their profession, they would not be subject to blame. And he was clearly influenced by the Melanchthonian conception of the stars as teachers of the law. Preachers, he wrote, should explain the signs appearing in the sun, moon, stars, and on earth as signs of pure joy to the faithful. "To the others," he added, "the stargazers should interpret them to mean nothing other than war, bloodshed, death, and every misfortune."[67] As both messengers of hope and instrument of warning, the heavens had appropriate Christian uses after all.

Other evangelical works from the 1560s reveal a similar ambivalence toward the art of the stars, and reflected a genuine questioning and debate in some minds about the proper role of the art in the life of the faithful. Ludwig Milich, for example, a learned pastor who wrote two of the most celebrated Lutheran "Devil-books" of the later sixteenth century, presented a judgment that was far from straightforward. Milich's famous *Zauberteufel* of 1563 typified a lively Lutheran discourse on the devilish temptations ever-present in human life. His goal was vaguely similar to that of Peucer in his *Commentary* of a decade earlier, namely to distinguish between legitimate and illegitimate ways of pursuing knowledge of the future. Thus various sorts of astrological practice were to be distinguished. "Choosers of days" (*Tagwehlern*) were those who determined good or bad days or times for undertaking particular tasks. Those who did this by following inherited popular superstitions were to be dismissed outright. So too were those who followed the "foolish planet books" (i.e., nativity books) issued by greedy printers in order to make money from gullible folk; regrettably, even faithful people of high status were caught up in such dubious games. On the other hand, astrologers who sought to determine the best times for undertakings by careful inquiry into natural causes were on firmer ground. In a later section "On Pharisaical Elections" Milich agreed with the natural astrologers on a key point; here he discussed the perverse belief that some days and times were holier than others, and thus more appropriate for worship or service to God. The truth was "that all days and times are alike to the Christian good and holy, since God has created and blessed one day just as the next, and one time just as the next." The faithful were to pray all days, fast all days, live piously all days.[68]

Milich did not hide his reservations about stellar prediction, but he had to acknowledge that many learned people defended it vigorously. For his part, he wrote, "I truly do not know whether their opinion is to be accepted." He notably left open the possibility that greater precision might lead to improved results in this field. His uncertainty was reflected in numerous equivocations. On one hand, he called astronomy a true gift of God, useful not only for keeping track of years, seasons, months, and days, but also for various practical ends such as weather prediction. He was wary of too-precise forecasts, but here, as he acknowledged, he merely echoed the calendar and practica writers: "These things a Christian should regard not as certain prophecies, but rather as conjectures, which might happen or not happen and which remain in God's discretion." At one point he called it "a demonic presumption" to plant, sow, or undertake other work according to the positions of the planets rather than simply when sunshine and good weather allowed, yet elsewhere he admitted to ambivalence about how far one was justified in determining one's schedule of work by the stars. Even with regard to predictions about individual people, he could finally say only that he would "take nothing away from the account of one more knowledgeable."[69]

Milich's ambivalence was actually a reflection of his honesty. For it was next to impossible, even for hard-line Gnesio-Lutherans, to dismiss the art altogether. Far more common than outright rejection were expressions of the critical yet ultimately tolerant attitude that Luther himself had generally taken. When the theologian Jacob Andreae tried to show the foolishness of particular astrological forecasts, as he did in a series of sermons in the 1560s, he did not assert that such efforts were positively contrary to the gospel; rather he offered the traditional and far less damning argument that since God could alter nature's course at any moment, astrological predictions were inherently uncertain and were thus mainly a waste of time. The noted Swabian preacher Moses Pflacher, who had studied under Andreae at Tübingen, could not quite decide whether the heavens offered some legitimate basis for natural predictions, or whether the pursuit of such knowledge was opposed to true faith.[70] We have seen evidence that most evangelical attacks on the astrologers were in any case not primarily indictments of the stellar art itself, but above all tactical attempts to discredit the Philippists. If Gnesio-Lutherans saw danger in the tendency of popular astrologers to become preachers and polemicists, their more basic effort was to discredit Melanchthon's theological supporters. While they had some success on this score, they had little to none in turning the faithful away from their almanacs.

Isolated cases of principled hostility actually help prove the larger point. Toward the end of a long sermon delivered in 1577, for example, Andreae moved well beyond his earlier depiction of the stellar art as a foolish waste of time. Here he harshly denounced the practica and calendar writers as "Devil's prophets" hawking dangerous perversions in these Last Times. While the great comet of 1577 was unquestionably a heaven-sent sign of deepest urgency, the readings of these "diviners" were utterly false; indeed "their calendars, practicas, and interpretations are so full of lies that they should be ashamed not only before God and all pious people, but for themselves." Andreae lamented openly that people paid more attention to the practicas than to God's Word; indeed "the calendars and almanacs have become our Bibles." His sermon echoed points that Aurifaber and Stoltz had made in vain nearly a quarter-century earlier, and it was surely no coincidence that he delivered it at Weimar, where these earlier preachers had been active and where party hostility to the Melanchthonians was still strong. Notable as well is that here as in many of his other writings, Andreae spent far more energy exposing the falsehoods of the Papists and other confessional enemies than in criticizing the omnipresent obsession with stellar science.[71]

The nasty factional spats among Luther's heirs eased off especially after the 1577 Formula of Concord brought theological agreement between the major feuding parties; not coincidentally, open questioning of the stellar art now grew rarer than ever. Naturally the animosities that had wracked an entire generation did not disappear all at once. In 1578 the Kitzingen astrologer Georg Meder was still railing against "the secretly malicious [crypto-] Calvinists and Flacianists (who can hide under the cloak of Luther, and of whom Germany is now full)." Meder predicted much continuing strife on account of these deceivers, and called on Christian rulers to fulfill their office by fully extirpating their errors, which implicitly included their hostility to stellar forecasting. Christoph Stathmion could still complain in his practica for 1578 that a main cause of disunity in the Church was the unwillingness of some theologians to acknowledge the force of natural scientific demonstrations. Clearly he believed that stellar science could provide objective grounds upon which theological differences might be reconciled. But once those quarrels were actually settled by theologians on theological terms, the astrologers were free to pursue their enterprise with fewer entanglements. In 1577 Andreas Musculus, the zealous Gnesio-Lutheran preacher and writer at Frankfurt an der Oder, could refer in warmly positive terms to "our astrologers," whose predictions for coming earthly disasters complemented both biblical prophecy and the outlook of a number of old vaticinations recently recovered.[72]

Most practica writers did not cease to include at least some words of defense. Yet as the second half of the century wore on even the stock arguments came to seem unnecessary, mere rote recitals of obvious truths. Georg Meder, the passionate Kitzingen commentator cited earlier, opened his practica for 1578 with a brief stock defense. "But now enough of this," he impatiently broke in. "Others have already written enough on the usefulness of this art, so I will omit it here; in this sort of introduction it would take too long to deal with it."[73] Many other writers just barely continued to go through the motions of explaining the differences between their natural art and the demonic practices of divination and sorcery. Stathmion's forecast for the same year forebore to defend its basis in the stars, since its author had "earlier by necessity responded and proved sufficiently how thoroughly natural and workable this art is." In 1580 the prolific Nicholas Winckler issued a brief Latin *Tractatus de Astrologiae*, evidently at the request of his city council, "against certain anonymous persons who contend that the stars have no effect." A formal refutation of a nameless opponent, the work seems almost to have been designed to demonstrate its own superfluity.[74]

The increasingly isolated publicists who sought to oppose all astrological study and practice on theological principle had little solid ground on which to stand; at best they could merely denounce particular abuses. A scattering of evangelical preachers and authors kept the art at arm's length and took the position that it was essentially irrelevant to the faith, but few were as direct as Andreae in rejecting any use of astrological principles in order to issue warnings about anticipated disasters and exhortations to repentance. In the 1550s and 1560s a handful of vocal critics may have pushed some calendar men into a slightly more humble posture, but their efforts were soon overwhelmed. By the time the factional squabbles among Lutherans waned in the 1570s, the stargazers had successfully reinforced their place in an emerging confessional culture.

A Saturated Atmosphere

In a 1584 letter to the Altdorf professor Johannes Praetorius, the Hungarian humanist Andreas Dudith echoed the perceptions of many earlier observers, writing of his amazement that "here in our Germany there are so many, especially among those who come from the University of Wittenberg, with whom these [astrological] prophecies enjoy great authority." Just a couple of years later the Tübingen poet and satirist Nicodemus Frischlin noted that Wittenberg had educated and sent forth mathematicians "almost without number."[75] Scholars have often suggested that after the imprisonment of Caspar Peucer on charges of crypto-Calvinism in 1574, the school began to lose its reputation as the premier center of astronomical and astrological study in Germany. While this point is not to be dismissed, it is also true that both here and at other Lutheran universities, including Tübingen, Leipzig, Erfurt, Rostock, Greifswald, and Helmstedt (founded 1575), these disciplines remained in extremely high regard. One minor but revealing piece of evidence is that the vastly adventuresome Italian philosopher Giordano Bruno, whose travels had taken him to many European centers of learning and who would be burned at the stake in Rome in 1600, developed a serious interest in astrology only in the late 1580s, when he was happily engaged at Wittenberg.[76]

In humanist circles outside the universities as well, Lutherans had long since become the most prominent promoters of mathematics. No late-Reformation scholar was more zealous in cultivating and promoting astrology than Heinrich von Rantzau (1526–1598), the long-time Statthalter for the Danish kings in the duchy of Schleswig-Holstein. A student of Melanchthon from 1538 to 1546, Rantzau devoted his intellectual life to making the art more widely accessible and appreciated. For years he was in close correspondence not only with his Wittenberg mentors but with princes, councilors, and many leading thinkers of the day, including Tycho Brahe, Gerhard Mercator, Cyprian Leowitz, Justus Lipsius, and Sixtus ab Hemminga. His letters to these and other figures show an intense and unflagging preoccupation with the construction and interpretation of horoscopes. His own publications were essentially redactions of older work, compilations and guides rather than substantive contributions. He clearly saw himself in the line of reformers and reconcilers that went back through his teachers to Regiomontanus. Although he wrote in Latin rather than German, several of his works quickly appeared in translation, and most saw repeated reprintings. They included a handbook on astrological medicine (1574), a historical catalogue of famous stargazers (1576), a multiyear calendrical work (1590), and at least two instructional texts on celestial science (1591 and 1593). The 1593 text, *Tractatus Astrologicus*, was so highly regarded that it was adopted for use in schools. It is no surprise that Rantzau was among the contemporary authorities the practica writers liked to cite. His writings echoed the Melanchthonian conception that the revival and progress of astrological science provided the philosophical complement to evangelical faith.[77] Indeed while not himself an academic, Rantzau took up at least a corner of Melanchthon's mantle as the most prominent evangelical advocate of celestial studies.

Not many stargazers enjoyed such an elevated position as Rantzau's, which afforded him the luxury of engaging with his studies precisely as he pleased during the latter decades of the century. At the same time, fewer were able to retain the prestige of functioning simultaneously as professors, princely consultants, and urban practitioners, as a substantial number had been able to do in earlier generations. As counsel to the courts grew more exclusive, and as at least some elite mathematicians began slowly inching away from openly prophetic and polemical uses of the art, those who more and more dominated the realm of astrological publicity were the physicians, schoolmasters, pastors, printers, and educated burghers—in other words the middle and lower intelligentsia of the German evangelical towns. This development seems to have reflected a broader trend: while the courts and universities certainly retained great weight in shaping the lives of burghers, the common culture of the evangelical cities had by now established an independent momentum.

Among the astrological publicists, physicians continued to predominate. Scholars have often assumed that Protestant clergymen felt their own roles and status threatened by these stargazing physicians, who often took upon themselves the tasks of moral counsel and prophetic warning. Although we noted a certain rivalry and tension between preachers and medical practitioners during the earliest phases of the evangelical movement, during the second half of the century any lingering notions of competition were increasingly outweighed by mutual respect and perceptions of shared aims. Questions about professional competence or vocational sanction to preach the word received little attention during this period. On this point the calendar writers might have adverted in theory to the principle of the priesthood of all believers, as the Stargard physician David Herlicius would do early in the next century. But over several generations the actual circumstances made it unnecessary to evoke this idea explicitly. In the Lutheran schools and universities, after all, students were trained to see the clerical and mathematical callings as closely related, even fully complementary. Already by the 1560s we find pastors and astrologers beginning to attest directly to a sense of overlapping responsibilities. In a 1562 pamphlet that sought to establish proper Christian guidelines for reading of natural signs, the preacher Johann Pfeffinger claimed for his office the role of considering phenomena from a biblical and prophetic perspective. But natural interpretations were appropriate as well; these should be left largely to the mathematicians and astronomers, so long as their readings remained "conformable to faith" and served "the betterment and building up of God's church."[78] The more fully this Melanchthonian understanding established itself, the rarer open disputes became between pastors and astrologer-physicians, and the more frequently we find expressions of cooperative attitudes. Thus it is hardly surprising that the two roles came closer together, and in many cases merged almost completely.[79]

Another likely reason for the remarkable accommodation between pastors and astrologers had to do with their mutual and profound concerns for public instruction and public order. What, in these fast-changing times, were the most effective ways of instructing the people? We know that evangelical leaders of the mid- to late-sixteenth century were by no means consistently eager to encourage independent Bible-reading among laypeople. Those with only a basic education who studied the scriptures without theological guidance were liable to slip easily into error. Many preferred that their parishioners receive instruction through sermons and catechisms, which helped insure a proper and consistent understanding of the Word.[80] In the German towns, however, where anticlerical attitudes were deep-seated, the moral authority of pastors was inevitably surrounded by suspicions. Moreover, irregular attendance at sermons was becoming a matter of serious concern; preachers could not easily impress a message on people who came grudgingly or sporadically to regular services. These perspectives may help explain the general willingness of clergy to sanction other channels that could serve this function of proper teaching as well. Few forms reached as broad an audience as the popular calendars and practicas, and here after all were media that emphasized the moral lessons of the law, the need to discipline oneself in every aspect of one's daily existence, and the divine sanction of political power structures.

No development is more revealing of the unique relationship between German Lutheranism and the science of the stars than the emergence of the pastor-astrologer. The late-Reformation phenomenon of the active pastor who also wrote practicas and cast horoscopes continues to draw amazement from scholars, who betray in this way their own metahistorical assumptions.[81] But for generations of men who studied in the Lutheran universities from the 1530s on, above all those who absorbed the natural philosophical teachings of Melanchthon and Peucer at Wittenberg, preconceptions about the incompatibility of astrology with biblical faith were utterly foreign. A notable early example was Johann Garcaeus the Younger, who after studying at Wittenberg became a professor and then pastor at Greifswald; later he served the Church at Neustadt in Brandenburg. Best known for his massive text of 1570, *Astrologiae methodus*, he gained influence as a serious promoter of the art, but apparently did not take up the practice of issuing calendars or prognostications.[82] Among the first Protestant clergymen who did put out an annual calendar was the Saxon pastor Johann Paceus, whom we encountered above as a combatant in the factional wars. Starting around 1560 he published a series of such works, which fit the already common model combining natural forecasts and pro-phetic warnings.

The pastor-astrologer trend seems to have picked up especially in the 1570s. While it is often difficult or impossible to determine the back-ground or status of the popular writers, many did give some indication on their title page or at the end of a dedicatory preface, often simply "pas-tor and astronomer." Some of those who identified themselves as pastors were among the most prolific practica producers of the entire century. Albin Moller, for example, who grandly designated himself "Ecclesiastes, Theologus, und Astronomus" of Straupitz, wrote in 1595 that this was the twenty-sixth consecutive year for which he had composed a practica.[83] By far the most famous of the stargazing pastors, however, was Georg Caesius, who studied under Peucer at Wittenberg and then undertook what he saw as closely intertwined responsibilities in his hometown of Rothenburg. After moving to Ansbach, residence city of the Brandenburg princes in southern Franconia, he became official calendar-maker to the Margrave; he continued to enjoy this high-profile position even as he became a locally beloved pastor at nearby Burgbernheim. For nearly forty years he issued annual calendars and practicas, giving highly dependable business to the printer Valentin Fuhrmann at Nuremberg. When he died in 1604 his fellow citizens and clergymen celebrated his life as a pastor, astrologer, and preacher of repentance in the face of the Last Judgment.[84]

In Caesius the elements of caution and defensiveness that had appeared in midcentury practicas effectively disappeared. As early as 1575, he argued without hesitation that a proper understanding of Holy Scripture positively required a knowledge of astronomy. To reject this art was therefore indeed to reject the Bible itself. Caesius quoted the astrologers' favorite lines from Luther to prove his point: "While astrology involves many superstitions, it is not therefore to be rejected entirely. For it consists entirely in attention to and observation of the divine creation, and such observation serves and is proper to a man. This is why the finest and most ingenious minds engage in this study and have found joy in it." He shrugged off Catholic attacks on his evangelical astrology, including "the slanders of [Georg] Scherer, the Jesuit of Vienna"; likewise he often took the opportunity to denounce the errors of the Calvinists.[85] The great success of this preacher-forecaster reflected the overwhelming triumph of evangelical astrology as a tool of both teaching and propaganda.

In addition to pastors, a growing number of educated burghers who were neither physicians nor pastors entered the business of calendar and practica production by the last third of the century. A modest but growing number of authors gave no indication of a profession, and if an author did not identify himself as either a physician or a pastor, we can generally assume that this was because he was not active in either calling. Some writers, such as Caspar Pontanus of Lübeck, referred to themselves as "Magister," which probably meant that the writer held a degree and taught in a local school. The titles "mathematicus" and "astronomus" were more ambiguous, and might have been used by a variety of educated towns-men. Wolff Geuss, "Astrologer" of Nuremberg, was among the earlier likely examples of a nonprofessional author. Georg Busch called him-self "painter and burgher in Erfurt." Toward the end of the century we find many similar designations. Typical was Matthias Fischer, "student of astronomy and burgher in the Free Imperial City of Schlackenwald."[86] While physicians and pastors continued to dominate the market, the expanding involvement of men outside these callings clearly shows that the stellar art was a general preoccupation of the culture.

Supplying basic data for the ordering of daily life as well as an orien-tation in nature and in history, the calendars and prognostications took on a role in the culture of the evangelical towns that is difficult to weigh with precision, but equally difficult to dismiss. In his famous *Aller Praktik Grossmutter*, the Reformed satirist Johann Fischart agreed: the annual prognostications had essentially taken the place of the Bible, so that one no longer undertook any dispute, medical treatment, harvest, or other enterprise at all without consulting the omnipresent booklets full of little crawling numbers.[87] Supplying the basic data for directing one's life in nearly every respect, the almanacs and practicas had become something like the personal digital assistants of evangelical burghers. Censorship, meanwhile, appears to have played a very limited role in the market for the annual works. To be sure, city councils sought to maintain some sort of control over the circulation of the ephemera along with other popular literature. As we have noted, most towns of any size continued the practice of appointing an official calendar writer, whose works were to guide local barber-surgeons and other medical practitioners. This function held such importance that when the designated writer for Nuremberg, the Altdorf professor Johannes Praetorius, once failed to publish a practica to accompany his annual calendar, he received a stern reprimand from the city council.[88]

But it was one thing to insure the production of official works, another to prevent the circulation of competing editions each year. Printers, sellers, and buyers had countless ways to skirt local ordinances, which were in any case often shifting and inconsistent. Restricting the circulation of the annual ephemera proved such an impossible task that most local authorities gave it up, and moved to suppress only those writings that included religious or political material deemed dangerous. Cases of prepublication censorship were rare, probably because those astrologers who were prepared to submit their works to official scrutiny were unlikely to overstep implicitly understood limits. Minor scandals caused little more than wrinkles in a highly competitive but lucrative enterprise. The Nuremberg Council, for example, was upset to find noted in Joachim Heller's practica for 1564 the best times not to "wean children," but rather to "make children." In this case the trail of guilt led to the typesetter, who was thrown in jail.[89]

Throughout the second half of the century the publishing situation for the popular astrologers remained a virtual free-for-all. Several of the bigger-name writers worked with printers in a number of cities at once, reaching in this way a broader audience than ever before. Hoping to prevent pirated printings, a series of prominent forecasters sought the Imperial privilege for their annual works, which meant that unauthorized printings were officially banned. A line of authors starting with Johann Virdung in 1522 had been granted this privilege. Notably, it appears that most of the sixteenth-century practica writers who held this right after Virdung himself were evangelicals. Some, like Georg Caesius, sought the privilege but never managed to receive it. The large number of authors who hoped to gain such official protection was yet another reflection of the social importance contemporaries saw in these yearly booklets.[90] Yet neither Imperial sanctions nor local restrictions appear to have had any serious limiting effects.

The printing of calendars and practicas did become gradually more concentrated in the major centers of commercial publication. This trend was owing partly to economies of scale in mass printings, partly to an ongoing swelling of the ranks of itinerant booksellers, and perhaps also to the growing renown of the most successful authors, whose fans eagerly awaited their predictions year after year. Since as early as 1500 Nuremberg had been the leading center for astrological publication of all sorts, and so it remained throughout the century. In fact more and more almanac makers had their works printed here even though they lived and worked elsewhere. Gradually the Nuremberg printers absorbed much of the production that had been scattered among numerous smaller cities of the Empire. But towns such as Augsburg, Ulm, Strasbourg, Frankfurt am Main, Leipzig, and Erfurt remained in this race. Printers in Vienna, Ingolstadt, Cologne, and a handful of other Catholic towns continued to issue far thinner streams of annual works, thus showing signs of much stricter and more successful control by local authorities.[91]

The soaring commercial success of the annual works was aided by innovations that made these genres handier, and indeed useful in new ways. The most notable change in format came with the widespread introduction of the calendar in booklet form. Starting around 1550 and taking off quickly over the next twenty years, these new quarto-sized calendars devoted a single opening to each month, thus escaping the increasingly crowded confines of a single broadsheet. The added room allowed printers to leave a large open space on one side of each opening, an invitation for the user to record memorable events or the weather day by day, or to schedule their affairs for the coming weeks and months. Known as the *Schreibkalender* (writing calendar), this form proved immensely appealing, and soon gained dominance in the market. At least part of the reason for the enormous jump in the numbers of surviving annual works from the 1560s to the 1580s was that at year's end the calendar now retained its function as a personal or family record; the new form engaged readers with the past as well as with the present and future. More than ever, the calendars helped evoke a sense of time's unbroken march in relation to the life of the individual, his family and community, and the larger unfolding of history. Scholars have found strong connections between the emergence of the personal or family astrological calendar and the development of a specifically "bourgeois" historical awareness around this time.[92] Evidence such as we find in the 1595 inventory of a Braunschweig burgher's library is revealing; at his death this apparently quite conventional head of household left Bibles, works by Luther and Chemnitz, books of sermons, hymnals, devotional tracts, medical manuals, some travel volumes, and also "a large stack of old almanacs."[93]

Astrologers and their printers also introduced more superficial changes aimed at boosting the already huge market appeal of the annual works. Over the last half of the century, the traditional title of *Practica Teutsch* (or *Deutsch*) or simply *Practica* gradually ceded ground to the fancier *Prognosticon* or *Prognosticon Astrologicum*. The new style was really nothing but a veneer meant to celebrate the supposed Latinate learning of the author, and in many cases publishers sought to insure clarity and reassure vernacular readers by including both styles: *Prognosticon Astrologicum oder Practica Deutsch*. By 1600 some practicas were fronted with titles and title pages of nearly baroque complexity, perhaps an indirect reflection of a genre just starting to go to seed. But if so the seeds kept sprouting; according to one report, a practica for 1610 by Simon Marius, inheritor of Georg Caesius's official mantle at Ansbach, was printed in as many as 11,000 copies.[94]

So strong was the demand for the popular annual works that even a hustler such as Leonhard Thurneisser (1531–1597), a Basel native with little formal education, could enjoy meteoric success in this market despite his professional reputation as a charlatan. This man's almost incredible career of self-promotion in medicine, alchemy, astrology, and magical speculation got a kick-start in 1572 when he successfully healed the ailing wife of the Brandenburg Elector Johann Georg. With the Elector's support he set up a laboratory and his own press in Berlin; he then gained an exploding popular following with his graphically innovative almanacs and practicas, as well as notoriously cryptic longer works on "natural magic." A declared disciple of Paracelsus, Thurneisser departed from the Melanchthonian consensus in basic ways; as we will see in a later chapter, he was in this respect an early forerunner of trends that would emerge strongly only after 1600. Both his methods and his marketing triumphs incurred tremendous resentment and harsh criticisms from more mainline physicians and calendar-writers. Yet Thurneisser's yearly forecasts, especially his calendars, did not differ dramatically in outward form from those of his competitors. And his insistence that the stars warned people to amend their lives agreed broadly with the goals of his more conventional Lutheran contemporaries.[95]

The depth of the art's penetration into evangelical culture is also evident in the frequency with which other writers adopted the vocabulary, imagery, and forms of the star literature, especially of the practicas. To some extent this trend merely picked up on the tradition of the Christian practica, which sought to drain the star-talk of its astrological meanings

and turn it to biblical lessons. But the rapid escalation in the use of astrological terms as advertising suggests a truly pervasive presence and influence. So for instance it quickly became common for preachers to adopt the
designation "Practica" for their popular sermonic works. In 1563 Thomas
Roerer issued *A New and Truly Spiritual Practica for these hard and perilous
times until the End of the World*, which presented no astrology at all, but biblical apocalyptic preaching of the starkest, most intense kind. Similar was
Georg Breuning's *Christian Sermon, or, Universal Practica* of 1588. In the
following year Kaspar Lutz issued *A Christian Practica or Prognostication
for All Years*. Collections of Luther's prophetic utterances were promoted
the same way. In 1578 Johann Lapaeus gathered some of the reformer's
darkest warnings under the title *Practica and Prognostication, or terrifying
Prophecies of Dr. Martin Luther.*[96]

Other genres are equally revealing of a culture immersed in stellar
forecasting. In the 1560s, just as the production of annual calendars and
practicas was expanding more dramatically than ever, parodies and satires on popular astrology also rose quickly in number. From the earliest
spread of the printed calendars and practicas the works of the stargazers
had drawn a range of reactions combining humor, ridicule, and rejection
in various proportions. Because of their imaginative and literary qualities,
these genres of mockery and scorn have drawn nearly as much scholarly
attention as the works of the sixteenth-century astrologers themselves.
Whether or not we view such writings as fundamentally antiastrological, it is noteworthy that in the later sixteenth century they came mainly
from the pens of Catholics and Calvinists. We noted earlier the *Practica
Practicarum* of the Franciscan Johann Nas, often reprinted after its first
appearance at Ingolstadt in 1566. Nas drew heavily on a caustic 1565 satire on the annual forecasts by the Reformed writer Johann Weyermann,
whose attitudes were in line with the broader rejection of popular astrology among Zwingli's heirs. These works were among the varied sources
for the most famous of all the late-sixteenth-century astrological satires,
Johann Fischart's *Aller Practick Grossmutter* of 1572. Fischart, also of
Reformed background, provided the classic German literary spoof on the
widespread obsession with stellar forecasts, and inspired a gaggle of eager
imitators.[97]

At least a few satires did come from the evangelical fold. The poet
and dramatist Georg Rollenhagen, for instance, a product of Wittenberg
schooling and by no means an enemy of the astrologers generally, could
not resist issuing verses in which he parodied the pervasive obsession

with the stargazers' long-building preoccupations with 1588. Similarly the Tübingen humanist Nicodemus Frischlin published his *De Astronomicae Artis* at Frankfurt in 1586; here he mercilessly mocked the pretentions of the calendar makers and the horoscope casters by whom he felt surrounded. But Frischlin was a notorious maverick, an unhappy man alienated from his colleagues; he was clearly not representative of views at Tübingen, where astrological study was generally held in high regard. He was moreover neither a mathematician nor a theologian, and his indictment of the stargazers, issued in Latin, was of little concern to those who sailed the seas of vernacular publication.[98] More earnest and straightforward criticisms did come from the pen of a highly respected Tübingen mathematician who advocated reforms that could bring universal respectability to the science of the stars. Michael Maistlin, the revered teacher of Johannes Kepler, thought the worst abuses were found in the popular planet books, which taught laymen crudely and misleadingly about the reckoning of horoscopes. All right-minded mathematicians and astrologers, he wrote, "hold as worthless the planet booklets such as are produced and sold everywhere, and see them as far more harmful than useful." Similarly Tycho Brahe and Kepler would express deepening disdain for the confusions and inaccuracies that were common in popular publications and practices.[99] But such complaints attest primarily to the near-ubiquity of stellar preoccupations among the heirs of the Wittenberg reformers.

This brief survey leaves little room for doubt that in its early defining stages Lutheran confessional culture integrated astrological teachings in ways that were essentially foreign to the other emerging religious blocs of the mid- to late-sixteenth century. John Calvin's harsh attack anticipated and helped to set the tone among most Reformed Protestants, who favored very different tools of discipline. A Papal bull of 1586 reinforced the already strong Tridentine strictures against this and other forms of divination, while Catholic polemicists ridiculed the astrological obsessions of Luther's followers. Among both Catholics and Calvinists, clerical opposition tended to restrict the art to elites, and thus limited its influence on broadly shared perceptions. Nicholas Campion is therefore on the right track in noting that in the Reformation era traditional arguments against stellar science as idolatrous "were recycled by Puritan divines in northern Europe and Catholic priests in the south."[100] The great majority of Lutheran clerics, on the other hand, indulged and even promoted a popular astrological culture that complemented and strongly articulated their own biblical preaching. Evangelical preachers had little motivation to denounce the sort of popular astrology that now flourished among them; indeed they had potent reasons to embrace it. The art of the stars made manifest the power and glory of the creator, even as it provided essential tools for the ordering of earthly life and of time itself. In ways that Chapter 6 will explore more fully, it exposed the growing corruption of nature and the decline of faith, warning sinners and perhaps strengthening hearers of the word in the face of the nearing Last Judgment. Throughout the late sixteenth century, the broad alliance between preachers and astrologers held persistent sway; it was questioned only sporadically and with little result. The pedagogical and polemical advantages of this fraternity far outweighed the abstract concerns of a few cranky theologians.

6

Fate and Faith

Preaching Worldly Pessimism

Through the middle decades of the sixteenth century, evangelical preachers and publicists showed a deepening historical pessimism that sometimes came to border on outright despair. As the years passed the prospects for Germany, Christendom, and the whole world seemed to grow continually darker, while warnings about imminent divine punishment and the Last Judgment itself took on greater weight among those who saw themselves as Luther's inheritors. Several general reasons for this trend are not hard to discern. The reform movement had done much to turn religious attention away from medieval ritual traditions, focusing it instead on prayer and prophecy. But the early excitement over Luther's recovery of the gospel and his discovery of the Antichrist in the Roman papacy were gradually dampened by time and by a host of dispiriting circumstances. From the 1540s, these developments included the war of the Protestant cities and territories against the emperor, the hugely divisive religious and political temporizing measures known as the Interims, intense intra-Lutheran theological conflicts, new challenges within the Empire from both Catholics and Calvinists, and a somber apprehension that the progress of the gospel had stalled. The intensification of an apocalyptic worldview among evangelicals in this era was both a reaction to deepening disappointment over the world's stubborn refusal to take God's word to heart, and a result of the need to maintain a sense of prophetic assurance in the face of disorienting changes.

In seeking out causes of this darkening mood, however, we also need to consider the inherited culture of popular astrology in the German towns, channeled and reinforced from the 1530s on by the campaign headquartered at Wittenberg, and booming to unprecedented levels in the second half of the century. Throughout the later Reformation era the ubiquitous popular practicas and related genres grew ever fuller with predictions of calamity, suffering, divine punishment, the Last Judgment, and the end of the world. This aspect of harsh admonitory preaching gained powerful sanction from the Melanchthonian doctrine that the stars were teachers of the law. As in the pre-Luther era, the practicas would prove a nearly perfect vehicle for the articulation and channeling of vague but widely shared fears; the astrologers were always on the lookout for future threats, imbalances, and disasters. And as we have seen in earlier settings, it was but a short step from predicting worldly catastrophe to denouncing human sin and announcing the inevitable punishment to come. At the same time, advocates of the stellar art remained wedded to the notion that some sort of cosmic order would carry through to the end of time; God's glory and grace would remain for faithful eyes. The practica writers thus embraced at least implicitly a paradoxical vision of the natural creation as hopelessly corrupt and yet divinely structured to maintain life. This vision allowed these publicists to cooperate closely with the evangelical clergy in preaching a highly conservative and defensive apocalyptic message that shaped Luther's movement into a distinct confession.

In the late 1520s most forecasters had tended to ease off the disaster sirens of the flood panic. Over the following generation this partial pullback helped make room for the cautious hope of evangelical humanists that Christians were teachable, and that at least some worldly problems might be ameliorated. In the practicas of city physicians such as Anton Brelochs of Schwäbisch Hall, the belief often peeked through that a newly revived and reformed mathematics might overcome a host of social ills, including those caused by the irregular, confusing, and burdensome demands of the traditional religious order. Thus too these forecasts could include modestly reassuring visions of prosperity for at least the near future. Brelochs declared that in 1535 Germany and neighboring lands were likely to enjoy "a highly fortunate and happy condition" on the whole, even if several high rulers would be plagued by enemies and fatal illnesses. While astrologers' predictions about the crops were most often hedged with major qualifications, they occasionally allowed hopes for an abundant growing season. Achilles Gasser of Feldkirch expected a generally good and fruitful year for 1545, though naturally he did not rule out major mishaps, especially in light of an expected eclipse of the sun and an ominous planetary opposition. In some cases writers tried to soften the grim outlook they found in the stars by working to head off needless and excessive alarm. In his predictions for 1540, Johann Schöner counseled his readers "not to be so very terrified" over the likelihood of dread diseases, "for they will not all come at one time." In fact the cycle of seasons ahead would see its share of peace and happiness.[1] These writers shared with many in their network a guarded notion that with proper star-guided discipline the German faithful might mitigate their vices, and thus enjoy some measure of stability and peace.

But if such efforts at public reassurance were partly related to the positive thrust of an educational campaign, they also revealed persisting, even rising fears of social disorder. Most practica writers tended to tiptoe around any potentially volatile social or political issue; this was especially the case in making predictions about "the common people." Several of Brelochs's forecasts anticipated great suffering among the peasants. Many would rise up against their rulers, but "a quick death and many grievous illnesses" would be their main rewards. Here was far less a prognosis than a reflection of prevalent social dread and a barely veiled warning. Obvious worries about public order also surfaced in continued dwelling on the evils of usury and speculation. Just as in the practicas of earlier decades, authors of the 1530s and 1540s fretted openly about the use of their predictions by those who would unscrupulously play on public nerves. Thus Schöner refused to say much about how the crops would do in 1534, lest he lead the usurers to gouge the poor. The moneylenders always turned first to the chapter on fruitfulness, he wrote, "and as soon as they see the least indication of a shortage, they yell in all the streets 'Hunger! Hunger! Thirst! Thirst!'" Nicholas Pruckner of Strasbourg made a related point: no one was to think that his predictions gave any basis for speculation or hoarding. The local authorities should guard against future emergencies by keeping adequate stores of grain, and should at all costs avoid joining the Jews in riding down the poor. Matthias Brotbeihel likewise acknowledged that he avoided talk of shortages so as not to harm the common good by encouraging the speculators and usurers.[2] Admonitions and moralizing about economic crimes and abuses would continue through the sixteenth century, though they would gradually fade in the shadow of a broader and deeper sense of worldly despair.

Among the majority of the calendar and practica writers, the anticlerical tendencies of the pre-Reformation era did not wane. We have seen that both implicit and explicit attacks on the traditional calendar of saints' days and related practices remained common fare. The priestly hierarchy was similarly a continuing target, again often indirectly through unfavorable forecasts. Bartholomew Mangolt predicted that in 1532 Christendom would suffer all sorts of shocks and troubles, but among those he singled out were "the clerics, such as bishops, nuns, monks, and priests, [who] will be scorned and persecuted, and their worldly rule will be reduced." Equally typical was a prediction of Brelochs about the effects of Saturn and Mars in Leo: those who adhered to the Roman Church and clergy would see "nothing but envy, hatred, [and] hostility from princes, lords, knightly men, and the common people too." While such wishful expressions may have complemented the aggressive campaign of the evangelical humanists against anything viewed as superstition, they also reflected ongoing fears of priestly power at a time when everything about the religious and political future of the Empire seemed uncertain. Even Peter Apian perpetuated this well-established trend among German humanists, writing in his practica for 1532 that "the holy father the Pope and his cardinals will have little good fortune this year; the same goes for priests . . . and in general all spiritual persons."[3]

Yet priests and monks posed only one sort of danger to a world in crisis. Indeed, even as the growing network of physicians, teachers, pastors, printers, and publicists worked to give the stars a central role in ordering the burgeoning lay culture of the evangelical towns, perceptions of the worldly future grew grimmer. Already with the great comet of 1531, a new wave of threats and warnings arose. Broadly representative was Johann Schöner's pamphlet, which combined a fully Aristotelian and Ptolemaic analysis of the phenomenon with earnest preaching on its signification of the divine punishments that would herald the Last Day itself. The Nuremberg mathematician also made reference to apocalyptic passages from Matthew, Mark, and Luke, echoing Luther's affirmation that such wondrous heavenly signs were multiplying quickly with the nearing end. Several writers, including the Zurich city physician Christopher Clauser, claimed to have predicted the comet even as they expounded on its awful meanings for the earthly future. Warnings of widespread calamities in the comet's wake came from formal adherents to the traditional faith such as Apian and Johann Virdung as well. While these older humanist astrologers preferred to play down direct end-time references, their chilling forecasts were unlikely to hinder the evangelical cause.[4]

Like the comet tracts, the annual practicas presented their grim forecasts as consistent with the best natural evidence and careful reckonings. Schöner's yearly works showed his concern with mathematical precision, but also expressed his fervent longing that the heavenly signs should spur his readers to return to the way of the Lord, "which we have long since put aside for the sake of worldly honor and riches." In his practica for 1538 he followed the standard form, offering a typical prefatory assertion of astrology's value to the Christian life, then supplying astronomical data and weather forecasts along with expectations for illness, health, the harvest, and other mundane matters. Yet he also included predictions that recent eclipses and coming planetary conjunctions would lead to widespread war and bloodshed, to "scorning and destruction of good, godly laws and customs," and to falsehood and injustice in hearts and minds, "not of the common man alone, but also among the great lords, and especially among middle-aged persons," who were especially prone to the baleful influence of Mars. This sort of admonitory moralizing emerged seamlessly from the astrologer's reckonings. Similarly in his *Practica Teutsch* for 1539 the Ulm physician Gregor Saltzmann offered detailed data, and went on to explain that an expected eclipse of the sun would be a clear warning from on high. "We have the day, the light, the gospel, Christ," wrote Saltzmann, but now like the sun the saving light of the world was being darkened. No one watched out for his neighbor any longer; all were growing blind as the golden rule was simply forgotten. The world had failed to come together in Christ, and the miseries portended by the stars would be the righteous punishments of the Lord.[5]

The mood among these publicists was evidently sinking fast when in 1544 Walter Hermann Ryff predicted "much unrest, quarrelling, contention, fighting, murder, and many sorts of misery on all sides." Among the major causes of open wars and violent hatred would be "matters of religious belief." The city physician Dionysius Sibenburger was increasingly strident in denouncing threats to the community; he worried that "all sorts of financial swindling, subtle underhandedness," and a thousand other kinds of greed were infecting the lives of citizens. In the eyes of the Strasbourg astronomer Nicholas Pruckner, the princes and ruling classes were as guilty as anyone else. Some mighty ones were "so drunk in their own dreams and fancies that they completely scorn [the astrologers' warnings]," and were thus like unreasoning beasts who look upon the heavens without knowledge or understanding, "as a cow stares at a new gate." Pruckner predicted that the influence of Mars in Cancer would mean radical upsets in all realms of life. "But what does it help to warn?" he asked in near hopelessness. "The counsel of poor people goes for nothing." One tried to make holders of power aware of the dangers, "but it is all in vain. Their scorn is without end or measure."[6]

The stargazers were by no means alone in their slide to pessimism. Toward the end of his life, Martin Luther grew notoriously gloomy and despairing about worldly conditions. The outlook of the practica writers broadly paralleled his emotional trajectory. And as the tone of the annual forecasts began to grow notably bleaker, they incorporated more and more explicit religious preaching. Just as the Weimar critics Aurifaber and Stoltz noted, the years around 1540 saw a swift rise in the number of openly religious and especially biblical references. In his forecast for that year Burkhard Mithob dwelled emphatically upon Leviticus 26, a litany of the harsh punishments the Lord would send upon those who failed to keep his commandments. And the larger meaning was clear: "we are those over whom the end of the world is come."[7] This even as Mithob presented an otherwise upbeat Melanchthonian lecture about the enormous benefits of stellar study for practical human welfare. His approach to the art, like that of most practica writers for decades to come, was largely shaped by a more or less self-conscious limitation to the realm of law. Yet within this realm these astrologers could and did denounce ever more severely the sin they saw metastasizing around them, drawing freely and with rising frequency on the words of the Old Testament prophets.

Imbuing their forecasts with more and more sermonic content, popular forecasters such as Anton Brelochs turned to the angriest passages of the prophets to show God's ire at the sinfulness, disobedience, and ungratefulness of his people. In his practica for 1545, for example, Brelochs prominently cited verses from Isaiah and Jeremiah. In Isaiah 13:11, the Lord warned that "I will punish the world for its evil, and the wicked for their iniquity; I will put an end to the pride of the arrogant, and lay low the haughtiness of the ruthless." Jeremiah 9: 9 bewailed the lies and iniquity of Israel: "Shall I not punish them for these things? says the Lord; and shall I not avenge myself on a nation such as this?"[8] Again, these biblical warnings did not displace the nature-based observations and forecasts; rather they appeared as virtually inescapable complements and conclusions. Indeed the analysis of the natural signs afforded a nearly perfect platform for pounding home the message of divine wrath over a world mired in sin. Even practicas that advertised themselves as purely natural in content began to include Old Testament references showing God's wrath at the sinfulness, disobedience, and ungratefulness of his people. Without abandoning their goal of supplying the data needed to guide an ordered personal, family, and civil life, the practica writers seized eagerly upon the potential of their medium to stoke elemental fears, and thus finally perhaps to awaken minds and hearts.

Prevailing perceptions grew even uglier during the years of war, factionalism, and confusion that followed Luther's death in 1546. To be sure, hopes for the future could still surface when circumstances appeared momentarily propitious. In 1548, for instance, despite the defeat of the Protestant League of Schmalkalden by the Emperor Charles, the medical doctor Balthasar Eisslinger could still see a glimmer of promise in the Elector Frederick III's introduction of Lutheran teaching and practice in the Palatinate. Considering the thoroughly awful heavenly aspects for the year ahead, he nonetheless consoled himself and his readers with a prayer "that the greater part of these stellar effects will be prevented or greatly softened by the currently undertaken Reformation and amendment, as the Almighty will allow this to happen."[9] But it seems unlikely that Eisslinger found his prayer answered, for the broader trajectory of events was accompanied by a deepening general gloom.

Anton Brelochs foresaw shattering conflicts and wasting diseases breaking out in 1548; he called for zealous prayer that the Almighty God might turn away his furious wrath. Dionysius Sibenburger was plainly disgusted with all the fools who cried out "Dear Astronomer, when will things go better for once?" His reply revealed apprehensions inseparable from his study of celestial science: "Never," he wrote, " for not until the world betters itself will the influence of the stars improve." Melanchthon's learned associate Georg Joachim Rheticus issued a popular practica for 1551 fronted by a sensationally grisly woodcut depicting death hewing down the human race, while above the clouds a judging Christ appeared. In the text that followed, natural predictions were accompanied by heavy preaching against the sinful lives of his contemporaries. "Although all of this is zealously expressed by Christian preachers," explained Rheticus, "I wished to offer here a short and not unsuitable reminder." According to Simon Heuring, physician at Hagenau, impiety and wickedness now reigned more fully than in any age since the world had begun; hypocrisy and lies infected not only the common people, but also those who were supposed to rule. Hate, vice, and division could hardly grow any worse. "I will leave it to almighty God, who knows how to deal with these things, and thus move on to conclude [my prediction] with Messahala."[10]

The famous Peace of Augsburg in 1555 failed utterly to impress our commentators, whose warnings about war, disease, natural catastrophes, moral breakdown, treachery, ecclesio-political chaos, and the spreading reign of death painted an ever more fearsome picture. And while attacks such as those of the Weimar theologians and Thomas Erastus may have pushed a few writers to greater caution in making direct appeals to scripture, any such hesitations about connecting the stars with the words of the prophets proved short-lived. We are already laid waste by diseases, wrote Jerome Brotbeihel in 1559, but surely far worse was coming, for rarely if ever had the heavens indicated such a terrible change in nature as they did now. Year after year, drawing on sources from Jeremiah to the Arab authority Haly Abenragel, Brotbeihel foresaw the planets bringing nothing but injury, destruction, and suffering, and called in earnest but often nearly hopeless words for each and every person to repent. Similar uses of the prophets along with natural-scientific authorities abounded in the works of major publicists such as Joachim Heller, whose Nuremberg practicas were among the most widely read and imitated of all by the early 1560s. Heller's forecast for 1561 pointedly adverted to Amos 8:11: "Behold the days are coming, says the Lord God, when I will send a famine on the land: not a famine of bread, nor a thirst for water, but of hearing the word of God." In Heller's eyes, the Lord's punishments were already falling heavily on high and low, young and old, clergy and laymen; the causes included "scorn and persecution of the divine word, tyranny, the shedding of innocent blood . . . every sort of horrible error, factions and sects overriding the acknowledged truth of the gospel, war and murder, stealing and robbing, usury, fleecing and hoarding, lies and offenses, adultery and lewdness, gluttony and drunkenness, every pomp and excess." Such vices were no longer counted sins. Every estate had taken a filthy path, so that no true improvement of any sort could be hoped for. This wild and godless world could look forward to nothing but the most painful penalties.[11]

For Christian Heiden, Heller's successor as head of the Nuremberg Gymnasium, unworthy pastors who failed to uphold the gospel held a notable share in the universal guilt. One might perhaps still cling to shaky hopes that secular rulers would act to defend God's Word, but in truth every person was responsible for the desperately needed general repentance. Georg Meder of Kitzingen posed the question squarely: "Have not all sins mounted to the highest degree among the great lords just as among the common people?" Nothing more was to be expected before the end than the horrific advent of Gog and Magog. But whatever form the coming calamities might take, no one was immune. Mainly on the basis of a 1560 solar eclipse, Jerome Brotbeihel foretold that even pious and peaceful princes would be swept into shockingly bloody and destructive wars, resulting in "more sin, shame, vice and danger than a mouth can express." We will take no warning, he wrote, no matter what one writes or says; "thus all is lost." Caspar Pontanus of Lübeck foresaw an infinity of troubles coming for everyone, including "both spiritual and worldly Lords"; horrors ranging from deadly plagues to unprecedented social breakdown were announced by shocking monstrous births as well as by the stars.[12]

While the astrologers often made predictions for lands outside Germany or the Empire, these were on the whole much briefer and more general than those about matters closer to home. Moreover, if any nation or group deserved singling out for its sins and guilt, the Germans held center stage. As the element of sermonic chastisement intensified in the annual forecasts, the overwhelming culpability of the German people was rarely absent from the picture. Several forecasters appear to have drawn on published collections of Luther's bleak prophecies for Germany and Christendom that began to appear in the 1550s.[13] Looking ahead to 1562 and subsequent years, Gregor Fabricius foresaw the coming of ever-greater religious error and disunity. The Germans, he observed despairingly, were tired of the gospel. Always searching for something new and exciting, they were taking on the characteristics of Epicureans or Jews; as a result God would inflict the most horrible forms of justice upon them. Victorin Schönfelt's practica for 1563 showed the forces of the Empire gambling perilously with the Pope, the Turks, and death itself (see Figure 6.1). Another of his yearly forecasts illustrated its central theme with a personified Germania consigned to storms and flames. Yet another was fronted with a phrase from Isaiah 47 inscribed on a coffin: "VLTIONEM CAPIAM": "I will take vengeance"; the booklet concluded with a gruesome scenario of destruction at the hands of Gog and Magog, either Turks or Muscovites. Johann Hebenstreit castigated readers for failing to reform their sinful lives, so that "faith, love, and trust wane from day to day, while God's word is daily falsified by unlearned, prideful, fanatical asses." The Almighty was preparing to deal the Germans the full deserts of their ingratitude. The same author's forecast for 1568 depicted Germania as a woman under attack from the East, losing her crown and her riches.[14] No informed reader would fail to realize that the demise of the Empire would mark the end of the fourth Danielic imperium, thus the end of the world. Through both words and images, Hebenstreit's works poured out a bitter brew of astrological and biblical end-time imagery (see Figure 6.2).

FIGURE 6.1 The forces of the Empire gamble with Death, the Pope, and the Turks under the influence of eclipses and a conjunction of Saturn and Jupiter in Cancer. Title page illustration from Victorin Schönfelt's practica for 1563. Reproduced from Heinz Artur Strauss, *Der astrologische Gedanke in der deutschen Vergangenheit* (Munich, 1926).

Although Schönfelt, Hebenstreit and their fellow students of the stars regularly appealed to history and experience to show that certain heavenly signs had always been followed by this or that sort of punitive disaster, they left little room for doubt that all these earthly calamities and sufferings were but anticipations of the final reckoning for eternity.[15] The punishments were multiplying as the end approached; they were above all prefigurings and preparations inseparable from the apocalyptic context. The Last Judgment was to be the final and most terrible correction to a sinful world, as well as the final testing of the faithful in the fire. Heller made the point plainly in his outlook for 1561: the chastisements announced by the stars would culminate in "final destruction and collapse." Commenting on the terrible effects expected from the 1564 great conjunction of Jupiter and Saturn, Gregor Fabricius railed against the sinful and "epicurean" lives of his day, foreseeing wasting waves of disease,

PROGNOSTICON
HISTORICVM vnd PHY=
SICVM.

Auffs M. D. LXbj. Jhar/ Darinne al
lerley künfftige voranderung/ auff vorgangene gleiche
Exempla / gegründet werden/ Warnungs
weise gestalt.

Magog Papa, petent Arctoas milite terras.

imperijs victus Morte Monarcha cadet.

Cæsareo dabitur digna Corona viro.

Fact conuersa, renouatio fiet in ipsis.

Durch Joannem Hebenstreidt/ PHILO=
SOPHIAE & Medicinæ Doctorem, der Friedestadt
Erffordt Phisicum, vnnd Medicinæ lectorem
Ordinarium.

FIGURE 6.2 Title page from Johann Hebenstreit's *Prognosticon Historicum und Physicum* (Erfurt, 1565). Eclipses at the dragon's head and tail (ascending and descending nodes of the moon) threaten the northern lands. Courtesy of the Bayerische Staatsbibliothek München, Res/4 Astr.p. 446#Beibd.21.

enormous upheavals in both the worldly and spiritual realms, a bloody onslaught of the Turks, intense persecution of God's Word, and finally the Last Day itself; he prayed that the Lord might "graciously protect his scorned little band of Christians, and hold them steady in the true faith until the end." The young pastor-astrologer Hieronymus Wilhelm insisted that the warnings of the stars merely confirmed a clear Old-Testament truth: as soon as God's people turned away from him, he placed them in their enemies' hands and sent every sort of affliction upon them. Wilhelm emphasized that no lesson was more important "in these last times," when even the sordidness of Sodom and Gomorrah was outdone.[16]

What we might see as a logical inconsistency between an ongoing pattern of conditional punishments on one hand, and an apocalyptic vision of inevitable finality on the other, was merely one manifestation of the existential paradox that stood at the very heart of Christian teaching, especially in the Augustinian tradition: God was in full control, his plan eternal, yet his word called upon humans to change their hearts, minds, and lives. The abstract discordance between concepts of the ineluctable and the possible posed no more trouble for our practica writers than it did for evangelical pastors in their preaching. As the astrologers repeatedly reminded their readers, their forecasts were always less than certain because of God's power to answer prayer. It was indeed standard for a practica to include prayers in the dedicatory preface, in the conclusion, or scattered throughout, that God would turn away the expected disasters and sufferings and send instead the blessing of a peaceful, healthy, and fruitful year. These were by no means stock formulaic expressions, but rather earnest appeals to the Almighty for mercy. Typical was Nicholas Caesarius's call to repentance, clinging to the possibility that the Lord would "turn aside the well-deserved punishment that shall fall upon us Germans."[17] Just as in countless Lutheran sermons, the story of the Ninivites from the Book of Joel became stock material in the yearly practicas; here God withheld his punishment from a people whose repentance was full and sincere.

Yet the example of the Ninivites did not soften the hard truth that a frightful and eternal judgment loomed over all, especially those to whom the gospel had been preached openly and clearly but who now ignored this greatest of gifts. Any lightening of the punishments would be purely an act of grace, and as the atmosphere of fearful expectancy continued to feed on itself, it seemed less and less likely that the Lord would actually turn away the disasters heralded by the stars; the only true escape for the faithful would be at the Last Day. Hopes that any true inner transformation might actually be forthcoming and that God would overrule the stars grew ever more tenuous. This sort of heavy pessimism toward the earthly future, often joined with fervid appeals for repentance on both personal and communal levels, became a remarkably consistent feature in the writings of the popular astrological literature. The perspectives they conveyed were by no means incidental accretions to evangelical culture; rather they both reflected and helped to shape the outlook of Luther's heirs toward themselves and their movement.

Once more we see how important it is to avoid reading back into this sixteenth-century world an inherent and inevitable opposition between humanistic astrology and biblical apocalypticism. Scholars who adopt this model of irreconcilability argue that the principles underlying astrology ultimately implied ongoing natural cycles and historical continuity, while a perspective stressing New Testament prophecies of the end and Luther's discovery of the Antichrist in the Roman Papacy posed a vision of radical historical discontinuity and finality.[18] But this supposed incompatibility does not appear to have weighed on the minds of our Lutheran preachers and practica writers. Just like biblical texts, the stars could be deployed either to support or to oppose apocalyptic expectancy. Rather than assuming a fundamental conflict between astrological and evangelical biblical outlooks, we need to recognize two forms of apocalyptic imagery, which in the setting of Reformation Germany were mutually and powerfully reinforcing. Both moved increasingly toward a stark pessimism regarding the worldly future. Both presented an essentially paradoxical juxtaposition of divine order and sinful disorder in nature and history, a paradox that resonated, if perhaps only vaguely and unconsciously, with evangelical teachings on law and gospel. Recognizing this resonance helps us see that the pervasive mixing of astrological and biblical themes and imagery was anything but a peripheral influence on the formation of a Lutheran confessional culture.

Order, Chaos, and the Last Day

The theological quarrels of the Reformation intensified basic questions about the ways in which God exercised his rule in the natural world, and how he revealed his power in that world. The problem of whether the Almighty governed through an unchanging order ("general providence"), or through direct and unpredictable acts of will ("special providence") was an old scholars' debate that went back centuries in medieval thought. But as Charlotte Methuen points out, "it was in the sixteenth century, and particularly in the thought of the forerunners of Lutheran orthodoxy, that it gained importance."[19] The issue had basically to do with perceptions of order and disorder in nature itself. Did God rule the world essentially through secondary causes predictable by natural law, or did absolute divine control at every moment mean that nature posed mainly a field of wonder and awe? If one acknowledged—as virtually everyone did—that stellar patterns and events were causes of, or at least powerful influences on, earthly events, could acquired knowledge about such patterns and causes offer some sort of insight into the divine plan? Or was it the case that while one could learn about natural patterns just as the ancient pagans had done, these regularities had no meaning in themselves; when God used the natural world to convey supernatural messages, he did so directly through highly unusual, unpredictable, and even unique phenomena? As we noted earlier, historians have often analyzed the differences between Melanchthon and Luther on the value of astrology in some such terms, but in a way that overemphasizes the contrast and tensions between them.

These issues took on new weight at this time partly because Reformation thinkers approached them not simply as abstract scholastic problems, but against a background of ever more pressing questions about history and apocalyptic prophecy. Did the unfolding of God's plan for history mean that he would uphold the basic order of his creation to the very end? Could one depend on nature's gifts from day to day? Or did the providential plan to punish sin mean that God was allowing the natural order to crumble, so that it became mainly a medium for miraculous signs that pointed to crisis and the Last Judgment? Evangelical thinkers such as Jacob Andreae, Jacob Heerbrand, and Matthias Haffenreffer debated the matter at length in learned treatises.[20] But while these and other scholars argued over the priority of one or the other sort of divine governance, none could finally avoid acknowledging at least implicitly with Melanchthon that both were at work; the Lord's rule over creation was manifest in his maintenance of nature's established order as well as in his breathtaking violations of that order. This dual perspective came across often in published evangelical sermons as well as in the yearly stellar forecasts.

Speaking in 1558 about the certainty of God's judgment over all crea-tures, for instance, the highly active preacher Tilemann Heshusius expounded on the ways in which nature revealed the almighty power behind such judgment. While "the beautiful, orderly, and certain course of the heavens" testified to this power, so too did "the great, shocking, unusual acts of God, which transcend the understanding of all men and angels." The preacher and sometime church superintendent Johann Wigand, a passionate adherent to Gnesio-Lutheran views, acknowledged both perspectives, if less consciously, in a 1571 sermon on the Last Times and the coming judgment. In one passage he stressed that an aging and tired world was patently cracking up: "now it comes to its sad end, groaning, cracking, and crashing in every corner and part, and nature becomes feeble and exhausted." Yet soon thereafter he stated in equally plain terms that God had maintained the structure and the elements of his creation unchanged since the beginning, and would so keep them until the very end.[21] Matthew Zeysius, "student of physics and medicine" at Frankfurt an der Oder, offered an analogous double understanding. His practica for 1577 began with a classic lecture on the enormous benefits of the stellar art, and its potent testimony that an eternal and almighty creator continued to rule over and maintain the beautiful structure of the world and all that lived and moved within it. A few pages on, the author drew on prophecies of both the Old and New Testaments to show a world staggering under a burden of sin, already reeling as God prepared to deliver the final blow.[22] Consciously or not, preachers and practica writers not only accepted but promoted the same apocalyptic paradox. Life in these last times meant a tense suspension—and at times a wild vacillation—between polar perceptions of universal order and disorder.

No doubt instances of disorder were the easier to advertise. Strange and shocking events had an immediate appeal in the mass market, and the 1550s and 1560s brought a surge of publications dedicated to broadcasting news of them. This acceleration paralleled not only the tremendous proliferation of calendar and practica editions in these decades, but also the advent of printed collections of Luther's dark predictions for whatever time was left before the end, and a thickening swarm of apocalyptic sermons and didactic eschatological tracts.[23] A sustained cloudburst of cheap broadsides and pamphlets fell in the burgher realm, illustrating and describing an almost limitless range of weird phenomena, both celestial and terrestrial, from monstrous births to deadly earthquakes, from visions of armies clashing in the night sky to massively ruinous lightning strikes. Most of these announcements included heated warnings and moralizing about the ominous meanings of such happenings; many spoke openly of divine punishment and judgment. More expansive and systematic were the larger bound collections that formed the genre of the evangelical wonder book. As Philip Soergel has shown in a penetrating study, these works evolved in a process of "continual cross-fertilization" with the proliferating pamphlets and broadsides. Major wonder books by authors such as Job Fincel (1556, 1559, 1562), Caspar Goltwurm (1557), and

Christoph Irenaeus (1556, 1578, 1584) worked to assemble the myriad, multiplying freaks and rarities into fearsome lessons for a sinful world desperately in need of discipline.[24]

The wonder books painted a picture of a weakening nature, ever more subject to satanic subversion, on the verge of collapse. Yet even these works had to recognize the continuation of some sort of order as long as the world stood. Most of them were organized chronologically, so that by studying wondrous appearances and events in the past one might learn something about how particular signs were related to one another and to subsequent events. This approach was especially notable in the collections of Fincel, the most widely read of all the evangelical wonder-writers. But ultimately more significant for the majority of these authors was a sort of order in disorder, namely the eschatological order revealed by the dramatic multiplication of freakish phenomena in the recent past, evidence of the divine intention to bring all to closure. It was hardly possible to reject the overwhelming evidence that the wondrous signs in all nature had proliferated wildly, especially in the years since Luther had begun his great prophetic work; indeed Fincel's collections began with the year 1517. The sudden mushrooming of signs revealed at least the basic outline of God's plan in these Last Times. The wonder book authors were not greatly concerned with a problem that had nagged at Luther, namely that strange and shocking events might come from the Devil as easily as from God. They seem to have assumed that dramatic warnings about divine punishment and the nearing Judgment would not serve the Devil's purposes very well. The accelerating pace of amazing phenomena in the Last Days made sense not as a rash of demonic delusions, but as a series of ever-clearer announcements of God's intentions. In all these ways the wonder literature reflected assumptions shared by the practica writers as well.

Unlike the annual stellar predictions, though, the wonder books did not take as their starting point the goal of establishing a secure orientation in natural time and space. They presented no data so basic and mundane as a calendar, weather predictions, or the best days to bathe; they made no claim to practical daily uses. Despite the profoundly sober messages their authors sought to convey, their public appeal was rooted first and foremost in rank sensationalism and an often morbid curiosity. Their exclusive dwelling on weird, upsetting, largely unpredictable happenings could easily evoke a world in such thorough disarray that the gritty concerns of everyday life virtually faded into insignificance. As Soergel puts it, for readers of such a collection "it might have been difficult to presume that any order was present in nature at all."[25] In the eyes of Christoph Irenaeus, the creation had become so corrupted that it was loathsome to God; here the world was so utterly fallen that forecasts about next season's crops or the likelihood of winter agues were not only impossible, but utterly beside the point. In short, while these authors spoke in terms of God's rule over nature, their interest in the realities of human life in the natural world remained fairly abstract. They were "theological commentators" concerned more with eternal than with practical truths.[26] As massively popular as the literature of wonders became, then, these writings were arguably less intimately connected than the annual astrological publications with the lived experience of evangelical townsfolk, and revealed less about the complex mixture of human hopes and fears that defined their culture.

Although terrestrial freaks and disasters of all sorts drew intensive attention in broadsheets and wonder books, for virtually all observers the signs in the heavens above were the most dramatic as well as the most necessary to describe and interpret. From midcentury on the question loomed ever larger: were these signs to be understood as those predicted by Christ himself in the gospels, or even those mentioned in the Book of Revelation? Some preachers and writers showed concern about the danger of equating the current signs of corruption directly with the final collapse at the time of the Last Judgment. Andreas Musculus argued that recent and current eclipses and other natural movements in the heavens were not actually the signs of which the Lord spoke in Luke 21 and elsewhere. Only when the sun and moon went dark and the skies truly caved in would the final destruction come. The wonder book author Fincel basically agreed on this point: regular events such as eclipses and conjunctions could not be counted as those that the Lord had meant when he spoke of the sun and the moon going dark and the stars falling. Nor indeed could the freakish occurrences that were so obviously multiplying in the heavens and in terrestrial nature. The world was full of countless signs of divine wrath and intent, but when Christ finally returned, he would truly come without warning, "as a thief in the night."[27] We noted Johann Wigand's similar insistence that although the wondrous signs of the approaching Last Day were evident everywhere, God would maintain the basic order and the elements of the world until the very moment when he brought it all to an end. When the time came at last, the entire earth and the heavens together would burn up in an instant.[28] Yet most preachers and practica writers did not distinguish consistently between past or present signs and those

that the Bible prophesied as announcing Christ's return. The key scriptural passages were themselves open to interpretation in regard to which
signs would precede the end, and which would immediately announce
and accompany it.

Nor for most was it possible to see wondrous phenomena as fully separate from predictable patterns. To be sure, almost all informed observers
acknowledged a theoretical difference. Yet Luther himself, we remember,
had not hesitated to recognize predictable planetary conjunctions and
eclipses as biblical signs, and for the stargazers even the most freakish
heavenly apparition was subject to analysis in terms of its time and its
placement in relation to the planets, the zodiac, the terrestrial houses, the
horizons, and so on. Any phenomenon appearing to the external senses
had a natural aspect, after all, however the Almighty had chosen to work
it. Some astrologers contended that many of the strange and frightening
signs God was sending were not in fact violations of the natural order;
rather, they simply transcended human understanding of that order. But
such points of principle had limited weight in practice. In his forecast for
1572 the pastor Johannes Rhau explained what amounted to the prevailing
view: all the heavenly phenomena, not just wondrous appearances but also
regular ones such as conjunctions, oppositions, quadratures, and eclipses,
had to be regarded as signs with prophetic meaning in these final, desperate times. Even such an ardent Gnesio-Lutheran preacher as Bartholomew
Gernhard stood fast in agreement on this point.[29]

Again, while the nearly universal assumption was that the world was
indeed growing old, clouds of ambiguity surrounded this notion. Did
the decrepitude of age mean that some normal natural functioning had
already ceased? Or would all the essential life processes continue until the
heart stopped beating? The teaching that the fundamental constitution of
nature would stand as long as the world itself had inherent appeal for any
astrologer who saw himself as a scientist inquiring into natural laws, but
also for any theologian who insisted that a good God would not abandon
his creation before he chose to renew it altogether. Thus when Christoph
Stathmion instructed readers of his 1551 forecast that the existing natural order would remain until the end, he was commenting not only on
the astrologer's ability to make natural predictions, but also on an issue
of theological import.[30] On the other hand, the calendar makers could
not easily ignore Melanchthon's sobering acknowledgment that the sun
had sunk closer to the earth. The pastor-astrologer Johann Garcaeus was
among thinkers who picked up on this notion, asserting that the central

and most brilliant star had not only hung lower; it had also become weaker. The sun—indeed the entire firmament—was like a feeble old man, losing strength from day to day. The breakdown that clearly marked the Last Times was thus not only moral, spiritual, and social; it was evident in all nature and in the very condition of the cosmos.[31] But as the final death of the old creation approached, could nature still perform its daily functions? Was it still of any use even to take a pulse? Caspar Peucer, Melanchthon's closest colleague in matters of natural philosophy, came to reject the conclusion that the heavens had contracted because it seemed to threaten any systematic reading of nature at all. Such a view, he thought, did not accord with God's own intention.[32]

In addressing such questions, neither the evangelical astrologer nor the biblical theologian could avoid dealing at least implicitly with matters of world history. Just how far might one be able to discern an overall order, a divine plan, in the course of historical time? The student of the Bible and the fathers had ready at hand such well-established schemes as the four empires of Daniel and the Augustinian six ages of the world. In addition, through his edition of Johann Carion's *Chronicle* Melanchthon had popularized the apocryphal but now increasingly revered "Prophecy of Elias," according to which the world would stand two thousand years before the time of the Mosaic law, another two thousand under the law, and an equal period under the gospel; Luther had used this scheme in structuring his own effort to discern the outlines of world history, the *Supputatio annorum mundi* of 1545.[33] If an extrabiblical scheme such as this might prove so very useful, then what about theories about the periodic conjunctions, which despite their more controversial origins remained as intensively studied and discussed as ever?

The efforts of humanist reformers to distance themselves publicly from the teachings of the Arabs had not deterred the editing and printing of texts from this tradition, and scholars such as Rheticus showed serious interest in historical conjunction theory.[34] Yet the Melanchthonians' strong public advocacy of a return to Ptolemaic purity probably did help dampen open attention to the twenty-year great conjunction of 1544. Thus even as they ramped up their preaching on the need for general obedience and repentance in the 1540s, practica writers devoted far more attention to other threatening stellar phenomena, especially eclipses. In the years following Luther's death, however, perceived prospects for the evangelical movement grew so stunningly negative, and threatening portents appeared to multiply so dramatically, that fewer hesitations arose about exploring the world-historical meaning of the great conjunctions. It now seemed increasingly pointless to play down or ignore the likelihood that these major celestial events held clues to God's design in these last times.

It was no accident that the most notoriously influential of all sixteenth-century writings on the theme came from within the ranks of the Melanchthonians. In 1564 Cyprian von Leowitz issued at Lauingen his *Historical Account of the Great Conjunctions of the Upper Planets, Eclipses of the Sun, and Comets, with their Effects in the Fourth Monarchy* in both Latin and German editions.[35] Presented as a chronicle and analysis of all significant conjunctions, solar eclipses, and comets since the beginning of the fourth Danielic (i.e., Roman) empire along with predictions "for the next twenty years" (i.e., 1564–1584), this was essentially a work of Lutheran apocalyptic interpretation and propaganda. The book made an enormous international splash, but it would reverberate most deeply among German evangelicals, for many of whom it focused a host of vague fears in a way that would show some parallels with the run-up to the supposed flood year of 1524.

Of Bohemian noble background, Leowitz had pursued mathematics at Wittenberg in the 1540s, and he remained in close contact with Melanchthon thereafter. As a young man he stood squarely in the ranks of the evangelical campaign against superstition, fully sharing the view of his own time as bringing both a great recovery of the gospel and an associated flowering of the arts and sciences. Highly active as an author and editor of astronomical and astrological works, including his own annual almanacs reckoned for Augsburg, he first gained widespread notice with his *Eclipsum omnium* of 1556, a computation of all eclipses expected for the period 1554 to 1604. But his renown skyrocketed with the *Historical Account*, which went through multiple editions and was translated into several languages. Leowitz apparently composed the work at the request of the newly elected "Roman King" Maximilian, soon to ascend the Imperial throne as Maximilian II (1564–1576), whose rumored openness to Lutheran teachings fueled furtive dreams of a Protestant *Imperium* among evangelical rulers and elites.[36]

Leowitz did his best to find order, and even a slice of worldly hope, in the mounting chaos. He took a good deal of his material from the major world-chronologies of his day, especially from the *Chronicle* of Carion and Melanchthon in its later, revised editions. But his *Historical Account* placed far more emphasis on stellar patterns, especially those of the great, greater, and greatest conjunctions.[37] Leowitz followed numerous precedents in theorizing that the world would see a total of seven of the greatest kind, each separated by just under 800 years, and each marking a hugely significant transition from the watery to the fiery trigon. The last three all fell within the span of the final world monarchy, that of the Romans. The first had come in 6 B.C., shortly before the birth of Christ, the second during the crucially important reign of Charlemagne. The third and last would come in 1584, with a final transition out of the water and into the fire. In each case, the prior twenty-year conjunction was highly significant as well, which meant that the 1564 meeting of Jupiter and Saturn in Leo (very close to the fiery sign of Cancer) merited the closest possible attention.

While the order of the great conjunctions supplied his basic structure, Leowitz gave only a brief and incomplete explanation of this matrix. In fact, few readers were likely to have discerned clearly the regular periods marked by these planetary events as he presented them. Most numerous by far in his chronological list of some 126 celestial events were solar eclipses and comets, for which Leowitz found no consistent historical pattern, but which had nearly always been followed by some sort of calamity. What was evident—indeed obvious—was a dramatic acceleration in the overall frequency of the phenomena. As his narrative reached the sixteenth century, it bristled with signs of major events. In 1513 a solar eclipse in Pisces combined with a dramatic opposition of Mars and Saturn to help bring about a world-historical change. Under these influences "God in his majesty mercifully led us out of the horrible darkness and the shadows of death, namely out of the terrifying tyranny of the Pope and his wicked avarice . . . [and] idolatry, and called us to the bright clear light of his holy gospel, by his chosen instrument Doctor Martin Luther."[38] Over fifty pages of this 120-page history were devoted to the years since Luther had begun to preach. During this time, even as the pure gospel had spread unstoppably, war, murder, natural disasters, disease, and other horrors had thrown the Empire and Christendom into a near-total chaos. More and more outstanding heavenly phenomena piled on top of one another in a way that bore out Luther's comments about the multiplication of divine warning signs before the End. The narrative approached its prophetic epilogue with a feeling of rushing into the maelstrom.

In his appended prophecy, which was integral to the work as a whole, Leowitz pictured a redoubled surge in the pace of worldly changes, offering a scenario that swung wildly between extremes of hopeful dreaming and dark despair.[39] A startling eclipse of the sun in June 1563 would be followed by a series of threatening conjunctions that would continue into

the following year. Then in June and July of 1564 nearly all the planets
would come together in Leo in a congress that could only be compared
to one that had come at the opening of Charlemagne's reign. Just as God
then raised a great ruler to restore both Empire and Church, so now he
would surely bring forth a heroic figure to bring peace, to drive out superstition, and to support the good and useful arts. Here Leowitz addressed
Maximilian directly, explaining that all signs pointed to his taking up this
role. During his reign the momentous shift from the watery to the fiery
trigon would occur. As the most crucial historical moments had come
with such transitions at the times of Caesar Augustus and Charlemagne,
so the way was now open for their final great successor.

But precisely how or when any of this would happen was less than
clear, for immediately after expressing these hopes, Leowitz predicted a
"very great" solar eclipse to come in Aries in April of 1567, and turned to
a forecast of unprecedented division, violence, crime and misery in the
Empire. In 1573 and 1574 the effects of the eclipse would be redoubled by
those of a great opposition of the upper planets and yet another eclipse.
Unspeakably horrifying changes would follow, and then the final flurry of
celestial events: a major conjunction in May of 1583, followed early in 1584
by the great 800-year conjunction along with almost all the other planets
in Aries; then a solar eclipse in Taurus, a congress of the planets in the
twelfth house, a brilliant comet, and a crowd of "wondrous signs" as the
watery trigon came to an end.[40]

Many centuries would have to pass before similar conditions could
recur. But according to the Prophecy of Elias the world could not possibly
last that long; therefore the impending transition to the Fiery Trigon would
surely usher in the end of time. The Lord's own assurance that the days
would be shortened for the sake of the elect made likely the imminence of
his return. An analogy between the six prior 800-year conjunctions and
the traditional Augustinian six ages of the world underlined the point that
Creation had reached the extremity of decrepitude, and was now about to
enter a presumably eternal seventh age. And the association between the
"fiery trigon" and the final flames in which God would destroy the old
creation were too obvious to be ignored. Unlike a number of prominent
sixteenth- and seventeenth-century thinkers such as Jerome Cardano and
Tommaso Campanella for whom the transition to the fiery trigon held out
the promise of a new age of peace, Leowitz and the popularizers who drew
on him associated this event with the combustion of the world at the Last
Judgment.[41] Here Leowitz cited a famous quatrain about the likely end

of the world in 1588; indeed he gave this prophecy its main punch-up in public currency. Yet the particulars of his scenario in this final part of his work tended to fade in a storm of urgency, as Leowitz burst out repeatedly into pained cries over the sinful state of the world, passionate repentance preaching in light of the fearsome chaos to be seen on all sides, and earnest warnings of the approaching Judgment.

Suddenly, at the very end of his text, Leowitz swung to a bold insistence upon the fundamental stability of the natural order. While God was totally free and in no way bound by his creatures, he would not lightly upset or confuse the structure he had established: "As this order has stood from the beginning of the world until now out of God's wondrous and unfathomable decree, so no one should doubt, but rather one should conclude with certainty, that he will maintain this order undisturbed and inviolate to the end of this last age of the world."[42] We can understand this statement only if we appreciate that for Leowitz, as for so many of his evangelical contemporaries, both sin and grace were always at work among his creatures. The perception of ubiquitous disorder and breakdown could never completely cancel the faith that God would somehow sustain his own until he delivered them from this world; indeed given Leowitz's multiple aims it could not even entirely vanquish the slim hope that a divine intervention might effect a final earthly victory of truth. In a sense Leowitz presented one scenario for the old man living under the law, and another for the new man of faith. But the matter was not simply one of threatening disorder versus a consoling order. The regular order of the heavens—revealed most dramatically in the pattern of great conjunctions—could provide assurance that God was following his eternal plan for final and universal justice, and perhaps even a brief worldly glimpse of that reality; yet it also carried warnings about the inevitable judgment that lay ahead. Likewise the mounting signs of celestial disorder may have pointed most directly to the fearsome prospect of the final trials and judgment, but at the same time they promised joyful deliverance to the faithful. Here was a view essentially in line with Luther's own.

In Leowitz's eyes, as in those of the calendar makers and the wonder writers, the more immediate and pressing need was to warn. During the 1560s and 1570s, under the reign of Maximilian II, his work may have helped keep alive a thin and brittle strand of hopes for an empire finally unified under the gospel. But such political dreams never came close to outweighing the terrifying truths that the stars announced more loudly almost every year. In the end Leowitz himself seems hardly to have put much stock in the prospect of a final worldly gospel triumph to be led by the emperor. Instead both celestial order and disorder pointed to the overriding reality of the nearing end. This sort of paradox was basic to the apocalyptic perceptions that prevailed increasingly among his evangelical contemporaries.

Fifteen Eighty-Eight

Tausent/fünffhundert/achtzig acht
Das ist das Jahr/dass ich betracht
Geht im dem die Welt nicht vnter
So geschieht doch sonst gross Wunder.[43]
[Fifteen hundred eighty-eight
That is the year I contemplate
If then the world does not go under
Surely comes some other great wonder.]

The year 1588 stood second only to 1524 as a focus of apocalyptic expectancy and speculation in the sixteenth century. But we know less about the specific origins of the anxious attention to the later year, and almost nothing about the original source of the famous quatrain that anchored it in the realm of mass publicity. The earliest known reference to the 1588 prophecy came from the evangelical humanist Caspar Brusch in the preface to a 1553 Latin work on the fate of the Roman Empire by Engelbert von Admont. Brusch claimed that he had discovered the written prophecy at a monastery in "Noricum" (most likely Austria), and that its author was none other than Regiomontanus, revered as a heroic reviver of astronomical and astrological learning by virtually everyone who felt the influence of the Melanchthonian campaign.[44] Brusch also offered a Latin translation of the prediction which would make it known far beyond the German lands. As in the years before 1524 the anticipations spread on a pan-European scale, yet there can be no question that just as before, the discussion of the prediction grew especially intense among the intelligentsia of the Empire, who learned about it mainly through Leowitz. He repeated Brusch's claim that the prophecy had come from Regiomontanus, which was by itself enough to give it virtually unquestionable authority, although later writers attributed it to various other figures, including Stöffler and Melanchthon. Well-connected and influential humanist astrologers such as Heinrich

Rantzau took the prediction with profound seriousness and discussed it in their correspondence, but the idea would gain its loudest report among German evangelical townsfolk, who read and heard about it through hundreds of practicas, sermons, apocalyptic tracts, pamphlets, and poems.[45] Yet despite all the attention to 1588, the practica writers would tend to keep apocalyptic date-setting at arm's length. In fact, their yearly forecasts showed a general reluctance to present precise prophetic scenarios; like most of their ministerial colleagues, they believed natural evidence should be used to support biblical truths and to keep their evangelical brethren on their toes, but not to forecast the details of the Lord's plan.

A handful of practica writers had called attention to the twenty-year conjunction of 1564 before Leowitz's work appeared. Wolff Geuss, an independent astrologer at Nuremberg, reckoned that the key conjunction would begin in 1563, citing the Jewish-Arabic authority Messahala. Because this meeting would come in the watery trigon, it indicated heavy rains, shipwrecks and much loss of life on the seas, the rise of divisive sects, the clergy drawn into perversion and error, the people seduced into an uproar. But for him as for Leowitz the conjunction was only one of the scores of signs in nature to which preachers, astrologers, and publicists properly called attention more energetically each year.[46] Writing his annual practica for 1564 at Marburg, Victorin Schönfelt stressed that all the regular planetary conjunctions, oppositions, and eclipses together with the recent eruption of countless miraculous signs meant, if not the outright destruction of the world, at least an unprecedented punishment upon mankind. Without doubt they were common indicators of imminent social, political, and even cosmic disintegration. Already the high rulers were so divided that the public welfare and defense had been abandoned. Churches and schools were forsaken; outright anarchy loomed. Nearly all that was left was to call sinners to awaken and repent. None of this, however, prevented either Schönfelt or Geuss from charting out the times of the year ahead, providing weather forecasts, and dwelling on the need for personal and public order.[47]

Other annual writers soon joined in the commentary on the disasters that would no doubt follow the great conjunction of 1564 as well as several recent and anticipated eclipses. In his forecast for 1565 Gregor Fabricius, a physician at Schweinfurth, added to his analysis of these natural effects that "in fact they signify great future upheavals in both spiritual and worldly regiments, a bloody attack of the Turk against us Christians, also other persecutions of the divine word, and finally the Last Day." The hugely successful, ardently Melanchthonian physician Johann Hebenstreit of Erfurt, an energetic propagandist to say the least, drew directly on Leowitz in his *Prognosticon Historicum et Physicum* for 1566. This rambling, heated work, bristling with ominous words about the future of Germany and true gospel teaching, advertised itself with a sensational title page woodcut combining astrological, biblical, and anti-Roman apocalyptic symbolism. Hebenstreit followed the Bohemian astrologer's analysis of recent signs, above all those that happened together in 1563 and 1564, "the like of which we have never heard about in 800 years." He speculated vaguely about some sort of worldwide spread of the truth before the Last Judgment; at the same time he presented an overall prospect rife with terrors and end-time expectancy. He did not, however, refer directly to the 1588 prophecy.[48]

Notably, in fact, most popular astrological writers did not leap right away to include predictions about the great conjunction of 1584 or the prophecy for 1588 in their annual works. Over the decades after Leowitz's work appeared most practicas remained focused primarily on the year ahead, an approach that left room for general forebodings over an indefinite future. Longer-range forecasts necessarily sacrificed some of the more immediate practical purposes of the annual works, but were also probably less attractive because they did not quite suit the sense of urgency in the face of intense theological quarrels, the apparent threat of imminent anarchy, and the genuine conviction that the time was very short. Concentrating on the more immediate tomorrows allowed the annual writers full scope for warnings about punishments and judgment that might be expected at any moment. Tellingly, Hebenstreit offered an alternative to the 1588 quatrain suggesting that the most dangerous times—or even the end itself—might be coming in the years directly ahead, before 1570.[49] Similarly, although the Dresden astronomer Nicolaus Orphanus saw the need to look past the next twelve months, he may have been deliberately short-circuiting the 1588 prophecy by restricting his 1573 *Ivdicivm Astrologicvm* to the years from 1574 to 1578. Orphanus presented what amounted to an astrological repentance sermon, focusing on quickly worsening disease, wars, and upheaval to come. In 1577 and 1578 several eclipses would exercise horrible combined effects; Christendom would fall under attack from the Turks, and misery would have the upper hand everywhere. In 1576 or early 1577 Orphanus issued an updated version for the following two years, foreseeing little except complete breakdown, and calling for each person to turn at once to God: "The time is near and hard by the door, and the golden age is over."[50]

Once again the pattern is familiar: while the popular calendars and practicas were designed in the first place to offer practical orientation in the world, their inherent concern with the threat of future imbalance and corruption lent them a powerful potential to evoke fear and anxiety. The Melanchthonian astrologers increasingly adopted this potential to serve a deliberate strategy. The signs in the heavens became more and more an open commentary on human sin and earthly corruption. This was a mentality that could and did feed on itself, as predictions of degeneration became psychologically self-fulfilling. Few if any channels of mass publicity sounded this drumbeat of imminent punishment and the approaching Last Day more loudly and consistently than the annual stellar forecasts. More and more, a vision of universal natural, moral, and spiritual decline grew dominant; Luther's oft-painted picture of an aging creation on the eve of destruction became an ever more pervasive theme. In his practica for 1571 the Tonndorf pastor-astrologer Adam Ursinus stressed that while the first Adam and his offspring had been learned in all the arts of nature and gifted with profound understanding, since then the world had been growing weaker and more infected with evil by the day. Shortly later Ursinus issued what amounted to a small apocalyptic wonder book surveying the rush of heavenly warning signs from 1568 to 1570; how many more, he asked, could one possibly expect? Johann Reinstein's forecast for 1573 fell in with the chorus of lamentations: one should expect more murderous crimes, more terrible conflicts, and more agonizing suffering than the world had ever known, "for the ancient serpent will not rest, but will stir up with God's permission every sort of anguish before the Last Day."[51]

If a profound worldly pessimism and apocalyptic expectations were already pervasive by the early 1570s, a potent new charge to the atmosphere came with the appearance of the famous new star of 1572, best known to readers today because of its presumed role in helping to bring about the decline of Aristotelian natural philosophy, particularly the assumption that the superlunary heavens were perfectly unchanging. Probably no natural event of the sixteenth century has evoked more attention from modern scholars, who often note the general astonishment it caused throughout Christendom. For learned astronomers it was a thing of awe as well as an object of intensive study; Tycho Brahe's early reaction was to see it as announcing the great transition to the fiery trigon, and as a creation of God that he now "exhibited to a world hastening to its end."[52]

Leading Wittenberg academics including Caspar Peucer and Erasmus Reinhold likewise took it an unprecedented divine sign of the nearing Last Judgment, not least because it had appeared in the twelfth house, which bore especially on the realm of religion. Attention to the nova extended well beyond the bounds of German Lutheranism, to be sure, but in no setting was it more intensively publicized by churchmen, astronomers, and calendar-writers as a supernatural wonder indicating the advent of the Last Times. Typical of dozens of other reactions was a brief Latin tract by Leowitz, which revealed its main theme by prominently citing apocalyptic passages from Luke 21 and Daniel 11.[53]

In his annual forecast for 1574 the Wittenberg-trained Franconian pastor-astrologer Georg Caesius explained the mainstream interpretation. The nearer the Last Day approached, he wrote, the more signs appeared that were clearly opposed to nature, and the greater too were their variety. Now a brilliant new star had appeared, and remained visible for so long that the like had never been seen since the creation. In addition strange rainbows, multiple suns, and other supernatural signs had suddenly come into view; all of them had a special hidden meaning. At the very least one could say that together these signs threatened immense upheavals, wars, plagues, and storms. These sorts of supernatural signs, wrote Caesius, often hindered the regular effects of the stars and planets, so that otherwise accurate prognostications were thrown off the mark. Yet people were by no means to devalue the systematic art on this account; indeed it was to be esteemed all the more, since it was the very basis on which one came to understand which phenomena were usual and natural, and which violated the natural order. Not that Caesius himself made much of this distinction; for him as for most of his evangelical contemporaries, God acted and spoke through both order and disorder. Unfortunately the world would be changed neither by such knowledge nor by preaching and warning from God's Word; hence the near certainty of disasters before the Last Judgment itself.[54]

The new star thus merely confirmed and deepened attitudes that were already securely embedded in an intensive evangelical discourse. In his 1575 practica Caspar Bucha, appointed *medicus* at Quedlinburg, catalogued the many sins that were evoking such stunningly unprecedented stellar spectacles. Because of these evils "the entire framework of heaven and earth no longer wants to serve the purpose for which it was created by God." Clearly, any larger hope had to reside elsewhere. Nicholas Winckler's outlook for 1576 projected a nearly unbroken series of misfortunes, from deadly outbreaks of plague to religious division, idolatry, personal and public vices, broken marriages and hatred among relatives; one could only pray for God to see his people through the horrifying trials ahead. Georg Meder, the prominent Kitzingen stargazer, reported along with his weather forecasts that nothing better was to be expected before the end of the world than the advent of Gog and Magog: "Yet the world pays no attention to such prophecies, but goes on in its security and casts them to the wind." The Wittenberg-trained and widely read Amberg astrologer Andreas Rosa was moved by such convictions to dwell repeatedly on the transience of all things, the vanity of life in general, and the imminence of judgment.[55] A fundamental tendency in the popular forecasts remained, as it had been since the prior century, to stress the inevitability of imbalance and conflict, and thus to fix anxious attention on the future.

In the 1570s some astrologers, spurred no doubt in part by the astounding new star, began to extend their forecasts to include a period of several future years. The result was an almost separate genre of astrologically based repentance sermons. We noted the *Iudicium Astrologicum* of Nicholas Orphanus covering the years from 1574 to 1578, and its updated version for 1577 to 1578. With the prediction commonly attributed to Regiomontanus in mind, the *mathematicus* Nicolaus Weiss issued a prognostication looking to the period from 1572 to 1588. While he referred to numerous eclipses, conjunctions, and other celestial events, he offered little in the way of technical astrological analysis. For as he made clear, his main aim was to foretell the punishments that God would certainly inflict upon his people if they did not repent and return to obedience. One might expect a gracious break or two as 1588 drew nearer; 1579 might see a good deal of peace and plenty, for instance. But in the years before then and especially afterward, little except misery and suffering were likely. The half-decade after 1584, the year of the greatest conjunction, would bring trouble and evil beyond description. In 1578 Weiss issued an updated *Practica for Ten Years* that distilled masses of anxiety, especially in regard to the disasters to befall the Germans; here he placed even more emphasis on 1584, the entry into the fiery trigon, the horrors to follow, and the desperate need for repentance.[56]

The decisions of Orphanus and Weiss to update their multiyear predictions in the late 1570s may have had something to do with events that deepened the gloom and thus further intensified the despairing tone of apocalyptic speculations. In 1576 came the unexpectedly early death of Maximilian II; whatever misty dreams still lingered about an Empire

unified under the purified gospel now came close to evaporating altogether. At the same time, new challenges were arising from both Jesuits
and Calvinists in the Empire; evangelical astrologers would show no less
vituperation than the most committed evangelical churchmen against
these threatening forces. Then, almost as if on cue, the great comet of
November 1577 appeared, drawing at least as much publicity as the new
star of five years earlier. Like that prior event, the comet evoked not only
scores of astronomical and astrological tracts, but also published sermons
from prominent preachers such as Jacob Heerbrand and Sigismund
Suevus; these clerics cast the spectacle as the clearest sign yet of imminent punishment and final judgment. Here again the broad alliance of
preachers and astrologers made itself felt. In a popular verse work the
theologian Heerbrand expressed his respect for those who studied such
phenomena in physical terms, but made it clear that his exclusive concern
was with the more urgent matters of sin, punishment, and the Last Day,
which stood "at the door."[57] The physician Winckler told readers of his
German practica for 1579 that he had reserved his technical analysis of the
comet to his Latin tracts; he would report to the common man only the key
points, as far as human reason could determine them, about this "great
wondrous work and image of God's wrath." On account of our ungratefulness, he wrote, "there must finally follow a universal punishment of the
whole world, which we can expect to come from 1584 to 1588." Winckler
followed up with an urgent call for personal repentance. Meanwhile the
1577 appearance prompted Georg Caesius to publish a chronicle of all comets from the time of the biblical flood to his own day, showing both their
unquestionable signification of harsh corrections in the past and their
unique meaning for his own critical time. The normally quite restrained
and prophetically reticent Johannes Praetorius, the official Nuremberg
calendar writer, was so deeply affected by the phenomena of 1572 and 1577
that he approvingly cited current predictions that the world might end in
1580 or shortly thereafter. It was entirely proper for faithful Christians to
grant some authority to natural reckonings that agreed so well with the
prophecies of scripture.[58]

Around this time Georg Meder's yearly forecasts groaned repeatedly
and harrowingly with extended descriptions of suffering to come, along
with earnest biblical exhortations and prayers. He joined to his practica for
1579 an analysis of the comet of 1577, which made the outlook for subsequent years look as awful as his readers' imaginations allowed. Presenting
a list of wondrous celestial signs that had appeared over the past decade, he

expounded on their message to the Germans as the latter-day Israelites. So many and clear were these signs that "heaven and earth preach and announce to us nothing other than the final downfall of the Empire and the advent of Gog and Magog on the Mount of Israel." But the world utterly ignored these warnings, and so sin spread everywhere and final punishment neared. Nothing was more urgent, wrote Meder, than that preachers of the word should shout their warnings to repentance.[59] Such admonitions, of course, repeated themes by now many decades old in evangelical culture. But they were kept fresh partly by the commitment of the calendar makers to renewing their forecasts year after year with reference to the most recent and the anticipated evidence of the heavens. The astrologers were after all the most careful charters of time; their observations and calculations lent a concreteness and immediacy to discussions of past, present, and future that might otherwise have been lacking.

With few exceptions, the stellar interpreters continued to acknowledge that all their nature-based predictions were finally no more than admonitory conjectures. The ideal of pious speculation regarding God's plan for historical time was in fact a main pillar of early evangelical humanism, one consistently encouraged by a wide range of Lutheran theologians and scholars. A tradition of "Christian conjectures" went hand in hand with the burgeoning interest in history and chronology, and thus continued to flower throughout the sixteenth century.[60] When it came to chronological or astrological calculations bearing on the nearness of the Last Day, evangelical clergy showed a general openness as long as efforts at precision did not go too far. In 1581 the Hohenlohe church superintendent David Meder cited a raft of evidence from the Bible, history, and nature about the imminence of the end, including the great conjunction expected in 1583 and 1584. Luther himself, wrote Meder, had often repeated the now-famous rhyme about 1588. Pious calculations and reckonings were not to be scorned, as long as one kept firmly in mind that the actual time of the end was hidden to all creatures. This speculative openness was manifest in tomes such as Leonard Krentzheim's *Christian Conjectures on Future Conditions* (1577; first German edition 1583), and Nicolaus Winckler's *Reflections on Future Changes in the Worldly Regiment and the End of the World* (1582).[61] These and an expanding array of similar works were rooted in the synthetic culture of stellar science and biblical prophecy epitomized in the practicas; we might see here too a process of cross-fertilization between the cheapest and most widespread works and the larger publications that sought to gather various perspectives and to offer a more broadly informed speculative picture. Krentzheim explored scenarios that extended well into the seventeenth century; Winckler paid most attention to 1588, but he too offered a variety of possibilities.

Like the practicas, these longer tracts included heavy repentance preaching and conveyed strong apocalyptic convictions. In nearly all such speculations the influence of Leowitz was evident. Georg Ursin, a "lover of the astronomical art" at Magdeburg, offered in 1575 a survey of all expected eclipses and major planetary aspects up to 1600; here he directly imitated the famous Bohemian's approach, giving most concentrated heed to the 1584 conjunction and to 1588. A few years later Ursin issued *Two Practicas* offering alternative projections. The first covered the years from 1582 to 1600, the second extended only to 1588. Both were packed with references to upcoming conjunctions and eclipses, along with a nearly constant heavy stream of consequent evils and misfortunes; meanwhile the threat of a bloodbath at the hands of the Turks always loomed. By presenting two possible schemes Ursin acknowledged the conjectural nature of his work, but he left few doubts that he thought the second more likely: the "wondrous year" would bring the cumulative effects of the 1584 conjunction in the fiery trigon along with several eclipses, meaning a change of unimaginable scope for the entire world. Although Ursin was apparently neither a formally trained mathematician nor an ordained preacher, his work was in essence an evangelical sermon combining both astrological warnings and biblical exhortations to repentance in the face of God's awful wrath.[62]

Coming close upon the eve of the great conjunction and the fiery trigon, the promulgation of the new Gregorian calendar in 1582 could not have been better timed to stoke the apocalyptic anxiety among evangelicals still further. The Tübingen-trained city physician of Hagenau, Helisaeus Roeslin, immediately linked this latest Roman outrage with these widely feared celestial events and with the likely imminent fulfillment of all scriptural prophecies.[63] Many calendar-makers, who saw their very calling as the proper keeping of time, joined the chorus of furious outcries against the Antichrist for this blatant example of satanic corruption: the pope and his learned hirelings were trying to confuse the temporal order itself. Georg Caesius called the new calendar a test to see who held to the pope's vicious superstition, and who clung to true evangelical teaching. Doctor Luther's predictions were coming to fulfillment in the wake of this satanic outrage, and things would only get worse after the coming conjunction and entry into the fiery trigon. Johann Schulin, yet another pastor-astrologer who had studied at Wittenberg, denounced the change as an abomination. Christoph Stathmion drew extensively on the Book of Revelation to demonstrate the involvement of the Papal Antichrist in this innovation, one of many monstrous tricks to mislead the faithful in the last days of the world. These views would not prevent many of the most widely published authors from adopting within a few years a new format supplying both the "old and new" dates. This was mainly a matter of pragmatism. It remained unclear where the new calendar would be officially or popularly accepted, and since reaching the largest possible market remained a priority for the leading calendar makers, it made sense to try to minimize the inevitable disorientation by including both forms.[64]

The new star, the great comet, and countless other teeming wonders had all come more or less unexpectedly, but the conjunction of 1583 to 1584 was clearly anticipated; for many it explicitly evoked the vision of a final world conflagration. In his practica for 1583 Winckler digested in a few pages much of the evidence, both natural and biblical, for approaching worldwide upheaval, and quite possibly the universal consummation in 1588. Georg Meder declared that in the following year "the fiery trigon begins, which will kick the bottom out of the barrel and make an end of the world in fire." He explained that when astronomers described the transition to the fiery trigon, they also pointed out that this trigon would last for two hundred years: "This does not mean that the Last Day will come at the beginning, or in the middle, or at the end of this period," but rather that within this time "we have certainly nothing more to expect." Although he left no doubt that the 1588 prophecy should carry great weight for his readers, Meder's approach thus ultimately reinforced the notion that the time of the end was necessarily hidden; the point was to be ready at every moment. In his practica for 1585 Jacob Cnespel noted the conclusion of "many venerable astrologers" that the years from 1584 to 1588 would be a time of unimaginable shock and anguish, and Cnespel was certain that events were already bearing out these fears. Adding to the already profoundly frightening effects of the conjunction, a major solar eclipse would have "great power and influence," bringing yet more evils beyond imagining. The Almighty, he wrote, can and will ease our suffering if we earnestly repent and pray to him unceasingly. In his forecast for 1588 Georg Caesius gave a long list of all the wondrous signs that had appeared since 1572, and likewise engaged in

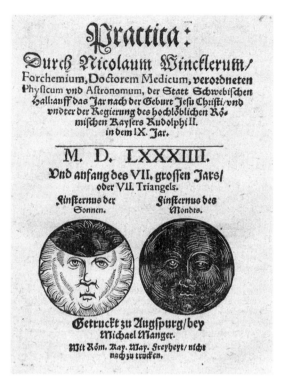

FIGURE 6.3 Practica for 1584 by the city physician Nicolaus Winckler, title page. Courtesy of the Bayerische Staatsbibliothek München, Res/4 Astr.p. 446#Beibd.7.

full-fledged repentance preaching.[65] (For typical title pages, see Figures 6.3 and 6.4.)

In disseminating such speculations and expectations the astrologers never lacked for cooperation, especially from evangelical preachers. As noted earlier, Andreas Musculus bolstered his apocalyptic warnings by referring to the frequent predictions of "our astrologers." The world would surely overflow with suffering, perhaps until 1588 unless the Last Day came sooner. In explaining the signs of the end around 1580, the learned Breslau preacher Lucas Pollio did not hesitate to discuss the expected "Great Sabbath Conjunction" of 1584. "All men of high understanding" had concluded that if this seventh conjunction did not bring the world to an end, it meant at the very least some enormous and unprecedented change.[66] In his lengthy sermon collection of 1585 titled *The Plain Truth*, the Neumark pastor Bartholomew Ringwaldt expounded energetically on "the rotting of the world, the decline of faith, the coming punishment of all hypocrisy," and the imminent final stroke. These realities were announced to the world not only by ordained servants of Christ out of God's unchanging word;

FIGURE 6.4 Practica for 1590 by the pastor-astrologer Georg Caesius, title page. Courtesy of the Bayerische Staatsbibliothek München, Res/4 Astr.p. 515, 22.

they were also made clear "by the mute preachers of the heavens," which included comets, meteors, and frequent eclipses, as well as conjunctions and equally portentous planetary configurations, "about which the astronomers have written abundantly, and continue to make predictions yearly."[67]

Worth noting, however, is a new reticence in the years immediately prior to 1588 among many of the practica writers themselves, including several whose earlier works had overflowed with horrific images of punishment and judgment. These figures, including Tobias Moller, Nicolaus Winckler, Andreas Rosa, and Johann Schulin among others, probably preferred not to commit themselves on particulars at such a late moment. But it seems equally likely that they were collectively holding their breath, waiting in nervous awe for momentous changes that might come at any time. Winckler interrupted his quite mundane predictions for 1587 with only a "brief admonition" dealing in more or less vague terms with the likelihood of massive upheavals under the new trigon, and exhorting readers to turn at once to the Lord. In 1587 Victorin Schönfelt issued warnings of terrible wars and divine chastisements, but declared that he would "let rest other conjectures about the year 1588 and the next following." God willing he would deal with them in future writings; meanwhile prayers to the Almighty were in order. We should not read too much into these cases of reticence, since reactions varied as the "wonder year" drew near. The Augsburg physician Georg Henisch, for example, was a notably restrained forecaster who generally avoided open references to sin, divine wrath, the Last Judgment, or even earth-shaking natural disasters. But in his practica for 1588 even he could cite the famous prophetic quatrain, while referring to "tremendous changes in religion, laws, and worldly rule" as likely results of coming eclipses.[68]

The powerful evangelical discourse of apocalyptic imminence showed no immediate signs of weakening with the passing of 1588. In fact, many if not most preachers and astrologers continued to insist that now the closeness of the end was more certain than ever. This point should remind us once more that conjectures or expectations focusing on any particular date were merely crystallizations of deeper, more enduring attitudes.[69] Again, while astrologers had long been subject to criticism for too-precise forecasts, the late-sixteenth-century practicas do not show a marked penchant for apocalyptic date-setting. On the contrary, these omnipresent guides repeatedly emphasized essential evangelical teachings about the radical contingency of this world, stressing that future hope should focus on deliverance at the Last Judgment. Indeed the presumed seventh world-historical great conjunction in 1583 and 1584 may have proved more significant as a historical datum once it was past than it had been earlier as a focus of anticipation. That neither the end of the world nor earth-shaking changes affecting the Empire had come in the years immediately after that event posed no stumbling-blocks for those astrologers and preachers who noted the transition to the fiery trigon. Now it was clearer than ever that the time God had charted for the world was over; that every remaining day was a gift of grace. With growing urgency toward the turn of the century, the practica-writers preached that not a moment in this life could be taken for granted; in so doing they reinforced a standard evangelical doctrine.

Naturally we cannot discount the effects of external circumstances in helping to perpetuate and even intensify the overall outlook of gloom for this world. As Hartmut Lehmann and others have shown, the last decades of the sixteenth century witnessed climatic disaster, widespread agrarian crisis, and mounting social unrest in the Empire.[70] The 1590s brought the onset of what is sometimes called the Little Ice Age, a rapid cooling that has been plausibly linked to poor harvests, years of famine, and high mortality. On a more local front, war with the Turks had flared up again in 1593, reviving nightmares of a bloody scourge in preparation for the Last Judgment. Even more threatening in the eyes of many Lutherans was the further stiffening competition from both Catholics and Calvinists; Ingolstadt and Heidelberg had by now become the spearheads of aggressive programs of clerical training and propaganda. Between 1588 and 1591, the Saxon elector Christian I had tried to introduce Calvinism in the very cradle of the evangelical movement, and though the effort failed, the shock waves continued to reverberate.[71] Many practica writers joined their clerical colleagues in lashing out more energetically than ever at such enemies of the truth. Albin Moller predicted staggering misfortunes to come in 1595, especially in lands to the west, "because of the malicious Calvinists." Equally if not more typical was Caesius's scornful response to the "blasphemies" of the Jesuit Georg Scherer, a prominent vilifier of the evangelical stargazers.[72]

But decades of apocalyptic preaching and writing had by now created their own momentum, so that new dangers and hardships merely fed the sense of universal breakdown and the nearing end that had come to distinguish German Lutheranism. The Stendal preacher Daniel Schaller insisted in his *New Theological Prognostication for 1589 and Following Years* that God's grace alone had allowed the world to remain standing. The astrologers had not been wrong; rather, the Almighty had stepped in miraculously to delay the punishment he had long promised. The natural predictions of the learned were not to be scorned, but rather studied the more closely with a strengthened awareness that all finally depended on the divine will, to which scripture remained the unfailing guide.[73] In practice, of course, such a view by no means precluded further forecasts, and most practica writers wasted little time in explaining away what they never really saw as a problem at all. Instead they moved on, keeping up as always with the latest natural conditions, anticipating the near future, and fulfilling their duty to warn. Looking to 1592, Tobias Moller affirmed that the rod of eternal justice would fall upon Germany for her sins: "For the very last times are here, and now brother rises against brother, one friend against another; and since unrighteousness gains the upper hand, love and all true friendship shall freeze up in nearly everyone." The Nuremberg preacher and astrologer J. P. Sutorius emphasized year after year that worldly conditions had never been worse; every possible sign pointed to the coming day of resurrection and judgment.[74]

The generation of practica-writers who closed out the sixteenth century continued to preach insistently on both the manifest order and the
spilling turmoil of the heavens. Caspar Bucha was among those who
stated openly that the celestial realm was the great book of God, "in which
much is to be read and understood" and which thus clearly declared God's
glory. At the same time he insisted that evidence of breakdown was everywhere, and especially in the heavens the signs of disaster and wrath were
"mounting up as a world-ending flood" (*Süntflut*). All of nature witnessed
to the fulfillment of biblical prophecy and the nearness of Christ's return.
The Amberg city physician Andreas Rosa likewise typified the continuing Melanchthonian tradition, drawing on a wide range of sources from
Haly Abenragel to Luca Gaurico, from Luke 21 to Cyprian von Leowitz.
Starting from astronomical data and the usual mundane predictions, he
moved into a heavy message of repentance, with emphatic warnings to the
Germans to waken to their sins. In 1595 he declared that if in the following
year Germany escaped destruction by the Turks it would not be because
of natural strength but only because of earnest prayer and repentance to
God; in any case, mortal sufferings would be rampant. The clergy and
church would be poisoned with falsehood and strife. Despite indications
of an abundant growing season, a far darker and deadlier outlook prevailed. Rosa concluded with a line from Jeremiah 15: "I have stretched out
my hand against thee to destroy thee; I am weary with repenting."[75]

Similar continuities are evident in both published sermons and the
annual practicas right through the turn of the century. Another major
comet in 1596 evoked intensely sobering comments from a host of writers;
here was further confirmation of unprecedented changes in the heavens.[76]
While the number and thus the year 1600 did attract a good deal of excited
attention in works of chronological and prophetic speculation, for most
practica writers it did not particularly stand out as a focus of expectancy.
In his forecast for that year Albin Moller anticipated crises in virtually
every realm of life, but for him such predictions were nothing out of the
ordinary. Even as he offered practical recommendations about precautions
the physician or layman might take in the face of these perils, he recognized that special caution was needed "above all in these final, fleeting
and dangerous times before the nearing Last Day, when almost no trust or
faith is at hand." A solar eclipse in Pisces, along with unmistakable natural signs everywhere, gave "certain announcements not only of the Last
Day, but also of other horrible punishments of God that shall fall upon
unrepentant men as well as on unreasoning creatures." Likewise Johann

Krabbe of Wolfenbüttel thought the signs clearly showed "the dangerous and evil condition" of the year 1600, yet his outlook did not differ notably from what he presented in earlier or later editions.[77]

Along with these continuities, the last years of the sixteenth century did bring some significant shifts in the evangelical discourse of the stars. As Chapter 7 will strive to show, preachers and practica writers faced a variety of new challenges that prompted reintensified efforts to achieve a fully refined Christian science of the heavens. Ironically, these same efforts would lead in opposing directions, ultimately breaking down the potent brew of preaching and prognostication that is our main focus. Yet this eventual disintegration should not lead us to underestimate popular astrology's role in shaping the confessional outlook and identity of German Lutherans through the early generations of their movement.

Pragmatic Defense

Recent scholarship has tended to see the threats of punishment and judgment that so pervaded evangelical literature in the late-Reformation era as fundamentally part of a project of social control, a means by which elites could impose new levels of discipline and obedience. This interpretation does have valid grounds; we have seen that the Melanchthonian program sought to establish a solid natural basis for the ordering of personal, family, social, and even political life. One might reasonably characterize this program as a form of Aristotelian patriarchalism. The writers of the popular almanacs and related works reflected a fundamental conservatism, expressed in deference to secular authorities, frequent defenses of the well-ordered household, and fear of deteriorating economic conditions. When they foresaw political or social disturbances they rarely failed to predict bloody but divinely ordained punishment for those involved. They sought to make clear that children were to obey their parents, wives to obey their husbands, citizens to obey their rulers, and all to obey God.

But terms such as "patriarchalism" can be seriously misleading, especially when they evoke a picture of order imposed essentially from above. It is hard to read scores of the annual astrological ephemera without concluding that they represented more than the purposes of educated elites, whether lay or clerical; rather these mass publications both reflected and reinforced broadly shared perceptions among Lutheran townsfolk. The calendar and practica writers were not simply mouthpieces for local authorities, nor were they simply disillusioned intellectuals. Nearly always they were well integrated members of burgher society: pastors, physicians and teachers; by the latter part of the century more than a few were simply educated laymen with access to a press, such as Paul Leopold, "a lover of God's word and the liberal art of astronomy."[78] Their critical commentaries, their laments and dark predictions about social, moral, and spiritual conditions, and their apocalyptic anticipations were scattered through pages of detailed and earnest astrological reckoning in works intended for the benefit of both individuals and civic communities. We cannot fully explain their increasingly intense expressions of warning as reactions to the mounting worldly problems and tensions that affected life in the evangelical cities, in the Empire generally, and throughout Europe. The astrological publicists not only reflected but also cultivated among burghers an apocalyptic sensibility that saw little hope for this world, yet sought to protect what remained of its gifts and its goodness.

Neither the calendar-writer nor his readers could simply forego the need for worldly order and understanding. The very nature of the astrologer's work required that he offer data that bore on the practical matters of life day by day, month by month, year by year. Even in the most despairing prognostications we find continuing regard to the recurring patterns of nature and the tools needed to order life in good Melanchthonian fashion. Though the world may have been declining into old age and toward collapse, people still wanted to orient themselves in the cycles of the seasons, still wished to know when best to undergo therapeutic bleeding, whether the spring would be wet or dry, whether they should travel in the summertime or wait until fall, whether or not the planetary aspects made likely another outbreak of the plague. The stellar publicists saw no contradiction between this acknowledgment of cyclical regularities and their emphasis upon the unique degeneracy of their world. In their eyes God's purpose was manifest both in the cycles of nature and in evidence for the coming consummation of all things. Just as each year the warmth of spring and summer could only follow after the cold and dark of winter, so in the universal scheme the world had to descend into darkness before the coming of the eternal summer. The renowned Nicolaus Winckler wrote in detail about practical matters of weather, health, and daily chores, admonishing at the same time that no one should wonder or whine about the future calamities of the world, for it was all ordered according to the wisdom of divine providence. The same combination of down-to-earth yearly predictions with fervent repentance preaching marked the practicas of lesser-known writers such as Matthew Bader and Heinrich Maius. These writers, like dozens of others each year, paid attention to realities both mundane and spiritual.[79]

The Melanchthonian campaign had placed a strong emphasis on the positive benefits of the stellar art for daily life. These advertisements were sincere, yet at the same time they could not and did not cancel persisting fears of social disorder. As the century progressed and evangelicals saw their movement more and more severely threatened by internal division and external challenges, both practica writers and pulpit preachers dwelled ever more intensively on the near-certainty of general disaster, divine punishment, and the last judgment. And the more starkly divine punishment and judgment loomed, the more these publicists reflected and reinforced a defensive mentality that looked primarily to protect whatever forms of worldly security could still be found. If, as it seemed, God was allowing the whole earthly order to disintegrate, then beyond preaching full and sincere repentance all one could do was to defend the most immediate, pragmatic forms of order, those that applied directly to one's immediate community, family, and personal life, along with the traditional practical freedoms that these forms of order made possible. In this sense the popular astrologers became contributors to the profound conservatism of evangelical culture.[80]

Scholars have noted that something approaching a spiritual and cosmic siege mentality came to characterize the outlook of German Lutherans in the later sixteenth century, Robert Kolb has described the Lutheran position at this time as a "battle on two fronts"—that is, against the other two major confessions.[81] We might go further and add that many of Luther's heirs saw themselves fighting on innumerable fronts at once. While Luther had identified only one genuine Antichrist, by the end of the century his followers were discovering a whole host of Antichrists, not only Papists and Calvinists but Turks, enthusiasts, false prophets, magical dreamers, warmongers, murderers, adulterers, usurers, thieves, tyrants: the world swarmed with enemies. The natural parallel to this complete moral and spiritual collapse was the breakdown of the cosmic order itself. As a perfectly practical matter the task was now to circle the wagons, to hold out until the day of judgment and deliverance by protecting those structures most crucial to sustaining life.

The role of established authorities was to maintain a modicum of stability for believers in a crumbling world from which they would soon be delivered. Thus secular power was itself restricted to an essentially conservative role, maintaining traditional freedoms as well as order. To defend an existing order was not the same as mobilizing a new one; in a disintegrating world, new structures merely added to the chaos. The prominent Brandenburg pastor-astrologer George Caesius repeatedly offered high praise and support to the electoral house and its agents. But he made it clear that neither the elector nor his subjects would be around for long; hence the attention of all classes should be on the coming end. The physician-astrologer Nicholas Weiss railed against the ungratefulness and corruption at every level of society; the coming divine punishments would include unprecedented disasters for the great lords as well as for the common folk. He predicted that in the years before 1588, "many lands and peoples will be piteously wasted, and there will be many new laws and regulations; similarly the old freedoms and civic statutes will be much altered." Christian Heiden's popular practicas similarly warned that zealous efforts would be needed to maintain the "old freedoms" in whatever time remained before the last judgment.[82] The civic ideal represented in the popular forecasts was to allow as little change as possible until God himself brought about the promised final and total transformation.

The staunchly Lutheran Andreas Rosa ominously predicted innovations and alterations not only in worldly matters, but also and especially among the clergy and in religious affairs.[83] Among the greatest dangers that he and other astrologers perceived was any significant strengthening of clerical power, or clerically enforced moral discipline. Despite the growing number of evangelical pastor-astrologers, and despite the overall complementarity of the messages that came from the pulpits and the practicas, popular astrology remained essentially a lay business, reflecting mainly lay values. Physicians such as Rosa, after all, still comprised the majority of the calendar makers. As in the fifteenth century, the stargazer's art showed some inherently anticlerical aspects; it called for an unmediated reading of the natural text, a book that lay open, at least potentially, to everyone. The practica-writers acknowledged the responsibility of clergymen to preach the word of God, but rarely implied that clerical authority should extend any further. With reference to a later English setting, Bernard Capp has referred to "the astrologers' ferocious anti-clericalism," directed against both priests and Puritans. Such attitudes were not always so obvious among our Lutheran publicists, yet they most often lay just beneath the surface. Both Romanists and Calvinists posed threats to the cherished old freedoms.[84]

Thus even as the tone of the practicas grew more negative and despairing over time, a basic social defensiveness remained a consistent note in these writings, a defensiveness of established order as well as of established liberties. The need to maintain civic peace remained a central obsession. Typical of countless practicas was Georg Busch's 1573 admonition to his readers to obey their rulers so that "Christian civic peace" might be upheld. Such peace naturally meant more than political obedience; it meant mutual forbearance and support among all classes in the face of manifold threats. In 1570 Victorin Schönfelt offered his predictions about coming scarcity so that the needy "might better order their household economy and might have the necessary food when the time comes." Some years later Tobias Moller offered suggestions about a new system by which each city or village might effectively care for the local poor. In his forecast for 1595 Winckler prayed for God's help "that rich and poor may live together peacefully, [and] that no unrest will be awakened among subjects against *Reich* and government." Although they often seemed to suggest that earthly hopes were utterly exhausted, most late-sixteenth-century calendar men continued to show concern for "the common good"; in this they were maintaining a theme that had been powerfully present already in forecasts of the late fifteenth century.[85]

The goal was to maintain a modicum of stability in a swiftly crumbling world. In light of this basic aim, the mass-market astrological works can hardly be understood as reflecting any new movement of social discipline. What was central in Lutheran settings, it appears, was rather a sense that the open preaching of the gospel had failed to bring about any meaningful transformation of lives. The more evident it became that the Word had not done its work, the more frustration and pessimism mounted, the clearer it became that what defined Lutheran evangelicals was precisely their conviction that the gospel hope lay entirely beyond this world. Melanchthonian teachings and the ready-made forms of popular astrological literature offered precisely what was needed for preaching this message while also driving home the defensive need for personal discipline and social order. Practica writers clearly shared with official evangelical preachers a conception of their own prophetic role, which was to sound an urgent and universal alarm. The striking and undeniable adoption of a popular astrological culture among German Lutherans therefore reinforces the general picture presented over a century ago by Ernst Troeltsch, who argued that early Lutheranism was supportive of a highly traditional social order, and thus did little to promote political modernization.[86]

In sum, we cannot fully understand the early formation of a Lutheran confessional culture and identity apart from the intense preoccupation with celestial prediction among evangelical burghers. An apocalyptic outlook strongly linked with astrological images and habits of thought had been integral to evangelical publicity and propaganda from the beginning. As the sixteenth century progressed, the authors of the almanacs and prognostications worked alongside preachers and pastors—indeed often as preachers and pastors themselves—to sustain a sense of prophetic certainty among evangelicals; their reading of the heavens became one main means by which Luther's heirs sought to reassure themselves that an all-powerful God was fulfilling his plan for the world. But paradoxically once again, the stars would prove far less a source of assurance than a mirror of sin. For even as popular astrology retained its practical and mundane goals of bodily health and social stability, it helped fuel a deepening historical pessimism among Luther's heirs, a growing sense of alienation from a world on the very eve of destruction.

The denizens of the late-sixteenth-century Lutheran towns surely had objective reasons to feel increasingly disgusted with the outward conditions of their world. But together with the pulpit preachers, the huge publicity machine of cheap astrological literature amplified such perceptions by promoting skepticism about virtually all hopes for significant worldly betterment, and by cultivating a common apocalyptic vision of impending disaster, punishment, judgment, and deliverance as the only possible resolution of worldly problems. The faithful were thus taught to protect what thin remnants of stability they could find remaining in their lives and surroundings. If God turned away the expected evils, this was purely a matter of unmerited grace. This outlook was profoundly conservative and defensive; it legitimized established authority as a final bulwark of order, but distrusted all new forms of political or social control. In these ways popular astrology was integral to early evangelical culture, and tied up with the emergence of a Lutheran confessional identity.

7

Centrifugal Forces

BY THE END of the sixteenth century the first serious cracks began to appear in the German evangelical synthesis of astrological prediction and biblical preaching. After 1600 it suffered new internal divisions as well as renewed assaults from without, and by the early phases of the Thirty Years' War it was quickly breaking down. The reasons for this disintegration were complex to say the least, connected as they were with no less a historical problem than the transition from the Reformation era to the age of Lutheran Orthodoxy and Pietism in Germany. Continuing the general approach we have taken throughout, this final chapter focuses mainly on trends among the major writers of popular calendars and practicas, and works to place them in a larger context. Through these channels more than any other, stellar prognostication had become integral to evangelical culture as it was actually experienced in the towns through most of its first century. Through them too we can develop a basic picture of the centrifugal forces that worked to pull apart the broad Melanchthonian consensus, and that would ultimately drive the stargazer's art to the margins of the Lutheran confessional world.

Generational changes can help shed at least a little light on the shifting and often dizzying scene in the years around and after 1600. As the pastors, teachers, and physicians who had formed the network of the Wittenberg-led offensive began to die off in the later sixteenth century, their common program came gradually to lose its main drivers. By the turn of the century or shortly later, several of the most prominent practica writers, including Georg Caesius, Andreas Rosa, Caspar Bucha, Georg Meder, and Tobias Moller, had passed from the scene. The younger publicists who moved to the fore in this era were a more diverse lot, less united in those assumptions that had allowed pastors, physicians, and teachers to cooperate over several generations. A related factor was the ongoing increase in the varieties and the sheer volume of popular literature. With the German Protestant cities still setting the pace for all Europe, the world of mass publication witnessed a ballooning array of prophetic, polemical, didactic, devotional, historical, natural-scientific, medical, magical, and occultist tracts and pamphlets.[1] We have seen that the total number of annual practica editions began to fall off slowly by the 1590s, and while these works certainly retained a huge market appeal, they were beginning to lose weight in proportion to the swelling masses of print, cheap and otherwise. Amid the varied aims and often sensational contents of pro-liferating vernacular genres, the role of the calendar makers became less central, and their overall influence began to ebb.

Over these years around and after the turn of the century, a quickly rising tide of public speculations about the status of the past, present, and future in relation to God's plan for the world pressurized the atmo-sphere of apocalyptic expectancy in the Lutheran cultural sphere as never before. Urgent efforts to unlock the mysteries of the Last Times produced a seemingly endless array of new prophetic visions of imminent disaster, upheaval, world-transformation, and deliverance. From one perspective, the victory of Lutheran orthodoxy involved a reaction against this cha-otic scene. But the story was more complex, for the mystical and magi-cal questings of this era were by no means limited to fringe thinkers. On the contrary, many well-established evangelical teachers and preach-ers were caught up in the atmosphere of anxious exploration. Students of this period have often referred to a *Frömmigkeitskrise*, a crisis of piety, among Luther's heirs at this time, when basic issues of confessional iden-tity were at stake.[2] Taking care not to oversimplify a tremendously complex scene, we can picture German Lutheranism beginning to divide into two broadly opposed currents. In one general direction moved seekers and soul-tenders who were coming to regard the prevailing biblical and astro-logical discourse as fundamentally limiting and oppressive. A different route was followed by scholars and churchmen who increasingly saw this very discourse as the slippery slope to a dangerous and often heretical cacophony of voices in the public market. In the middle, feeling pulled in several directions at once, stood a dwindling band of more or less tradi-tional prognosticators, struggling to defend their evangelical humanism even as they competed and quarreled among themselves.[3]

We will see that by the second and third decades of the new cen-tury, representatives of an accelerating orthodox campaign worked energetically to discredit any reading of the stars they could not square with their own approach to biblical prophecy, which grew more and more severely delimited. In the process they lumped forms of stellar reading that had long been standard fare together with quite different pansophic and "chiliastic" notions that they had come to see as deeply subversive. Their task was made easier by the outbreak of war in the Empire, which led a number of otherwise cautious calendar men to speculate in ways that would undermine their status as the conflict wore on. The trials of the war era not only reinforced overall disillusionment with the art of the calendar-writers; they would also hasten the disintegration of the independent burgher culture that had brought preachers, physicians, and practica-writers together for several generations. The disappearance of the common ground on which these and other evangelical townsmen had stood—a dissolution clearly evident by the 1630s—would mean nothing less than a fundamental reorientation of Lutheran confessional culture.

A *Purer Christian Mathematics*

The Melanchthonian ideal of a reformed, purified science of the stars had both natural-philosophical and theological aspects. We have seen that these motives were mutually reinforcing: a truly scientific study grounded in proper mathematical and cosmological principles would approach nature as God intended it to be approached, without any taint of idolatry, superstition, or human imaginings. At the end of the sixteenth century this ideal was still shared by nearly all active readers of the heavens: university and court mathematicians, the writers of calendars and practicas, preachers and publicists who looked to the stars for confirmation of biblical and historical prophecy. While by the 1570s and 1580s the broad astrological discourse promoted by the evangelical humanists had drowned out nearly all resistance, it also encouraged continuing efforts to enhance stellar interpretation as a true instrument of Christian understanding. In fact, the increasingly chaotic atmosphere of expectancy that was building by 1600 was both cause and effect of quickening efforts to pursue the goal of a refined and fully Christianized art. As before, this drive was certainly not limited to the evangelical realm. Yet in those German towns where preaching from the Bible and from the heavens had been closely connected for generations, the growing debate over what it meant to pursue a true Christian reading of the skies was far more public, and thus had more direct and obvious reverberations, than in other settings.

The renewed push for a purified art was associated with what Robert Westman views as mounting "epistemological uncertainty" toward the end of the sixteenth century, especially in regard to stellar phenomena. Westman notes a swiftly advancing openness to criticisms of Aristotle and to a variety of speculative currents among cosmological thinkers around this time.[4] Leading mathematical experts such as Tycho Brahe, David Fabricius, and Johannes Kepler began to approach both predictable and unpredictable heavenly appearances in ways that avoided a good deal of the inherited intellectual baggage. These new approaches showed both continuities and breaks from the Melanchthonian tradition in which such men were mainly trained. Steven Vanden Broecke describes the Lutheran astronomer Brahe as "a reformer who pursued the humanist track of restoring and purifying ancient judicial astrology," and whose early goals included demonstrating the stellar influences through detailed weather observations. By 1588, however, Tycho began publicly to put at arm's length the traditional practice of weather prediction; he also issued sharp criticisms of the sorts of natal and conjunctionist astrology practiced by figures such as Leowitz.[5] Moreover, Tycho argued more and more forcefully in his later years that no creature could calculate the time of the Last Day, though this growing caution never undermined his evangelical conviction that the end could not be far off. Tycho's yet more renowned intellectual heir Kepler likewise owed much to the Melanchthonian heritage even as he broke away in important ways. In his efforts to reject all astral magic and occultism, he was fully in the traditional line, and he presented himself in this light. "I am a Lutheran astrologer," he famously explained, "I throw out the nonsense but keep the hard kernel."[6] It is no secret that over much of his career Kepler issued annual calendars as well as practicas for the mass market. Yet his interests became more and more purely mathematical, so that the hard kernel came to mean only very general "natural" predictions. At the same time, we find in Kepler—as well as in Tycho and among other learned mathematicians—a marked willingness to pursue speculations in a Neoplatonic, even reverential vein about cosmic harmonies and the very structure of the universe.

The spirit of questioning epitomized by these figures was no doubt connected with the humanist eclecticism of the age. Yet it owed at least as much to the intense air of expectancy and the celestial preoccupations that prevailed especially among their fellow Lutherans. To be sure, as Kepler and other thinkers in his league developed more sophisticated applications of mathematics to observed phenomena, they grew ever more disdainful of those whom they regarded as incompetent popularizers. Already in the wake of the 1572 nova, Tycho had attacked "the vain and worthless authors of annual prognostications"; Kepler came to express similar disdain despite his own place among those very authors. Increasingly these men saw themselves as members of a small cadre of experts set apart from the common ranks of calendar-makers; their reform efforts were of a piece with their conscious desire to rise above the blunderings and contradictions that filled the yearly predictions. As Westman points out, members of this elite group came to enjoy exclusive court patronage, which allowed them a new and separate intellectual space.[7] But it is also clear that these thinkers were not pushing the planetary envelope in isolation from the star-obsessed culture that surrounded them. They were participants in a swiftly intensifying debate about the nature and meaning of cosmic phenomena. Again, while this exchange certainly extended across confessional boundaries, it took on particularly strong public dimensions in the Empire, above all in those settings where it was shaped by the inherited astrological and prophetic emphases of the evangelical movement.

Toward century's end we find a new zeal to pursue a perfected Christian art of the stars emerging among the calendar men. Their writings, however, reflect mounting worries about trends within their own ranks that seemed to threaten that very ideal. Caesius, always a prominent model, preached more strongly than ever a good Melanchthonian line presenting the proper study of the heavens as a natural science admitting of no superstitions. In reinforcing his position he cited not only Luther and Melanchthon, but also figures such as Johannes Brenz, Lucas Osiander, Johann Paceus, and Leowitz. In 1596 he castigated the many young climbers who had taken to filling their calendars with racy news, quarreling, childish sensationalism, and mistaken reckonings. He supported his predictions each year with long lists of events that had followed similar celestial events and aspects in the past, especially over the course of his own lifetime, thus demonstrating the sober observations and experience on which he based his work. At the same time, he repeatedly acknowledged the ongoing need for improved accuracy and refined methods. None of this precluded the same sort of earnest apocalyptic warning he had included in virtually every annual edition for decades; the preface to his 1601 edition, for instance, was almost entirely given over to a pounding sermon on the coming Judgment.[8]

The widely known writer Andreas Rosa showed parallel concerns. In 1595 he pointedly mentioned his thirty-four years of experience, drawing on teachers both ancient and modern to produce his "annual, natural, unsuperstitious prognostications" out of the truest Christian motives. Together with several other well-established calendar men, Rosa grew markedly critical of recently introduced methods that appeared thoroughly ill-founded. He understood and praised any pious longing to know about the future; he did not dismiss efforts to make natural conjectures about the Antichrist and the Last Day. But of those upstarts who followed Faustus, Paracelsus, or their ilk out of a vain curiosity, he thought the less said the better. Again like Caesius and many others who shared his perspective, he supplied his readers with detailed astronomical, calendrical, and meteorological data. Both his natural predictions and his prophetic warnings were utterly serious business, not to be abused or trivialized by the new crowd of inexperienced and even fraudulent speculators.[9]

While the practica writers had long pointed out that their predictions were grounded in natural observations, this assurance now grew more frequent and insistent. Nicholas Winckler and others took to advertising the point prominently, with title page assurances that their forecasts were taken "ex Lege Naturae," or "from true astronomical principles." Winckler left no doubt that the Roman Empire stood on its last legs and would soon see final destruction. He implied that since the entry into the Fiery Trigon in 1583, the truths Luther had rediscovered had been preached with renewed purity. With the coming of the year 1600, one could expect more dramatic signs than ever that God's plan was coming to culmination. Yet Winckler criticized other prognosticators for their errors and abuses in trying to calculate the time of the end. He inveighed most harshly against those who arrived at questionable forecasts by reckoning from Hebrew or Greek Letters in a supposedly "cabalistic" way; such methods smelled of "curiosity and superstition." In 1602 Georg Friedrich Caesius, following in his father's celebrated footsteps, sharply denounced the spread of "magical" predictions as well as too-definite political vaticinations. Errors of this sort had all come with a revival of Chaldean, Egyptian, and Arabic perversions.[10]

A heightened reserve toward the Arabic heritage in particular is evident among several of the mainline forecasters. This trend no doubt had connections with broader anti-Aristotelian currents on the rise among European physicians and philosophers, but again we have reasons to see developments within the Lutheran sphere as uniquely tied up with a public discourse in which the popular astrologers were intimately involved. As early as the 1580s we find some practica writers distancing themselves with new energy from Albumasar and other medieval Arabic sources. In his annual works from those years, for instance, the astrologer and pastor Johann Schulin avoided the theory of periodic conjunctions, rarely if ever cited the Arabs, and essentially ignored the general obsessions regarding 1588, although he did not fail to issue strong warnings to repentance. This trend became more common and explicit in the 1590s and thereafter. Caspar Bucha criticized Arabic methods of predicting the fruitfulness of the coming year, and turned to Ptolemy and Cardano instead. While Johannes Krabbe of Wolfenbüttel could give a quick prefatory nod to the "old monuments of the Arabs," he named none of them, and generally avoided citing them as the century wound down. His preferred authorities included Italians such as Guido Bonatti and Cardano, and also Melanchthon, whose memory he clearly adored.[11]

Around this time we also find students of the stars paying less attention to the Zodiac and more to planets themselves, especially the sun. Students of this era have noted a general movement in the direction of a more sun-centered astrology, a tendency revealing the new willingness to engage in cosmological speculations, which extended well beyond the bounds of court-sponsored elites. While in many annual forecasts the Zodiacal signs and the terrestrial houses did retain a major role in analyzing the planetary aspects, by the 1590s several of the most widely read writers were devoting more time and mental energy to eclipses, with only limited mention of the constellations in which they appeared. Practica chapters devoted to both solar and lunar darkenings and their expected effects during the coming year grew longer, more detailed, and generally more prominent. It is surely not entirely coincidental that this was precisely the period when Kepler himself began to reject the natural reality of the Zodiac, the houses, and other traditional elements of the art.[12] Related changes were evident on the title pages of the annual forecasts, which since the fifteenth century had most often included anthropomorphized images of the ruling planets for the coming year. By the end of the sixteenth century these more or less standardized woodcuts had almost entirely disappeared, no doubt at least partly because they did not sit well with the resurging ideal of a fully Christian mathematics.

A Way Out

One reason for the intensifying reform impulse around 1600 may have been what Will-Erich Peuckert long ago described as the quest for "a way out," meaning the growing need for some sort of psychological escape from the potentially crushing worldly pessimism that preachers and astrologers alike had cultivated since at least the 1540s.[13] We saw earlier that up at least through the 1580s, expressions of expectancy had taken shape overwhelmingly as warnings. The stars revealed and enforced the law, both natural and spiritual. Thus whether addressed primarily to the individual sinner or to the whole German people, the message had focused on the urgent need for repentance as the terrors of the Last Times unfolded. Evangelical publicists had rarely omitted altogether the message of grace for the truly repentant, yet they had dwelled so heavily on the heavens as conveyors of the law and teachers of discipline that the more positive aspects of the Melanchthonian message could fade perilously. The passing of the "wonder year" certainly brought no relaxation in the public air of apprehension; instead it appears that apocalyptic expectancy remained as high as ever well into the new century. Yet by this time hints emerged of growing unease with the unremitting emphasis on utter human helplessness in the face of worldly doom. In the predictive and prophetic literature we find new signs of a desire to read the message of the stars less exclusively in terms of divine wrath and warning, and more directly in connection with positive tidings of consolation. This newly affirmative aspect included the hope of insights deeper than those afforded by the art of the calendar men. Thus the task of reading now grew more complicated as a new range of stellar observations and possible meanings emerged.

For evangelicals, one simple if paradoxical response to the need for a way out was to point with yet greater force than ever before to the testimony of expert stargazers that the heavens themselves were mutable. As we have noted, the idea that the sun itself was sinking had appeared earlier in Melanchthon and among some of his students, though it had not led them to doubt that the beauty of the heavens revealed the glory of God. The great 1572 nova and the comet of 1577 had fanned an intense flareup of questioning about the possibility of change in the celestial realm, and in the eyes of most Lutheran observers change inevitably meant degeneration. In the wonder books and in much evangelical preaching the idea that all creation was weakening had been at least implicit, but only after the surge of expectancy associated with 1588 did an explicit vision of cosmic breakdown begin to appear with any real frequency in mass publications. In the period around 1600 we more and more often find writers citing the evidence of decline not only in the terrestrial world, but also in the heavens themselves, which in the inherited Aristotelian cosmology stood above and apart from the corruption of earthly matter. The producers of annual practicas helped popularize this idea that the sky was literally falling. Tobias Moller of Zwickau, for instance, explained in 1591 that the sun, "as the learned understand, has fallen fully twenty-eight degrees from where it stood shortly before the time of Christ."[14] This sort of data strongly reinforced the notion that decrepitude and disorder were affecting the entire natural universe.

Especially welcoming to the idea of a collapsing cosmos were popular preachers such as Daniel Schaller, whose intensely apocalyptic *Herolt* of 1595 included it among one of many proofs for the closeness of the Last Day and the deliverance of the faithful. All creation, wrote Schaller, showed clear signs of ebbing vitality. The most noble creatures of all, namely humans, had often lived one thousand years in the first age of the world; now people seldom lived to fifty or sixty. Thus too "all other creatures grow weaker ... in sum all the powers of the heavens now move and prepare for their departure." As the astronomers reported, the firmament had sunk some 9,967 miles, and the sun had come much closer; the final and utter disintegration would come with the son of righteousness himself. To be sure, Schaller was a fully eclectic gatherer of evidence, and he did not neglect stellar phenomena that might suggest a more regular natural unfolding. He could cite the theory of the great conjunctions, for instance, and the widely shared belief that the seventh such meeting, in 1584, was itself among the key final signs. But his overall emphasis fell heavily on extraordinary celestial events as revealing the radical uniqueness of the present day. Other highly active preachers such as Ambrosius Taurer of Wettin and Philipp Nicolai of Hamburg joined Schaller in pointing vigorously to the sinking sun as a key piece of apocalyptic evidence. "The substance or structure of the heavens is growing tired," asserted Taurer, "and as the astronomical experts write and can demonstrate, they have bent under and sunk like an old house, as a sign that all will soon collapse." Nicolai affirmed that the sun had come so much nearer "as a sign and evidence that this present heaven will soon come to an end, and the Sun of Righteousness, our Savior, will soon appear to melt this world and to create a new heaven and a new earth."[15]

For writers such as Schaller, Taurer, and Nicolai the collapsing cosmos theme served to fix the eyes of the faithful firmly on the new life to come. Their intention was to emphasize anew the need to turn entirely to the New Testament promise of resurrection and a radically reformed creation. Nicolai elaborated theologically on the idea of cosmic collapse by linking it with the Lutheran doctrine of Christ's ubiquity. The entire edifice of the heavens and of earth, he explained, were the "world-body" of Christ, "which he fills everywhere with his ruling presence." But that body, like the human body of the savior, had to be abandoned to suffering and death before the final resurrection, the birth of a new heaven and earth. This was the meaning of the Last Day, which would see all present nature consumed in flame, then miraculously revived. In a cosmos that appeared to be disintegrating, the only fully meaningful order lay in the vision of a total transformation, both spiritual and material. Thomas Kaufmann has pointed out how fully such apocalyptic ideas could be integrated into mystically tinged Lutheran teachings: as one could anticipate that the whole world would soon be burned up in fire, the only hope lay in the advent of the fire of the Holy Spirit in dark and blinded hearts.[16]

The mystical, even escapist element in such teachings was certainly not new, but now appeared more consistently and forcefully than ever in evangelical publicity. This was true not only of explicitly devotional materials, but of the common astrological works as well, where direct references to New Testament promises of deliverance became notably more frequent. We have seen that at least until the late 1580s the astrologers' biblical references were mainly to the Old Testament prophets, an approach directly reflecting the Melanchthonian emphasis on the stars as manifestations of natural and divine law. By the end of the century, however, the gospels and the Book of Revelation provided a growing proportion of the passages cited. Not surprisingly, the gospel chapters most often mentioned included Matthew 24, Mark 13, and Luke 21, all of which included the savior's foretelling of the end-time signs in the sun, moon, and stars. These heavenly signs, along with those featured in the Book of Revelation and elsewhere, were announcements not only of the final tribulations to come over the earth and the ultimate destruction of the world, but also of eternal deliverance for the faithful. The astrologers' waxing attention to the New Testament promises was consistent with the general spiritualizing trends we have noted, with a growing need to find more in the stars than the terrors of the law. Thus for instance in his practica for 1596 Matthias Fischer several times interrupted his natural forecasts of imminent mortal dangers with petitions that the Lord might "draw [believers] under the wings of his grace, and in his time guide and lead them out of this wasteland into eternal joy."[17]

Again, the quest for a way out inevitably involved a wide-ranging exploration of stellar meanings, and thus increased the appeal of various departures from the typical self-limitations of evangelical astrology. In the 1530s Paracelsus had rejected the art's traditional principles, and sought his own distinctive, highly unorthodox path to a truer and more Christian way of reading the stars. He had issued annual practicas of his own, as well as longer-range forecasts of a generally delphic character that had continued to appear under his name in later decades. As we noted in Chapter 5, however, the first avowed Paracelsian to gain a notable presence in the market for yearly editions was the mercurial Leonhard Thurneisser, who gained the patronage of no less a figure than the Elector of Brandenburg. An advocate of the doctrine of "sympathies" or magical correspondences in nature, this adventurer and entrepreneur came to oppose more and more stridently all "heathen" astrology, meaning essentially any sort grounded in Aristotelian or Arabic teachings. He argued that unlike many of his critics he did not depart from Ptolemaic and Christian doctrines; thus for instance he interpreted the stars as signs only, and not causes. Indeed he posed as a true reformer, attacking his critics and competitors for depending on outdated tables and confused reckonings. Denouncing all dark and demonic arts, he claimed that his own predictions were based purely in nature for the sole purpose of pious warning and consolation. Under repeated attacks in the 1570s and 1580s he grew ever more pugnacious, contending that he had introduced nothing novel or heretical. Yet much in his writings appeared deliberately obfuscatory. He posed as master of ancient languages including Hebrew, Arabic, Persian, and Syriac, all of which helped him discover profound secrets; his longer publications remained notorious for their flights into the clouds of mystery.[18]

In the eyes of most contemporary calendar men, Thurneisser was merely a fraud. Yet by the 1590s it is hard to miss broader signs of a similar desire to move beyond the pervasive sense of doom, to overcome what had evidently become a nearly paralyzing fear among evangelical townsfolk. Lucas Bathodius, for instance, a physician in the Palatinate of uncertain confessional orientation, wrote yearly forecasts with the broad goal of drawing attention beyond the physical heavens to the true spiritual prophecies of scripture. Possibly showing influence of Paracelsianism but also echoing broader spiritualizing tendencies among many evangelicals, Bathodius did not abandon natural prediction, but insisted forcefully that true prophecy was something altogether different. "Whoever trusts in God needs no weather register," he wrote in a practica for 1594; "this we present merely for the children of this world, whose curiosity has no end." His works bore similarities to some of the Christian practicas of the 1520s and 1530s, first offering apparently standard astrological data and predictions, but then moving to denounce Aristotelian natural philosophy as a basis for expounding biblical truths. At the same time, Bathodius rejected the notion that the heavens were growing naturally old and weak as an explanation for the spreading chaos among humans and in the whole cosmos. This was a "foul physic," which mistook causes and effects. A universal breakdown was indeed evident, but its ultimate causes were not natural at all; the real explanation lay in human sin, which was ultimately manifest in the very condition of the heavens. For Bathodius the central lesson of the stars was that nature itself required a radical transformation, one that could come only through an inner spiritual renewal, a change in human hearts.[19]

While in basic respects Paracelsian astrology departed from Melanchthonian principles, it shared just enough with the established emphases to filter gradually into many of the annual publications without any dramatic changes to the outward form or to much of the content. The assumption that true insight into nature looked beyond appearances to deeper realities that could confirm and strengthen faith provided a strong common ground, as did the strong prophetic element in many Paracelsian and pseudo-Paracelsian writings. It is not hard to see why by the end of the century some Lutheran physicians and pastors were beginning to appropriate Paracelsian notions for popular preaching and medical practice, or why even as they denounced various magical and "superstitious" trends, well known calendar writers such as Caesius and Winckler felt the allure of various Neoplatonic and mystical currents.[20] When referring to extra-biblical and extra-Christian texts, for instance, both these men increasingly favored ancient Neoplatonists such as Proclus, as well as famous moderns such as Cardano, over the Arabs. Winckler grew increasingly fond of ancient mystical sources such as the pseudo-Dionysius, and in 1599 described the world as a great divine circle, suggesting that all creation would ultimately return to its source. In the same year, Caesius referred to Paracelsus himself as a "wondrous philosopher." Along with his typical invocations of Luther, Melanchthon, and figures such as Leowitz, Caesius could now even cite Hermes Trismegistus, the imagined mouthpiece of highest ancient pansophic wisdom.[21]

Thus too terms such as "natural magic" appeared more frequently in the practicas of the 1590s, along with allusions to the possibility of divining crucial mysteries through the heavens in these last times. Caspar Bucha cited the heavily Neoplatonic church father Origen to the effect that the heavens were a great book through which the Creator revealed himself to his creatures. Straying from the otherwise generally conservative orientation of his practicas, Johann Krabbe of Wolfenbüttel could by 1596 refer admiringly to the "subtle, secret, hidden philosophical art of alchemy," a subject suggesting forms of human agency that had always been largely foreign to such works. These and other popular calendar writers clearly felt the pull of new perspectives that seemed to offer promises of deeper insight, a fuller and truer astrological art. The ideal of a reformed Christian astrology still showed a typically Melanchthonian capaciousness; a more precise, penetrating, and inspired understanding of nature could only help to illuminate more clearly the prophetic truths of the faith. Jole Shackelford has argued that in Lutheran Denmark at the opening of the seventeenth century "there was no telling conflict between Paracelsianism and acceptable Lutheran doctrines"; evidence from our popular practicas suggests that the German scene was not greatly different. But this situation would soon begin to change.[22]

Pansophists and Skeptics

Not long after 1600 a serious public divide began to open up among German Lutherans, evoking a true crisis of piety. The essential questions did not revolve around cosmic order or disorder, fatalism or freedom; nor were they centrally about chiliastic hopes for a new age, a worldwide triumph of the Spirit. Rather the basic issue was epistemological: were the fundamental, saving, prophetic truths to be found equally and identically in the books of nature and scripture, or was it necessary to separate these books and to show that the genuine saving truth came only through one of them? Not surprisingly, the matter would become increasingly tied to questions of authority. The full equation of the two books implied a universal revelation of truth through texts that stood potentially open to everyman; this perspective helped inform a powerful if disorganized movement of mystical devotion that flowered above all in the period c. 1605 to 1625.

On the other hand, insistence on the exclusive verity of scripture could and did help justify the notion that a proper reading required academic training, not least for the purpose of defending the gospel against all way-ward interpretations. Thus during these same years we see swiftly rising concern among many theologians, physicians, and mathematicians about the uncontrolled spread of mystical, magical, and prophetic ideas. Here the typical evangelical humanist, for whom the stars complemented the scriptures but could not reveal the saving truth itself, stood awkwardly in the middle.

A full discussion of the opposed trajectories of pansophic specula-tion and biblical orthodoxy in the early seventeenth century would take us beyond the scope of this study. But we do need to sketch a picture that allows us to see the struggles of the Lutheran calendar men in rela-tion to the general crisis of piety and its eventual outcome. One pivotal point in this unfolding was the appearance of the astounding new star of 1604, which accompanied the much-discussed twenty-year conjunction of Saturn and Jupiter in that same year. As Westman points out, this bril-liant nova helped spur a turn to more purely natural analyses of such phenomena among some interpreters. But for most the nova provided a "divine exclamation point" to the conjunction, which underscored the whole series of unprecedented cosmic signs stretching back most notably to 1572.[23] The notion that a visibly changing cosmos pointed to the immi-nence of universal changes now spurred more intense debate than ever. For evangelicals searching anxiously for signs of promise and a "way out," and especially for those drawn to Neoplatonic visions of a fallen creation coming full circle to its original purity, the new star became a glorious announcement of approaching transformation. Wilhelm Eo Neuheuser of Strasbourg analyzed the phenomenon through a combination of bibli-cal and "cabalistic" means, leading to the conclusion that a rebirth of both spiritual and worldly dimensions was imminent. Another major comet in 1607 further reinforced the vision of a cosmos on the verge of sudden and radical transformation.[24]

Publicists such as Neuheuser worked to accelerate the emergence of a newly eclectic apocalypticism drawing on mystical, magical, and prophetic traditions both old and new. Among the sources contributing to this mix were the writings of the Lutheran mystic Valentin Weigel (1533–1588), who emphasized the need for inner transformation on the basis of a profoundly personal relationship with Christ and the Holy Spirit; this transformation could then become manifest on the macrocosmic level. Perhaps the most widely influential synthesis of mystical and apocalyptic currents came in the writings and sermons of Johann Arndt (1555–1621). In some ways Arndt was typical defender of evangelical astrology. In his famous work *True Christianity* (1605–1610) he denounced misuses of the art that led to curiosity, idolatry, and superstition. Because the Creator ruled all nature through the stars, the natural man was subject to them. Yet by the gift of grace one could become a child no longer of Saturn or Venus, but of God. Arndt also drew on the idea of celestial degeneration; here again a vision of natural decline and hope for a redemptive spiritual transformation were intimately related. Moving beyond these common themes, however, Arndt engaged in a heavily Neoplatonic discourse of macrocosm and microcosm that approached an outright magical pansophism. The heavens were a divine text meant for human reading and illumination; the truly faithful person could become a ruler over nature for whom all things were possible. It would be difficult to overstate the appeal of Arndt's writings during the years of soaring confessional tensions, dearth, inflation, and general anxiety that preceded the outbreak of war in the Empire. Yet at the same time he came under heavy attack from a number of prominent orthodox academicians, and his immensely popular works drew even more intense denunciations in the years immediately after his death. Arguably no one was more central than Arndt to the early-seventeenth-century crisis of piety.[25]

Although astrologers in the Melanchthonian tradition had always given a wide berth to divine messages in the heavens, their approach to the stars did not satisfy the spiritual sensibility of Paracelsian, Arndtian, Weigelian, and other mystically inclined interpreters. These figures felt constrained by any mere "science" of astrology conceived essentially as "a part of physics." Even the long-venerated ideal of returning to a purified Ptolemaic art seemed too limiting, since all such heathen practices pursued only the outward knowledge of physical forces. The proper approach to the stars required a spiritual understanding that grasped the profound correspondences between external signs and inner experiences. Proponents of this emerging pansophic perspective often cultivated the ideal of a higher, more comprehensive mathematics, in which the mysteries of number became the essential keys to a unified knowledge of the Bible, nature, and history. A main if still obscure figure in this development was Eustachius Poyssel, who in the 1590s conceived a dizzying mix of biblical numbers, conjunction theory, and pseudocabalistic reckoning, and was among the first writers to cite 1623 as the likely year of universal transformation, looking past 1603 and 1604 to the time of the following great conjunction. Since in their eyes the usual mundane predictions, forecasts of disaster, and prayers for divine intervention failed to touch the crucial correspondences, seekers in this vein tended to abandon the annual calendar and practica as vehicles for their explorations; the production of the yearly forecasts thus remained mostly in the hands of more restrained evangelical pastors and physicians.[26]

The most dramatic public eruption of pansophy and magical reformism came with the printing of the first Rosicrucian manifestos in 1614 and 1615. Both the *Fama Fraternitatis* and the *Confessio Fraternitatis* had originated around 1610 within a circle of thinkers that included the Swabian pastor and theologian Johann Valentin Andreae, along with his teacher Tobias Hess. Well before these tracts were printed, passionate Protestants across the Empire had eagerly copied, read, and issued responses to these writings, which purported to reveal the formation of a secret society of enlightened men devoted to the realization of a universal spiritual and social transformation in the last days of the world. Both works conveyed a burning anti-Romanism along with intense anticipation of an imminent worldwide reform. Central was the notion that the secrets of scripture and nature were fully identical; with their dawning revelation in these final times, the creation was coming full-circle to its original pristine condition. These texts built directly on the doctrine of the great conjunctions and on the astounding series of recent new stars and comets, but insisted that reading these signs required a "new language" transcending all school doctrine. The idea of a secret society whose members were alone worthy to understand this language inevitably contributed to an atmosphere of cloudy speculation and even mystery mongering among the spiritual explorers of the day. Many of the "new prophets" whom the Rosicrucian tracts helped inspire seized upon the idea that saving truths were to be learned only in the "school of the Holy Spirit," emphasizing in this way their rejection of academic theology and philosophy. The tremendous publicity evoked by the Rosicrucian tracts thus did much to speed up the polarization of perspectives within German Lutheranism.[27]

Even as mystics and pansophists turned against the heathen astrology of the still-omnipresent annual works, a surge of new and harsh attacks on the evangelical calendar men came from another flank. Indictments against them grounded in a combination of strict biblicism and natural-philosophical skepticism had never disappeared entirely, as we saw in the case of Jacob Andreae's sermon of 1577. But this sort of outright denunciation of the astrologers as purveyors of a false and unchristian temptation had remained exceptional through the sixteenth century. Now, in the midst of an ever more tangled scene of published prophecies and revelations, a solid oppositional front began to form. While some critics focused on the presumed proclivity of the practica-writers to offer specific forecasts about the end of the world, the real issues were nearly always broader and deeper.

Thus for instance in his *Regentenspiegel* of 1607 the Ulm preacher Thomas Birck included a long blanket attack on the "star-gawkers" whose superstitions had infected everything. This thick advice-book was formally addressed to "all lords and noble rulers," but offered an easy vernacular style accessible to a broader lay readership. Birck's targets included both the casters of private nativities and the annual publicists. He cited Luther at great length, who along with the Bible, the fathers, and even wise pagans such as Cicero had shown the perversity in trusting to this and all "demonic arts," which were closely allied with Papist superstition. Likewise he drew directly on Andrea's 1577 sermon: the latter-day calendars and practicas were "so full of lies that [their authors] should be ashamed not only before God and all pious people, but for themselves." He saw no essential differences between these writers and a long line of notorious sorcerers stretching back to ancient times. Birck described the sun, moon, and stars simply as "the ornaments of God's heavenly seat," from which one could tell nothing at all about divine intentions.[28] Despite his goal of defending supposedly orthodox evangelical teachings, he presented here a brand of skepticism at which Luther himself would surely have balked.

The size of Birck's tome might have limited its audience, but similar arguments were also spreading through shorter, more accessible tracts such as Philipp Fesel's 1609 *Gründtlicher Discurs Von der Astrologia Judiciari*. Fesel's writing was prompted above all by the annual practicas of the Mentzingen pastor-astrologer Melchior Schaerer, a figure solidly ensconced in the Melanchthonian tradition. But his goals were much larger: he sought to discredit the entire industry of stellar publicity. Holding the post of physician to the staunchly evangelical Margrave of Baden-Durlach, Fesel was probably a Lutheran, at least for political and professional purposes; it is notable, though, that he maintained numerous and close contacts in Calvinist circles. He placed himself in a line of thinkers who had supposedly opposed astrology outright, including not only Luther and other evangelicals such as Johannes Brenz and Jacob

Andreae, but also Reformed figures such as Erastus. He took hot exception to Schaerer's argument—by now common in the mass literature—that Luther had opposed only the astrological abuses of his day; indeed he worked hard to present evidence to the contrary. Melanchthon naturally posed a problem; one could merely observe that this teacher had given himself "more than excessively" to the stellar art, and had thus perpetrated "many gross errors."[29]

Fesel tried to ground his own contentions both philosophically and theologically, pointing out contradictory assumptions and inconsistent conclusions among various astrologers, while also making frequent references to scripture. In a twist that might amuse us today, he dismissed the belief of "some of the most prominent astrologers" that the earth, rather than the sphere of the fixed stars, rotated; this notion violated both scripture and common sense. Fesel also denied that the heavens were weakening, an idea that he knew had fed into mystical currents. Following Erastus, he denounced the deeply entrenched practice of timing medical treatments according to the common calendars, holding that it had far more often damaged than helped bodily health. Like Birck, Fesel drew on Jacob Andreae's sermon of 1577, one of only a handful of sixteenth-century evangelical works that a writer hostile to the stellar art might cite. He lifted a long section from Andreae asserting that the sign-readers finally led people away from the gospel; indeed "they come to believe such a practica and the devilish stargazer more than the divine word itself." Fesel's sweeping condemnation included predictions from a practica of 1604 that had appeared under the name of Leonhard Thurneisser. He thus implicitly linked Schaerer's form of astrology with the work of a writer whom many if not most calendar men regarded as a dangerous charlatan and a hawker of fables.[30]

Schaerer himself had in fact not entirely resisted the spreading Paracelsian and Neoplatonic trends. He stressed the close complementarity between the book of nature and the scriptural word in a powerfully suggestive way, and included much talk of correspondences between microcosm and macrocosm. But his writings from this period also reflected a hesitation to move further along this path, and even a certain retrenchment. In the preface to his practica for 1609 he vigorously presented the standard justifications in a traditional Melanchthonian mode; at the same time he hurled abuse at the art's opponents, calling them "Cyclopes" emitting "bovine and asinine sounds."[31] His main response to Fesel took form in a work of 1611, actually little more than an expansion of points he had already presented in his earlier practicas, adducing arguments from authority, experience, reason, nature, and scripture in an effort to prove that astrology was a fully Christian science. He sought to turn Fesel's evangelical authorities fully around, repeating the now-standard line that Luther's attitude had been largely a response to abuses that had since been corrected in tandem with the gospel teaching itself. "Today through the special grace of God," he wrote, "not only have theology and the Holy Scriptures been purified of all sorts of corruptions and human inventions, but also the noble liberal arts have been reestablished and arranged so that they now nobly flourish and bloom, and may together with the divine word be useful and of help to the human race." His own position, Schaerer insisted, was the true middle way. He sought to defend "only genuine and sober astrology, which is nothing other than a part of physics, and is grounded on purely natural causes." To identify this noble art with magic, conjuring, and the demonic arts was simply wrong; on the contrary, a proper reading of the heavens helped reveal both divine omnipotence and the glory of the creation.[32] Here Schaerer seems deliberately to have skirted questions about the prophetic and apocalyptic dimensions of stellar science.

The dispute between Fesel and Schaerer has escaped oblivion mainly because it would draw in the most renowned reforming astrologer of the day. In 1610 Johannes Kepler stepped into the ongoing feud with his *Tertius interveniens*, presenting his now-famous appeal to Fesel and other critics "not to throw the baby out with the bathwater." We have noted that Kepler had reason to see himself as a perpetuator of the Lutheran reformation of astrology, though in fact he had already departed significantly from the main emphases of that tradition. Many old-style calendar men clung to the belief that he was one of their own, an expert vindicator of their calling. His name appeared frequently, often together with those of the pagan and Arabic masters, but more emphatically in association with the line of great recent reformers going back to Regiomontanus. Yet his intervention, which saved the art by reducing it to barest bones, could have brought little real comfort to those still convinced that astrology was both a part of physics and a means of reading divine signs. Kepler's *Astronomia nova* had appeared in 1609, muddying the mathematical waters in ways that were immensely difficult for even the most sophisticated astrologers to digest.[33]

Meanwhile, critiques from the side of the theologians grew more insistent. In 1612 the Giessen professor Caspar Finck added to a growing

chorus of complaints about astrologers' speculations on the nearness of
the Last Day. Two years later Daniel Cramer of Stettin argued strenuously
against the calendrical astrologers who made a hash of stellar computation
and prophetic visions.[34] Such attacks reinforced growing doubts among
the calendar men themselves. The pastor-astrologer Nicholas Eberhard
Winckler had followed in the footsteps of his famous forebear, Nicholas
Winckler, undertaking annual forecasts starting around 1602. But he
soon began to downplay the stars as causes of predictable human events,
and he grew more and more critical of the abuses, errors, and incompetence he found in many, even most of his competitors' works. The elder
Winckler continued to publish yearly until around 1612 and lived into the
following year, which may explain the son's hesitation to make a public
break any sooner than he did. But in 1615 the younger man issued a scathing attack on "the ubiquitous misuse of astrology, which in these days has
been ever more commonly and shamelessly introduced into calendars and
practicas." Despite its title, this was more than a condemnation of novelties; it came close to a general indictment of the evangelical stargazers.
Winckler appealed repeatedly to scripture and the church fathers, arguing
that the prevailing modes of stellar reading were unnecessary, ill-founded,
and indeed sins against God that should be opposed by all pastors and
church leaders. Evidently feeling that his admonitions were having little
effect, he gave up entirely on calendar writing by 1618. Parallel shifts in
attitude appear in the writings of other prominent evangelical publicists
around this time. By 1617, even Johann Valentin Andreae came to ridicule not only the sort of apocalyptic astrology that had shaped the early
Rosicrucian writings, but the whole enterprise of reading prophetic truths
in the stars, nature, and numbers.[35]

Holding the Center

Confused and conflicted, traditional mainstream Melanchthonians began
to feel the ground slipping from under their feet. Especially from around
the time of the "divine exclamation point" of 1604, we find the prominent
calendar men struggling to maintain an approach to the heavens that was
both mathematical and prophetic, neither a fully rationalized science nor
a spiritualized pansophic quest. One way in which more traditional students of the stars began to draw lines was by resisting visions of a firmament in collapse. In his forecast for 1605, for example, Sebastian Koestner

energetically denied that the stars were already literally falling. The hands of the Almighty himself were the true pillars of heaven; he held them up "strongly and securely." And although they had spun about the earth once every twenty-four hours since the creation, "the great firmament does not grow tired, and it is not breaking down." Heaven and earth were indeed the books of God, which revealed his omnipotence, goodness, and mercy. To be sure, Koestner expressed a typically intense apocalyptic outlook; he had no doubt that the judgment was coming soon. But to hold that the heavens themselves were disintegrating was to suggest that God's goodness was no longer evident in nature at all. Evangelical astrology had always left room, at least implicitly, for the chaotic workings of the devil, but it had never admitted that this fallen world would ever be lost entirely to the forces of evil. As long as the world stood, nature would continue to manifest both order and disorder. So too David Herlicius denied the possibility of a complete natural breakdown before the end itself. Amid detailed reckonings about looming waves of disease and death, he clung to a positive hope: "Yet surely our dear God will not leave the lowest [elemental] world entirely wasted, but will keep a seed [of life] on earth until the longed-for Last Day." And after further painstaking figurings and forecasts, he assured his readers that "in sum, God orders all, rules all, and eases all so that we poor humans can bear it. To him be praise and honor in eternity. Allelujah."[36]

Herlicius learned from his own experience about the perils of unrestrained speculative adventures. This renowned professor and Stargard physician had begun to produce more or less standard annual forecasts in the 1580s, when he had humbly described himself as "still a pupil in this high art."[37] But soon afterward he was allowing himself to calculate daringly on prophetic matters. His *Tractatus Theologastronomistoricus* of 1596, for example, drew on history, scripture, and the stars to predict the imminent demise of the Turkish Empire, hard on the heels of which would follow the end of the world itself. Page upon page of calculations and prophetic evidence pointed to 1600 as a crucial date in this final unfolding.[38] The work brought its author much attention and no little notoriety. As time passed with no earth-shaking developments Herlicius appears to have felt chastened; his subsequent practicas, as well as his tract on the 1604 nova, showed a more modest mix of natural analyses and warnings to repentance. Nonetheless in 1606 he came under heavy fire from a Riga calendar-writer named Bernhard Messinger, who charged him outright with making false predictions,

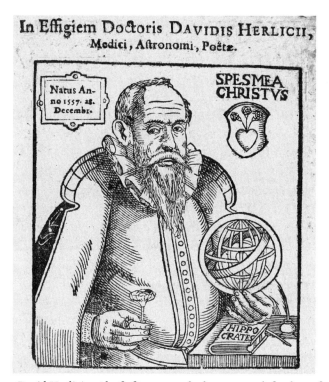

FIGURE 7.1 David Herlicius (d. 1636), among the last strong defenders of evangelical astrology in the Melanchthonian tradition. Image from Herlicius's practica for 1610. Courtesy of the Herzog August Bibliothek Wolfenbüttel, Xb 5126 (3), A/v.

especially regarding political affairs. Herlicius replied in a hot-tempered tract of the same year, defending his own reputation and expertise while impugning those of his critic.[39] His career suffered no obvious harm from such spats; indeed he would go on to enter the service of the Brandenburg Elector. Yet like others trained in a tradition now starting to wane he felt mounting hostility, both from those who cast his art as blind philosophy, and from those who feared it as an encouragement to mystical fantasies.

Working to show the care with which he pursued his science, Herlicius packed more and more detail into his practicas; his forecast for 1610 stretched to over sixty pages (see Figures 7.1 and 7.2). Here he led a general trend: in the face of an ever more crowded and sensation-filled market, the typical annual prognostication grew longer and more elaborate. While in most cases the motive was to offer fuller and clearer astrological reasoning, the overall result was that these works grew more characteristically baroque in both form and content. For Herlicius, though, more verbiage

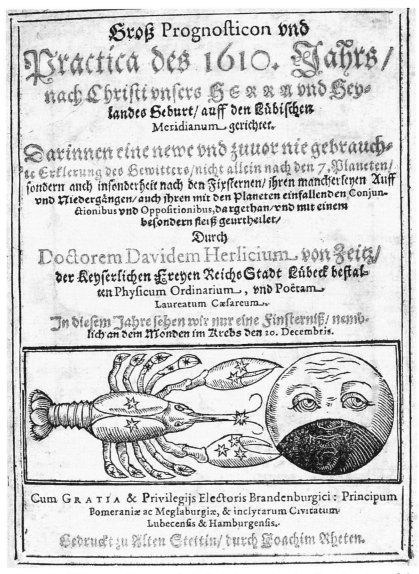

FIGURE 7.2 Title page from David Herlicius's practica for 1610. Courtesy of the Herzog August Bibliothek Wolfenbüttel, Xb 5126 (3).

did not mean any dilution in the defense of Melanchthonian principles. He asserted the profound necessity of the stellar art not only in his own professional field of medicine, but also for the proper understanding of Holy Scripture and thus for theology. The end of the world, he stressed, could not be calculated, "though learned fantasts have tried to do so."

Filling leaf after leaf with analyses of the predicted planetary aspects and their mainly negative effects, Herlicius could still mix references to Albumasar and the great conjunctions with biblical citations and preaching on the need of every person to repent and prepare himself for death. His worldly pessimism echoed themes still deeply rooted in evangelical preaching. As the old creation approached its limit, peace had all but fully retreated to heaven; it would not return until the heavenly king himself came for the judgment.[40]

In his practicas through most of the subsequent decade, Herlicius referred repeatedly to his ambitious plan for a work to be titled *Calendarographia*, a comprehensive and definitive exposition of the calendar-maker's art. Tellingly, though, the book never appeared. Herlicius implied that he was unable to find a willing publisher, and the claim was quite possibly true, for with each passing year of the sixteen-teens, the very idea of fulfilling such aims would appear more suspect in many eyes. Meanwhile the physician responded to critics by stressing over and again the tremendous difficulties facing anyone who hoped to predict atmospheric conditions and their effects. He opened his practica for 1617 with the argument that of all the branches of stellar science, the hardest lay in yearly predictions for the weather, health and illness, fruitfulness, war and peace, the outlook for travelers, and similar basic matters of practical concern. Many who had lately entered this field had no conception of its challenges, and imagined that guesswork was a substitute for the daunting labors it actually required. To the almost infinite range of variables one had always to take into account, expert astronomers such as Tycho Brahe, Kepler, and David Fabricius had lately added new observations and mathematical hypotheses, making the task more complex than ever. Only time would tell where these new ideas would lead; "God help us," he exclaimed in apparent exasperation. His words reveal the growing strain on evangelical stargazers and preachers as they tried to maintain their characteristic balance of faith and philosophy.[41]

Following what had by now become almost a convention among the better-known calendar men, Herlicius spat out scorn for ignorant, self-appointed writers who managed to do nothing but smear the paper with their nonsense. They spent their energies in attacking one another while stealing data and insights from authors such as himself. But they failed to understand or even to state accurately what he had presented. And this was not even to mention the dreamers who offered nothing but crazed delusions disguised as stellar prognostications. Making much of his own experience over more than three decades, he wrote that he had continually directed all his skills to the correction and right use of the art. Yet he now stressed more strongly than ever the limits of mathematical reckoning. While the natural signs indicated a cold, hard winter to come and an even worse spring, "we appeal from the unsure calendrical art (by which no one can swear an oath that it will so happen) to our dear God, who is a merciful and almighty father." With earnest prayer and repentance the practica-writer might prove far, far wrong, and this was his sincere hope.[42] As we know, this sort of self-limitation and hopeful disavowal had been common among evangelical stargazers for nearly a century; Herlicius was simply voicing it with new force in the face of challenges on every side. Indeed the more he felt the need to justify and rectify his science, the more sweeping his qualifications became.

The efforts of mainline astrologers to fend off multiple assaults and to maintain the Melanchthonian tradition are similarly evident in the works of Simon Marius (1573–1624), successor to Georg Caesius as the appointed calendar writer at Ansbach and court astronomer to the Margrave of Brandenburg. Like fellow writers such as Herlicius, Marius did his best to distance himself from a presumed mob of ignorant writers who thrived on guesswork and wild sensationalism. He explained that he drew his data not from any of the inherited and conflicting ephemerides, but rather from the tables of Tycho Brahe, which marked a patent advance in his eyes. Marius was in fact a more careful observer and a more able mathematician than most of his competitors. We know for instance that he discovered Jupiter's moons independently of Galileo, also using a telescope. In his practicas he devoted much more attention to careful meteorological reckonings than to the more human vagaries such as war and peace.[43] He conformed to the general trend by packing his annual works with more and more historical evidence to bolster his readings. Continuing in a spirit of Melanchthonian eclecticism, he did not entirely reject the Arab authorities. On the other hand he did denounce the new chemical medicine of the Paracelsians, and scoffed at the quest for the "philosopher's stone," a universal cure. He also consistently sought to distance himself from any definite political forecasting, though he left a good deal of ambiguity about the possibilities. If he wanted to employ "Thurneisserish" methods, he wrote in 1614, he might predict the demise of a great ruler for the following February. But he would refrain from dealing with such things in print, for "they bring great dangers."[44]

Nonetheless, in his forecast for 1612 Marius noted that for more than a few years astrologers had predicted some enormous world-change or Reformation, and he clearly placed himself among them. Though nothing of the sort had yet come to pass, he maintained that the expectation was still valid. He disavowed any association with those who wrote practicas out of "an angry, pernicious, or troubled spirit"; he hoped to make his own predictions as simple, straightforward, and honest as possible. Beyond his painstaking forecasts of atmospheric conditions, Marius thought it crucial to note the striking series of celestial signs that had appeared since 1572, "the likes of which have never occurred and been observed in any age from the beginning of the world." One did not need to be an expert mathematician to draw appropriate conclusions. Again in his annual outlook for 1615 Marius acknowledged that he and many other "excellent mathematicians" had expected some "universal change" to come around 1612; while none had yet happened, he thought the current celestial aspects reinforced the anticipation of terrible events that would transcend all prior human experience: "God grant that it will turn out better than we astrologers state or hope."[45] Among other challenges, Marius and his fellow evangelical prognosticators faced the problem of an increasingly glaring gulf between the knowledge of expert cosmologists and the culture of astrological publicity. They were increasingly unsure of just how to position themselves. In the preface to his forecast for 1610, Marius discussed the question of whether "high matters of philosophy" should be translated into or discussed in the German language rather than in Latin. On one hand, he complained about the new flood of vernacular medical and alchemical works that led the common folk into error, confusion, and harmful practices. It was necessary, he thought, to maintain a clear distinction between the learned and the uneducated masses. Yet in this very same work he followed a pattern long typical of the mass-market calendars and practicas, mixing in many Latin phrases and passages along with learned references in ways that implicitly undermined any clear barriers between lay and learned cultures. And he included discussions of astrological methods "to encourage other free and sharp minds to consider these [philosophical] issues energetically."[46]

Indeed, for all his concern to set his works apart from the writings of ignorant sensationalizers, Marius shared more than he care' o admit with other astrological publicists who remained within the M anchthonian orbit. For years he carried on a bitter dispute with Georg Halbmayer (d. 1637), who borrowed material heavily and shamelessly from his work, and who even half-stole his identity by using the pseudolatinized name of Albanus Marius. Halbmayer took his marketing tricks yet further, calling himself the disciple of the renowned Georg Caesius, and putting out calendars under the names of other popular astrologers such as Georg Kreslin, yet another stargazing pastor. The Albanus Marius forecasts for 1613 and subsequent years perpetuated familiar themes, mixing astronomical data and weather forecasts with terrifying scenarios of disasters, frequent biblical citations, invective against the Papal Antichrist, appeals to the prophecies of Luther regarding Germany, warnings of the imminent Judgment, and fervent calls to repentance.[47] Certainly Halbmayer showed less real mathematical expertise than Marius, and he was far more open in expressing evangelical and anti-Roman convictions. Yet it is hard to see any basic divide between the aims of these publicists; Halbmayer's thefts and imitations finally amounted to statements of agreement. The spats among such figures were nothing new, and were not a major cause of their slipping public status. While they may have struck different balances of mathematical precision, religious preaching, and propaganda, the two men stood on a common inherited ground.

With growing difficulty, these Lutheran prognosticators fought to maintain their art amidst the opposing barrages of hostile claims from the new biblicists, mathematical reformers, skeptics, mystical seekers, Rosicrucian enthusiasts, and spiritualist prophets. Their plight is reflected in a 1616 work by Christopher Cnoll, a church deacon at Sprottau, titled *Prognosticon Generale Perpetuum*. Clearly familiar with a wide range of recent trends in stellar science, Cnoll made ready reference to the debate among Schaerer, Fesel, and Kepler. Denouncing what he saw as a recent surge in superstitious and harmful abuses of the stars, he strongly implied that his views were in agreement with Kepler's. His actual position, however, was much closer to that of the more popular and mainstream calendar men. He engaged in what was by now an almost tortured debate over what sorts of things could and could not be predicted from natural signs. Generally rejecting the Arabs, he drew on Peucer in an attempt to distinguish between legitimate and illegitimate kinds of divination. Without doubt the stars were a necessary instrument of Christian understanding and warning. But while predictable events such as eclipses and conjunctions might indicate all sorts of earthly disasters, they were not themselves signs of the imminent Last Judgment. On the other hand, the Almighty did intend the natural eclipses that occurred each year to be reminders of the nearing day on which the sun and moon would lose their shine supernaturally and forever. God's beneficial natural order would remain until the very end, yet indicators of disorder and wrath were visible everywhere in creation; passages from scripture and Luther underlined this latter point. For all his earnest wrestling with these issues, in the end Cnoll failed—or rather refused—to draw a precise line between an art of natural prediction and a theological reading of the heavens. Such a line would have violated his deep desire to hold together a cosmos at once mathematically ordered and filled with uniquely urgent divine messages. His conclusion was revealing: the best-qualified students of the stars, he wrote, were mathematically trained theologians.[48]

Mounting Crossfire

The most serious blows to the Melanchthonian tradition came only after the outbreak of war as announced by the famous Defenestration of Prague in May, 1618 and by a great comet later in that same year. From this point through the middle of the next decade, the confrontation between a newly consolidating orthodoxy and the pansophic currents of the day surged to a head and burst entirely open. The studies of Leigh Penman have explored this critical phase in Lutheran confessional history mainly through the lens of the controversy over chiliasm, understood as any belief in an age of peace to come before the Last Day itself. But as Penman himself points out, orthodox critics of chiliasm were themselves unable to define the error clearly, so that the term came to mean little more than any teaching without the approval of academic theologians. While predictions of a new age offered a relatively easy if superficial target for these critics, the confrontation between the so-called "new prophets" and the agents of an emerging academic departmentalism reflected the broader and deeper issues of prophetic knowledge and authority we have outlined, which now reached full crisis stage. Caught in the heavy crossfire of this battle, the evangelical astrologers sustained serious wounds from which they would never recover.

One figure arguably epitomizes better than any other the churning mix of biblical apocalypticism, astrology, Paracelsianism, pansophism, number mysticism, and magical chiliasm that drew a storm of orthodox condemnations by the late sixteen-teens. Paul Nagel (c. 1580–1624) emerged in the early years of the century as a more or less typical evangelical commentator on the nova of 1604, a hotly anti-Roman preacher of repentance in the face of the nearing Last Judgment. Nagel had studied first at his hometown university of Leipzig; he then took the master of arts degree at Wittenberg. Sustaining himself as a private tutor and astrologer, in 1609 he was appointed official calendar writer at Torgau by the Leipzig city council. His writings from this period, such as his *Catoptromantia Physica* for 1610, continued to boil with apocalyptic excitement, but also revealed an urgent striving for deeper and fuller wisdom. Indeed by this time Nagel was becoming immersed in Paracelsian magical and alchemical writings, as well as in the mystical thinking of figures such as Johann Arndt and Valentin Weigel (1533–1588). Soon he would encounter the theosophy of Jacob Böhme, today the best-known Lutheran mystic of all. In fact, as Penman has shown, he read Böhme's *Morgen Röte im Aufgang* (1612) before it appeared in print, and later he would work sections of this treatise into his own publications. Similarly, even before the first of the famous Rosicrucian tracts was printed in 1614, Nagel had read and transcribed the text; not surprisingly he would join the chorus of praise for the presumed wisdom of the secret society. He probably also became familiar with the pseudo-Weigelian text *Astrologia Theologizata*. Not printed until 1617 but circulated in manuscript for years earlier, this work stressed the need to move beyond the common stellar art to a fully spiritualized understanding of nature.[49]

Until at least 1617, Nagel appears to have refrained from open criticism of more conventional evangelical teachers and preachers. Not coincidentally, this year also brought the centenary jubilee celebrations looking back to 1517, which afforded clerics and academics an obvious opportunity to expound on their understanding of Luther's heritage, to defend it against the Jesuits and the Calvinists, and to combat what they saw as threats from within the fold.[50] The rifts between Lutheran pansophy and orthodoxy were quickly growing wider and more public when in September Nagel was first called before the Saxon church inspectors and questioned about his teachings and writings. Shortly later he published his *Prognosticon Astrologo-Cabalisticum* for 1618, a work that according to Nagel himself came under attack from both the learned and the ignorant, and "even seemed to raise the ire of the Devil."[51] While this tract is apparently lost, it likely marked its author's first unrestrained expression of a pansophic and prophetic vision, a kaleidoscopic mix of biblical prophecy, astrology, numerology, and anticipation of a soon-to-dawn new age. Then in November of 1618, the appearance of the brilliant comet yet further crystallized Nagel's convictions. Coming as it did just as interconfessional and political animosities were exploding into war, this event evoked literally hundreds of pamphlets, broadsheets, and tracts from interpreters through-out Europe. In dozens of his own publications over the next several years, the Torgau theologian and astronomer—as he called himself—preached a message combining passionate calls for inner spiritual transformation with an almost incredible array of biblical, mathematical, and historical reckonings to show that a age of peace and fulfillment would dawn in 1624 if not sooner. This final flowering of the spirit would be as brief as it was beautiful; Nagel thought the Last Judgment itself would likely come after forty-two years, in 1666.

Although as early as 1619 his worldly predictions looked ahead to 1624, most of Nagel's writings were based at least loosely on the traditional form of the annual practica. He saw himself as an astronomer whose eyes had been opened to God's wonderful revelation, expressed identically in the heavens and scripture. His was thus an "astronomy of grace" quite unlike the heathen astronomy of Brahe, Kepler, and the mainline calendar writers. He rejected their worldly mathematics, while at the same time he criticized more and more boldly the emerging academic orthodoxy. Every person could ultimately find within himself the "golden instrument" or measure by which truth would be revealed to him. "Pray that your eyes will be opened to see," he preached against his critics. "Throw away your art, your logic and metaphysics, become fools with us before the world, and children of the new birth before God the Lord; thus will you be helped, otherwise you remain blind and deluded."[52] Although he dismissed the school doctrines of his day, Nagel never decisively rejected his evangelical heritage; indeed he saw himself as Luther's true heir, preaching the same message of repentance in the Last Days but gifted with a fuller and truly final revelation. It seems likely that the coming of his personal last day, late in 1624, was connected with the evident failure of his dream for a new age.[53]

The torrent of publications that flowed from Paul Nagel's pen formed only a small portion of the literature produced by the nature-mystics and new prophets of this era, but no one did more to solidify and accelerate the orthodox drive to reject the book of nature as a source of prophetic insight. In 1620 the Mecklenburg court preacher Georg Rost could still defend the astrologer's cautious use of the stars along with the Bible to make predictions about events on the eve of the Last Day. Only two years later, however, Rost expressed himself far more vigorously and negatively, arguing that Nagel and his ilk had introduced "a confused chaos between theology and philosophy"; these, he insisted, were entirely different forms of knowledge, which could not be mixed together.[54] As Penman shows, Rost was soon accompanied by a flock of orthodox critics who were united in denouncing virtually everything associated with the supposed party of the Rosicrucians and with the cabalistic reckoning, pansophic striving, and chiliasm of the new prophets. But the key point is that in reacting to what they perceived as a dangerous chaos, orthodox thinkers were led to dismiss an entire tradition of pious conjecture, a tradition that included uses of astrology still embraced by many preachers and calendar men.

The frightening events of the day certainly facilitated this dismissal by placing new liabilities on almost anyone engaged in the business of prediction. The comet of 1618 was a screaming siren not only for the likes of Nagel, but for nearly all evangelical commentators; coming at a time of peaking political crisis in the empire, it drew a new wave of intensely excited responses.[55] Despite their denunciations of the pansophic "fantasts," calendar men such as David Herlicius could not resist the pressure to engage in a range of prophetic speculations that would open them even more fully to criticism from the consolidating orthodox ranks. Like many others, Herlicius interpreted the comet as both a divine warning and as a public sign of God's grace, which had to be understood in the series of astounding new stars and comets going back to 1572. Other recent appearances such as a triple sun brought yet more urgency. And the conjunctions remained crucial: the expected meeting of Jupiter and Saturn in 1623 and 1624 carried enormous if literally incalculable apocalyptic import. The famed physician defended himself more vigorously than ever against those theologians who would accuse him of binding God to the stars, while at the same time he preached more earnestly than ever his message of repentance in the face of the coming end. Melchior Schaerer's practica for 1620 sounded many parallel points, but ventured just a bit further: the whole array of comets, novas, eclipses, and other signs since 1572 pointed to "a general Reformation to come around the year 1623, when there will occur the great conjunction of the planets in the fiery triangle and indeed in the sign of Leo." Schaerer left the precise nature of this coming general Reformation to individual speculation, and ultimately to God's infinite freedom. He retained a traditional emphasis on future wrath and judgment, preaching that God would lighten the deserved punishments for those Germans and Christians who were truly repentant.[56]

Other practica writers expanded on the hints of hope conveyed in terms such as "general Reformation," taking their speculations in more concrete political directions that carried serious risk. The Nuremberg mathematician Mauritz Huberin was among those who indulged the prospect that "a great change in the entire Holy Roman Empire is at hand." Although the final hour of the world was certainly imminent, the coming great conjunction and complementary signs indicated that God in his grace would allow a union of German princes, who would overthrow the forces of evil. In fact the preface to Huberin's forecast for 1621 included a slobbering celebration of the newly elected but soon-to-be-deposed King and Queen of Bohemia, Frederick V and Elizabeth. This was an unusual step among the generally cautious calendar men; enthusiasm for Frederick often went together with a magical reformism that sought to transcend Protestant confessional differences. But Huberin's writing shows how quickly the outlook of the popular astrologers could become politicized and confused in the intensely pressurized atmosphere of the early war years. After the Battle of the White Mountain in 1620, as Habsburg advances made conditions in the Empire appear more and more desperate, calendar writers were further tempted to offer alternative speculative scenarios. In his annual work for 1624, for instance, Georg Halbmayer revived the predictions of Johannes Lichtenberger from a century and a half earlier, turning them into Protestant propaganda. He foresaw countless horrors, but such special disasters for "spiritual princes and prelates" that one might hope for "a New Order" in Germany. He prayed that God might bring the current afflictions to an end, and "maintain the true saving religion among us, and protect us in peace."[57]

In 1624, in the very last practica he composed before his death, Simon Marius concluded that the great reformation and upheaval he had long predicted for Germany and indeed the whole world had in fact begun four years earlier. Having been announced and partly brought on by celestial events such as the new star of 1604, this change was in fact the great and high work of the almighty God, and thus beyond explanation through the constellations and heavenly aspects. Marius carefully pointed out that he had never used methods such as the "foolish and superstitious cabala" in an effort to discern the divine plan. But even those more sober and responsible astrologers who had a good knowledge of political affairs would have to admit that much had happened and was now happening that they had never foreseen, and that none of them could say with certainty how affairs in the Empire would turn out. Marius did think one could reasonably hope for a great unifying Diet, thus revealing his own move toward a more mundane style of anticipation. But "further than this

I can say or predict nothing of these matters. Others may give lofty prophecies according to their pleasure; I leave them responsible. I will not do as they do but will remain with my orderly constellations, and commit the rest to the dear true God in my prayers, along with many thousands of other pious Christians who long greatly with fervent sighs for this peace and prosperity in the Empire." The words of this bewildered astrologer anticipated a trend that would grow notably more marked after 1624 and 1625: in the place of apocalyptic warnings or hopes of deliverance through the Last Judgment, practica writers now began to issue far more modest prayers for earthly peace, the restoration of lost freedoms and a lost political order.[58]

But prudence and modesty were not enough to reverse a tidal shift taking place, above all in the Lutheran universities. The most notable development in the curricula of the schools during the early seventeenth century was the "return to metaphysics," meaning above all the revival of Aristotelian philosophy as a crucial tool in the defense of evangelical doctrine.[59] This largely academic movement involved deep opposition to the mystical and pansophic strains that had emerged within the Lutheran sphere. Strikingly and even ironically, however, it also involved a general turning away from the teachings of Melanchthon. Although the decline of Melanchthon's academic authority was far from sudden or uniform, signs of irreversible erosion were clear by the 1620s and 1630s. From the perspective of prominent orthodox theologians such as Balthasar Meisner (d. 1627), Johann Gerhard (d. 1637), and Jacob Martini (d. 1649), the lectures and writings of the very figure whose curricular ideals had dominated throughout the prior century now seemed increasingly out of date. They appeared too humanistically eclectic, not strictly philosophical enough, not sufficiently grounded in logically consistent principles; rather they presented a disorienting combination of Aristotelian, Platonic, Galenic, biblical, and other elements. These and other Lutheran academicians showed mounting hesitancy to recommend the works of the famed preceptor, even as helpful starting-points, in the study of fields ranging from ethics to natural philosophy.[60] As a result, the universities no longer sanctioned the sort of learning that had produced pastor-astrologers and physician-preachers for the evangelical towns.

While orthodox teaching generally emphasized the fundamental agreement of nature and scripture, the movement's prominent representatives approached questions about the book of nature in largely abstract terms, avoiding as far as possible the whole epistemological tangle over celestial

readings. Indeed its leading representatives brought to the orthodox program an ever-greater emphasis on scripture as the only valid source of
prophetic truth. To be sure, no one could doubt that God had created the
heavens both to reveal his glory and to help order human life by marking out times and seasons. The labors of the expert astronomers might
be prized as a way of celebrating cosmic order and divine omnipotence.
Beyond this, however, thinkers such as Martini and Meisner pursued a
form of Aristotelian philosophy shorn of all additions and interpretations
that had contributed to the art of stellar forecasting, especially those that
sanctioned readings of the human future. In a sermon of 1624, Meisner
stressed that the heavens were a pure "fifth essence" that would stand
beautiful and unchanging until the end of the world; at the same time
he notably avoided any mention of the many heavenly signs that contemporaries regarded as announcements of Christ's imminent return.
His approach, now growing common among a new generation of orthodox writers, dealt with the popular science of the stars at least partly by
ignoring it.[61]

Especially from the mid-1620s, many Lutheran academics deliberately and increasingly limited their work to academic publications in
Latin, isolating their educational enterprise from the ferment of the vernacular market and thus from the dizzying realm of popular prediction
and prophecy. At the same time, university theologians were becoming
ever more heavily involved in programs of censorship.[62] Their perspective quickly showed its influence in works intended for general consumption. A tract published at Erfurt in 1624 by the Saxon pastor Henning
Friedrich titled *Gründliche Widerlegung der Abergläubischen Astrologorum*
clearly mirrored the goals of orthodoxy; a vaguely scholastic ordering
and the inclusion of long Latin passages suggest that this work was
aimed above all at pastors and students. Decrying the ubiquitous practicas, astrological calendars, planet books, nativity manuals, and the like,
all of which were "as soon to be found in our houses as the Holy Bible,"
Friedrich presented a long and detailed diatribe against a pervasive
obsession that amounted in his eyes to heathen magic, sorcery, and an
idolatrous violation of the first commandment. He associated astrology
with the superstitions of women, and made much of every hint of a dismissive attitude he could cull from Luther's writings. In order to counter oft-cited evidence that Luther himself was not entirely opposed to
astrology, he resorted to declaring early editions of the reformer's works
corrupt. Much as Fesel had done some years earlier, he also worked to

cast Melanchthon's commitment to stargazing as a deeply misguided superstition.[63]

For his main source, Friedrich looked all the way back to the 1554 work of the Gnesiolutherans Aurifaber and Stoltz, whom he quoted and paraphrased repeatedly. As we know, the arguments of that work had faded almost entirely from the field, and scattered protests such as Andreae's 1577 sermon had gone all but entirely unheeded among evangelical publicists. But now Friedrich did everything he could to update the polemic in ways that served the theological and polemical goals of orthodox leaders. He posed an entirely novel parallel, for example, between the astrologers and the hated Calvinists. Just as the Calvinists placed Christ in the heavens (opposing the doctrine of ubiquity), so the astrologers would make Christians subject to external heavenly influence; and just as the Calvinists restricted divine grace by making God responsible for eternal damnation, so the astrologers' teachings limited the saving power of the divine Word. At the same time the astrologers could also be compared with the Papists, who taught that it was not enough to believe what was clearly revealed in Holy Scripture, but clung to foolish human inventions and traditions.[64] These analogies amounted to imaginative twists in light of prevailing attitudes among the three main confessions over the seventy years since the attack of Aurifaber and Stoltz.

We might be tempted to see in the orthodox program the triumph of an original evangelical self-understanding that had become confused and obscured by the popular astrological culture of the sixteenth century. In this view, Luther's supposed discovery of the Roman Antichrist and a specific biblically based vision of the ever-imminent Last Judgment formed the foundations of the apocalyptic outlook that defined the movement. Stellar prognostications had become mixed up superficially with these convictions, though they were essentially incompatible with them. In the course of the early seventeenth century the prophetic uses of astrology were discredited, and the supposedly central apocalyptic teachings reasserted in ways that clarified what it meant to be a good Lutheran.[65] As we have seen, however, it is hardly possible to disentangle celestial prognostication and scriptural prophecy as elements of the public discourse that actually prevailed in the sixteenth-century evangelical towns. From the very start the burghers' reception of the reform had been shaped by the assumption that visible nature, especially the heavens above, offered messages of both practical and prophetic significance. We therefore have strong reasons to see the antiastrological movement of orthodox writers in the early to mid-seventeenth century representing not the recovery of an original and authentic confessional identity, but rather something new: the rejection of an established evangelical tradition.

Enduring Eclipse

The seventeenth-century decline of stellar science as a respected element of western culture was a complex and uneven process, impossible to encompass in a single coherent narrative. Especially if we survey the entire European scene, we see that the arguments and motives of the art's various defenders and attackers were highly varied.[66] The nature and pace of astrology's retreat differed greatly between learned classes and layfolk, between townsmen and peasants, and among regional, political, and confessional settings. One might even question whether terms such as "decline" or "retreat" validly describe the outlooks of a majority of western and central Europeans before 1700; much depends on just how we define the art of the stars itself. When in 1682 the French Calvinist Pierre Bayle famously derided the assumption that comets portended evils and suffering, this belief still retained much greater currency than, say, the notion that an eclipse of the sun following a conjunction of Saturn and Mars in Aries would result in a specific sort of disaster. Historians of science have shown little consensus on the role of the "new philosophy" and of Copernicanism's quickening advance; certainly there was no simple correlation between the spread of heliocentrism and the marginalization of the stargazers.[67]

In the case of the evangelical towns of the Holy Roman Empire, however, home to the most powerful, pervasive, and public astrological discourse anywhere in Christendom during the Reformation era, unmistakable signs of a dramatic loss of status mark the era from around 1625 to 1650. We have noted one main factor in this development, namely the orthodox drive to settle the crisis of piety by discounting virtually all prophetic uses of the book of nature. A second cause lay in the waves of suffering, confusion, skepticism, and disillusionment that swept over the prognosticators, their patrons, and their audiences during the chaotic wartime decades. The relatively quick displacement of the physical heavens from their earlier role in the lives and outlooks of Lutheran burghers is manifest in the changing form and content of the popular publications as well as in the shifting circumstances of their production.

While most of the calendar men seem to have resisted jumping openly on the bandwagon of political dreams spurred by Frederick V's election to the Bohemian throne in 1618, over the course of the 1620s it became increasingly difficult for them to isolate their predictions, warnings and hopes from the realities of the wartime situation. The most fervent hopes of all among German Lutherans arose with the entry of the Swedish king Gustavus Adolphus into the picture in 1630. Now even the aging David Herlicius, having been chastened many times for mistaken forecasts over his long career, could not resist the temptation once again to pay close attention to political events. His calendar for 1631, for example, openly celebrated this new advent, adding to the chorus singing the promise of the Protestant hero.[68] But after the King's death at the battle of Lützen in November of 1632, he quickly returned to a more modest and sober mode. Herlicius was indeed one of the very last prominent representatives of the Melanchtonian tradition, combining a fundamentally practical concern with mundane matters of weather, health, and overall well-being with warnings about God's judgment and the nearing end. His own personal Last Day was ushered in mainly by the grinding demolition of war. In 1535 during the Imperial siege of Stargard, all his possessions were burned in a fire that destroyed much of the city. He died in the following year after writing his final calendar and practica.[69]

Younger contemporaries in the profession tended to become caught up more consistently than Herlicius in wartime politics and polemics. David Beineken's *Astrologische Wunder-Schrifft* of 1633 expressed the typically intense Protestant disillusionment following the death of Gustavus Adolphus, harping on God's punishments and judgments on the German people. At the same time, this work showed an ongoing preoccupation with the state of affairs in the Empire.[70] The Bohemian stargazer Martin Horky, driven from his native land after the Imperial victory there in 1620, became an ardent partisan of "the Lion of the North," but his writings lost no polemical steam after the disaster at Lützen; he continued to lace his practicas with furious antipapal and anti-Imperial thrusts. His hatred of the Jesuits was intense, for "they alone are the principal reason that now (God have mercy) the Holy Roman Empire suffers such bloody chaos." Never would the Empire see lasting peace, he added, as long as the Jesuits remained within it. He called for a united front of the German princes against the Spaniards and the power of Rome; only thus could "Germany remain Germany." Here Horky revealed a new political pragmatism, for his vision of German unity included both Lutherans and Reformed. In

1632, despite the devastating conflicts and shocking mortality that he foresaw for the year ahead, he continued to predict the advent of a great military hero who would wage successful war against the forces of Antichrist.[71]

Since the overwhelming majority of stargazing publicists favored the
Protestant cause, their works were inherently suspect in Imperial circles.
Catholic Bavaria had long since banned all calendars and practicas published outside the reach of its censors, and the prohibition was renewed in
1639. But so unsettled and confusing was the scene that at least one popular Lutheran calendar-maker, Hermann de Werve, could express explicit
support for the Emperor from the mid-1630s into the following decade.
His position allowed Habsburg partisans to encourage the distribution
of his works in both Catholic and Protestant regions. Here again, the circumstances of the war raised pressures on stargazers to take more open
and definite political stances, and thus worked to hasten the breakdown of
the intimate relationship between evangelical preaching and the business
of popular astrology.[72]

But whatever their political orientation, writers such as de Werve could
no longer count on the same level of public attention that many of their
predecessors had been able to take for granted. We saw that already in the
years around 1600 the annual works were starting to lose visibility amidst
a blizzard of vernacular publications, many of which indulged in sensational speculations about the future of the gospel, or its enemies, or the
faithful, or the Empire, or the whole world. This crowding by no means
eased during the era of the war. The 1620s and 1630s brought scores of
cheap tracts reporting prophetic visions based on dreams, personal revelations, amazing apparitions, and mysteries hidden in the Bible. At the
same time there appeared a rush of new editions of vaticinations attributed to figures such as Lichtenberger, Grünpeck, Carion, Paracelsus, and
the Sibyls, among others. Often the writings that appeared under the
names of famous stargazers included no actual astrological reckoning at
all; many, on the other hand, presented visions bearing on the raging military and political conflict. The openly political prophecies of Paul Gräbner,
a Saxon writer of the 1570s who had foreseen a great Protestant victory
over all antichristian forces, were among the older works that were now
first adapted, published, and widely distributed.[73]

Also pushing into the markets of mass publicity were broadsheets and
pamphlets that were far less concerned with predicting the future than
with simply reporting and commenting on recent and current events.
The mounting challenges to normal everyday life ultimately worked to

deflate the appeal of speculative forecasting among townspeople in the Empire, and correspondingly increased the value of concrete news about actual dangers and human disasters. Indeed this era saw the first publications that we can properly call newspapers, whose beginnings suggest a fundamental shift in attitudes about present and future knowledge.[74] Newly insistent preaching to the effect that only God could see the future went hand in hand with growing skepticism about any valid art of divination, raising the premium on direct information about the present state of affairs. These changes were far from sudden or uniform, but they showed clearly even in the annual works. David Froehlich's calendar for 1649, for instance, included a long section, entirely devoid of astrological analysis, reviewing the major events of the terrible conflict just ended.[75]

Not only among orthodox critics but in the broader public eye, the practicas were increasingly subject to scorn, ridicule, and satire, denounced more and more as books of lies. As their predictive failures became more glaring, the astrologers' confidence in their own art waned. In many cases the yearly forecasts became thoroughly bland recitations of stereotypical formulae. By the 1630s it became more or less standard for the annual calendar and practica to be bound and sold together in a format that made it easy to regard the latter as a mere appendix to the more immediately useful listing of days.[76] Yet another sign of waning vitality was that at Nuremberg, whose printers had increasingly dominated production of the annual works since at least the mid-sixteenth century, the entire business fell more and more into the hands of a single publisher, Wolfgang Endter. In the 1630s, during the height of the Thirty Years' War, he was already close to cornering the market. He did not hesitate to publish any calendar or practica he thought would sell, including works by the notorious Paul Nagel and by the pro-Imperial Hermann de Werve. By 1653 he held a monopoly in the city; by the time he died six years later he was publishing sixteen different book-form calendars annually. In many cases these later works included no supplementary practica at all.[77]

But of all the circumstantial changes to which the wartime upheavals contributed, probably none was more significant than the decline of direct civic patronage for the calendar writers. At the opening of the seventeenth century, many annual works still carried dedications to burgermeisters and city councils. While such expressions of honor and deference did not always imply that the author received formal sanction or support from these officials, they did reveal the continuing rootedness of astrologers in the fabric of urban life. In fact, despite the transregional sales and fame of the best-known writers, most still saw their primary markets, and the locus of their main responsibilities, in the towns where they practiced, pastored, or taught. Gradually over the first third of the century, however, dedications to city councils disappeared almost entirely; in their place we find electoral or territorial princes, or powerful nobles and their families, as potential or actual patrons. Here was one sign of the dissolution of the independent burgher culture in which the early evangelical movement and popular astrology had their common roots.[78]

The shift to princely and noble patrons may have resulted partly from a heightened need for security in the face of newly palpable dangers. But we also have good evidence that the traditional civic networks in which the calendar writers had an established place were no longer willing or able to maintain them. In Reutlingen, Bayreuth, and in several other cities where the annual works had long appeared, the councils simply did not bother to name successors as the older generation of Melanchthonian writers faded by the 1630s. Nuremberg continued to sponsor an official calendar maker through that decade, but the council proved increasingly unwilling to pay any stipend for the service. In 1641 the printer Georg Rhete reported on the now frequently voiced opinion that the annual works were no longer helpful or needed. In many eyes they evoked a harmful curiosity among the common folk, and each year they clogged up the presses, taking valuable time and attention away from more useful publications. Unsurprisingly Rhete himself did not share this view; he looked mainly to his bottom line. But his comments add weight to the argument that public attitudes were in rapid flux. By midcentury many if not most evangelical towns had ceased to require or formally sanction the production of the annual stellar guides.[79]

As wartime disillusionments and the loss of civic patronage eroded what resistance remained to orthodoxy's antiastrological campaign, the last defenders of the traditional Melanchthonian position fell away. One apparent sign was a swift decline in the numbers of active pastor-astrologers; the generation that included Melchior Schaerer, Christopher Cnoll, and Georg Kreslin was all but gone by the 1630s.[80] While calendar-writing city physicians in the mold of Herlicius may have been a little slower to disappear, they too were a dying breed. As they slid from the scene, the remaining calendar men continued to move down diverging paths. On one side we find figures such as Johannes Rummel (Rhumelius), who issued practicas with titles such as *Prognosticon Magicum et Cabalisticum*, attacking the old "rational" forms of astrology and drawing on a wide range of prophecies to feed hopes for some kind of transformation—either personal, cosmic, or both.[81] More widely read though at least equally obscure were the works of Andreas Goldmayer, no less than Nuremberg's appointed calendar-writer, whose practicas fairly oozed with baroque complexity and mystery. He used cryptic methods unknown to traditional astrology, introducing so many confused novelties that Klaus Matthäus declares him simply "a quack." He dedicated a number of his annual works to Catholic rulers, further evidence that by the later stages of the war the long-standing ties between popular astrologers and the evangelical cause had come largely undone. As the years passed Goldmayer's relationship with the town fathers became rockier; these conflicts helped undermine the council's willingness to continue funding for his office. His service ended with his dismissal in 1556.[82]

In 1642 the Rochlitz pastor Matthaeus Lungwitz could still invoke a long line of authorities, from Luther to Leowitz to Kepler, in a survey of all the comets, eclipses, new stars, and major conjunctions since 1524. His combined goals included explaining Germany's desperate plight, attacking all enemies of the gospel, and preaching repentance in the face of the end. Yet this aging, world-weary cleric was no longer in step with most of his contemporaries. Caught between the baroque mystery-hawkers on one flank and mathematical reformers on the other, he clung to a fast-fading outlook.[83] Indeed, the reforming astrologers who continued to write for the general public included men who had left the preaching aspect largely behind; by the 1630s and 1640s these figures worked to delimit the art in newly strict and clear ways. Lorenz Eichstädt, for instance, having preached zealously on the celestial signs as apocalyptic warnings in the 1620s, came in later years to emphasize more modest uses of the stars, largely within the realm of medicine. In fact by the 1640s the yearly calendars were losing even their long-time connections with health and healing.[18] The last officially authorized calendar writer at Nuremberg, the Altdorf professor Abdias Trew, labored consistently through the midcentury period to make astrology purely a matter of physical science, to restrict severely the scope of the stargazer's potential knowledge in any field, and to deny all associations with biblical prophecy or claims to insight into the divine will. He thus clearly rejected attitudes that had reigned among evangelicals for generations.[84]

Writers far less sophisticated than Trew were by this time sounding clear notes of humility, showing that the tradition of prophetic stargazing among German evangelicals was essentially defunct. In a practica for 1651 written at Berlin, Johannes Magirus insisted that conjectures about "future storms" and "political affairs" were not merely inherently uncertain, but "they will be revealed as largely false because of their weak foundation." This author celebrated the great progress in astronomy achieved by mathematicians such as Kepler and the Danzig professor Peter Crüger; this sort of ongoing work meant that "the principles of astrology are far truer and more natural than they have been before now; in fact they are studied and improved daily." At the same time he could appeal to the opposite wing of anti-Melanchthonian criticism, referring to Paracelsus as among the greatest men of medicine, "an experienced and highly influential physician." Equally if not more telling was Magirus's ready acceptance of the Gregorian calendar reform as good and necessary. Although most writers had long since incorporated both old and new systems for practical reasons, this full embrace of the latter marked a significant change; no longer was the reform in any sense the work of the Antichrist.[85]

Indeed by this point almost all notes of prophetic tension had disappeared from the practicas; Magirus's work typified this deep shift in outlook. We must not fear what the heavens portend, he wrote, but rather turn to God, "for we can expect all good things from his hand, just as he promised us in his Word." Here was no mention of divine punishment or judgment, no talk of sin, no hint of the world's end. What Magirus offered instead was a wandering discussion peppered with household advice, historical tales, bits of poetry, and various other diversions. Although brief histories both biblical and classical had begun to appear in the month-by-month columns of the calendars as early as the 1570s, the fashion of including much broader and larger selections of incidental material did not really take off until decades later. By the time Magirus wrote the annual works were evolving mainly into vehicles for popular entertainment, and this trend would only accelerate in the second half of the seventeenth century. The century-old form of the *Schreibkalender* faded away; in its place emerged a variety of annual calendars designed to appeal to different interests and tastes. The practica, meanwhile, largely shed its claims to serious astrological reckoning.[86]

Reinforcing the orthodox campaign to divorce the stellar art from biblical preaching, the all too real disasters of the Thirty Years' War certainly contributed to and accelerated the demise of evangelical astrology. The chaos ultimately highlighted the futility of any meaningful forecasting of human events, and of efforts to understand God's will through the heavens. As German Lutherans retreated from revelatory readings of the stars, the art rapidly lost the role it had played as an integral element of evangelical culture in its first century. Although Luther's seventeenth-century heirs certainly continued to employ astrology in their everyday lives, its broader status fell precipitously. Neither Lutheran orthodoxy nor Lutheran Pietism would have much room for stargazing pastors; indeed orthodox academics worked hard to ignore and even deny this increasingly distasteful element of their heritage. The decline of evangelical astrology marked the end of a distinctive sixteenth-century world in which broadly shared assumptions about the lessons of stellar science prompted an unusually intense and complex dialectic between notions of nature and spirit, freedom and order, hope and despair, sin and redemption. As this long past world of perception dissolved, so too did the original culture of the evangelical burgher, in which celestial meanings were knit together in a common fabric with both everyday experience and the hopes and fears of prophetic faith.

Postscript

"That the Providence of God is knowable through *this world*," writes Sachiko Kusukawa, "is a specifically Lutheran interpretation." These words, intended to illuminate the significance of sixteenth-century Melanchthonian natural philosophy, recall another observation made long ago by Ernst Troeltsch, that "the relative uniformity of early Lutheran culture" was based on "the assumption of an inward unity and conformity of Natural Law with the Christian Spirit."[1] The former insight points to a distinctive feature of Reformation-era Lutheranism that set it apart from other emerging confessional cultures, while the latter points to an element that bound evangelicals together. But both strongly complement the argument that over the first century of their movement most Lutherans saw especially close connections between their knowledge of celestial nature and their sense of the divine. Our study has tried to make this perspective more central than it has been for most students of the period, and to show that attention to the heavens had an integral role in shaping the religious orientation of German evangelicals during their foundational era.

We began by observing that over the half-century or so before 1520, the printing press helped bring a tremendous proliferation of astrological images and ideas in the German towns, and that the main vehicles for this development were the annual vernacular calendars and prognostications. So rapid and intense was this process that by the time Martin Luther appeared on the scene, these cities were home to a more pervasive popular astrological culture than any other part of western Christendom, including even the urban centers of Italy. The widespread adoption of the stellar art, both as a practical tool of everyday life and as a catalyst for changing religious and social attitudes, undeniably helped prepare the cultural ground on which the early evangelical movement would build. These conclusions tend to undermine the traditional notion that Protestants adopted astrology in order to compensate for the loss of medieval ritual equipment for dealing with everyday adversities; in the settings we have studied, at least, the relationship between astrology and reform was more complex.² As we saw in the case of the flood panic, the publicity surrounding astrological forecasts was integral to the fears, hopes, and excitement of the nascent reform era. While Luther himself often expressed skepticism toward scientific astrology, he never took a consistent public stance to oppose it the way John Calvin did. Even more important, his own urgent concern with heavenly signs and wonders ultimately helped boost the status of stellar interpretation among his followers and heirs.

Despite some evident tensions between evangelical preachers and physician-astrologers during the earliest years of the Reformation, Luther's followers soon appropriated the main genres of popular astrology, and came to regard the properly understood art as a godly gift with manifold uses. In particular, the teachings of Melanchthon reinforced trends already evident in the popular star-literature of the pre-Reformation era: a paradoxical recognition of both human bondage in the face of universal forces and practical freedom in human affairs. Indeed Melanchthon worked to synthesize astrological teachings with the central evangelical doctrine of law and gospel. More explicitly and forcefully than virtually any earlier Christian theologian, he taught that the stars revealed and enforced divine rule over the natural world. Their very beauty and magnificence declared the glory of God. At the same time, they embodied and expressed God's law, at once natural and spiritual. Thus they showed the ultimate helplessness of the "old man," and demonstrated at least indirectly the complete dependence of every person on the gift of grace, the only source of true freedom. On a more mundane level, stellar study supplied humankind with means for adapting to the laws by which God governed all creation.

Under the influence of evangelical humanism as taught by Melanchthon, his colleagues, and his intellectual heirs, many if not most Lutheran townsfolk came to regard the popular calendars, practicas, and related materials as practical and even moral guides that complemented biblical faith. A quickly expanding network of professors, physicians, pastors, schoolmasters, and literate burghers insured that this art, grounded in the assumption that the stars were significant both as divine signs and as natural causes, became integral to daily life in the Lutheran sphere. In this way the science of the stars became for all practical purposes the philosophical complement to the evangelical movement in its first century. The data of the heavens served as a central means of connecting history, nature, politics, and much everyday experience to biblical truth. Like the message of scripture, the testimony of the stars was unmediated, coming from beyond all human authority and terrestrial confusion. Despite the training and expertise that were presumed to lie behind the work of the mathematicians, the celestial art was ultimately open to all, or at least to all who read the signs through eyes enlightened by faith. While the reader of the calendars and practicas did not need to look directly to the skies, these ubiquitous printed texts demanded a mental picture of the entire cosmos as the sphere of divine operation. Here was perhaps the most powerful way in which German Reformation piety, so often associated with an emphasis on the word as heard, the ear more than the eye, in fact extended its appeal to the visual imagination.[3]

Over the second half of the sixteenth century, as both Catholic and emerging Calvinist clerical establishments sought to control and dampen astrological publicity, Lutheran preachers not only tolerated but most often welcomed and encouraged the work of the stargazers; often they joined their ranks and became calendar writers themselves. The popular almanacs presented virtually every person with the tools presumably necessary to order his or her own life, while they also offered preachers and lay critics ready channels for public warnings and exhortations. The publicists who issued these works year after year worked mainly to sanction existing structures of power, but at the same time they cast suspicion on innovations that appeared to threaten traditional burgher freedoms; in both these ways, astrology worked to reinforce a thoroughly conservative outlook. We also saw that as the sixteenth century progressed, the authors of the almanacs and prognostications contributed to a deepening sense of alienation, worldly despair, and defensiveness among evangelicals. They continued to cultivate a basic existential paradox: while on one hand they tried to offer an orientation in the cosmos and a sense of security in everyday rhythms, their warnings about divine punishment and judgment served to intensify anxiety in both public and personal spheres. Indeed, as they labored to reconcile polar perceptions of natural order and chaos, regularity and novelty in the heavens, evangelical students of the stars in effect projected the basic evangelical dialectic of law and gospel onto the plane of natural philosophy and cosmology. This tense dialectic demanded a vision of resolution; hence the culture of stellar forecasting strongly reinforced anticipations that the world was literally coming to an end. Along with biblical prophecy, popular astrology remained throughout the century a key element of the apocalyptic outlook on which Lutheran confessional identity was originally founded.

The eventual breakdown of this complementarity between stellar prediction and biblical prophecy may or may not have been inevitable. What seems clear is that by the end of the sixteenth century, Lutheran preachers, teachers, and calendar men were beginning to search for ways to escape the heavy psychological pall created by decades of disaster forecasts and apocalyptic warnings. Their earnest strivings for a purer, more affirmative Christian astrology soon began to draw them down diverging paths, one combining scripture and nature as fully parallel sources of revelation, the other calling for a clear separation between the two books, only one of which could be the standard of truth. The resulting early-seventeenth-century crisis of piety, essentially a conflict between preachers of a pansophic mysticism and representatives of a newly skeptical biblicism, left the last generation of Melanchthonian astrologers struggling to hold on to their synthesis of scriptural truth and stellar science.

They failed for at least two main reasons. First, in the contest for epistemological and ultimately for ecclesiastical authority, the orthodox biblicists almost inevitably gained the upper hand over the popular mystics. It was then an easy step to discredit the more traditional calendar men by associating them with a broad range of newly and loosely defined heresies. Second, the unfolding disasters of the war posed impossible challenges to forecasters; the resulting disillusionment reinforced and hastened the success of the orthodox campaign. When the alliance between evangelical preaching and popular astrology finally collapsed altogether in the 1630s and 1640s, what survived were doctrines that disavowed all forms of apocalyptic prophecy, biblical as well as astrological. The leaders of seventeenth-century Lutheran orthodoxy would successfully present themselves as the upholders of pure teaching, even as they abandoned the testimony of the heavens that had helped shape the very movement they inherited.

Our exploration of astrology's role in the German Reformation helps us understand this movement as neither medieval nor modern, but as a distinctive early modern cultural configuration among evangelical townspeople. Within that culture, astrological publicity functioned in paradoxical ways. It contributed to an enlarged and abstracted sense of the divine that led away from clericalism, sacramentalism, and the cult of the saints; at the same time, it sought to ground people more squarely in practical matters of daily life. Many advocates of the Melanchthonian art who saw it as part of a general enlightenment had such effects in mind. On the other hand, the apocalyptic astrology that came to prevail among evangelicals involved a perpetuation, even a strengthening of ties between faith and cosmology, which played out in beliefs about nature and the supernatural that later centuries would come to regard as rank superstitions. This was therefore a world neither traditionally enchanted, nor rationally disenchanted, but very differently enchanted from the one it worked to displace. For most sixteenth-century Lutherans, the stars were a God-given text that complemented the Bible, a text that mirrored both the divine order of the world and its imminent disintegration. We cannot properly understand the historical realities of their Reformation unless we open our eyes to this aspect of their faith. Nor should we condescend to their beliefs as precritical myths, for surely they reveal no more pathetic weakness than our own postmodern gropings for any meaning at all.

Notes

PRACTICA CITATIONS

The following list includes only those annual practicas cited in the notes, along with bibliographic identifiers as follows:

HPB – Consortium of European Research Libraries, Heritage of the Printed Book database.

VD16 – *Verzeichnis der im deutschen Sprachbereich erschienenen Drucke des 16. Jahrhunderts.*

INKA – Inkunabel-Katalog deutscher Bibliotheken

WLS – Württembergische Landesbibliothek Stuttgart

HAB – Herzog August Bibliothek Wolfenbüttel

GNM – Germanisches National-museum (Nuremberg)

Adler, Bartholomaeus
1597 HPB DE-601.GVK.471188328

Anonymous
1489 INKA 10007592
c. 1492 (fragment) INKA 10007593

Apian, Peter

1524 VD16 A 3101
1532 VD16 A 3105

Aurifaber, Andreas
1541 VD16 G 2563

Bader, Matthäus
1579 VD16 B 119

Bathodius, Lucas
1594 HPB DE-601.GVK.471203769

Brelochs, Anton
1528 VD16 B 7415
1535 VD16 B 7417
1544 VD16 ZV 15794
1545 VD16 ZV 2415
1548 VD16 ZV 2416
1559 VD16 B 7424

Brotbeihel, Jerome
1560 VD16 B 8400
1561 VD16 B 8401

Brotbeihel (Brotbeyhel), Matthias
1527 VD16 ZV 23331
1538 VD16 ZV 25083
1545 HPB DE-604.VK.BV001564139
    (English)

Bucha, Caspar
1575 VD16 B 8967
1594 VD16 B 8971

Busch, Georg
1573 VD16 B9875

Caesarius, Nicolaus
1577 VD16 C 92

Caesius, Georg
1574 VD16 C 156
1575 VD16 C 157
1583 VD16 C 167
1584 VD16 C 168
1588 VD16 C 172
1596 VD16 C 176
1597 VD16 C 177
1598 VD16 ZV 25042
1600 VD16 ZV 22589
1601 VD16 ZV 22585
1602 VD17 23:288609Y

Caesius, Georg Friedrich
1603 VD17 23:288265L

Cnespel, Jakob
1585 VD16 C 4226

Copp, Johannes
1521 VD16 C ZV 3859
1522 VD16 C 5022
1524 VD16 C 5024

Eisslinger, Balthasar
1549 VD16 E900

Engel, (Angelus) Johannes
1488 HPB GB-Uk.ISTC.ia00712300
1497 HPB GB-Uk.ISTC.ia00712400

Eyssenmann, Simon
1516 VD16 E 4761
1520 HPB DE-604.VK.BV001418290

Faber [von Budweis], Wenzel
1483 HPB GB-Uk.ISTC.if00005100
1487 HPB GB-Uk.ISTC.if00005300
1492 HPB GB-Uk.ISTC.if00006000
1499 HPB GB-Uk.ISTC.if.00008780

Fabri [von Prustat], Sigismund
1496 HPB GB-Uk.ISTC.if00026400
    (facimile in Pascher,
    Praktiken)

Fabricius, Gregor
1562 VD16 F 404
1565 VD16 ZV 5726

Fischer, Matthias
1596 VD16 ZV5880
1597 HPB DE-601.GVK.413047938

Froelich, David
1649 VD17 27:711887D

Gasser, Achilles Pirmin
1545 VD16 G 498
1547 VD16 G 499

Gereon, Johann
1524 VD16 G 1481

Germanus, Christoph
1573 HPB DE-601.GVK.15034757X

Geuss, Wolff
1564 VD16 G 1915

Goetz, Johannes
1486 HPB GB-Uk.ISTC.ig00319000

Halbmayer, (Albanus Marius), Georg
1613 WLS HFB 3711
   (bound with *Alter und Newer Schreibkalender*)
1618 WLS HFB 3716
1624 WLS HBF 3722
   (bound with *Alter und Newer Schreibkalender*)

Hebenstreit, Johann
1559 HPB DE-601.GVK.149931557
1566 VD16 ZV 7498
1568 HPB DE-601.GVK.149931522

Heiden, Christian
1567 HPB DE-604.VK.BV001492928
1568 VD16 H 3321

Heller, Joachim
1549 HPB DE-601.GVK.386201226
1553 VD16 ZV 18215
1557 HPB DE-601.GVK.153547332
1559 VD16 H 1694
1561 VD16 ZV 7609

Henisch, Georg
1588 HPB DE-604.VK.BV001433455

Herlicius (Herlitz), David
1610 VD17 23:285555G
1617 WLS HBF 3715
   (bound with *Alt und Neu Schreibkalender*)
1631 VD17 23:264161A

Heuring, Simon
1551 VD16 H 3293

Hoffmann, Erhard
1571 HPB DE-601.GVK.150680562

Huberin, Moritz
1621 WLS HBF 3719
   (bound with *Alt und Neu Schreibkalender*)
1629 VD17 56:736178V
   (bound with *Alt und Neu Schreibkalender*)

Klain, Johannes
1578 HPB DE-601.GVK.486267032

Koestner, Sebastian
1605 VD17 23:287276V

Krabbe, Johann
1597 HPB DE-601.GVK.471148814
1599 VD16 ZV 22580

Leopold, Paul
1594 VD16 L 1252

Luginsland, Urban
1553 VD16 L 3198
1558 VD16 L 3203
1570 VD16 L 3200
1576 VD16 ZV 9946

Lutz, Bernhard
1512 VD16 L 7648
1513 VD16 L 7649

Maius, Heinrich
1574 VD16 M 1978

Mangolt, Bartholomaeus
1532 VD16 ZV 10338-E

Marius, Simon
1610 WLS HBF 3708
   (bound with *Alter und Newer Schreibkalender*)
1612 VD17 75:696601R
1615 WLS HBF 3713

(bound with *Alter und Newer Schreibkalender*)

1625 WLS HBF 3723
   (bound with *Alter und Newer Schreibkalender*)

Meder, Georg
1577 VD16 ZV 10565
1578 HPB DE-601.GVK.471153761
1579 VD16 M 1851
1583 HPB DE-601.GVK.471154415

Magirus, Johann
1651 HPB DE-601.GVK.154420328

Mangolt, Bartholomaeus
1532 VD16 ZV 10337

Misocacus, Wilhelm
1580 VD16 M 5480
1583 VD16 M 5482
1590 VD16 M 5487

Mithob (Mithoff), Burkhard
1540 HPB DE-601.GVK.15164554X

Moller, Albin
1587 VD16 ZV 25614
1592 HPB DE-601.GVK.397008902
1595 VD16 ZV 11093
1600 VD16 ZV 22596

Moller, Tobias
1592 VD16 ZV 11119

Paceus, Johannes
1561 VD16 P 55

Pollich, Martin
1490 HPB DE-601.GVK.630684715
   edited version in Eis,
   Warsagetexte

Pontanus, Caspar
1566 VD16 P 4240

Pruckner, Nicolaus
1533 VD16 P 5160
1543 VD16 P 5156

Reinstein, Johann
1573 VD16 R 1022

Rheticus,
1551 HPB DE-601.GVK.150874022

Rosa, Andreas
1586 VD16 R 3068
1587 VD16 R 3069
1593 VD16 R 3071
1596 VD16 R 3073

Ryff, Walther Hermann
1544 VD16 ZV 27117

Saltzmann, Gregor
1543 VD16 S 1499

Schaerer, Melchior
1609 WLS HFB 3707
1620 WLS HFB 3718

Schöner, Johannes
1534 VD16 S 3492
1538 VD16 S 3496
1539 VD16 S 3497
1540 VD16 S 3498

Schynnagel, Marcus
1500 HPB GB-Uk.ISTC.is00336300
   (facsilime in Pascher, *Praktiken*)

Schönfelt, Victorin
1562 VD16 S 3706
1563 VD16 S 3708

1564 VD16 S 3709
1570 VD16 S 3713
1588 HAB A: 202.47 Quod. (12)

Schoder, Georg
1551 HPB DE-601.GVK.151319162

Schulin, Johannes
1585 VD16 S 4333
1586 VD16 S 4334

Seger, Johannes
1517 VD16 S 5307

Sibenburger, Dionysius
1546 GNM Postinc 8° Nw 2139i
1547 VD16 S 6189

Stathmion, Christoph
1551 HPB DE-601.GVK.150989490
1555 VD16 ZV 18254
1563 VD16 S 8653
1578 VD16 ZV 22643
1584 VD16 S 8664

Sutorius, Johann Paul
1596 VD16 S 10321
1599 HPB GB-UkLU.01.19941213

Tannstetter, Georg
1505 VD16 ZV 14859
1506 VD16 T 170

Titius, Simon
1556 VD16 T 1391

Tockler (Noricus), Conrad
1515 VD16 T 1454

Uberling, Johann
1514 VD16 O 53

Ursinus, Adam
1571 VD16 U 251

Virdung, Johannes
1495 INKA 10009202 HPB GB-Uk.
   ISTC.iv00302235
1497 HPB GB-Uk.ISTC.iv00302259
1503 facsilime in Pascher, no. 13
1521 VD16 ZV 21865
1524 VD16 V 1281

Volmar
1524 VD 16 V 2301

Wilhelm
1567 VD16 W 3092
1571 VD16 W 3093

Winand, Heinrich
1590 HPB DE-601.GVK.471153885
1594 HPB DE-601.GVK.476704634
1595 VD16 ZV 20562

Winckler, Nicolaus
1576 HPB DE-604.VK.BV001746923
1579 VD16 W 3452
1583 HPB DE-601.GVK.396998380
1587 VD16 ZV 24152
1595 HPB DE-604.VK.BV001746928
1599 VD16 w 3464

Winckler, Nicolaus Eberhard
1606 VD17 23:288600E
1613 VD17 1:643325P

Zeysius
1577 VD16 Z 258

INTRODUCTION

1. Thomas Erastus, *Astrologia Confutata. Ein warhafte Gegründte Vnwidersprechliche Confutation/der falschen Astrologei* . . . (German translation of Savonarola's work against astrology; Schleusingen, 1557), A2.

2. Aby Warburg, *Heidnisch-antike Weissagungen in Wort und Bild zu Luthers Zeiten* (Heidelberg, 1920). Reprinted in *Gesammelte Schriften*, vol. 2 (Nendeln, 1969), 487–558.

3. Thus for instance Diarmaid MacCulloch's tome of nearly 800 pages *The Reformation* (New York, 2004) makes but two passing references to astrology. Ulinka Rublack's study of *Reformation Europe* (Cambridge and New York, 2005) never mentions the subject. A 2009 survey of writings on the German Reformation in English over thirty-five years says not one word about the topic; see Thomas A. Brady, "From Revolution to the Long Reformation: Writings in English on the German Reformation 1970–2005." *Archive for Reformation History*, 100 (2009): 48–69. A major collection on *Lutheran Ecclesiastical Culture, 1550–1675* edited by Robert Kolb (Leiden and Boston, 2008) includes not a single reference to either "astrology" or "prophecy."

4. Robert Westman offers a helpful discussion of the term "the science of the stars" and its usefulness with reference to the history of astronomy and astrology; see his *The Copernican Question: Prognostication, Skepticism, and Celestial Order* (Berkeley, CA, 2011), 34, 40.

5. Johann Friedrich, *Astrologie und Reformation. Oder die Astrologen als Prediger der Reformation und Urheber des Bauernkrieges. Ein Beitrag zur Reformationsgeschichte* (Munich, 1864).

6. Friedrich von Bezold, *Geschichte der deutschen Reformation* (Berlin, 1890); Willy Andreas, *Deutschland vor der Reformation* (Stuttgart, 1959; 1st ed. 1932); Will-Erich Peuckert, *Die Grosse Wende: Das Apokalyptische Saeculum und Luther*, 2 vols. (Darmstadt, 1966).

7. The classic art-historical study is Raymond Klibansky, Erwin Panofsky, and Fritz Saxl, *Saturn and Melancholy* (London, 1964). For the history of science, Lynn Thorndike's work remains nearly as useful as it is famous: *A History of Magic and Experimental Science* (New York, 8 vols., 1923–1958). Still indispensable in the realm of late medieval astrology and prophecy in Germany is Dietrich Kurze, *Johannes Lichtenberger (†1503). Eine Studie zur Geschichte der Prophetie und Astrologie* (Lübeck and Hamburg, 1960).

8. The studies of Wilhelm Maurer devoted attention to this aspect of Melanchthon's thought: *Der junge Melanchthon zwischen Humanismus und Reformation* (Göttingen, 1967); *Melanchthon-Studien* (Gütersloh, 1964). Among Anglo-American scholars in the middle decades of the last century, a remarkable exception to the overall inattention to the topic was John Warwick Montgomery; see his *Cross, Constellation and Crucible: Lutheran Astrology and Alchemy in the Age of the Reformation* (Ottowa, 1963).

9. Anthony Grafton, *Cardano's Cosmos: The Worlds and Works of a Renaissance Astrologer* (Cambridge, MA, 1999).

10. An important study drawing on communications theory is Jonathan Green, *Printing and Prophecy: Prognostication and Media Change 1450–1550* (Ann Arbor, 2012). The most comprehensive treatment of the broader issues of astrology and prophecy in this period is Gert Mentgen, *Astrologie und Öffentlichkeit* (Stuttgart, 2005).

11. Claudia Brosseder, *Im Bann der Sterne: Caspar Peucer, Philipp Melanchthon und andere Wittenberger Astrologen* (Berlin, 2004); Westman, *The Copernican Question;* Euan Cameron, *Enchanted Europe: Superstition, Reason, and Religion 1250–1750* (Oxford, 2010).

12. Steven Vanden Broecke, *The Limits of Influence: Pico, Louvain, and the Crisis of Renaissance Astrology* (Leiden and Boston, 2003), 17.

13. Eugenio Garin, *Astrology in the Renaissance: The Zodiac of Life* (London, 1983), 93.

14. Scholars who maintain that a separation was generally recognized in the sixteenth century include Brian Vickers; see his "Kritische Reaktionen auf die okkulten Wissenschaften in der Renaissance," in Jean-François Bergier, ed., *Zwischen Wahn, Glaube und Wissenschaft: Magie, Astrologie, Alchemie und Wissenschaftsgeschichte* (Zurich, 1988), 167–239; here 169–70. But most studies acknowledge that the distinction was neither so clear nor so widely accepted. See for example Franz Boll, Carl Bezold, and Wilhelm Gundel, *Sternglaube und Sterndeutung: Die Geschichte und das Wesen der Astrologie* (Darmstadt, 1966), 72–75; Garin, *Astrology in the Renaissance*, 14, 25; Wolfgang Hübner, "Astrologie in der Renaissance," in Bergier, ed., *Zwischen Wahn, Glaube und Wissenschaft*, 241–79; here 249.

15. Vanden Broecke, *The Limits of Influence*, 17. On the theoretical/practical idea: Jim Tester, *A History of Western Astrology* (Woodbridge, UK, 1987), 19, 55, 124–25.

16. Gerhard Adler and R.F.C. Hull, eds., *The Collected Works of Carl Jung*, vol. 13, *Alchemical Studies* (Princeton, 1968), 237.

17. Valerie Flint, *The Rise of Magic in Early Medieval Europe* (Princeton, 1991). Older but still useful is M.L.W. Laistner, "The Western Church and Astrology in the Early Middle Ages," *Harvard Theological Review* 34, no. 4 (1941): 251–75.

18. On D'Ailly see the excellent work of Laura Smoller, *History, Prophecy and the Stars: The Christian Astrology of Pierre D'Ailly* (Princeton, 1994).

19. Theodore Wedel, *The Medieval Attitude Toward Astrology, Particularly in England* (New Haven, 1920; repr. Hamden, CT, 1968), 78; John D. North, "Astrology and the Fortunes of Churches," *Centaurus* 24, no. 1 (1980): 181–211; here 182–83. On the medieval background see also Otto Mazal, *Die Sternenwelt des Mittelalters* (Graz, 1993), and Wolfgang Hübner, *Zodiacus Christianus: Jüdisch-christliche Adaptionen des Tierkreises von der Antike bis zur Gegenwart* (Königstein, 1983).

20. Basic background: Richard Kieckhefer, *Magic in the Middle Ages* (Cambridge and New York, 1989).

21. Garin, *Astrology in the Renaissance*, 27.

22. Tamsyn Barton, *Power and Knowledge: Astrology, Physiognomics, and Medicine under the Roman Empire* (Ann Arbor, 1994), 69; Barton here cites the medievalist Peter Brown.

23. Even scholars who certainly know better have continued to make blanket references to "occult pseudo-sciences such as astrology." See e.g. Charles Nauert, *Humanism and the Culture of Renaissance Europe*, second ed. (Cambridge and New York, 2006), 63.

24. Don Cameron Allen, *The Star-Crossed Renaissance: the Quarrel about Astrology and its Influence in England* (Durham, NC, 1941), 99–100.

25. Wolfgang Hübner argues persuasively that studies of Renaissance astrology have focused too much on the debates rather than on the art's role in particular cultural settings: "Astrologie in der Renaissance," 253–55.

26. See my "Note on Sources," xi.

27. Johannes Kepler, *Tertius Interveniens* (Frankfurt am Main, 1610), 3/v. The phrase "new, useful and entertaining matter" is from the oldest line of American almanacs, *The Old Farmer's Almanac*, founded by Robert B. Thomas in 1792 and currently published by Yankee, Inc. at Dublin, NH.

28. Scholars who have looked at all closely into the question generally agree that the annual astrological works likely reached a broader public than any other sort of publication in the sixteenth century; see for example Pfister, *Parodien*, 15. Jonathan Green properly points out that in regard to the early history of printing "prophecy, astrology, and literacy are near neighbors to each other": *Printing and Prophecy*, 31. An inevitably incomplete but still valuable and readily available bibliographic source is Ernst Zinner, *Geschichte und Bibliographie der Astronomischen Literatur in Deutschland zur Zeit der Renaissance* (Stuttgart, 1964).

29. In this study I have essentially bracketed out the question of how fast and how far the popularized science of the stars penetrated peasant or village culture. For an informal and engaging discussion bearing on the question see Arthur Imhof, *Lost Worlds: How Our European Ancestors Coped with Life, and Why Life is So Hard today* (Charlottesville, 1996), 139–61.

CHAPTER 1

1. Hilary M. Carey, *Courting Disaster: Astrology at the English Court and University in the Later Middle Ages* (Houndsmills, Basingstoke, 1992), 16. See also Carey's "Church Time and Astrological Time in the Waning Middle Ages," in R. N. Swanson, ed., *The Use and Abuse of Time in Christian History* (*Studies in Church History*, 37; Woodbridge, UK, 2002), 117–32; also Jan R. Veenstra, *Magic and Divination at the Courts of Burgundy and France: Text and Context of Laurens Pignon's "Contre Les Devineurs" (1411)* (Leiden, New York, Cologne, 1997), 21.

2. Warburg, *Heidnisch-antike Weissagungen*; also A. Warburg, "Orientalisierende Astrologie," in *Gesammelte Schriften*, Vol. 2, 561–65; here 565.

3. Blume, *Regenten des Himmels*, 163–64. Johannes Wissbier von Gmund should not be confused with the famous Johannes of Gmunden, a professor of astronomy at Vienna. See Francis B. Brévart, "The German Volkskalender of the Fifteenth Century," *Speculum* 63, no. 2 (April, 1988): 312–42; here 312.

4. Brévart, "The German Volkskalender," 322n; 337. The *Lucidarius* was a popular encyclopedia of knowledge both religious and natural. The earliest known German manuscript is from the late twelfth century. See Karl Schorbach, *Studien über das deutsche Volksbuch* Lucidarius (Strasbourg, 1894); also Becker and Overgaauw, *Aderlass und Seelentrost*, 376–78.

5. Blume, *Regenten des Himmels*, 159ff.

6. Blume, *Regenten des Himmels*, 160–67.

7. Brévart, "The German Volkskalender," 314ff. See also Brévart, "Chronology and Cosmology: A German *Volkskalender* of the Fifteenth Century," *Princeton University Library Chronicle*, 57, no. 2 (Winter 1996): 225–65. Brévart uses the term "Volkskalender" to designate a genre of practical instructional collections that saw many variations. Blume, *Regenten des Himmels*, 167–76 uses the broader term "Kalendarische Hausbücher." For a careful study of one version of this genre, the *Passauer Kalender* of 1445, see Markus Mueller, *Beherrschte Zeit: Lebensorientierung und Zukunftsgestaltung durch Kalenderprognostik zwischen Antike und Neuzeit* (Kassel, 2009). Another version has been edited and studied by Lorenz Welker: *Das "Iatromathematische Corpus": Untersuchungen zu einem alemannischen astrologisch-medizinischen Kompendium des Spätmittelalters* (Zurich, 1988). Older but still worth consulting is Viktor Stegemann, *Aus einem mittelalterlichen deutschen astronomisch-astrologischen Lehrbüchlein* (Reichenberg, 1944).

8. Brévart, "The German Volkskalender," 322–23.

9. Brévart, "The German Volkskalender," 338–39 et passim; see also Adolf Dresler, *Kalender-kunde, Eine kultur-historische Studie* (Munich, 1972), 30–32. Variations of the genre appeared in the sixteenth century under titles such as *Calendarius teutsch Maister Joannis Küngpergers* (Augsburg, 1512), *Astronomia: Teutsch Astronomei* (Frankfurt a. M., 1545), *Das gross Planetenbuch* (Frankfurt, 1554).

10. Mieczyslaw Markowski, *Astronomica et astrologica cracoviensia ante annum 1550* (Florence, 1990); also Markowski, "Die Astrologie an der Krakauer Universität in den Jahren 1450–1550," in *Magia, Astrologia e Religione nel Rinascimento* (Wroclaw, 1974), 83–89.

11. Garin, *Astrology in the Renaissance*, 26.

12. Paul Joachimsen, "Humanism and the Development of the German Mind," in Gerald Strauss, ed., *Pre-Reformation Germany* (New York, 1972), 162–224; here 188–89.

13. Rudolf Klug, *Johannes von Gmunden: Der Begründer der Himmelskunde auf deutschem Boden* (Vienna, 1943). Essential on Vienna is Helmuth Grössing,

Humanistische Naturwissenschaft: Zur Geschichte der Wiener mathematischen Schulen des 15. und 16. Jahrhunderts (Baden-Baden, 1983). Here as elsewhere I have benefited from the references in Darin Hayton, "Astrologers and Astrology in Vienna During the Era of Emperor Maximilian I (1493–1519)" (Ph.D. dissertation, University of Notre Dame, 2004).

14. Ernst Zinner, *Leben und Werken des Johannes Müller von Königsberg, gennant Regiomontanus* (Osnabrück, 1968); also Zinner, *Geschichte und Bibliographie*, 3–11; Dresler, *Kalender-kunde*, 24–25.

15. Regiomontanus's 1474 Kalender is available in an edited facimile edition: Ernst Zinner, ed., *Der deutsche Kalender des Johannes Regiomontan, Nürnberg, um 1474* (Leipzig, 1937).

16. Jakob Pflaum, *Kalender 1477–1512* (Ulm, 1478); *Kalender 1477–1554* (Ulm, 1478). See Grössing, *Humanistische Natwissenschaft*, 121–22.

17. On Stabius and Perlach, see Hayton, "Astrologers and Astrology," 72–90, 215–91 et passim.

18. Johannes Essler, *Speculum Astrologorum* (Leipzig, 1508).

19. M. Manilius, *Astronomicon* (Nuremberg, c. 1472); [Pseudo-] Ptolemy, *Quadripartitum ... [et] Centiloquium cum commento Hali* (Venice, 1484); *Epytoma Ioa[n]nis de mo[n]te regio in almagestu[m] Ptolomei* (Venice, 1496).

20. On Ratdolt: Green, *Printing and Prophecy*, 135–36.

21. On the 1472 edition of Sacrobosco, see Zinner, *Geschichte und Bibliographie*, 8; Petrus de Alliaco (Pierre D'Ailly), *Concordantia astronomiae cum theologia* (Augsburg, 1490); Guido Bonatti, *Decem tractatus astronomiae* (Augsburg, 1491).

22. On court astrologers in the Empire see Mentgen, *Astrologie und Öffentlichkeit*, 161–216; 253–56.

23. Walter J. Ong, *Interfaces of the Word: Studies in the Evolution of Consciousness and Culture* (Ithaca, 1977); Ong, *The Presence of the Word: Some Prolegomena for Cultural and Religious History* (Minneapolis, 1981). See also Elizabeth L. Eisenstein, *The Printing Press as an Agent of Change: Communications and Cultural Transformations in Early Modern Europe*, 2 vols. (Cambridge, 1979); Eisenstein, *The Printing Revolution in Early Modern Europe* (Cambridge, 1983).

24. In Karl Schottenloher's view it was above all through the annual calendars and practicas that printing caused belief in the power of the stars to become more securely rooted than ever among the people. Schottenloher, *Flugblatt und Zeitung: Ein Wegweiser durch das Gedruckte Tageschriftum* (Berlin, 1922), 191. Parts of this section are adapted from my essay "Astrology and Popular Print in Germany," in Robin B. Barnes, Robert A. Kolb, and Paula L. Presley, eds., *Habent sua fata libelli: Books Have Their Own Destiny: Essays in honor of Robert V. Schnucker* (Kirksville, MO, 1998), 17–26.

25. Brévart, "The German Volkskalender," 339. Dieter Blume sees a near-total disappearance of the *Teutsch Kalender* tradition after c. 1522; see his *Regenten des*

Himmels, 168. But see Chapter 4 on the continuing tradition of popular planet books in the sixteenth century.

26. On the early broadsheet calendars: Zinner, *Geschichte und Bibliographie*, 11–13; also Paul Heitz and Konrad Haebler, eds., *Hundert Kalender-Inkunabeln* (Strasbourg, 1905), 1–14; Brod, *Mainfränkische Kalender aus vier Jahrhunderten* (Würzburg, 1952); Dresler, *Kalender-kunde*, 19–24 et passim; Wolf-Dieter Müller-Jahncke, *Astrologisch-magische Theorie und Praxis in der Heilkunde der frühen Neuzeit* (Stuttgart/Wiesbaden, 1985), 175–84; Hayton, "Astrologers and Astrology," 292–369.

27. Brévart, "The German Volkskalender," 339; also Klaus Matthäus, "Zur Geschichte des Nürnberger Kalenderwesens: Die Entwicklung der in Nürnberg gedruckten Jahreskalender in Buchform," *Archiv für Geschichte des Buchwesens* IX (1969): 965–1396; here 981ff. The earliest printed calendar was long thought to date from 1448; Zinner accepted this dating (*Geschichte und Bibliographie*, no. 1, 93), but the more likely date is c. 1457–58, as Matthäus points out (981n).

28. Zinner, *Geschichte und Bibliographie*, 12.

29. Schottenloher, *Flugblatt und Zeitung*, 36.

30. Zinner, *Geschichte und Bibliographie*, 13; Dresler, *Kalender-kunde*, 26, 44–48; Matthäus, "Zur Geschichte," 995–1001, 1165ff.

31. Jonathan Green describes the 1482 practica of Wenzel Faber von Budweis as "an exercise in chaos"; see *Printing and Prophecy*, 117; also 112–15. A selection of facsimile examples is available in Hans-Peter Pascher, *Praktiken des 15. und 16. Jahrhunderts* (Klagenfurt, 1980).

32. Tester, *A History*, 183; Gustav Hellmann, "Versuch einer Geschichte der Wettervorhersage im XVI. Jahrhundert," *Abhandlungen der Preussischen Akademie der Wissenschaften*, 1 (Berlin, 1924), 8.

33. Keith Thomas, *Religion and the Decline of Magic* (London, 1971), 334.

34. Matthäus, "Zur Geschichte," 967–1006. On the practica genre: Green, *Printing and Prophecy*, 109–30 et passim.

35. Hellmann, "Versuch," 3–4.

36. The idea of a market crash has been suggested by Green, *Printing and Prophecy*, 121–22. Matthäus more properly emphasizes the lower survival rate for works published early in the new century. Johann Schöner of Nuremberg almost certainly published broadsheet calendars for most if not all years between 1504 and 1529, but no copies remain from this period. It is also likely that by 1500 the exploding competition among printers drove smaller operations out of the market, and often out of business altogether; thus fewer editions appeared, but probably in greater numbers. See Matthäus, "Zur Geschichte," 1013, 1023.

37. These numbers, which include both Latin and vernacular editions, are derived from my own count of works listed in Zinner, *Geschichte und Bibliographie*. (Matthäus counts 392). Jonathan Green, *Printing and Prophecy*, counts 212 practicas from Germany before 1501; thus Hellmann's original figures for calendars

and practicas have not changed a great deal. See also Westman, *The Copernican Question*, graphs on 26, 44, drawing on Zinner.

38. The numerous genres not covered in this count include the popular planet books, frequently reprinted works such as the astrological folk-book *Lucidarius*, medical tracts, and other vernacular writings that included astrological references. And finally they do not take into account sensational bestsellers such as Johann Lichtenberger's *Pronosticatio* (note 46).

39. See Geneviève Bollème, *Les Almanachs Populaires aus XVIIe et XVIIIe Siècles: Essai d'histoire Sociale* (Paris, 1969), 18; also Capp, *Astrology and the Popular Press*, 272–74. On Simon de Phares (c. 1444–1500): Jean-Patrice Boudet, "Simon de Phares et les rapports entre astrologie et prophétie à la fin du Moyen Age," in *Mélanges de l'Ecole française de Rome. Moyen-Age, Temps modernes*, 102, no. 2 (1990): 617–48. On the importance of national context and the special place of Germany in the printing of almanacs and practicas: Green, *Printing and Prophecy*, 8–9, 121.

40. Parron: Carey, *Courting Disaster*, 161. On sixteenth-century England as an "astrological backwater": Capp, *Astrology and the Popular Press*, 180.

41. On the Laet publications, see Vanden Broecke, *The Limits of Influence*, 36–40, 91–95 et passim; Thorndike, *Magic* IV, 445–46; Capp, *Astrology and the Popular Press*, 27.

42. My count is again based on Zinner, *Geschichte und Bibliographie*. Gustav Hellmann's studies still offer a good indication of the comparative trends; see Hellmann, "Versuch," 4ff. His figures, and Zinner's listing, have been updated by Jonathan Green, but without changing the overall picture significantly; see Green, *Printing and Prophecy*, "Appendix," 155–94. Robert Westman draws on both Hellmann and Zinner in charting and graphing works of prognostication in the German lands, concluding that "the Empire led the way with an enormous production of . . . annual forecasts": *The Copernican Question*, 71. Neither Green nor Westman devotes much attention to the annual astrological calendars.

43. Rudolf Hirsch, *Printing, Selling and Reading 1450–1550* (Wiesbaden, 1974), 134; Hans-Joachim Köhler, "The Flugschriften and their Importance in Religious Debate," in Zambelli, ed., *"Astrologi hallucinati"* (Chapter 3, note 4), 153–75; here 155.

44. My estimates are based on the listing in Klaus Wagner, "Judicia Astrologica Columbiniana: Bibliographisches Verzeichnis einer Sammlung von Practiken des 15. und 16. Jahrhunderts der Biblioteca Columbina Sevilla," in *Archiv für Geschichte des Buchwesens* 15 (1975): 1–98.

45. Pascher, *Praktiken*, 12–14; also Zinner, *Geschichte und Bibliographie*, 94–135. On Nuremberg overtaking Augsburg: Heitz and Haebler, *Hundert*, 7; Dresler, *Kalender-Kunde*, 20.

46. The first edition of Lichtenberger's *Pronosticatio in latino* was published anonymously at Heidelberg in 1488; the German version, *Pronosticatio zu theutsch*,

followed no later than 1490. The essential study is still Kurze, *Johannes Lichtenberger*. See also Kurze, "Popular Prophecy in the Fifteenth and Sixteenth centuries: Johannes Lichtenberger," in Zambelli, ed., *"Astrologi hallucinati,"* 177–93.

47. Jobst Hord, Calendar (Almanach) 1477: Heitz and Haebler, *Hundert*, 17; no. 13. On the increasing frequency with which authors' names appeared on calendars: Matthäus, "Zur Geschichte," 993–94.

48. Manfred Stürzbecher, "The Physici in German-Speaking Countries from the Middle Ages to the Enlightenment," in Andrew W. Russell, ed., *The Town and State Physician in Europe from the Middle Ages to the Enlightenment* (Wolfenbüttel, 1981), 123–29; G. A. Wehrli, "Der Ärzt als Kalenderschreiber," *Internationale Beiträge der Medizin: Festschrift Max Neuberger* (Vienna, 1928), 308–15. On the efforts of city governments to enforce uniform calendrical and medical practice: Matthäus, "Zur Geschichte," 994.

49. Fabri 1496, preface. On Crakow and John of Glogau: Thorndike, *Magic*, IV, 449–51; also Westman, *The Copernican Question*, 70–71.

50. The story about the Wittenberg foundation has been disputed, but remains entirely plausible. See Mentgen, *Astrologie und Öffentlichkeit*, 256; Jürgen G. H. Hoppmann, *Astrologie der Reformationszeit: Faust, Luther, Melanchthon und die Sterndeuterei* (Berlin, 1998), 11–13; Thorndike, *Magic*, V, 379. For an edited version and discussion of Pollich's practica for 1490 see Gerhard Eis, *Wahrsagetexte des Spätmittelalters* (Berlin, Bielefeld, Munich, 1956), 17–24, 55–65.

51. John D. North, *Horoscopes and History* (London, 1986), 153.

52. Faber 1492; Engel 1497, A2.

53. Matthäus, "Zur Geschichte," 1007.

54. On Augsburg and early German printing, see Hans-Jörg Künast, *"Getruckt zu Augsburg": Buchdruck und Buchhandel in Augsburg zwischen 1468 und 1555* (Tübingen, 1997). Also Heitz and Haebler, *Hundert*, 4–9; Dresler, *Kalender-kunde*, 19–20. On competition among printers: Martha Tedeschi, "Publish and Perish: The Career of Lienhart Holle in Ulm," in Sandra Hindman, ed., *Printing and the Written Word: The Social History of Books, circa 1450–1520* (Ithaca and London, 1991), 41–67.

55. Ludwig Rohner, *Kalendergeschichte und Kalender* (Wiesbaden, 1983), 27; Martin Brecht, "Kaufpreis und Kaufdaten einiger Reformationsschriften," *Gutenberg Jahrbuch* (1972): 169–73; here 173.

56. Moritz Sondheim, *Thomas Murner als Astrolog* (Strasbourg, 1938), 7ff.

57. Konrad Haebler, "Paulus Eck gegen Wenzel Faber," *Zeitschrift für Bücherfreunde*, n.f. 6 (1914–1915): 200–204.

58. Pascher, *Praktiken*, 15.

59. On Schynnagel and Faber: Thorndike, *Magic*, IV, 456–57.

60. On Virdung: Green, *Printing and Prophecy*, 119–24 et passim; Max Steinmetz, "Johann Virdung von Hassfurt: sein Leben und sein Astrologischen

Flugschriften," in Zambelli, ed., *"Astrologi hallucinati,"* 195–214; see also the older literature cited by Steinmetz. On Melanchthon's horoscope: Müller-Jahncke, *Astrologisch-magische Theorie und Praxis,* 142.

61. Lutz 1512; Lutz 1513.

62. On Tannstetter see Hayton, "Astrologers and Astrology," Ch. 5 et passim.

63. On Eyssenmann: Gerhard Eis, "Beiträge zur spätmittelalterlichen deutschen Prosa aus Handschriften und Frühdrucken," *Journal of English and Germanic Philology* 52, no. 1 (1953): 76–89; here 82–86. On Etzlaub: See Fritz Schnelbögl, "Life and Work of the Nuremberg Cartographer Erhard Etzlaub (†1532)," *Imago Mundi* 20 (1966): 11–26.

64. Green, *Printing and Prophecy,* 79–84.

65. Vanden Broecke, *The Limits of Influence,* 91–94.

66. Vanden Broecke, *The Limits of Influence,* 143, 261 et passim.

67. Mentgen, *Astrologie und Öffentlichkeit,* 283.

68. Wolf-Dieter Müller-Jahncke has noted the general resistance of early sixteenth-century German astro-medical writers to Neoplatonic or demonological themes: *Astrologisch-magische Theorie und Praxis,* 138, 150.

69. Zinner, *Geschichte und Bibliographie,* 18; Eberhard Knobloch, "Astrologie als astronomische Ingenieurkunst des Hochmittelalters. Zum Leben und Wirken des Iatromathematikers und Astronomen Johannes Engel," in *Sudhoffs Archiv* 67, no. 2 (1983): 129–44; here 134.

70. On planetary imagery in Italy and the North: Warburg, *Orientalisierende Astrologie,* 563; Blume, *Regenten des Himmels,* 105ff. 125.

71. Tester, *A History,* 220.

72. Thomas Murner, *Practica anno domini* [1498] ([Freiburg], [1498]) edited and translated in Sondheim, *Thomas Murner,* 62–89; here 76–77; Johann Virdung, Practica for 1503 (Cologne, [1502]): facsimile in Pascher, *Praktiken,* 114, 118.

73. Rolf Engelsing, *Der Bürger als Leser: Lesergeschichte in Deutschland 1500–1800* (Stuttgart, 1974), 12.

74. Jakob Schonheintz, *Apologia Astrologiae* (Nuremberg, 1502).

75. J. R. Hale, *The Civilization of Europe in the Renaissance* (New York, 1994), 472. On the lack of almanac production at Cologne: Heitz and Haebler, *Hundert,* 5. On the Dominican Observants and Cologne see D. J. Collins, "Albertus, Magnus or Magus? Magic, Natural Philosophy, and Religious Reform in the Late Middle Ages," *Renaissance Quarterly* 63, no. 1 (Spring 2010): 1–44.

76. Thorndike, *Magic,* IV, 544ff. Nicholas Campion, *History of Western Astrology,* Vol. 2 (New York, 2009), 99–100. According to Gert Mentgen, the Hartung Gernod case suggests that astrologers were generally more subject to clerical sanctions in Germany than in Italy, the "paradise of astrologers"; see Mentgen, *Astrologie und Öffentlichkeit,* 283. But the atmosphere in Cologne was untypical; official press censorship was introduced here as early as 1487. In any case the moves against Lichtenberger and Gernod did not amount to much.

77. Benedikt Ellwanger, *Judicia vel prognostica astrologorum superstitiosa quam nefanda sint et saluti animarium contraria* (Erfurt, c. 1490).

78. Christoph Burger, "Volksfrömmigkeit in Deutschland um 1500 im Spiegel der Schriften des Johannes von Paltz OESA," in Peter Dinzelbacher and Dieter R. Bauer, eds., *Volksreligion im hohen und späten Mittelalter* (Paderborn, 1990), 307–27; here 324–25.

79. Murner, *Practica* [1498], in Sondheim, *Thomas Murner*, 87; on the *Invectivo contra Astrologos* (Strasbourg, 1499): 90–126.

80. Eis, *Wahrsagetexte des Spätmittelalters*, 20–21. On Pollich's dispute with Pistoris see also Grafton, *Cardano's Cosmos*, 52. On Schedel's comment: Dietrich Kurze, "Astrologie und Prophetie im spätmittelalterlichen Geschichtsdenken," in Anita Mächler, et al., eds., *Historische Studien zu Politik, Verfassung und Gesellshaft* (Bern, 1976), 164–86; here 166.

81. Faber 1499; Latin calendar for 1492: Heitz and Haebler, *Hundert*, no. 72. On the "fallback" argument: Sondheim, *Thomas Murner*, 48–49.

82. German Calendar for 1480: Heitz and Haebler, *Hundert*, no. 34.

83. On Brant's attitude, see Dieter Wuttke, "Sebastian Brants Verhältnis zur Wunderdeutung und Astrologie," in Werner Besch, et al., eds., *Studie zur deutschen Literatur und Sprache des Mittelalters* (Berlin, 1974), 272–86. Wuttke's other valuable essays on Brant include "Wunderdeutung und Politik: Zu den Auslegung der sogenannten Wormser Zwillinge des Jahres 1495," in K. Elm, E. Gönner, et al., eds., *Landesgeschichte und Geistesgeschichte* (Stuttgart, 1977), 217–44; "Sebastian Brant und Maximilian I. Eine Studie zu Brants Donnerstein-Flugblatt des Jahres 1492," in O. Herding and R. Stupperich, eds., *Die Humanisten in ihrer politischen und sozialen Umwelt* (Boppard, 1976), 141–76; "Sebastian Brants Sintflutprognose für Februar 1524," in Michael Krejci, ed., *Literatur—Sprache—Unterricht* (Bamberg, 1984), 41–46.

84. Still helpful on the astrological satires is Adolf Hauffen, "Fischart-Studien," *Euphorion* 5 (1898); see esp. 40–43.

85. Pamphilus Gengenbach, *Practica zu Teutsch vff das xv. vñ new Jar gemacht . . .* (Basel, 1515).

86. On the point that astrological parodies were not dismissals of the art, see Silvia Pfister, *Parodien astrologisch-prophetischen Schrifttums 1470–1590: Textform, Entstehung, Vermittlung, Funktion* (Baden-Baden, 1990), 426–28 et passim; also Müller-Jahncke, *Astrologisch-Magische Theorie und Praxis*, 185ff.

87. The classic argument about the "acceleration" of late medieval piety is Bernd Moeller, "Religious Life in Germany on the Eve of the Reformation," in Strauss, ed., *Pre-Reformation Germany*, 13–42.

88. Pfister, *Parodien*, 446.

CHAPTER 2

1. Franz Cumont, *Astrology and Religion among the Greeks and Romans* (New York, 1960; orig. ed. New York, 1912); see also K. Beth, "Astralmythologie," in Hanns

Bächtold-Stäubli, ed., *Handwörterbuch des deutschen Aberglaubens* (Berlin and Leipzig, 1927–1942), vol. 1, 632–45.

2. The term "economy of the sacred" comes from Robert Scribner, "Cosmic Order and Daily Life: Sacred and Secular in Pre-Industrial German Society," in Kaspar von Greyerz, ed., *Religion and Society in Early Modern Europe, 1500–1800* (London, 1984), 17–32; here 18.

3. Scribner, "Cosmic Order and Daily Life," 26.

4. Tester, *A History*, 126–28; on the medieval "computus" see also Mueller, *Beherrschte Zeit*, 39–49.

5. Peter Thaddeus Lang, "Würfel, Wein und Wettersegen: Klerus und Gläubige im Bistum Eichstätt am Vorabend der Reformation," in Volker Press, et al., eds., *Martin Luther: Probleme seiner Zeit* (Stuttgart, 1986), 219–35; here 234.

6. G. J. Whitrow, *Time in History: The Evolution of our General Awareness of Time and Temporal Perspective* (Oxford and New York, 1988), 83; see also Heinrich Schmidt, *Die Deutsche Städtechroniken als Spiegel des bürgerlichen Selbstverständnisses im Spätmittelalter* (Göttingen, 1958), 123.

7. Jaques Le Goff, "Au Moyen Age: temps de L'Église et temps du marchand," *Annales* 15 (1960): 417–33: Edward Muir, *Ritual in Early Modern Europe* (Cambridge, 1997), 75, 79; Gerard T. Moran, "Conceptions of Time in Early Modern France: An Approach to the History of Collective Mentalities," *Sixteenth Century Journal* 12, no. 4 (Winter 1981): 3–19; here 15, 18; Francesco Maiello, "Il Tempo dei Calendari in Francia (1484–1805)," *Studi Storici* 31, no. 2 (1990): 413–36.

8. William J. Bouwsma, "Anxiety and the Formation of Early Modern Culture," in Barbara C. Malament, ed., *After the Reformation: Essays in Honor of J. H. Hexter* (Philadelphia, 1980), 215–46; here 219.

9. Compare the argument of Tullio Gregory, "Temps Astrologique et Temps Chrétien," in *Le Temps Chrétien de la Fin de L'Antiquité au Moyen Age, IIIᵉ-XIIIᵉ Siècles* (Paris, 1984), 557–73; here 560–63, 566–68. Gregory proposes that late medieval astrology worked to "secularize" temporal awareness and thus to dispel the Christian sense of time. He certainly defines this "Christian" sense far too narrowly. See note 10.

10. Carey, "Church Time and Astrological Time," 128. Carey properly focuses not on a vaguely "Christian" or spiritual sense of time, but on specific aspects of medieval ecclesiastical time.

11. Peter Brown, *The Cult of the Saints: Its Rise and Function in Latin Christianity* (Chicago, 1981), 73, 80–81.

12. Zinner, *Geschichte und Bibliographie*, 13.

13. The belief that one did not grow older while attending mass is mentioned in the classic work of Johann Huizinga, *The Waning of the Middle Ages* (New York, 1985; first ed. 1924), 155. On conceptions of time in the late medieval calendrical tradition generally, see Mueller, *Beherrschte Zeit*, esp. 163–74.

14. Zinner, *Geschichte und Bibliographie*, 12.

15. On numeracy: Zinner, *Geschichte und Bibliographie*, 12; on clerical defense of the abacus: Georges Ifrah, *The Universal History of Numbers* (London, 1998), 590; for the quotation from Stöffler: Maurer, *Der Junge Melanchthon*, 136.

16. Anonymous (fragment) c. 1492 (Ulm).

17. Eustace Fulcrand Bosanquet, *English Printed Almanacks and Prognostications: a Bibliographical History to the Year 1600* (London, 1917), 2.

18. Anonymous 1489 (Reutlingen); Pollich 1490; Calendar for 1487: Heitz and Haebler, *Hundert*, no. 47.

19. Anonymous (fragment) c. 1492 (Ulm); *Prognostikon auf das Jahr 1495*, facsimile in Pascher, *Praktiken*, #6, 55; Heitz and Haebler, *Hundert*, no. 93; *Practica von Paris*, 1487: facsimile in Gustav Hellmann, ed., *Wetterprognose und Wetterberichte des XV. und XVI. Jahrhunderts* (Berlin, 1899). Jakob Pflaum, Calendar (Almanach) 1510: Pascher, *Praktiken*, 119–22.

20. On time "punctuated by the stars": Gregory, "Temps Astrologique et Temps Chrétien," 560. Alison Chapman's argument that early modern English astrology afforded a qualitatively differentiated time that functioned similarly to medieval sacred and profane times is fundamentally unconvincing; see her "Marking Time: Astrology, Almanacs, and English Protestantism," *Renaissance Quarterly* 60, no. 4 (Winter, 2007): 1257–90.

21. Fabri 1496: Pascher, *Praktiken*, 31–46; here 31; Memmingen broadsheet: Heitz and Haebler, *Hundert*, no. 51.

22. Capp, *Astrology and the Popular Press*, 147, 285.

23. For an admirably clear introduction to conjunction theory see Smoller, *History, Prophecy, and the Stars*, 16–22; also North, "Astrology and the Fortunes of Churches," 185–89.

24. Heike Talkenberger, *Sintflut: Prophetie und Zeitgeschehen in Texten und Holzschnitten astrologischer Flugschriften, 1488–1528* (Tübingen, 1990), 387.

25. *Calendarius teutsch Maister Joannis Küngspergers* (Augsburg, 1512), Ee4-Ff2/v.

26. On Behaim's globe see the wide-ranging exhibition catalogue produced by the German National Library: *Focus Behaim Globus: Ausstellungskatalog des Germanischen Nationalmuseums* (Nuremberg, 1992). For a discussion of cosmological space in the late medieval calendrical tradition, see Mueller, *Beherrschte Zeit*, 174–81.

27. For instance, an Augsburg calendar for 1492 specified that observers in other cities should add one minute for every four miles to the east of Augsburg, and likewise subtract one minute for every for every four miles to the west. Heitz and Haebler, *Hundert*, no. 71.

28. Quoted in Dietrich Kurze, "Astrologie und Prophetie im Spätmittelalterlichen Geschichtsdenken," in Anita Mächler et al., eds., *Historische Studien zu Politik, Verfassung, und Gesellschaft* (Frankfurt a. M. and Munich, 1976), 164–86; here 166.

29. Wolf-Dieter Müller-Jahncke offers an insightful discussion of astrological medicine, but arguably overemphasizes the magical elements. See his *Astrologisch-magische Theorie und Praxis*, esp. 139ff. The tendency to link

astrological medicine directly with magical and occultist notions is also evident in Becker and Overgaauw, *Aderlass und Seelentrost,* 359–63 et passim. On late medieval astrological medicine see also Mueller, *Beherrschte Zeit,* 189–97.

30. Brown, *Cult of the Saints,* 107, 113 et passim. The "casualty ward" reference is from Ronald C. Finucane, *Miracles and Pilgrims: Popular Beliefs in Medieval England* (Totowa, 1977), 67.

31. Brown, *Cult of the Saints,* 116–20.

32. On the saints as heavenly physicians: Maria Wittmer-Busch, "Pilgern zu himmlischen Ärtzten: Historische und Psychologische Aspekte früh- und hochmittelalterlicher Mirakelberichte," in *Wallfahrt und Alltag in Mittelalter und früher Neuzeit* (Vienna, 1992), 237–54; here 247ff.

33. Carey, "Church Time and Astrological Time," 125. On the role of physicians in undermining late medieval sacramental and clerical traditions see my essay "Alexander Seitz and the Medical Calling: Physic, Faith, and Reform," in Marjorie Elizabeth Plummer and Robin B. Barnes, eds., *Ideas and Cultural Margins in Early Modern Germany* (Burlington, VT, 2009), 183–99.

34. Capp, *Astrology and the Popular Press,* 64–65; Hoppmann, *Astrologie der Reformationszeit,* 75ff.

35. Becker and Overgaauw, *Aderlass und Seelentrost,* 452.

36. Here I have drawn broadly on Müller-Jahncke, *Astrologisch-magische Theorie und Praxis,* 166–80. See also by the same author: "Der Höhepunkt der Iatromathematik," *Berichte zur Wissenschaftsgeschichte* 4, no. 1 (1981): 41–50.

37. On the growth of popular Marian veneration, Otto Clemen, *Die Volksfrömmigkeit des ausgehenden Mittelalters* (Dresden and Leipzig, 1917), 16. On the image of Christ in the winepress: Horst Wenzel, "The *Logos* in the Press: Christ in the Wine-Press and the Discovery of Printing," in Kathryn Starkey and Horst Wenzel, eds., *Visual Culture and the German Middle Ages* (New York, 2005), 223–49; also Elina Gertsman, "Multiple Impressions: Christ in the Winepress and the Semiotics of the Printed Image," *Art History* 36, no. 2 (April 2013): 310–37. Examples of calendars using the imagery of Christ as fruit of the vine include Heitz and Haebler, *Hundert,* Nos. 28, 31, 37, 45, 50, 65, 74, 77, 82, 98.

38. A Strasbourg Calendar for 1500 shows the zodiacal man directly juxtaposed with St. Christopher (the Christ-bearer), suggesting that to be bled was reminder of the need to bear Christ in one's heart. Heitz and Haebler, *Hundert,* no. 99b.

39. Clemen, *Die Volksfrömmigkeit,* 24.

40. Peter Thaddäus Lang, "Würfel, Wein, und Wettersegen: Klerus und Gläubige im Bistum Eichstätt am Vorabend der Reformation," in Volker Press, ed., *Martin Luther: Probleme seiner Zeit* (Stuttgart, 1986), 219–42; here 235.

41. Engel 1488.

42. Leonhard Reynmann, *Wetterbuchlein: Von Wahrer Erkentniss des Wetters* (Augsburg, 1505). A later edition (Munich, 1510) was reproduced with extensive commentary and a full publication history by Gustav Hellmann (Berlin, 1893).

The work also saw many adaptations; large portions appeared unchanged in a work by the Frankfurt city physician E. Roesslin, *Kalender mit allen Astronomischen Haltungen* (1533, 1534, 1537). On this work see Chapter 4.

43. Hellmann, "Versuch," 40–54.

44. Johann Huizinga, *The Waning of the Middle Ages* (New York, 1985; 1st ed. 1924), 176.

45. Practica 1502: facsimile in Hellmann, *Wetterprognose und Wetterberichte*. On this work see Jan Knopf, *Die deutsche Kalendergeschichte: Ein Arbeitsbuch* (Frankfurt a. M., 1983), 31, 41–43. This work presented an explicit vision of *Natura naturata* (God in control) rather than *Natura naturans* (nature as independent).

46. Richard C. Dales, "The De-Animation of the Heavens in the Middle Ages," *Journal of the History of Ideas* 41, no. 4 (1980): 531–50; Blume, *Regenten des Himmels*, 22–33. See also the suggestion of Stegemann, "Planeten," (Chapter 1, note 6), 281: the late medieval German artists who depicted the planetary children may have been the first to work toward a renewed sense of the cosmos as a unity and to seek understanding of the planets as measurable powers that exercised influences on earth. On the qualities and "ruling" times of the planets see also Mueller, *Beherrschte Zeit*, 199–213 et passim.

47. Brévart, "Volkskalender," 322, 335.

48. Mainz calendar: Vita von Lieres, "Kalender und Almanache," in *Zeitschrift für Bücherfreunde* 18 (1926): 101–114; here 103; Goetz 1486 (*Practica von Ingelstat*), A; on Stöffler, see Maurer, *Der Junge Melanchthon*, 140; Virdung, 1497, B4/v.

49. Practica 1487 (*Practica von Paris*); "one God rules all things": *Practica auff das jar . . . 1502 . . . vnd weret xx. jar nach einander*" (N.p., 1501?), a/v; Eyssenmann 1520, A3.

50. Eyssenmann 1516, A3; Johann 1517, B4-B4/v.

51. On Tannstetter's *ex libris*: Grössing, *Humanistische Naturwissenschaft*, 124. For examples of images suggesting God's omnipotence, see H. A. Strauss, *Der Astrologische Gedanke in der deutschen Vergangenheit* (Munich, 1926), 12, 66.

52. The sun, moon, and stars all pointing to the star of Christ: Pascher, *Praktiken*, no. 6, 61; image of Christ as the Sun, the Virgin as Virgo: Boll, Bezold, and Gundel, *Sternglaube und Sternforschung*, 40; the woman of *Revelation* 12 as Mary: Heitz and Haebler, *Hundert*, no. 45; Faber 1492, A2/v. By the early sixteenth century we find fewer such depictions of the Virgin and Christ in the almanacs; in their place we find increasingly elaborate astronomical, astrological, and medical graphics.

53. In ancient Gnostic traditions the planetary spheres themselves were regarded as evil: Per Beskow, "Astrologie I," in Gerhard Krause and Gerhard Müller, eds., *Theologische Realenzyclopädie* (Berlin and New York, 1979), vol. 4, 277–80; here 279.

54. Virdung 1495; Murner, *Practica* [1498], in Sondheim, *Thomas Murner*, 67.

55. Peter Blickle, *Communal Reformation: The Quest for Salvation in Sixteenth-Century Germany* (Atlantic Highlands, NJ, 1992), 159. On the aspect of personal empowerment, see Mueller, *Beherrschte Zeit*, 351.

56. Boll, Bezold, and Gundel, *Sternglaube und Sterndeutung*, 80.

57. Thomas, *Religion and the Decline of Magic*, 327.

58. Peter Brown, *The Making of Late Antiquity*, 76, quoted in Tamsyn Barton, *Power and Knowledge: Astrology, Physiognomics, and Medicine under the Roman Empire* (Ann Arbor, 1994), 200, note 210.

59. Goetz 1486, A/v. On the idea of a "system of planetary anthropology": Stegemann, "Planeten," 71. Willy Andreas similarly argued that the doctrine of planetary children allowed extreme articulations of late medieval ideas about social classes and estates: Andreas, *Deutschland*, 191–92. See also Talkenberger, *Sintflut*, 8: the tensions and conflicts among the planets and their children worked against the ideal of harmony in human society. Cf. Tullio Gregory, "Temps Astrologique et Temps Chrétien" (note 9), who suggests that popular astrology worked to ease social tensions.

60. For background on ancient astrological geography: Boll, Bezold, and Gundel, *Sternglaube und Sterndeutung*, 64ff. Steven Vanden Broecke discusses aspects of the learned context of cosmography and geography: *The Limits of Influence*, 133–36.

61. Schynnagel 1500, b/v; see also Virdung 1503, in Pascher, *Praktiken*, 116. As Paul Russell points out, astrologers such as Joseph Grünpeck "reinforced an already negative view of the qualities of the female sex." See Russell, "Astrology as Popular Propaganda: Expectations of the End in the German Pamphlets of Joseph Grünpeck (†1533?)," in Antonio Rotondò, ed., *Studi e testi per la storia religiosa del Cinquecento*, 2 (1991), 165–95; here 191.

62. Engel 1488, A3/v; Murner 1498, in Sondheim, *Thomas Murner*, 85; "frölich, schympflich menschen": Mangolt 1532, B.

63. See the informative background supplied by North, "Astrology and the Fortunes of Churches."

64. The tripartite division appeared in a manuscript practica for 1476 by John of Glogau; see Thorndike, *Magic*, IV, 450. Printed forecasts using the scheme include Wenzel Faber 1499, Schynnagel 1500.

65. Zambelli, "Introduction," *"Astrologi hallucinati,"* 20.

66. Fabri 1496, in Pascher, *Praktiken*, 40.

67. Garin, *Astrology in the Renaissance*, 77. On the threat to Christianity's world-historical uniqueness: North, "Astrology and the Fortunes of Churches," 200–201 et passim.

68. On the stars as human equalizers: Capp, *English Almanacs*, 112–13. More often, scholars tend to stress the role of astrology in reinforcing social hierarchy; see

for instance Green, *Printing and Prophecy*, 128–29 et passim. But the issue is always one of particular circumstances and context.

69. Lichtenberger, *Pronosticatio zu theutch*, A3/v; see also Talkenberger, *Sintflut*, 63. Johann Friedrich Halbmayer, ed., *Joannes Indagine Astrologia Naturalis* (Strasbourg, 1630), A6.

70. Nicholas Campion, *History of Western Astrology*, Vol. 2 (New York and London, 2009), 101.

71. Carey, *Courting Disaster*, 16–17.

72. The classic essay on the acceleration of late medieval piety is Bernd Moeller, "Religious Life in Germany on the Eve of the Reformation," in Strauss, ed., *Pre-Reformation Germany*, 13–42.

73. *Practica von Paris*, 1487; Faber 1483.

74. Engel 1488, a2/v-a3; Virdung 1503, in Pascher, *Praktiken*, 116; Fabri, Calendar for 1493: Heitz and Haebler, *Hundert*, no. 79.

75. Lea Ritter-Santini, "Der Verwaltete Himmel: Sternzeichen und Kirchenordnung. Ein italienisches Beispiel der Gattung Almanach," in Ritter-Santini, ed., *Lesebilder: Essays zur europäischen Literatur* (Stuttgart, 1978), 140–75; here 151.

76. Anonymous (fragment) c. 1492.

77. Murner, *Practica* [1498], in Sondheim, *Thomas Murner*, 75, 81.

78. Anonymous, *Practica auff das jar* [1502] ... *vnd weret xx. jar nach einander* ... *durch gross maister & sternseher von Caldea auss babilonia* (N.p., c. 1501).

79. Tannstetter 1505 (*Ivdicium Viennense*), a3; similar statements in Tannstetter 1506, a3/v.

80. Lewis Spitz, *The Religious Renaissance of the German Humanists* (Cambridge, MA, 1963), 99–106.

81. Klibansky, Panofsky, and Saxl, *Saturn and Melancholy*, 133ff, 294–95, 393. See also Wolfgang Weber, "Im Kampf mit Saturn: Zur Bedeutung der Melancholie im anthropologischen Modernisierungsprozess des 16. und 17. Jahrhunderts," *Zeitschrift für historische Forschung* 17, no. 2 (1990): 155–92.

82. Engel 1488, a3. For a typical image of Saturn as reaper: Heitz and Haebler *Hundert*, no. 68.

83. Brown, *The Cult of the Saints*, 104–05.

84. Sondheim, *Thomas Murner*, 75. Robert Westman agrees that the popular prognostications "established a tone that was more often alarmist than consolationist": *The Copernican Question*, 63.

85. *Practica von Paris*, 1487. On the 1496 calendar: Bezold, *Geschichte der deutschen Reformation*, 146.

86. Engel 1497; Murner 1498, in Sondheim, *Thomas Murner*, 75, 77. On Tannstetter's pessimism, see Hayton, "Astrologers and Astrology," 359.

87. Faber 1487; Pollich 1490, in Gerhard Eis, ed., *Wahrsagetexte des Spätmittelalters* (Berlin, Bielefeld, Munich, 1956), 21, 64; see also G. Eis, "Martin Pollichs

Vorhersage für 1490," *Libri* 4, no. 2 (1954): 103–29. Stabius 1501 on the French disease: Hayton, "Astrologers and Astrology," 335–36.

88. William J. Bouwsma, "Anxiety and the Formation of Early Modern Culture," in Barbara C. Malament, ed., *After the Reformation: Essays in Honor of J. H. Hexter* (Philadelphia, 1980), 215–46; here 218.

89. Virdung 1503, in Pascher, *Praktiken*, 115–18.

90. Murner 1498, in Sondheim, *Thomas Murner*, 89; Tockler (Noricus), 1515 (*Practica Lipensis*), b2/v; Eis, "Beiträge zur spätmittelalterlichen deutschen Prosa," 85.

CHAPTER 3

1. Blickle, *Communal Reformation*, 184. On apocalyptic expectations in lay pamphlets, for example, see Paul A. Russell, *Lay Theology in the Reformation: Popular Pamphleteers in Southwest Germany, 1521–1525* (Cambridge and New York, 1986).

2. Parts of this chapter are adapted from my essay "The Flood Panic, Medieval Prophetic Traditions, and the German Evangelical Movement," in Roberto Rusconi, ed., *Storia e figure dell'Apocalisse fra '500 e '600: Atti del IV Congresso Internazionale di Studi Gioachimiti* (Rome: Viella, 1996), 145–62.

3. Von Bezold, *Geschichte der deutschen Reformation*, 140.

4. Green, *Printing and Prophecy*, 149–50. Green's approach has value as a corrective, but clearly goes too far in simply reversing causes and effects. The modern historiographical debate began with Zambelli, "Fine del mondo o inizio della propaganda? Astrologia, filosofia della storia e propaganda politico-religiosa nel dibattito sulla congiunzione del 1524," in *Scienze, Credenze Occulte, Livelli di Cultura* (Florence, 1982), 291–368. An important collection of studies is Zambelli, ed., *"Astrologi hallucinati": Stars and the End of the World in Luther's Time* (Berlin, 1986). An informative but rather ungenerous survey of the historiographical background is Zambelli's "Eine Gustav-Hellmann Renaissance? Untersuchungen und Kompilationen zur Debatte über die Konjunction von 1524 und das Ende der Welt auf deutschem Sprachgebiet," *Jahrbuch des italienisch-deutschen historischen Instituts in Trient*, 18 (1992): 413–55. Studies in conversation with Zambelli include Talkenberger, *Sintflut*; also Talkenberger, "'Die Bewegung der himlischen schar' ... Endzeitliche Denken und astrologische Zukunftsdeutung zur Zeit Martin Luthers," in Evangelisches Seminar, Wittenberg, *"Wach auf, wach auf, du deutsches Land!" Martin Luther, Angst und Zuversicht in der Zeitenwende* (Wittenberg, 2000), 25–47. See also Gert Mentgen, *Astrologie und Öffentlichkeit*.

5. Green, *Printing and Prophecy*, 9.

6. The classic study is Marjorie Reeves, *The Influence of Prophecy in the Later Middle Ages: A Study in Joachimism* (Oxford, 1969). See also Bernard McGinn, *Visions of the End: Apocalyptic Traditions in the Middle Ages* (New York, 1979).

7. On John of Lübeck see Thorndike, *Magic*, V, 179. Also still useful on learned speculations is Friedrich von Bezold, "Astrologische Geschichtskonstruktion im Mittelalter," in F. von Bezold, *Aus Mittelalter und Renaissance: Kulturgeschicht-liche Studien* (Berlin, 1918), 165–95.

8. In addition to Kurze, *Johannes Lichtenberger*, see Green, *Printing and Prophecy*, 43–55, 181–82 et passim. Engel's 1484 calendar: Heitz-Haebler, *Hundert*, no. 43; on Engel generally: Eberhard Knobloch, "Astrologie als astrono-mische Ingenieurkunst des Hochmittelalters. Zum Leben und Wirken des Iatromathematikers und Astronomen Johannes Engel (vor 1472–1512)," *Sudhoffs Archiv* 67, no. 2 (1983): 129–44.

9. Lichtenberger's general preoccupation with the German lands is emphasized by Talkenberger among others: *Sintflut*, 56–110 passim.

10. The fullest treatment of the images from Lichtenberger is that of Talkenberger, *Sintflut*, 82–110. Jonathan Green points out that such woodcuts were likely the products of several hands, and were not necessarily sanctioned by Lichtenberger; see his *Printing and Prophecy*, 85–108.

11. Hayton, "Astrologers and Astrology," 103 et passim. On Grünpeck's *Spiegel*: Talkenberger, *Sintflut*, 110–45; on other Grünpeck writings: Sarah Slattery, "Astrologie, Wunderzeichen und Propaganda. Die Flugschriften des Humanisten Joseph Grünpeck," in Bergdolt and Ludwig, eds., *Zukunftsvoraussagung*, 329–47; also Russell, "Astrology as Popular Propaganda," passim.

12. Joseph Grünpeck, *Ein hübscher Tractat von dem Ursprung des Bösen Franzos* (Nuremberg, 1496). Grünpeck was intensely conscious of his own role as a sin-ner needing deliverance; he suffered from syphilis himself, which he saw as a divine punishment; see Talkenberger, *Sintflut*, 124–25. See also Darin Hayton, "Joseph Grünpeck's Astrological Explanation of the French Disease," in Kevin Siena, ed., *Sins of the Flesh: Responding to Sexual Disease in Early Modern Europe* (Toronto, 2005), 81–106.

13. Grünpeck's *Spiegel* has been characterized as basically an abbreviated, popular-ized version of Lichtenberger's *Pronosticatio*, but as Talkenberger shows, this view must be qualified; the two works showed basic differences: Talkenberger, *Sintflut*, 142–45; on Grünpeck see also Green *Printing and Prophecy*, 47–48 et passim.

14. On Grünpeck's use of the "Ship of St. Peter" image, see Talkenberger, *Sintflut*, 116–18; also Slattery, "Astrologie, Wunderzeichen und Propaganda," 336–37.

15. On Stabius, see Hayton, "Astrologers and Astrology," 372–91; also D. Hayton, "Astrology as Political Propaganda: Humanist Responses to the Turkish Threat in Early-Sixteenth-Century Vienna," *Austrian History Yearbook* 38 (2007): 61–91; here 73–83. On the *Book of a Hundred Chapters*: Andreas, *Deutschland*, 181–83; Peuckert, *Die Grosse Wende*, 223ff.; also Gerald Strauss, *Manifestations of Discontent in Pre-Reformation Germany* (Bloomington, 1971), 233ff.

16. Among the versions of this "Anonymous Practica" were: *Ein ausszug etlicher Practica vnd Propheceyen auff vergangne vñ zükunfftige jar, Sibille, Brigitte, Cirilli, Joachim ... Methodii, vnd brüder Reinharts ...* (N.p., c. 1518); and *Disz biechlin zaygt an die weyssagung von zukünfftiger betrübnis ... Sannt Birgitta. Sannt Sybilla. Sant Gregorius. Sant Hilgart. Sant Joachim. Vnd wirt genant die Burde der welt* (Augsburg, 1522). See Talkenberger, *Sintflut*, 145–53.

17. Gregory, "Temps Astrologiques et Temps Chrétien," 566. Making a point that may hold better for the Italian than for the German scene, Ottavia Niccoli argues that "the affair of the deluge expected in 1524 is a good example of how prophetic culture could absorb, envelop, and to some extent annul astrological culture." See O. Niccoli, *Prophecy and People in Renaissance Italy* (Princeton, 1990), 166.

18. This is not to argue that astrological thinking inevitably worked in this way. In the case the French churchman Pierre D'Ailly, the science of the stars could serve to dispel visions of impending doom. See Smoller, *History, Prophecy and the Stars*. For a colorful picture of the prevailing sense of breakdown around 1500 see Peuckert, *Die Grosse Wende*, Vol. 1, 54ff. et passim.

19. Jean Céard, *La nature et les prodiges: L'insolite au XVIᵉ siècle, en France* (Geneva, 1977), 72.

20. Joëlle Ducos, *La Métérologie en français au Moyen Âge (XIIIᵉ-XIVᵉ siècles)* (Paris, 1998), 110.

21. Scholars who tend to overemphasize this distinction between wonder-interpretation and systematic astrology include Silvia Pfister; see her *Parodien astrologisch-prophetischen Schrifttums*, 424–25.

22. On Brant, see the essays by Wuttke cited in Chapter 1, note 83; also Hayton, "Astrology as Political Propaganda," 64–73.

23. *Die auszlegung Magistri Johannis Virdung von Hassfurt. . . vber die wunderbarlichen zaichen di do gesehen worden seind . . . Jm M.cccc.xiiii. jare* (N.p., 1515?); Alexander Seitz, *Ein Schoner Tractat darinnen begriffen ist die Art und Ursach des Traümes* (Landshut, c. 1515), in Peter Ukena, ed., *Alexander Seitz: Sämtliche Schriften* (3 vols., Berlin, 1969–75), Vol. 2, 2–55; here 50–55.

24. Mentgen, *Astrologie und Öffentlichkeit*, 54, 97–112, 148.

25. Mentgen, *Astrologie und Öffentlichkeit*, 113ff., et passim.

26. Klibansky, Panofsky, and Saxl, *Saturn and Melancholy*, 130–33, 143–44 et passim. Noteworthy also are the traditional associations between water, melancholy, and madness. As Michel Foucault put it, "water and madness have long been linked in the dreams of European man." See his *Madness and Civilization: A History of Insanity in the Age of Reason* (New York, 1965), 12.

27. Faber 1492, title page; also Faber 1499, title page; *Practica Teutsch auf die form Magistri venczlai von budveisz* (N.p., 1498), title page.

28. Lyndal Roper, *Oedipus and the Devil: Witchcraft, Sexuality, and Religion in early modern Europe* (London and New York, 1994), 23.

29. "Überflüssigem geblüt": Uberling 1514, a4/v; Andrew Cunningham and Ole Peter Grell, *The Four Horsemen of the Apocalypse: Religion, War, Famine, and Death in Reformation Europe* (Cambridge and New York, 2000), 254.

30. The 1496 broadsheet of Ulsenius is reproduced in Cunningham and Grell, *The Four Horsemen*, 250; also in Warburg, *Heidnisch-Antike Weissagung*, 525.

31. Grünpeck's 1496 tract, for instance, asserted that the stars were only a secondary, physical explanation; the first cause of the disease was divine punishment. See Hayton, "Astrologers and Astrology," 86.

32. Johannes Virdung, *Practica teutsch etliche jar werende* (1503), B4, C3/v-D, E. Virdung had in fact made similar points several years earlier in his practica for 1497.

33. Gerhard Zschäbitz and Annelore Franke, eds., *Das Buch der Hundert Kapitel und der Vierzig Statuten des sogennannten Oberrheinischen Revolutionärs* (Berlin, 1967); Friedrich Waga, ed., *Die Welsch-gattung* (Breslau, 1910).

34. Johannes Stöffler and Jacob Pflaum, *Almanach nova plurimis annis venturis inservientia* [1499–1531] (Ulm, 1499); see Thorndike, *History*, V, 181, and Thorndike's broader discussion re. 1524: V, 178–233.

35. See Paola Zambelli, "Many Ends for the World: Luca Gaurico Instigator of the Debate in Italy and Germany," in Zambelli, ed., *"Astrologi hallucinati,"* 239–63; also Talkenberger, *Sintflut*, 162–64. Gert Mentgen questions the argument that Gaurico began the debate. See his *Astrologie und Öffentlichkeit*, 118ff.

36. On Aventinus: Mentgen, *Astrologie und Öffentlichkeit*, 123–24; on Virdung's *Invectiva*: Talkenberger, *Sintflut*, 165–68.

37. Mentgen, *Astrologie und Öffentlichkeit*, 147; 275ff. See also Niccoli, *Prophecy and People*, 143f.

38. On Tannstetter's growing concern with weather prediction: Hayton, "Astrologers and Astrology," 349–50; on Johannes Werner in Nuremberg: Vanden Broecke, *The Limits of Influence*, 204–06.

39. Gustav Hellmann already recognized the key point that far more German than Italian flood works were issued in the vernacular: "Aus der Blütezeit der Astrometeorologie," in G. Hellmann, ed., *Beiträge zur Geschichte der Meteorologie* Nr. 1–5 (Berlin, 1917): 23–24. See also Zambelli, "Fine del Mondo," 297–98. On the English scene: Capp, *English Almanacs*, 19; on France: Jean-Patrice Boudet, "L'Astrologie, la recherche de la maîtrise du temps et les spéculations sur la fin du monde au Moyen Âge et dans la première moitié du XVIᵉ siècle," in B. Ribemont, ed., *Le Temps, sa mesure et sa perception au Moyen Âge* (Caen, 1992), 19–35; here 30; on Turrel, see Trevor Peach, "Un astrologue anti-luthérien en 1531. Pierre Turrel, *Le période du monde,*" *Bulletin de l'Association d'étude sur l'humanisme, la réforme et la renaissance* 55, no. 1 (2002): 25–40.

40. Niccoli, *Prophecy and People*, 152ff., 159–60. Denis Crouzet proposes that in early sixteenth-century Italy "the millennial dream takes priority over

apocalyptic anguish." See his "Millennial Eschatologies in Italy, Germany, and France: 1500–1533," *Journal of Millennial Studies* 1, no. 2 (1998): 1–8; here 1.

41. The basic statistical outlines remain unchanged since Hellmann's study of 1917 (note 39); he found a total of 133 works, 54 of which came from the German lands. Zinner gives a total of 59 authors and over 136 publications, the great majority from Germany and Italy: *Geschichte und Bibliographie*, 19. These figures do not include the many other published and unpublished writings that made reference to the flood fears. On Cervol, see Talkenberger, *Sintflut*, 273–75; a German translation of Cervol soon appeared: *Tröstliche Practica* (Nuremberg, 1523).

42. Albertus Pigghe, *Adversus prognosticatorum vulgus, qui annuas predictiones edunt* ... (Paris, 1518); see Talkenberger's discussion: *Sintflut*, 168–69; also Vanden Broecke, *The Limits of Influence*, 85–91, 137–43.

43. Eyssenmann 1520; "great changes": A/v.

44. Augustino Nifo, *De falsa diluvii prognosticatione* (Naples, 1519; Augsburg, 1520); see Talkenberger, *Sintflut*, 169–72.

45. Talkenberger, *Sintflut*, 172–74.

46. Pamphilus Gengenbach, *König Karl* (Basel, 1520); see Talkenberger, *Sintflut*, 173–74.

47. Johannes Virdung, *Ausslegung vnd Beteütung der Wůnderbarlichen zeichen/ wie die zů viel malen Jn den Lüfften vnd vff den Ertrich erscheinen vnd gesehen werden* ... (Oppenheim, 1520), E4. See Talkenberger, *Sintflut*, 177–79.

48. Alexander Seitz, *Ain Warnung des Sündtfluss*, in Ukena, ed., *Alexander Seitz*, vol. 2, 56–69; here 69. Seitz's biography is known only in broad outline; see *Allgemeine Deutsche Biographie* (*ADB*) 33: 653–55. Brief but still helpful is Karl Schottenloher, *Doktor Alexander Seitz und seine Schriften: Ein Kleinbild aus dem Münchner Ärzteleben des XVI. Jahrhunderts* (Munich, 1925); see also Talkenberger, *Sintflut*, 184–92.

49. On Brant's resignation by c. 1520: Talkenberger, *Sintflut*, 182–84.

50. Martin Luther, *On Christian Liberty*, in Charles M. Jacobs, et al., eds., *Three Treatises* (Philadelphia, 1947), 268; *D. Martin Luthers Werke: kritische Gesamtausgabe* (*WA*) 7, 20–38; here 23. See also Luther's sermon on John 20:19 from same period: *WA* 7, 803–13.

51. *WA Briefwechsel* 2, 248, no. 367; see Paola Zambelli, "Introduction: Astrologers' Theory of History," in Zambelli, ed., *"Astrologi hallucinati,"* 1–28; for the Luther quotation 1–2. On Seitz and the Diet of Worms see Zambelli, "Fine del Mondo," 336ff; Talkenberger, *Sintflut*, 184ff; Hellmann, "Aus der Blütezeit," 15.

52. Thomas Müntzer, *The Prague Protest*, in Michael G. Baylor, ed., *The Radical Reformation* (Cambridge, 1991), 1–10; here 7; Michael Stifel, *Bruder Michael Styfel Augustiner von Esslingen, Von der Christförmigen rechtgegrundten leer Doctoris Martini Luthers, ain überauss schönkünstlich Lied* ... (Augsburg, 1522) in Otto Clemen, ed., *Flugschriften aus den Ersten Jahren der Reformation* 3

(Leipzig, 1911), 261–352; here 274f.; see also Peuckert, *Die Grosse Wende*, 630. Melanchthon, Letter to Hugo von Einsiedelius, 5 Feb, 1522, quoted in Sachiko Kusukawa, *The Transformation of Natural Philosophy: The Case of Philip Melanchthon* (Cambridge and New York, 1995), 53.

53. On Zeno Rychard: Walther Ludwig, ed., *Vater und Sohn im 16. Jahrhundert: Der Briefwechsel des Wolfgang Reichart ... mit seinem Sohn Zeno (1520–1543)* (Hildesheim, 1999), 135–36, 204 et passim. See also H. Decker-Hauff, *Die Chronik der Grafen von Zimmern* (Constance and Stuttgart, 1967), 159. On Regensburg: Mentgen, *Astrologie und Öffentlichkeit*, 139–40.

54. On the Burgermeister: Hellmann, "Blütezeit," 17–18; Talkenberger, *Sintflut*, 336–39. On Kessler: Mentgen, *Astrologie und Öffentlichkeit*, 137ff.

55. Flooding in Germany: Mentgen, *Astrologie und Öffentlichkeit*, 152; Kaspar Ursinus Velius to Erasmus, in R. A. B. Mynors, ed., *The Correspondence of Erasmus ... 1522 to 1523* (Toronto, 1989), Letter 1280a: 82–83.

56. For Zambelli's major studies on the theme see note 4. On "fewer and less incisive Catholic elements": Zambelli, "Introduction," *"Astrologi hallucinati,"* 6. Robert Scribner basically agrees with Zambelli's interpretation; see *For the Sake of Simple Folk*, 123f.

57. Mark U. Edwards, *Printing, Propaganda, and Martin Luther* (Berkeley and Los Angeles, 1994), 106–08. On the question of the clarity and unity of the early Reformation message, see Susan Karant-Nunn, "What was Preached in German Cities in the Early Years of the Reformation? *Wildwuchs* versus Lutheran Unity," in Andrew Pettegree, ed., *The Reformation: Critical Concepts in Historical Studies*, Vol. 4 (London, 2004), 41–51.

58. Virdung 1521. On Carion's attack against Seitz: Zambelli, "Fine del Mondo," 342–45.

59. Johann Carion, *Prognosticatio und Erklerung der grossen Wesserung* (Leipzig, 1521; several later eds.). On Carion: Green, *Printing and Prophecy*, 55–61; Almut Fricke-Hilgers, "'. . . das der historiographus auch sei ein erfarner der gschicht des himels.' Die Sintflutprognose des Johannes Carion für 1524 mit einer Vorhersage für das Jahr 1789," in Stephan Füssel, ed., *Astronomie und Astrologie in der Frühen Neuzeit* (Nuremberg, 1990), 33–68.

60. Tannstetter, *Practica* (N.p., 1523?); see Talkenberger, *Sintflut*, 243–44. On Tannstetter's popular writings see also Hayton, "Astrologers and Astrology," 372, 432.

61. Apian 1524; see Talkenberger, *Sintflut*, 251–52.

62. *Doctor Joseph Grünpecks Warnunge auff das* [1524] *Jar* (N.p., 1523). See Talkenberger, *Sintflut*, 222–24.

63. Ottmar Nachtigall, ed., *Ain fast nutzlich büchlin zü diser zeit zülesen/Von dem Sindtflusz oder grossen wasser/das sochs durch den einflusz des Hymels nit bezaichent/wie etlich Astrologi vngeschicklich dauon geschriben ...* (Augsburg, 1524). See Talkenberger, *Sintflut*, 270–71.

64. Johann Carion, *Prognosticatio vnd erklerung der grossen wesserung* ... *So sich begeben* ... [1524] (Leipzig, 1521); Virdung, *Practica Teütsch. Vber die neüwe erschröckliche vor nie gesehen Coniunction* ... *der Planeten Jm Jare* [1524] (Oppenheim, 1521).

65. Johann Virdung, *Practica von dem Entcrist vnd dem jüngsten tag auch was geschehen sal vor dem Ende der welt* (N.p., n.d. [Speyer, 1523/4]), 3/v, 8/v.

66. Tannstetter, *Zw eren vnd gefallen den durchleuchtigsten Grosmechtigen Fursten vnd hern* ... *Hat Georg Tannstetter* ... *disz gegenwurtigs buechlen ausgeen lassen* ... ("*Trostbüchlein*") (Vienna, 1523); see Talkenberger, *Sintflut*, 244–45; Apian 1524; Leonhard Reynmann, *Practica vber die grossen vnd manigfeltigen Coniunction der Planeten die im jar M.D.XXIIII. erscheinen vnd vngezweiffelt vil wunderparlicher ding geperen werden* (Nuremberg, 1523). Reynmann referred to figures such as Joachim, Methodius, and Birgitta, (B4), and expressed hopes for a reforming emperor and council (B3/v). Lorenz Fries, *Ein zů samen gelesen vrteil* ... *über die grossen zů samen kunfft Saturni vnnd Jouis in dem M.D.xxiiii. iar* ... (Strasbourg, 1523), A3–A4 et passim.

67. Joseph Grünpeck, *Eyn Dylogus* ... *von dem glauben der Christen vnd von dem glauben des Machumeten. Nachmals von den vierundzweintzigisten jar* ... (Landshut, 1522).

68. Talkenberger reproduces (at reduced size) and discusses virtually all the relevant images: see *Sintflut*, 473–570.

69. Joseph Grünpeck, *Ain nutzliche betrachtung der Natürlichen/hymlischen/vnd prophetischen/ansehung aller Trübsalen, angst, vnd not/die über alle stände/geschlechte/ vnd gemainden der Christenhait/in kurtzen tagen geen werden* (Augsburg, 1522); Virdung 1521; Apian 1524.

70. Grünpeck, *Ain nutzliche betrachtung*, B2-B2/v; Virdung, *Auszlegung vnd Beteütung*, A4; Virdung, *Practica Teutsch. Vber* [1524] (1521), E2/v; on Stöffler: Talkenberger, *Sintflut*, 251.

71. Tannstetter, *Trostbüchlein*, D4-D4/v. On Stöffler: Talkenberger, *Sintflut*, 161.

72. Talkenberger, "'Die Bewegung der Himlischen schar'" (note 4), 30; Luther's sermon on the Ten Commandments: *Eine kurze Erklärung der zehn Gebote*, *WA* I, 247–56; on "Egyptian Days," etc., see 252. This was an abbreviated German version of a Latin sermon: *WA* 1, 422ff.

73. Lorenz Fries, *Ein kurtze Schirmred der kunst Astrologie/wider etliche vnverstandene vernichter* ... (Strasbourg, 1520), A4; see also Talkenberger, "'Die Bewegung der Himlischen schar,'" 28–30.

74. Fries, *Ein zů samen gelesen vrteil*, A2 et passim.

75. Gengenbach, *Ein Christliche vnd ware Practica* (N.p. [Basel], 1523), B2/v. On the Fries-Gengenbach exchange I have also benefited from Helga Robinson-Hammerstein, "The Battle of the Booklets: Prognostic Tradition and the Proclamation of the Word in Early Sixteenth-Century Germany," in Zambelli, ed., "*Astrologi hallucinati*," 129–51.

76. Seitz, *Ain Warnung des Sündtfluss*. In later years Seitz may have flirted with Anabaptism, and he was certainly always an agitator for the interests of the common man. See Talkenberger, *Sintflut*, 184–92.

77. Johannes Copp, *Judicium Astronomicum ad . . . Martinum Lutherum pro anno 1521* (Leipzig, 1520); Copp 1522, B2.

78. Johann Copp, *Was auff disz* [23] *vnd zum tail* [24] *jar. Des himels lauff künfftig sein . . . vrtayl* (N.p., n.d. [Augsburg, 1523]).

79. Copp, *Was auff disz* [23 & 24] *jar*, A3.

80. See the discussion of Copp in Talkenberger, *Sintflut*, 224–35.

81. Copp 1524.

82. See my essay "Alexander Seitz and the Medical Calling," (Chapter 2, note 33).

83. Conrad Gallianus, *Practica vff Drey ior Namlich des* [1522, 1523, 1524], a-b.

84. Gallianus, *Practica vff Drey ior*, a-a2, c2.

85. Gallianus, *Practica vff Drey ior*: "the just shall live": a2/v; images: c3–c4.

86. Gereon [Veit Bild] 1524, A4. Talkenberger argues persuasively against Zambelli's proposal (*"Astrologi hallucinati,"* "Introduction," 6–8) that Bild's work was essentially a satire on the predictions of Johann Carion; see *Sintflut*, 256–57.

87. Gereon [Veit Bild] 1524, B2; weather forecasts: B3–B4.

88. Sebastian Ranssmar, *Anzaygung. vnd Ausslegung. der grossen constellacion/vnd anderer aspectten/so sych in dem 1524 jar/in dem Februario erheben werden* (N.p., n.d. [Augsburg, 1523]). Accompanying the title page flood scene: "O got byss vns gnädig zů dyser zeyt / Wann wir schreyen zů dir / erhör vns wann es ist zeyt."

89. Volmar 1524 (*Practica Wittenbergensis teutsch*).

90. Martin Luther, *Ain Christliche vnd vast wolgegründe beweysung von dem Jüngsten tag vnd von seinen zaychen . . .* (Augsburg, 1522). On editions of this work see Johannes Schilling, "Der liebe Jüngste Tag: Endzeiterwartung um 1500," in Jakubowski-Tiessen, et al., eds., *Jahrhundertwenden*, 15–26; here 23–25. In the Weimar Edition of Luther's works the sermon is included in the *Adventspostille 1522*: "Evangelium am andern sontag ym Advent": *WA* 10, 1, 2: 93–120.

91. See Talkenberger's discussion of this sermon, *Sintflut*, 291–300.

92. Luther, *Ain Christliche*, C4; *WA* 10, 1, 2: 113.

93. Johannes Brenz, "Drei Adventspredigten vom Jahr 1524," in Martin Brecht, Gerhard Schäfer, and Frieda Wolf, eds., *Johannes Brenz: Frühschriften*, Pt. 1 (Tübingen, 1970), 23–32; here 27–28.

94. "Perish in water or fire": Heinrich von Kettenbach, *Ein Gespräch mit einem frommen Altmütterlein von Ulm* (Augsburg, 1523), in Clemen, *Flugschriften*, 2, 52–102; here 102; von Kettenbach, *Ein Practica practiciert aus der Heiligen Bibel auf viel zukünftig Jahr* (N.p. [Colmar], 1523), in Clemen, *Flugschriften*, 2, 192.

95. Heinrich Pastoris, *Practica Teütsch von vergangen/vnd zükünfftigen dingen/Auss der heyligen gschrifft gegründt vnd gezogen. Auf das. 1524. Jar* (N.p. [Zwickau], 1523). Cf. Talkenberger, *Sintflut*, 308–11.

96. Stefan Wacker, *Eyn warhafftig Practica Das keyn Syndfluss werd aus der heyligen geschrifft bewert vnd gezogen* ... (N.p. [Erfurt], 1523).

97. *Practica auff das* [1526] *vnnd all nachuolgende Jar* (N.p., n.d. [Nuremberg, 1525]), quotation on B4.

98. Otto Brunfels, *Almanach ewig werend/Teütszch, vnd Christlich Pracktik/von dem* [1525] *Jare bisz zů endt der welt aller welt* (N.p., n.d. [Strasbourg, 1525]); see title page.

99. Balthasar Wilhelm, *Practica Deutsch auss der Götlichen heyligen geschrifft* ... (N.p., c. 1525).

100. Green, *Printing and Prophecy*, 148 et passim.

101. Scribner, *For the Sake of Simple Folk*, 243, 269n.

102. Cited in Günther Franz, *Der deutsche Bauernkrieg* (Darmstadt, 1956), 92f.

103. On Tannstetter's prediction: Franz, *Der deutsche Bauernkrieg*, 92. On astrology as an inducement to mental violence, see Denis Crouzet, *Les Guerriers de Dieu: La Violence au Temps des Troubles de Religion* (Seyssel, 1990), 180 et passim.

104. On Apian and Virdung: Talkenberger, *Sintflut*, 340–42. On Caritas Pirckheimer: Zambelli, "*Astrologi hallucinati*," "Introduction," 10.

105. See A. Rosenthal, "Dürer's Dream of 1525," *Burlington Magazine* 69, no. 401 (1936): 82–85; also Talkenberger, *Sintflut*, 337–38.

106. On Carion and the Elector, see Thorndike, *Magic*, V, 202. Peter Creutzer, *Ausslegung ... über den erschröcklichen Cometen so im Westrich ... erschienen* (Nuremberg, 1528); on this work see Schottenloher, *Flugblatt und Zeitung*, 193–94, and Hayton, "Astrologers and Astrology," 407–08.

107. On editions of Lichtenberger, the basic work of Kurze, *Johannes Lichtenberger*, has been updated by Green; see *Printing and Prophecy*, 182.

108. See my introduction to "Martin Luther's Preface to Johannes Lichtenberger's Prophecy," in *Luther's Works, American Edition* (continued), Vol. 59 (St. Louis, 2012), 175–78.

109. Sermon of 1518: Talkenberger, *Sintflut*, 285. On Luther and the limits to any theologically based opposition to stellar science, see John D. North, "Celestial Influence: The Major Premiss of Astrology," in Zambelli, ed., "*Astrologi hallucinati*," 45–100; here 97–98.

110. Johann (N.p., [1525?]). So for example in his widely-read multi-year forecast *Bedeutnis vnd Offenbarung Warer Hymlischer Influxion* of 1526 Johann Carion stated—with more than a hint of irony, to be sure—that his work was not for the common man; since it dealt with high and potent matters, astrology should be a restricted art. A2/v-A3.

111. On Tannstetter's retreat from practica writing, see Hayton, "Astrologers and Astrology," 366. The Catholic Virdung denounced those who charged all astrologers with having caused "murder of bodies and souls through their false heretical teaching, by which they have not only stirred up constant

upheaval and slaughter, [but have also] led people away from the Christian faith"; *Ausslegung vnd bedeütniss des Cometen der gesehen worden ist* (N.p., n.d. [Speyer, 1531]), A/v. "Teneo medium": Brotbeyhel 1527, B4.

112. On new regulations in the cities: Talkenberger, *Sintflut*, 346–47; also Matthäus, "Zur Geschichte," 1016–20. On "a calling of God": Brotbeyhel 1527, A2/v.

113. Brelochs 1528; Matthäus, "Zur Geschichte," 1002.

114. Jonathan Green points out that by 1510, all of the practica writers who had been active before 1500 had disappeared from the scene except for Virdung (*Printing and Prophecy*, 122). But the older generation was soon replaced by city physicians who joined the evangelical movement. On Italy after c. 1530: Niccoli, *Prophecy and People*, 19, 190ff.

115. Robert Westman offers the pregnant observation that popular prognostications from city physicians and Lutheran pastors "mirrored the spread of the Reformation as it moved from the pulpit along the network of southwest German publishing cities"; see Westman, *The Copernican Question*, 71.

CHAPTER 4

1. Otherwise insightful and sophisticated studies often reflect the assumption that Melanchthon and his astrologically engaged associates were essentially on the defensive. For example, in her admirably comprehensive study *Im Bann der Sterne*, Claudia Brosseder suggests that the methodological discourse of the Wittenbergers sought to pacify the critics of astrology, to prove that the art was neither superstitious nor frivolous. See notes 7 and 23.

2. Brosseder, *Im Bann*, 256. Melanchthon's close colleague Caspar Peucer articulated similar connections at numerous points, as for example in his famous *Commentarius de praecipuis generibus divinationum* (first ed. Wittenberg, 1553; see for example the Wittenberg, 1576 edition, 111ff.).

3. These terms are Claudia Brosseder's: "The Writing in the Wittenberg Sky: Astrology in Sixteenth-Century Germany," *Journal of the History of Ideas* 66, no. 4 (2005): 557–76; here 557.

4. On the Reformation offensive against medieval superstition, see Cameron, *Enchanted Europe*, 156–218.

5. Heinrich Cornelius Agrippa von Nettesheim, *De Incertitudine & Vanitate omnium Scientiarium & Artium Liber* (Cologne, 1531).

6. The best-known antipractica of the 1530s and 1540s was *Der getrew Eckhart*; a typical edition: *Practica auff disz M.D. und xxxiij. Jar/vnd eyn trewe warnung an alle Stende wider den angezinnten zorn Gottes. Der getrew Eckhart* (N.p., c. 1533). Another example of the genre is Konrad Wickner's *Gewisse vnd Warhafftige Practica aus der heyligen geschrifft* (Nuremberg, 1530).

7. See Brosseder, *Im Bann*, 233, 268–70, 320.

8. Brosseder, *Im Bann*, 134–35.

9. In his *Heidnisch-antike Weissagung* Warburg helped strengthen the oppositional stereotype; see e.g. 497–99; 540–42. Anthony Grafton adopts this powerful conventional wisdom; see A. Grafton, "Some Uses of Eclipses in Early Modern Chronology," *Journal of the History of Ideas* 64, no. 2 (April, 2003): 213–29; here 227.

10. See Jaroslav Pelikan, "Cosmos and Creation: Science and Theology in Reformation Thought," *Proceedings of the American Philosophical Society* 105, no. 5 (1961): 464–69; here 468.

11. A good example of Luther's ongoing emphasis on heavenly signs of the end is his 1531 sermon *Ein tröstliche predigt von der zukunfft Christi und den vorgehenden zeichen des Jüngsten tags*, WA 34, 2, 459–82. See the commonly overlooked perspective of V. Stegemann, "Sterndeutung," in Bächtold-Stäubli, ed., *Handwörterbuch*, vol. 8, cols. 743–45.

12. Brosseder presents a fairly typical picture of opposition between Melanchthon and Luther, but does clearly acknowledge that Luther's position differed from Calvin's (*Im Bann*, 172, 257ff.); see also her "Writing in the Wittenberg Sky," 557–58. On the point that those who trained at Wittenberg came to see natural philosophy as entirely compatible with scripture see Günther Frank, *Die theologische Philosophie Philipp Melanchthons (1497–1560)* (Leipzig, 1995).

13. Stathmion 1551, A3.

14. Anton Brelochs, for instance, identified the ruling planets for the year 1559 as Jupiter and Venus, while Johann Hebenstreit pointed to Mars and Saturn (Brelochs 1559; Hebenstreit 1559).

15. For example, Heller 1549 denounced what he saw as recent innovations and errors in the timing of phlebotomy. Schönfelt 1564, E/v railed against those who ignored the proper astrological medicine.

16. Vanden Broecke argues that the sixteenth-century effort to reform the art and to "discipline" the popular prognosticators itself involved an appeal to the market, and that the more popular writers also encouraged reform by regularly criticizing one another. See Vanden Broecke, *The Limits of Influence*, 143.

17. Fabricius 1565.

18. Schöner 1539; Schöner 1534 dismissed the author of *Die Getrewe Eckhart* as "du grober kopff" (A/v). On Schöner as a calendar and practica writer, see Matthäus, "Zur Geschichte," 1020–25.

19. Stathmion 1555; 1563.

20. Fabricius 1562. He mistakenly cited Ecclesiastes; the words were actually from John 3: 8. Klain 1571, A3. In the late 1550s a number of other prominent calendar men such as Anton Brelochs also avoided preaching or biblical references; see e.g. Brelochs 1559.

21. Hebenstreit 1559, A2-A2/v.

22. Heller 1559; Paceus 1561; Schönfelt 1564, A3/v. On Tycho Brahe: Walther Ludwig, "Zukunftsvoraussagen in der Antike, der frühen Neuzeit und heute," in Klaus Bergdolt and Walther Ludwig, eds., *Zukunftsvoraussagen in der Renaissance* (Wiesbaden, 2005), 9–64; here 45–46.

23. Caspar Peucer, *Commentarius de praecipvis generibus divinationum* (note 2). See Brosseder's valuable contextualization: *Im Bann*, 235–56.

24. Brosseder, *Im Bann*, 250.

25. Peucer paralleled certain Roman Catholic beliefs and practices such as the eucharist and purgatory with illegitimate heathen and demonic arts. See his *Commentarius* (1576), 111-111/v; 153/v, 211-211/v.

26. The highly influential concept of a Melanchthon circle was shaped largely by Thorndike, *History*, V, 378–405. See also Kusukawa, *Transformation*, 38, 65. Westman, *The Copernican Question*, 143ff. continues to use terms such as "the Melanchthon Circle," but clearly stresses a very broad sphere of influence. Brosseder rightly qualifies the notion: *Im Bann*, 11–17 et passim.

27. Wolfgang Hübner, "Astrologie in der Renaissance," in Bergdolt and Ludwig, eds., *Zukunftsvoraussagen*, 264; Wilhelm Maurer, *Der Junge Melanchthon zwischen Humanismus und Reformation* (Göttingen, 1996), 131, 138.

28. Stefano Caroti, "Melanchthon's Astrology," in Zambelli, ed., *"Astrologi hallucinati,"* 109–21, esp. 113, 120; on Melanchthon and the flood debate: Talkenberger, *Sintflut*, 284; Müller-Jahncke, *Astrologisch-magische Theorie und Praxis*, 229. See also Charlotte Methuen, "The Role of the Heavens in the Thought of Philipp Melanchthon," *Journal of the History of Ideas* 57, no. 3 (1996): 385–403; Volkhard Wels, "Melanchthons Anthropologie zwischen Theologie, Medizin und Astrologie," in Kaspar von Greyerz, Thomas Kaufmann, et al., eds., *Religion und Naturwissenschaften im 16. und 17. Jahrhundert* (Gütersloh, 2010), 51–85; and the essays by Günter Frank, Karin Reich, and Georg Singer in Franz Fuchs, ed., *Mathematik und Naturwissenschaften in der Zeit von Philipp Melanchthon: Akten des . . . 2010 veranstalteten Symposions in Nürnberg* (Wiesbaden, 2012).

29. See my *Prophecy and Gnosis*, 298 note 19. In his *Historia Lutheri* of 1546, Melanchthon avoided controversy by affirming 1483 as the correct year. See K. G. Bretschneider, ed., *Corpus Reformatorum* (Halle, 1834–) VI, 155–70; German translation in Michael Beyer, Stefan Rhein, and Günther Wartenberg, eds., *Melanchthon Deutsch* (Leipzig, 1997), vol. 2, 169–88; here 171.

30. Aby Warburg noted the significance of Melanchthon's letter of inquiry to Carion: *Heidnisch-Antike Weissagung*, 493–96. On Melanchthon's reaction to the 1531 comet: Kusukawa, *Transformation*, 124ff. See also Stefano Caroti, "Comete, portenti, causalità naturale e escatologia in Filippo Melantone," in Istituto nazionale di studi sul Rinascimento, *Scienze, Credenze Occulte, Livelli di Cultura* (Florence, 1982), 393–426..

31. *CR* II, 530–37. See the modern edited translation in Sachiko Kusukawa, ed., *Philip Melanchthon: Orations on Philosophy and Education* (Cambridge, 1999),

105–12; German translation in Hoppmann, *Astrologie der Reformationszeit,* 123–28. See also Isabelle Pantin, "La lettre de Melanchthon à S. Grynaeus: les avatars d'une apologie de l'astrologie," in Ecole Normale Supérieure de Jeunes Filles, *Divination et Controverse Religieuse en France au XVIᵉ Siècle* (Paris, 1987), 85–101. Pantin rightly argues that this letter stood apart from any debate over stellar science, and that it was later attacked by Catholics for "une conception un peu trop luthérienne de la destinée humaine": 101.

32. Hans Blumenberg, "Melanchthons Einspruch gegen Kopernikus," *Studium Generale* 13, no. 3 (1960): 174–82; here 177.

33. *Oratio de Dignitate Astrologiae, CR* XI, 261–66; see the edited translation in Kusukawa, *Orations,* 120–25; here 120. See also Westman, *The Copernican Question,* 113.

34. *On the Dignity of Astrology,* in Kusukawa, *Orations,* 122.

35. Brosseder, *Im Bann,* 234. On the Neoplatonic elements in Melanchthon's thought, see Maurer, *Der Junge Melanchthon,* Vol. 1, 129–70. Maurer argues that Melanchthon inherited these elements from Johannes Stöffler, his teacher at Tübingen. See also Maurer, *Melanchthon-Studien* (Gütersloh, 1964), 39–66.

36. "Guided by divine providence": *On the Dignity of Astrology,* in Kusukawa, *Orations,* 122; see also Brosseder, *Im Bann,* 318.

37. Caroti, "Melanchthon's Astrology," 117–20; quotation: 120. See also Charlotte Methuen's excellent study, *Kepler's Tübingen: Stimulus to a Theological Mathematics* (Aldershot/Brookfield, 1998), 77; also Dino Bellucci, *Science de la Nature et Réformation* (Rome, 1988), 283, 606–07.

38. Bellucci, *Science de la Nature et Réformation,* 221; Frank, *Theologische Philosophie,* 307–08. On the stars as preachers of the law: Volker Leppin, *Antichrist und Jüngster Tag: Das Profil Apocalyptischer Flugschriftenpublizistik im Deutschen Luthertum 1548–1618* (Gütersloh, 1999), 156–59.

39. Bellucci, *Science de la Nature et Réformation,* 298; Troels Troels-Lund, *Himmelsbild und Weltanschauung im Wandel der Zeiten* (Leipzig, 1908), 201–02.

40. Bellucci, *Science de la Nature et Réformation,* 620–21. It is thus misleading to assert that Melanchthon adopted the Thomist solution to the problem of free will, as many scholars have done.

41. Bellucci, *Science de la Nature,* 317. Pierre Freyberger argues that while Melanchthon rejected Stoic fatalism, he stood closer to that doctrine than he wished to admit. See P. Freyberger, "Le Problème du Fatalisme Astral dans la Pensée Protestante en Pays Germaniques," in ENSJF, *Divination et controverse religieuse,* 35–55, esp. 45.

42. Ralph Keen, "Naturwissenschaft und Frömmigkeit bei Melanchthon," in Günter Frank and Stefan Rhein, eds., *Melanchthon und die Naturwissenschaft seiner Zeit* (Sigmaringen, 1998), 73–83; here 77–78.

43. *On the Dignity of Astrology,* 121.

44. *On the Dignity of Astrology*, 124.
45. *On Natural Philosophy, CR* XI, 555–60, translation in Kusukawa, *Orations*, 133–38; *On the Dignity of Astrology*, 124–25.
46. On Calvin's view of nature, see the comprehensive study of Susan E. Schreiner, *The Theatre of His Glory: Nature and the Natural Order in the Thought of John Calvin* (Durham, NC, 1991).
47. Brosseder, *Im Bann*, 274; Bellucci, *Science de la Nature*, 625 et passim.
48. On this aspect of Melanchthon's letters: Caroti, "Melanchthon's Astrology," 119; 1553 oration: *De Orione, CR* XII, 46–52.
49. On Luther and the old age of the world, see my *Prophecy and Gnosis*, 45 et passim. Melanchthon on "extreme dotage" and the decline of nature: Bellucci, *Science de la Nature*, 624–31; Brosseder, *Im Bann*, 250. Melanchthon shared this view with many expert astronomers of his time, including the Netherlander Joannes Stadius; see Vanden Broecke, *The Limits of Influence*, 192.
50. Melanchthon, *Initia*, 242, quoted in Brosseder, *Im Bann*, 273. For "an almanac on the wall": *CR* 20, 549ff. (Nr. 122), quoted in Beyer, Rhein, and Wartenberg, eds., *Melanchthon Deutsch*, I, 311.
51. Erika Rummel argues that the "confessionalization of education" was already well under way by the 1530s. See E. Rummel, *The Confessionalization of Humanism in Reformation Germany* (Oxford, 2000), Ch. 2. Still valuable on the Wittenberg interpretation of Copernicus as merely an acceptable basis for calculation is Robert S. Westman, "The Melanchthon Circle, Rheticus and the Wittenberg Interpretation of the Copernican Theory," *Isis* 66, no. 2 (1975): 165–93.
52. Brosseder, *Im Bann*, 49, 64ff. 71ff. On Spalatin, see Irmgard Höss, "Georg Spalatin and the Astrologers," in Zambelli, ed., *"Astrologi Hallucinati,"* 123–27.
53. Vanden Broecke, *The Limits of Influence*, 143, 261 et passim.
54. On Carion: Dietmar Fürst and Jürgen Hamel, *Johann Carion (1499–1537): Der erste Berliner Astronom* (Berlin, 1988). On the attack against Carion by the Habsburg propagandist Perlach, see Hayton, "Astrologers and Astrology," 262, 269–77.
55. Brosseder, *Im Bann*, 32–33.
56. On Osiander's astrology and astronomy see Gottfried Seebass, *Das reformatorische Werk des Andreas Osiander* (Nuremberg, 1967), 85–90.
57. For the Nuremberg context: Kurt Pilz, *600 Jahre Astronomie in Nürnberg* (Nuremberg, 1977). Brosseder stresses Wittenberg and Nuremberg as the most active European centers for astrological study and practice in the mid-sixteenth century: *Im Bann*, 137.
58. On Heller see Matthäus, "Zur Geschichte," 1025–38; also Brosseder, *Im Bann*, 151–53.
59. Petreius's role is emphasized by Brosseder, *Im Bann*, 147–49. Among the popular vernacular works he published were forecasts by Johann Carion (1532) and A. P. Gasser (1545).

60. On Schöner see the helpful essays by Christine Sauer and Monika Maruska in Fuchs, ed., *Mathematik und Naturwissenschaft* (note 28); also Brosseder, *Im Bann*, 153–57 et passim.

61. Gervasius Marstaller, ed., *Artis divinatricis, quam astrologiam seu iudiciarum vocant: encomia & patrocinia* ... (Paris, 1549). See Walther Ludwig, "Zukunftsvoraussagen in der Antike, der frühen Neuzeit und Heute," in Bergdolt and Ludwig, eds., *Zukunftsvoraussagen*, 9–64; here 34–35.

62. See Chapter 1, note 9, and below note 63. Also: Eucharius Roesslin, *Kalender mit allen Astronomischen haltungen* (1st ed. Frankfurt a. M., 1533); Peter Creutzer, *Planeten Büchlin* (1st ed. Frankfurt a. M., 1545); Nicolaus Rensberger, *Astronomia Teutsch* (1st ed. Augsburg, 1568). Brosseder essentially dismisses these works as beneath notice, and does not discuss their role in the booming stellar culture of the day: *Im Bann*, 147n. Also falling into the category of vernacular instruction books was the huge *Geburtsstundenbuch* of Martinus Pegius (Basel, 1570, 1572). A Salzburg jurist mainly known for his legal writings, Pegius was most likely a Catholic, but his work reflected a fully Melanchthonian spirit and numerous hints of evangelical sympathies.

63. *Astronomia. Teutsch Astronomei. Von Art/eygenschafften/vnd wirckung. Der xij. Zeichen des Himels. Der vij. Planeten* ... (Frankfurt a. M., 1545), G/v. Much of this work was adapted from the earlier planet book falsely attributed to Regiomontanus, *Calendarius Teutsch* (Augsburg, 1512).

64. On herbals and related genres, see Müller-Jahncke, *Astrologisch-Magische Theorie und Praxis*, 171–75. Müller-Jahnke points out that such works were probably aimed mainly at physicians or educated heads of families, while the great majority of the public turned to the almanacs or calendars as their main healing guides.

65. Hellmann, *Meteorologie*, 21; Vanden Broecke, *The Limits of Influence*, 204ff.

66. Aurifaber 1541, a2a. See Jonathan Green, "The First Copernican Astrologer: Andreas Aurifaber's Practica for 1541," *Journal for the History of Astronomy* 41, no. 2 (2010): 157–65. I follow Green's translation from Aurifaber's preface; here 162. On the questions of the extent to which Aurifaber actually used Copernican data and understood Copernican cosmology, see Richard L. Kremer, "Calculating with Andreas Aurifaber: A New Source for Copernican Astronomy in 1540," *Journal for the History of Astronomy* 41, no. 4 (2010): 483–502.

67. On "Lasszetteln": Müller-Jahncke, *Astrologisch-Magische Theorie und Praxis*, 147, 167; Brosseder, *Im Bann*, 56 et passim.

68. Terms such as "market scribblers" have been too often used in a way that discounts the networks linking elite and popular writers, thus implying that the mass of popular star-literature does not warrant serious historical study. Thus Brosseder, *Im Bann*, 39 refers to a class of "vagabundierender Jahrmarkts-astrologe[n]." On Sebastian Münster, see Hellmann, *Versuch*, 11.

69. On the idea of vernacular scientific and medical writers as cultural brokers see William Eamon, *Science and the Secrets of Nature: Books of Secrets in Medieval and Early Modern Culture* (Princeton, 1994); also Kathleen Crowther-Heyck, "Wonderful Secrets of Nature: Natural Knowledge and Religious Piety in Reformation Germany," *Isis* 94, no. 2 (2003): 253–73.

70. Virtually definitive on Gasser is Karl Heinz Burmeister, *Achilles Pirmin Gasser 1505–77: Arzt und Naturforscher, Historiker und Humanist* 3 vols. (Wiesbaden, 1970, 1975). On Gasser's practica for 1546 see Richard L. Kremer, "Copernicus among the Astrologers: A Preliminary Study," in Menso Folkerts and Andreas Kühne, eds., *Astronomy as a Model for the Sciences in Early Modern Times* (Augsburg, 2006), 225–52; also Green, "The First Copernican Astrologer," 157. On Mithob see Richard Cole, "Spreading Reformation Ideas: The Work and Medical Writings of Dr. Burchard Mithob in Sixteenth-Century Calenberg," *Zeitsprünge: Forschungen zur Frühen Neuzeit* 4, nos. 1/2 (2000): 72–80.

71. Mangolt 1532; Saltzmann 1543; Stathmion 1551; Schönfelt 1564, B3; Paceus 1561.

72. Schöner 1540, title page, A2.

73. Mithob, 1540, A2. On Regiomontanus: Zinner, *Geschichte und Bibliographie*, 15.

74. Germanus 1573; Heller 1549, 1553, 1557; Titius 1556; Klain 1578, A3/v: "Copernici fontibus (welchen auch die Obseruation zustimmet)." We find relatively little evidence in Lutheran Germany of what Steven Vanden Broecke calls a "remorseless debate between urban prognosticators and courtly practitioners." See Vanden Broecke, *The Limits of Influence*, 97, 260.

75. Hoffman 1571; Wilhelm 1567; Saltzmann 1539; Reinstein 1573; Brelochs 1548.

76. Matthias Brotbeihel, *Practica: von warer erkandtnus des Wetters* (Augsburg, 1540).

77. Schöner 1534, B4. On Matthias Brotbeihel and Jerome Brotbeihel, and on the likely evangelical leanings of the latter, see Chapter 5, note 9.

78. Schöner 1547, title page. Latin quotation in Matthäus, "Zur Geschichte," 1028: "Disce Deum Lector revereri, & conscia fati Sidera ne frustrum condita crede."

79. Stathmion 1551, A3; Stathmion 1563.

80. "COELUM TABELLA FATI": Schönfelt 1562, title page.

81. Wilhelm 1571; Rhau 1572, A2; Germanus 1573; Caesius 1583.

82. Fabricius 1565, A2/v; Brelochs 1548.

83. Mithob 1540, C4; Brelochs 1559, B4.

84. Stathmion 1563, 1, 2.

85. Reinstein 1573; Schönfelt 1564.

86. Stathmion 1555, A2/v; Schöner 1534; Gasser 1547.

87. Brelochs 1544; Gasser, Calendar for 1547.

88. On the antinomian impulse: Gerald Strauss, *Law, Resistance and the State: The Opposition to Roman Law in Reformation Germany* (Princeton, 1986), 192. On moral didacticism in the practicas: Barbara Bauer, "Sprüche in Prognostiken des 16. Jahrhunderts," in Burghart Wachinger and Walter Haug, eds., *Kleinstformen der Literatur* (Tübingen, 1994), 165–203, esp. 173–77.

89. Sachiko Kusukawa, "Melanchthon and Astrology for Lutheran Medics," in
    Ole Peter Grell and Andrew Cunningham, eds., *Medicine and the Reformation*
    (London, 1993), 46.

90. Schönfelt 1564, E/v; Reinstein 1573; M. Brotbeyhel 1545, C/v; I have borrowed
    the translation from Capp, *Astrology and the Popular Press*, 28. Geuss 1564.

91. Leppin, *Antichrist*, 156–59.

92. Schöner 1540; Stathmion 1551, A2; Titius 1556, B.

93. J. Brotbeyhel 1560; Wilhelm 1571.

94. Saltzmann 1539; Rheticus 1551, B2; Stathmion 1551, A3.

95. Among the matters of fundamental theoretical uncertainty was the method of
    dividing the twelve terrestrial houses; debate on the matter continued through-
    out the sixteenth century. See Vanden Broecke, *The Limits of Influence*, 238.

CHAPTER 5

1. Leppin recognizes this "especially free development": *Antichrist*, 286. Parts of
   this chapter are adapted from my essay "Astrology and the Confessions in the
   Empire, 1550–1620," in John Headley, Hans Hillerbrand, and Anthony Papalas,
   eds., *Confessionalization in Europe, 1555–1700: essays in honor and memory of
   Bodo Nischan* (Aldershot and Burlington, 2004), 131–53.

2. The figures used in the graph are approximations based largely on Zinner,
   Geschichte und Bibliographie. For the half-decades from 1531 to 1550 I have
   adopted the updated findings of Jonathan Green; see his graph in *Printing and
   Prophecy*, 123, as well as the valuable listing in Green's "Appendix." Before 1550 a
   small percentage of these works were still published in Latin, but after that date
   the percentage dropped to near zero. Robert Westman presents graphs similarly based on Zinner: *The Copernican Question*, 26, 44, 251. See also Westman's
   "Table 1," 71, drawing on Hellmann's figures comparing numbers of astrological prognostications published in various European lands. Comparable bibliographical data are not yet available for the period after 1630. The *Heritage of the
   Printed Book* database shows that numerous annual works continued to appear
   under titles such as *Prognosticon Astrologicum*, but these records suggest that
   the numbers never again approached pre-1620 levels. Far more important is the
   changing character of these works; see my discussion in Ch. 7.

3. Thomas Kaufmann, "1600—Deutungen der Jahrhundertwende im deutschen
   Luthertum," in Manfred Jakubowski-Tiessen et al., eds., *Jahrhundertwenden:
   Endzeit und Zukunftsvorstellungen vom 15. bis zum 20. Jahrhundert* (Göttingen,
   1999), 73–128; here 128.

4. My figures are again based on Zinner, *Geschichte und Bibliographie*. The available statistics indicate an almost limitless demand. In 1558 the Nuremberg
   printer Valentin Geyssler received a seller's order for over 37,000 copies of a
   broadsheet almanac. See Matthäus, "Zur Geschichte," 1119; also Dresler,
   Kalender-Kunde, 14.

5. Matthäus, "Zur Geschichte," 1069–70.

6. Hayton, "Astrologers and Astrology," 215–91, 329–69, 414–33, et passim. On the Perlach-Carion exchange see also Green, *Printing and Prophecy*, 134.

7. Apian 1532, Aiij. The warning verses to "Rome," which appeared on the title page, may of course have been added by the publisher. On the setting at Ingolstadt generally: Christoph Schöner, *Mathematik und Astronomie an der Universität Ingolstadt im 15. und 16. Jahrhundert* (Berlin, 1994).

8. On Virdung's loyalty to Rome see Steinmetz, "Johann Virdung von Hassfurt," 203.

9. M. Brotbeyhel 1528, 1533, 1538, 1548. Matthias Brotbeihel's earliest surviving practica is from 1527; his latest from 1551; see Green's listing, *Printing and Prophecy*, 162–63. For context see Siegmund Günther, "Ein Stück Meteorologie und Astrologie aus Alt-München," in K. von Reinhardstoettner and K. Trautmann, eds., *Jahrbuch für Münchner Geschichte*, Vol. 1 (Munich 1887): 75–92. Jerome Brotbeyhel issued similar works from at least 1529 to 1563. Leppin (*Antichrist*, 155) argues that Jerome Brotbeihel was a Catholic, citing evidence such as a dedication to the Archbishop, and later publications issued at Dillingen. But his several dedications to evangelical princes as well as the language of his practicas cast doubt on this claim. For the use of Luther's words on Micah: J. Brotbeihel 1560, A4/v.

10. R.J.W. Evans, *The Making of the Habsburg Monarchy 1550–1700* (Oxford, 1979), 396. In Italy, the popular prophetic atmosphere that did much to sustain astrological prediction waned rapidly after around 1530; on this point see Ottavia Niccoli, *Prophecy and People in Renaissance Italy* (Princeton, 1990), 19, 190–93.

11. Jonathan Green's study of German astrological and prophetic works extends only to around 1550, which partially explains his misleading conclusion that "the Catholic and Protestant divide does not form a boundary in the creation or reception of prophetic and prognostic works": *Printing and Prophecy*, 99.

12. Walter M. Brod, *Mainfränkische Kalender aus Vier Jahrhunderten* (Würzburg, 1952), 16; see also Matthäus, "Zur Geschichte," 973, 1104–05.

13. On the Catholic notion of "spiritual physic": David Lederer, *Madness, Religion and the State in Early Modern Europe: The Bavarian Beacon* (Cambridge and New York, 2006). On Counter-Reformation uses of the saints more generally: Philip M. Soergel, *Wondrous in His Saints: Counter-Reformation Propaganda in Bavaria* (Berkeley, 1993).

14. On the German Protestant connections of Gaurico and especially Cardano, see Grafton, *Cardano's Cosmos*, 71–90 et passim.

15. On the Index: Brosseder, *Im Bann*, 286. On growing Roman hostility to the astrologers and the Papal Bull of 1586, see especially Barbara Mahlmann-Bauer, "Die Bulle *contra astrologiam iudiciariam* von Sixtus V., Das astrologische Schrifttum protestantischer Autoren und die Astrologiekritik der Jesuiten. These über einen vermuteten Zusammenhang," in Klaus Bergdolt and Walther Ludwig, eds., *Zukunftsvoraussagen in der Renaissance* (Wiesbaden: Harassowitz, 2005), 143–222; here 152ff. Cf. Heribert Smolinsky, *Deutungen der Zeit im*

Streit der Konfessionen: Kontroverstheologie, Apokalyptik und Astrologie im 16. Jahrhundert (Heidelberg, 2000).

16. Schoder 1551.

17. Vanden Broecke, *The Limits of Influence*, 186–87, 190, 260ff. et passim.

18. Vanden Broecke, *The Limits of Influence*, 252ff.; Allen, *The Star-Crossed Renaissance*, 86.

19. Johannes Philognysius [Johann Nas], *Die vnfelig gewisest Practica Practicarum, auff das yetzig vnd nachvolgende jar* . . . (Ingolstadt, 1566), A2, F2, et passim; see Brosseder, *Im Bann*, 283–84; also my *Prophecy and Gnosis*, 161–62.

20. Theodor Graminaeus, *Erklerung oder Ausslegung eines Cometen, so nuhn* . . . *den dritten Februarij dieses jetzt lauffenden MDLXXIII Jars am himmel vernommen* (Cologne, 1573). On Graminaeus in the tradition of Lichtenberger: Kurze, *Johannes Lichtenberger*, 68.

21. Johann Rasch, *Practica Auff das grosswunder Schaltjahr* . . . (Munich, 1588). On Rasch, see Smolinsky, *Deutungen der Zeit*, 7–18 et passim; Mahlmann-Bauer, "Die Bulle *contra astrologiam*," 185–89.

22. Johann Rasch, *Cometen Büch. Von dem newen Stern des 73. vnnd von den Cometen des 77. vnnd 81 Jars* . . . (Munich, 1582), E4 et passim.

23. Rasch, *Practica auff das grosswunder Schaltjar*, Preface; Rasch, *Weissag der Zeit. Allgemaine Himels vnd Weldpractic* . . . (Munich, 1596).

24. Johann Rasch, *New Kalendar. Das erste büch* (Rorschach, 1590), cited in Smolinsky, *Deutungen der Zeit*, 25.

25. Mahlmann-Bauer, "Die Bulle *contra astrologiam*," 148–50.

26. On Jesuit efforts to exclude the art from university curricula: Brosseder, *Im Bann*, 286; Bauer, "Die Bulle *contra astrologiam*," 191. On Philip Apian's departure from Ingolstadt: Brosseder, *Im Bann*, 279–80. To be sure, as Brosseder notes, Apian also left Tübingen some fifteen years later, unwilling to subscribe to the Lutheran "Formula of Concord." Yet unlike the Tridentine strictures, the Lutheran statement said nothing about astrology; thus Apian's reasons for leaving Tübingen appear to have been unrelated to his stellar studies.

27. On Clavius, see Bauer, "Die Bulle *contra astrologiam*," 148–50. Pereira's work: *Adversvs Fallaces Et Svperstitiosas Artes, Id Est, De Magia, De Observatione Somniorum, et De Diuinatione Astrologica: Libri Tres* (Ingolstadt, 1591); esp. 246; on this work see also Mahlmann-Bauer, "Die Bulle *contra astrologiam*," 197–98; Allen, *The Star-Crossed Renaissance*, 90–91; Evans, *The Making of the Habsburg Monarchy*, 398.

28. Georg Scherer, *Antwort auff die zwey vnverschämpte vnd Ehrenschmähende Famos, Schandt vnd Lästercharten, M. Alexanders Vtzingers eines Predicanten zu Schmalkalden* (Ingolstadt, 1589), 149–50. The Jesuit Georg Scherer of Vienna (d. 1605) was a prominent Catholic reformer in the Habsburg lands, and the author of several severely anti-Lutheran tracts.

29. Lorenz Albrecht, *Evangelisch Prognostic. Ein bewärte augenscheinerfahrliche weissag . . . was das ketzerisch lutertumb . . . ergehn werde biss zu seinem end . . .* (Munich, 1589).

30. [Lorenz Albrecht], *Newe Predicanten Practica vnd Prognosticon. Darinn aigentlich der Predicanten Standt/Lehr/Leben/Frücht vnd Wandel beschrieben vnd . . . angezeigt wirdt . . .* (N.p., 1592), 13–15, 22 et passim.

31. On Pazmany: Evans, *The Making of the Habsburg Monarchy*, 398; Francisco de Osuna/Aegidius Albertinus, *Flagellum Diaboli: Oder Dess Teufels Gaissl* (Munich, 1602), 67/r; Adam Tanner, *Astrologia Sacra: hoc est orationes et quaestiones quinque . . .* (Ingolstadt, 1615); on Tanner's work see Brosseder, *Im Bann*, 291; on the Jesuit campaign, including Tanner: Mahlmann-Bauer, "Die Bulle *contra astrologiam*," 197–204.

32. Hippolytus Guarinonius, *Die Grewel der Verwüstung Menschlichen Geschlechts* (Ingolstadt, 1610), 30–37.

33. Adrianus Romanus: see for example Zinner, *Geschichte und Bibliographie*, Nos. 3792, 3793, 3865, 3866; and Hans-Joachim Vollrath, "Geschichte der Mathematik an der Universität Würzburg": www.didaktik.mathematik. uni-wuerzburg.de/history/mathematik/romanus.html. Wilhelm Upilio had published at Nuremberg as early as 1575; he had switched to Würzburg by 1588; see Zinner, *Geschichte und Bibliographie*, Nos. 2690, 3281. On Würzburg and Bamberg calendars, see also Walter M. Brod, *Mainfrankische Kalender aus vier Jahrhunderten* (Würzburg, 1952). Maximilian Tripet: the CERL database lists five annual prognostications by him from 1594 to 1598; I have seen those for 1594 and 1598. On Johann Gigas (Riese): *Neue Deutsche Biographie* 6, 390f.

34. Evans, *The Making of the Habsburg Monarchy*, 396.

35. John Calvin: *Avertissement contre l'astrologie judiciaire*; ed. Olivier Millet (Geneva, 1985); *A Warning against Judicial Astrology and other Prevalent Curiosities*, trans. Mary Potter, *Calvin Theological Journal* 18 (1983): 157–89. For the French context see J. Lewis, "Les Pronostications et la Propagande Évangélique," in *Divination et Controverse Religieuse en France au XVIᵉ Siècle* (Paris, 1987), 73–83.

36. Calvin, *A Warning*, 179.

37. Calvin, *A Warning*, 176–77; 187. Here Calvin cited Leviticus 20:6.

38. Max Engammare, "Calvin: A Prophet without a Prophecy," *Church History* 67, no. 4 (1998): 643–61; here 644.

39. Richard van Dülmen, "Volksfrömmigkeit und konfessionelles Christentum im 16. Jahrhundert," in W. Schieder, ed., *Volksreligiosität in der modernen Socialgeschichte* (Göttingen, 1986), 14–30; here 26–27.

40. Crouzet, *Les Guerriers de Dieu*, I, 135–53. Cf. Luc Racaut, "A Protestant or Catholic Superstition? Astrology and Eschatology during the French Wars of Religion," in Helen Parish and William G. Naphy, eds., *Religion and*

Superstition in Reformation Europe (Manchester, 2003), 154–69. On English Puritanism: Thomas, *Religion and the Decline of Magic*, 367–70.

41. Thomas Erastus, *Astrologia Confutata: Ein wahrhaftige Gegründte Unwiderspre-chliche Confutation/der falschen Astrologei oder abgottischen warsagung aus des himels . . .* (Schleusingen, 1557); Preface. On Erastus's comments see Mahlmann-Bauer, "Die Bulle contra astrologiam," 143–45; Müller-Jahncke, *Astrologisch-Magische Theorie und Praxis*, 252–53. Erastus's theoretical position is also discussed in Freyburger, "Le Problème du Fatalisme Astral," 53. Charles Gunnoe, Jr. has questioned whether Erastus's reaction "probably says as much about his expectations [regarding Protestantism] as [about] the conditions on the ground" in Germany and Italy. But it is clear that by this time the Italian production of vernacular calendars and practicas had fallen far below German levels. See C. D. Gunnoe, Jr., "German Protestantism and Astrology: The Debate between Thomas Erastus and the Melanchthon Circle," in von Greyerz, et al., eds., *Religion und Naturwissenschaften*, 86–101; here 88. Gunnoe does acknowledge a divergence between Reformed Christians and Lutherans regarding the role of astrology in their emerging confessional identities (100). See also Gunnoe's fine book, *Thomas Erastus and the Palatinate: A Renaissance Physician in the Second Reformation* (Leiden, 2010).

42. Gunnoe, "German Protestantism and Astrology," 87n, 96; and Gunnoe, *Thomas Erastus and the Palatinate*, 44–48.

43. Nikolas Gugler, *Prognosticon Astrologicum* (Heidelberg, 1563): Zinner, *Geschichte und Bibliographie*, 237; no. 2337.

44. Misocacus 1580, 1583, 1590. On Misocacus see Leppin, *Antichrist*, 46. On Gdańsk (Danzig), see Richard Kremer, "Mathematical Astronomy and Calendar-Making in Gdańsk from 1540 to 1700," in Klaus-Dieter Herbst, ed., *Astronomie, Literatur, Volksaufklärung: Der Schreibkalender der Frühen Neuzeit mit seinen Text- und Bildbeigaben* (Bremen, 2012). On Misocacus and Danzig, see also Derek Jensen, "The Science of the Stars in Danzig from Rheticus to Helvelius" (PhD dissertation, University of California at San Diego, 2006); esp. 28–36 on Calvinism. Perhaps mistakenly, Barbara Mahlmann-Bauer asserts that Misocacus was a Lutheran: "Die Bulle *contra astrologiam*," 185; Leppin (*Antichrist*, 181), and Smolinsky (*Deutungen der Zeit*, 9) call him a Calvinist.

45. On H. Zanchi, see Mahlmann-Bauer, "Die Bulle *contra astrologiam*," 178; Abraham Scultetus, *Warnung Für der Warsagerey der Zäuberer und Sterngücker, verfast in zwoen Predigten* (Amberg, 1609). Amberg, in the Upper Palatinate, was by this time officially Reformed, but it had long been Lutheran, and strong popular resistance to Catholic confessionalization continued.

46. *Assertio Io. Cratonis* (Frankfurt, 1585), 8; cited in Howard Lou⁴'an, "Johannes Crato and the Austrian Habsburgs: Reforming a Counter ᵣ ₑform Court," *Studies in Reformed Theology and History*, 2, no. 3 (Summer 1994): 8n. On Crato's opposition to Paracelsianism: Charles Gunnoe, Jr. and Jole Shackelford,

"Johannes Crato von Krafftheim (1519–1585): Imperial Physician, Irenicist, and Anti-Paracelsian," in Plummer and Barnes, eds., *Ideas and Cultural Margins in Early Modern Germany*, 201–16.

47. Pezel's one major astrological work was published posthumously: *Praecepta genthliaca sive de prognosticandis hominum nativitatibus commentarius eruditissimus* (Frankfurt a. M., 1607).

48. Brosseder, *Im Bann*, 22–25.

49. Hermann Witekind/Augustin Lercheimer, *Christliche Bedencken und Erinnerung von Zauberey, Woher, was und wie vielfeltig sie sey . . .* (First ed. Strasbourg, 1586; this ed. Speyer, 1597), 40, 79. For context see Hartmut Rudolph, "Das Faustbuch im kirchengeschichtlichen Zusammenhang," in Richard Auernheimer and Frank Baron, eds., *Das Faustbuch von 1587: Provokation und Wirkung* (Munich and Vienna, 1991), 41–57.

50. Howard Hotson, *Johann Heinrich Alsted: Between Renaissance, Reformation, and Universal Reform* (Oxford and New York, 2000), 185 et passim.

51. Hotson, *Johann Heinrich Alsted*, 54.

52. Irena Backus, "The Beast: Interpretations of Daniel 7. 2–9 and Apocalypse 13. 1–4, 11–12 in Lutheran, Zwinglian, and Calvinist Circles in the Late Sixteenth Century," *Reformation and Renaissance Review* 3, no. 1 (2000): 59–77; here 75.

53. On Clauser's astrology: G. A. Wehrli, *Der Zürcher Stadtarzt Christoph Clauser und seine Stellung zur Reformation der Heilkunde im XVI. Jahrhundert* (Zurich, 1924), 84–98.

54. Keller, *Jakob Ruf*, vol. 3; see Keller's introductions to and commentary on Ruf's *Ärzte- und Astrologenverzeichnis* (11–27, 47–75), and his *Astrologentafel* (79–96, 107–16).

55. Ruf 1558; see Keller, *Jakob Ruf*, vol. 4, 951–954; quotation: 951. For context, see Keller's introductions to and commentary on Ruf's annual calendars (899–913, 923–26), and prognostications (931–37, 957–62). Bullinger's *In Apocalypsim . . . Conciones centum* appeared at Basel in 1557; a German edition came out the following year at Mühlhausen.

56. Luginsland 1553, 1558, 1570, 1576. Bauer, "Sprüche," 186, counts Luginsland in the Lutheran biblical camp, but he certainly leaned more to the Swiss Reformed. The *Fröliche Practick* for 1588 (1587) was probably by Johann Hasler. A Swiss Reformed verse "Christian practica" appeared under the name of Severus Bersche, *Ein Geistlicher Kalender sampt der Practik, uff alle Jar, biss zu end der welt* (Zurich, 1543). At the Reformed city of St. Gall, Leonhard Straub issued practicas in the late 1570s and early 1580s; his forecast for 1583 foresaw enormous changes to follow the entry into the fiery trigon, but he was by no means as hotly apocalyptic as many evangelical practica writers.

57. Brosseder, *Im Bann*, 275–77.

58. Kaspar Brusch, *Ain uralte Practica auf das Jahr 1548 vnd alle andere Jare, biss zum ende der Welt* (Augsburg, 1548). On Brusch see *ADB* 3, 453–55.

59. Johann Aurifaber and Johann Stoltz, *Kurtze Verlegung der unchristlichen Practica Magistri Joh. Hebenstreito auff dar Jar 1554 zu Erffurd aussgangen* (Jena, 1554); quotation on A3. See Leppin, *Antichrist*, 175–76; Barbara Mahlmann-Bauer argues that the work was part of a largely fruitless effort to oppose Melanchthon's astrology: "Sprüche," 187–88.

60. Aurifaber and Stoltz, *Kurtze Verlegung*, E4.

61. On Heller: Matthäus, "Zur Geschichte," 1025ff; 1036–38.

62. Christoph Stathmion, *Astrologia Asserta. Oder Ein kurtzer vnnd gründtliche verlegung/der langen vnd vngegründten schrifft D. Thome Erasti . . .* (Nuremberg, 1558). On the Erastus-Stathmion debate generally, see Gunnoe, "German Protestantism and Astrology."

63. Johann Paceus, *Astrologia Vindicata. Warhafftige vnd gründtliche Ablainung der vngegründten vnd vnerfindtlichen aufflag/darmit yetziger Zeyt die Astrologey als Vnchristlich/Aberglaubisch/vnd Gotteslästerisch verdampt wirdt* (Nuremberg, 1562).

64. Heiden 1567; also Heiden 1568; on him see Matthäus, "Zur Geschichte," 1038–43.

65. Eucharius Gotthart, *Wider die Vnchristliche Heydnische Practicken/So Christian Heyde/Nürnbergischer Mathematicus/auff das 1567 Jar gestellet* (N.p., 1567 or 68). See also Bauer, "Sprüche," 187–88.

66. Waldner, *Defensio. Das ist: Entschuldigung und Ableinung, der Heidnischen unnd unchristlichen Verleumbdung und Lesterung, dess ubernatürlichen Sternsehers Christian Heiden . . .* ([Regensburg], 1568), D2. On Waldner vs. Heiden see Matthäus, "Zur Geschichte," 1042–43.

67. Waldner, *Defensio*, E4/v.

68. Ludwig Milich, *Der Zauber Teufel* (First ed. Frankfurt a. M., 1563), in Ria Stambaugh, ed., *Teufelbücher in Auswahl*, vol. 1 (Berlin, 1970), 115–26; 129–32.

69. Milich, *Zauber Teufel*, 115–25, 127; "a demonic presumption": *ein Zauberische Fürwitzigkeyt*.

70. Jacob Andreae, *Christliche/notwendige vnd ernstliche Erinnerung/Nach dem Lauff der irdischen Planeten gestellt . . .* (Tübingen, 1567). See my *Prophecy and Gnosis*, 162–63. Charlotte Methuen (*Kepler's Tübingen*; see Chapter 4, note 37) implies that these sermons constituted a frontal assault on popular astrology, but Andreae's tactics were more subtle than she suggests. Moses Pflacher, *Weinthewre. Oder Bericht auss Gottes Wort, woher und auss was Ursachen dise jetzige Weinthewrung entstanden . . .* (Tübingen, 1589), 4–7 et passim.

71. Jacob Andreae, *Ein Christliche Predig Vber das Euangelium auff den xxiiij. Sontag nach Trinitatis . . . Von vielen vnd mancherley verführungen in der Kirchen Gottes/vor dem Jüngsten tage* (Leipzig, 1578), K2/v-L/v.

72. Meder 1578, C4; on Georg Meder see Matthäus, "Zur Geschichte," 1103–04. In his practica for 1583, however, Meder was still attacking the "learned theologians" who opposed astrological reckonings about coming divine judgment.

By ignoring the signs in the heavens they opened the door to vice among the common people; indeed "they reject the law of God in Antinomian fashion, and even regard good works as harmful to salvation." Stathmion 1578, A3. On Musculus, see my *Prophecy and Gnosis*, 79.

73. Meder 1578, A2/v.

74. Stathmion 1578, A3-A3/v; Nicholaus Winckler, *Tractatus de Astrologiae* (Frankfurt a. M., 1580).

75. Brosseder, *Im Bann*, 11.

76. On the universities: Thomas Kaufmann, *Universität und lutherische Konfessionalisierung* (Gütersloh, 1997). On Bruno, see the essays in Thomas Leinkauf, ed., *Giordano Bruno in Wittenberg: Aristoteles, Raimundus Lullus, Astronomie* (Pisa, 2004); also Leen Spruit, "Giordano Bruno and Astrology," in Hilary Gatti, ed., *Giordano Bruno: Philosopher of the Renaissance* (Aldershot and Burlington, 2002), 242ff.

77. Günther Oestmann, *Heinrich Rantzau und die Astrologie: ein Beitrag zur Kulturgeschichte des 16. Jahrhunderts* (Braunschweig, 2004), 52ff. On Rantzau see also Brosseder, *Im Bann*, 163–64.

78. Johann Pfeffinger, *Christliche gewisse deutung der zeichen die für vnd in diesem 1562. Jar geschehen* (Leipzig, 1562), B4-B4/v.

79. Despite the prevailing assumption, we have little evidence to suggest that the issue of professional competence was a matter of active debate among Lutheran clergy and astrologers. Leppin argues rather abstractly that attempts to justify astrological predictions on the basis of the priesthood of all believers were unsustainable, but this approach seems to confuse the question of "cognitive competence," or inherent ability, with that of personal potential through education. See Leppin, *Antichrist*, 180–81.

80. See Richard Gawthrop and Gerald Strauss, "Protestantism and Literacy in Early Modern Germany," *Past and Present* no. 104 (1984): 31–55.

81. Leppin, *Antichrist*, 183; Brosseder, *Im Bann*, 159.

82. On Garcaeus see Brosseder, *Im Bann*, 44f., 158–60, et passim.

83. Albin Moller 1595, A4.

84. Michael Lochner, *Leich-Predig Vber der Bergräbnus dess Ehrwirdigen, Wolgelerten Herrn, auch weitberümbten Astronomi, M. Georgii Caesii, Weylandt Pfarrherrn zu Marck Burck Bernheim* (Nuremberg, 1604).

85. Caesius 1575, A3. Against the Jesuit Georg Scherer: Caesius, 1590, B2.

86. Burgher astrologers: Geuss 1564, Pontanus 1566, Busch 1573, Fischer 1597.

87. On the parodic works see Pfister, *Parodien*, and Hauffen, *Fischart-Studien* (Chapter 1, notes 84, 86).

88. Praetorius, officially appointed Nuremberg calendar-writer from 1576 to 1617, was not an eager pursuer of his duties and issued barebones calendars and practicas that appear never to have become very popular; meanwhile other writers crowded the market. See Matthäus, "Zur Geschichte," 1044–47.

89. On censorship: Allyson Creasman, *Censorship and Civic Order in Reformation Germany, 1517–1648: Printed Poison and Evil Talk* (Farnham and Burlington, 2012); Künast, *"Getruckt zu Augsburg"*; Leppin, *Antichrist*, 35–36; on the Nuremberg council: Matthäus, "Zur Geschichte," 1038.

90. Matthäus, "Zur Geschichte," 1108–10.

91. On concentration in larger cities see Künast, *"Getruckt zu Augsburg,"* 154; on Nuremberg: Matthäus, "Zur Geschichte," 1068 et passim.

92. The first annual calendar in booklet form was probably that of Anton Brelochs for 1545; see Matthäus, "Zur Geschichte," 1165. On the development of the *schreibkalender* see the essays in Herbst, ed., *Astronomie, Literatur, Volksaufklärung*. The Lutheran Paul Eber's *Calendarium Historicum* (Basel, 1551) helped shaped the development of the *schreibkalendar* and historical awareness; see Maiello, "Il Tempo dei Calendari in Francia" (Chapter 2, note 7), 421ff; Ludwig Rohner, *Kalendergeschichte und Kalender* (Wiesbaden, 1978), 97–98; Knopf, *Die deutsche Kalendergeschichte*, 46ff.

93. Michael Hackenberg, "Books in Artisan Homes of Sixteenth-Century Germany," in Donald G. Davis, ed., *Libraries, Books, and Culture* (Austin, 1986), 72–91; here 86, 88.

94. On Simon Marius: Matthäus, "Zur Geschichte," 1100, 1162; see also Chapter 7.

95. Fritz Juntke, "Über Leonhard Thurneisser zum Thurn und seine deutschen Kalender 1572–1584," in *Archiv für Geschichte des Buchwesens (AGB)* 19 (1978): 1349–1400; also Juntke, "Über Leonhard Thurneisser zum Thurn und seine Schriften nach seiner Fluch aus Berlin (1584)," *Archiv für Geschichte des Buchwesens* 21 (1980): 679–718.

96. Thomas Roerer, *Ein Newe vnnd Warhafftige geystliche Practica/in diser schwären vnd gefährlichen zeyt/bisz zum ende der Wellt* (N.p., 1563); Georg Breuning, *Ein Christliche Predigt Oder Vniversal Practica. Allgemeine verzeychnis/wie es nicht allein in diesen anwesenden 88. vnd zukünfftigen 89. Jaren/Sondern biß zum Ende der Welt/Ohnfelbarlich Wittern vnd ergehen werde* (Basel, 1588); Kaspar Lutz, *Ein christliche vnd Alljahrige Practika Oder Prognostication . . .* (1589); Johann Lapeus, ed., *Practica vnd Prognostica/Oder Schreckliche Propheceiung D. Martini Lutheri/des ausserwehlten Rüstzeugs vnd Propheten des Deutschen Landes* (Ursel, 1578; another ed. 1592).

97. Nas, *Practica Practicarum* (note 19); Johann Weyermann, *Practica vff das M.D.LXV. Jar von künfftigen Kranckheiten, Kriegen, Todt, Thüre vnd anderen Dingen . . .* ("Chillion," 1564); Johann Fischart, *Aller Practick Grossmutter* (Strasbourg, 1572–74).

98. On Rollenhagen, see Oestmann, *Heinrich Rantzau*, 53. Frischlin's work was the *De Astronomicae Artis, Cum Doctrina Coelesti, Et Naturali Philosophia, Congruentia* (Frankfurt a. M., 1586).

99. Michael Maistlin, *Notwendige vnd gründtliche Bedennken . . . von dem . . . Römischen Kalender* (Heidelberg, 1584), Preface; on the views of Brahe and Kepler, see Chapter 7.

100. Nicholas Campion, *A History of Western Astrology*, Vol. 2 (London and New York, 2009), 169.

CHAPTER 6

1. Brelochs 1535, A4; Gasser 1545, b2-b3; Schöner 1540, A3/v. Parts of this chapter are adapted from my essay "Hope and Despair in Sixteenth-Century German Almanacs," *The Reformation in Germany and Europe: Interpretations and Issues* (*Archive for Reformation History*, special volume), ed. Hans R. Guggisberg and G. Krodel (Heidelberg, 1993), 440–61.

2. Brelochs 1535, A4; Schöner 1534, A4/v; Pruckner 1533, A2/v; M. Brotbeihel 1538, A3-A4/v.

3. Mangolt 1532, A4; Brelochs 1535, A3; Apian 1532 B2/v.

4. Johann Virdung, *Auszlegung und bedeütnisz des Cometen der gesehen worden ist/im Augstmon im 1531. jare.* (Speyer, 1531); Johann Schöner, *Conjectur odder abnemliche auszlegung . . . vber den Cometen so jm Augstmonat des M.D.xxxj. jars erschinen ist. . .* (Nuremberg, 1532). Schöner also composed a brief pamphlet, *Was ein Comet sey: woher er komen/vnd seinen vrsprung habe. . .* (Nuremberg, 1531). On Clauser, see G. A. Wehrli, *Der Zürcher Stadtarzt Dr. Christoph Clauser und seine stellung zur Reformation der Heilkund im XVI. Jahrhundert* (Zurich, 1924); also Keller, *Jacob Ruf*, vols. 1–5, passim.

5. Schöner 1534, A3/v; Schöner 1538, A3; Saltzmann 1539, A3–A4.

6. Ryff 1544, A4; Sibenburger 1546, B2; Pruckner 1543, b/v.

7. Mithob 1540, A2.

8. Brelochs 1545, title page.

9. Eisslinger 1549, A2.

10. Brelochs 1548, A3, A3/v; Sibenburger 1547, B; Rheticus 1551, A2/v; Heuring 1551, A4/v. Sibenburger's lines to and from the "Dear Astronomer" were not new; earlier astrological texts had used essentially the same words, e.g. pseudo-Carion, *Bedeutnus vnd Offenbarung warer himlischer Influxion . . .* [1541–1550] (N.p., 1541), C.

11. J. Brotbeihel 1560, B2/v, B3; Heller 1561, B3/v.

12. Heiden 1567, A2/v-A3; Meder 1577, A2/v-A3; J. Brotbeihel 1561, B-B/v; Pontanus 1566, B/v-B2.

13. On these collections, see my *Prophecy and Gnosis*, 61–62.

14. Fabricius 1562, C/v; Schönfelt, 1571, title page; Schönfelt, 1564, title page, D/v-D2; Hebenstreit 1566, B2; Hebenstreit 1568, title page.

15. Volker Leppin divides the market for world-orienting ideas into three models or abstract categories: apocalyptic, astrological, and divine punishment. Only the first of these, he argues, served as the true basis for a Lutheran confessional identity. I maintain that these conceptual categories did not apply for most sixteenth-century evangelicals. See Leppin, *Antichrist*, 151–56; 163; 165ff., 278.

16. Heller 1561, "final destruction & collapse": B3/v; Fabricius 1565, B2; Wilhelm 1567, B3/v-B4.

17. Caesarius 1577, B3/v.

18. Like numerous other scholars, Volker Leppin argues for an essential divide between humanistic-philosophical and radical-bibliocentric perspectives; only the latter, in his view, became the basis for Lutheran confessional identity. I reject this perspective as ahistorical. See Leppin, *Antichrist*, 285–89 et passim.

19. Charlotte Methuen, "Special Providence and Sixteenth-Century Astronomical Observation: Some Preliminary Reflections," *Early Science and Medicine*, 4, no. 2 (1999): 99–113; here 102.

20. Methuen, "Special Providence," 102–06.

21. Tilemann Heshusius, *Eine Predigt vom Erkentnuss des waren Gottes* (Heidelberg, 1558), B; Johann Wigand, *Von den Letzten Tagen und verenderung der Welt. Eine Predigt Aus der Epistle 2. Pet. 3* . . . (Jena, 1571), D3–D4.

22. Zeysius 1577, A2, D3.

23. See my *Prophecy and Gnosis*, Chapter 2.

24. Philip M. Soergel, *Miracles and the Protestant Imagination: The Evangelical Wonder Book in Reformation Germany* (Oxford and New York, 2012).

25. Soergel, *Miracles*, 80.

26. Soergel, *Miracles*, 92.

27. Andreas Musculus, *Vom Mesech vnd Kedar, vom Gog vnd Magog, von dem grossen trübsal für der Welt Ende* . . . (Frankfurt a. O., 1577), K/v-L.

28. Wigand, *Von den Letzten Tagen*, 38.

29. Rhau 1572, A2; Bartholomew Gernhard, *Vom Jüngsten Tage Vier nützliche Predigten* (Erfurt, 1556), D2/v.

30. Stathmion 1551, A3.

31. See my *Prophecy and Gnosis*, 174.

32. Brosseder, *Im Bann*, 250.

33. Martin Luther, *Supputatio annorum mundi* (1541; 1545), WA 53, 1ff.

34. Westman, *The Copernican Question*, 120. See also Bellucci, *Science de la Nature et Réformation*, 229–30.

35. Cyprian Leowitz, *Grundliche, Klerliche beschreibung, vnd Historischer bericht, der fürnemsten grossen zusamenkunfft der obern Planeten, der Sonnen Finsternussen, der Cometen, vnd derselben wirckung, so sich in der vierden Monarchien erzeigt vnd begeben: sampt einem Prognostico von dem 1564. Jar biß auff nachvolgend zweinzig Jar werende gesteldt vnd beschriben* (Lauingen, 1564); Latin ed.: *De Coniunctionibvs Magnis* . . . (Lauingen, 1564). Walter B. Stone once called this work "in a manner of speaking the most successful astrological work of the century—in fact, astrology never recovered from its success." But while the book did draw widespread notice, we should not overstate its role in what was already a booming market in astrological publications and ideas. See Stone,

"Shakespeare and the Sad Augurs," *Journal of English and Germanic Philology* 52, no. 4 (October 1953): 457–79, here 461.

36. See Paula Sutter Fichtner, *Emperor Maximilian II* (New Haven, 2001); also Heinz Duchhart, *Protestantisches Kaisertum und Altes Reich: Die Diskussion über die Konfession des Kaisers in Politik, Publizistik und Staatsrecht* (Wiesbaden, 1977).

37. Philipp Melanchthon, *Chronica durch Magistrum Johann Carionis fleissig zusammengezogen, menigklich nützlich zu lesen* (Wittenberg, 1532). Helpful is Volker Leppin, "Humanistische Gelehrsamkeit und Zukunftsansage: Philipp Melanchthon und das *Chronicon Carionis*," in Bergdolt and Ludwig, eds., *Zukunftsvoraussagen*, 131–42. The Carion/Melanchthon work went through many later editions, most notably those expanded and updated by Caspar Peucer. On these editions see Uwe Neddermeyer, "Kaspar Peucer (1525–1602): Melanchthons Universalgeschichtsschreibung," in Heinz Scheible, ed., *Melanchthon in seinen Schülern* (Wiesbaden, 1997), 69–101. Johann Funck's somewhat less influential work was his *Chronologia: hoc est omnium temporum et annorum ab initio mundi . . .* (Nuremberg, 1545; later German eds.).

38. Leowitz, *Grundliche, Klerliche beschreibung*, J3.

39. *Prognosticon oder weyssagung, von dem 1564, jar nach Christi geburdt/bisz auff die zweintzig nachuolgende . . .*, in *Grundliche, Klerliche beschreibung*, P4-X.

40. Leowitz, *Prognosticon oder weyssagung*, S4/v-V2.

41. See Germana Ernst, "From the watery Trigon to the fiery Trigon: Celestial Signs, Prophecies, and History," in Zambelli, ed., *"Astrologi hallucinati,"* 265–80.

42. Leowitz, *Prognosticon oder weyssagung*, V2.

43. For general background see my *Prophecy and Gnosis*, 163ff. Helpful in regard to the 1588 prophecy is Leppin, *Antichrist*, 139–49, although Leppin is too ready to link such prophetic reckonings to a humanistic-philosophical perspective essentially at odds with biblical, evangelical apocalypticism.

44. Leppin, *Antichrist*, 144ff.; also Thorndike, *Magic*, V, 373.

45. Oestmann, *Heinrich Rantzau*, 61 et passim.

46. Geuss 1564, B, B2. Matthäus, "Zur Geschichte," 1044, calls Geuss a Paracelsian, but in 1563 he had apparently not yet moved strongly in that direction.

47. Schönfelt 1564, D/v-D2.

48. Fabricius 1565, B2; Hebenstreit 1566 (*Prognosticon Historicvm und Physicvm*), B2.

49. Hebenstreit 1566, C.

50. Orphanus, *Ivdicium Astrologicvm* [1574–78] (Nuremberg, 1573); *Iudicivm Astrologicvm* [1577–78] (Nuremberg. c. 1576), B7.

51. Ursinus 1571; Adam Ursinus, *Kurtze Beschreibunge der . . . Wunderzeichen am Himmel/im 1568. 69. vnd 70. Jhare* (Erfurt, 1570); Reinstein 1573, C4/v.

52. Quoted in Thorndike, *Magic*, VI, 69.

53. Cyprian Leowitz, *De Nova Stella* (Lauingen, 1573). On the reaction of the Wittenberg academics: Brosseder, *Im Bann*, 107–09. See also Charlotte

Methuen, "'This Comet or New Star': Theology and the Interpretation of the Nova of 1572," *Perspectives on Science* 5, no. 4 (1997): 499–515.

54. Caesius 1574, A2-A2/v.

55. Bucha 1575, B2; Winckler 1576; Meder 1577, A3, and Meder 1583, A4; on Meder see Matthäus, "Zur Geschichte," 1103–04; Rosa 1586; on Rosa: Matthäus, "Zur Geschichte," 1077–78.

56. Nicolaus Weiss, *Prognosticon Astrologicvm. Von dem 1572 biss auff das 1588 Jar wehrende* (Vienna, c. 1571; also Dresden, 1572, and Frankfurt a. M., 1573); N. Weiss, *Practica auff Zehen Jar . . . biss auff das 1588. Jar werende* (N.p., 1578). On Weiss see my *Prophecy and Gnosis*, 164–65.

57. Jacob Heerbrand, *Ein trewe Warnung vnd gutthertzige Vermanung zur Büss . . . vber das schröckliche Wunderzeichen, den Cometen . . . 1577* (Tübingen, 1578); Sigismund Suevus, *Cometen/Was sie für grosse Wunder vnd schreckliche ding zu bedeuten/vnd ankündigen pflegen . . .* (Görlitz, 1578).

58. Winckler 1579, A2-B; Georg Caesius, *Chronik, Oder Ordentliche verzeichnuss vnnd beschreibung aller Cometen, von der algemainen Sündflut an . . . biss auff dis gegenwertiges jtztlauffendes . . . 1579. Jar . . .* (Nuremberg, 1579); Johann Praetorius, *Narratio. Oder Historische erzelung dern Cometen . . .* (Nuremberg, 1578), B4/v. For related backgound see Sara J. Schechner, *Comets, Popular Culture, and the Birth of Modern Cosmology* (Princeton, 1997).

59. Meder 1579, E3/v-E4.

60. On the "conjectural" tradition among Lutherans, see my *Prophecy and Gnosis*, 126–39.

61. David Meder, *Zehen Christliche Busspredigten, Vber die Weissagung Christi dess grossen Propheten, vom Ende der Welt vnd Jüngsten Tage . . .* (Frankfurt a. M., 1581); Leonard Krentzheim, *Conjecturae. Christliche vermuttungen, von künfftiger Zeit, Zustand, in Kirchen vnd Regimenten . . .* (Görlitz, 1577; first German edition 1583); Nicolaus Winckler, *Bedencken von Künfftiger verenderung Weltlicher Policey, vnd Ende der Welt, auss heyliger Göttlicher Schrifft vnnd Patribus, auch auss dem Lauff der Natur . . .* (Augsburg, c. 1582). Provocative on Winckler is Helmut Häuser, *Gibt es ein Gemeinsame Quelle zum Faustbuch von 1587 und zu Goethes Faust? Eine Studie über die Schriften des Arztes Dr. Nikolaus Winckler (um 1529–1613)* (Wiesbaden, 1973). See also my *Prophecy and Gnosis*, 119–21 et passim.

62. Ursin 1575; Georg Ursin, *Zwo Practicken/Vom 1582. Jar/biss man schreiben wirt 1600. Jar . . . Die Ander weret biss man schreiben wirdt 1588. Jar.* (N.p., c. 1580).

63. Helisaeus Roeslin, *Kurtz Bedencken Von Der Emendation dess Jahrs . . .* (Heidelberg, 1584).

64. Caesius 1584; on Schulin, see Matthäus, "Zur Geschichte," 1093–96; Stathmion 1584.

65. Winckler 1583; Meder 1583, A3; Cnespel 1585, Preface; Caesius 1588. Walter Stone argued that in England the disillusionment following 1583 was intense, bringing a general reaction against apocalyptic astrology and end-time

predictions generally. No such disillusionment is evident in the German evangelical practicas. See Stone, "Shakespeare and the Sad Augurs," 471–72.

66. Andreas Musculus, *Vom Mesech vnd Kedar, vom Gog vnd Magog, von dem grossen trübsal für der Welt Ende* (Frankfurt a. O., 1577), Preface; Lucas Pollio, *Vom Jüngsten Gericht, Sechss Fasten Predigten. Anno MDLXXX* (Nuremberg, c. 1601).

67. Bartholomaeus Ringwaldt, *Der lauter Warheit Darinnen angezeiget, Wie sich ein Weltlicher vnnd Geistlicher Kriegssmann in seinem beruff verhalten soll . . .* (N.p., c. 1585?), A2/v-A3.

68. Schulin 1586; Winckler 1587; T. Moller 1587; Rosa 1587; Schönfelt 1588; Henisch 1588, B3.

69. On the passing of 1588 see my essay "Der herabstürzende Himmel: Kosmos und Apokalypse unter Luthers Erben um 1600," in Manfred Jakubowski-Tiessen, et al., eds., *Jahrhundertwenden: Endzeit- und Zukunftsvorstellungen vom 15. Bis zum 20. Jahrhundert* (Göttingen, 1999), 1129–45; also my *Prophecy and Gnosis*, 165ff.

70. Scholars have noted several external causes for a mounting sense of crisis in the 1590s and subsequent decades, including the onset of the Little Ice Age and the resumption of war against the Turks. See e.g. Hartmut Lehmann, "Endzeiterwartung im Luthertum im späten 16. und im frühen 17. Jahrhundert," in Hans-Christoph Rublack, ed., *Die lutherische Konfessionalisierung in Deutschland* (Schriften des Vereins für Reformationsgeschichte 197; Gütersloh, 1992), 545–54, and the literature cited there.

71. Still the basic study of the Second Reformation attempt in Saxony under Christian I is Thomas Klein, *Die Kampf um die Zweite Reformation in Kursachsen 1586–91* (Cologne and Graz, 1962).

72. Caesius 1590, B2; A. Moller 1595, D2/v.

73. Daniel Schaller, *Ein New Theologisch Prognosticon auff das 89. vnd folgende Jar . . .* (Magdeburg, 1589). For further context: Hartmut Lehmann, "Weltende 1630: Daniel Schallers Vorhersage von 1595," in Jakubowski-Tiessen et al., eds., *Jahrhundertwenden*, 147–61.

74. T. Moller 1592, D; Sutorius 1596; Sutorius 1599.

75. Bucha 1594, A2/v, D2. Rosa 1593, B; Rosa 1596. From the 1580s until after 1600 the city of Amberg remained largely evangelical, despite repeated attempts by the Palatine electors to impose Calvinism.

76. See Thomas Kaufmann, "1600—Deutungen der Jahrhundertwende im deutschen Luthertum," in Jakubowski-Tiessen, et al., eds, *Jahrhundertwenden*, 73–128. While Kaufmann finds many speculations focusing on the year 1600, he ultimately recognizes that this date was by no means uniquely important as a focus of expectancy for Lutherans.

77. Adler 1597, C4/v; A. Moller 1600, D2/v, E/v. On Krabbe, See Dieter Kertscher and S. Karr Schmidt, "Johannes Krabbe (1553–1616), ein Astronom am Wolfenbütteler Hof," in Christian Heitzmann, Stefanie Gehrke, Sigrun Haude,

et al., eds., *Die Sterne lügen nicht: Astrologie und Astronomie im Mittelalter und in der Frühen Neuzeit* (Wolfenbüttel, 2008), 111–21.

78. Leopold 1594, title page.

79. Bader 1579; Maius 1574; Winckler 1587.

80. Scott Dixon has argued that the adoption of popular astrology by Lutherans resulted above all from the sense that "the Reformation movement had not succeeded in its essential task, that of winning hearts and minds to the new faith"; indeed many preachers "saw the last chance for the faith in these 'astral sermons.'" But this argument does not do full justice to Dixon's own recognition that preachers "were able to invest the natural world—in this instance, the heavenly bodies—with the essentials of the Lutheran religion." This latter statement implicitly recognizes that evangelical astrology had roots deeper than waxing despair. See Dixon, "Popular Astrology and Lutheran Propaganda," *History* 84, no. 275 (1999): 403-18; here 416, 418. Thus I also need to qualify my own statement (*Prophecy and Gnosis*, 154–55) that "the distinctive Lutheran attitude toward astrology arose from the need to retain prophetic certainty in a time when the whole evangelical heritage seemed increasingly threatened."

81. Robert Kolb, "Die Umgestaltung und theologische Bedeutung des Lutherbildes im späten 16. Jahrhundert," in Rublack, ed., *Die lutherische Konfessionalisierung*, 202–31; here 213.

82. Caesius 1584, Preface; Nicolaus Weiss, *Practica auff Zehen Jahr* (1578), A3/v; Heiden 1567, B2.

83. Rosa 1596, C4/v.

84. Capp, *Astrology and the Popular Press*, 154.

85. Busch 1573, Schönfelt 1570; T. Moller 1592; Winckler 1595.

86. Ernst Troeltsch, *The Social Teachings of the Christian Churches*, trans. Olive Wyon; Vol. 2 (New York, 1931). As Volker Leppin rightly argues, Lutheran apocalyptic preaching was in part a form of "social disciplining," but one that operated less by means of external regulations than by publicizing certain norms of Christian conduct that individuals might internalize. The goal of social discipline did not exhaust the functional significance of such preaching, which extended to matters of confessional identity.

CHAPTER 7

1. On the distinctive features of Lutheran culture in the late Reformation era see Kaufmann, "1600—Deutungen der Jahrhundertwende im deutschen Luthertum." Also published as Chapter 10 in Thomas Kaufmann, *Konfession und Kultur: Lutherischer Protestantismus in der zweiten Hälfte des Reformationsjahrhunderts* (Tübingen, 2006).

2. The idea of a *Frömmigkeitskrise* or crisis of piety in early seventeenth-century Lutheranism goes back at least to Karl Holl: "Die Bedeutung der grossen Kriege

für das religiöse und kirchliche Leben innerhalb des deutschen Protestantismus," *Gesammelte Aufsätze zur Kirchengeschichte*, 3 vols. (Tübingen, 1921–28), vol. 3, 302–84. See also Johannes Wallmann, "Reflexionen und Bemerkungen zur Frömmigkeitskrise des 17. Jahrhunderts," in Jakubowski-Tiessen, ed., *Krisen des 17. Jahrhunderts: Interdisziplinäre Perspektiven* (Göttingen, 1999), 25–42.

3. On the polarization of views that divided a consolidating orthodoxy from the "new prophets" see my *Prophecy and Gnosis*, 231–49.

4. Westman, *The Copernican Question*, 252 et passim.

5. Vanden Broecke, *The Limits of Influence*, 264–67; see also Oestmann, *Heinrich Rantzau*, 246.

6. For the Kepler quotation and its context see J. V. Field, "A Lutheran Astrologer: Johannes Kepler," in *Archive for the History of the Exact Sciences* 31, no. 3 (1984): 189–272; here 220. Also on Kepler: Nick Kollerstrom, "Kepler's Belief in Astrology," in Anabella Kitson, ed., *History and Astrology: Clio and Urania Confer* (London, 1989), 152–70; Sheila Rabin, "Kepler's Attitude toward Pico and anti-Astrology Polemic," *Renaissance Quarterly* 50, no. 3 (1997): 750–70.

7. Tycho quoted in Westman, *The Copernican Question*, 234; on Kepler see Westman's discussion, 324–32 et passim; on the new intellectual space occupied by the expert court astronomers, 224–26 et passim. A partial corrective to the typical emphasis on the mechanistic character of Kepler's cosmology is Patrick J. Boner, "Kepler's Vitalistic View of the Heavens," in Miguel Á. Granada, ed., *Novas y cometas entre 1572 y 1618: Revolución cosmológica y renovación política y religiosa* (Barcelona, 2012), 165–93.

8. Caesius 1597, A/v; Caesius 1601, preface.

9. Rosa 1596, B3/v.

10. Winckler 1594, title page; Fischer 1597; Winckler 1599; G. F. Caesius 1603, Preface. On Georg Friedrich Caesius: Matthäus, "Zur Geschichte," 1092f.

11. Schulin 1585, 1586; Bucha 1594; Krabbe 1597, 1599. Matthäus sees the first distancing from the Arabs in the annual works coming only after 1600, but the trend is evident in the 1590s; see Matthäus, "Zur Geschichte," 1226.

12. On Kepler's rejection of the Zodiac: Field, "A Lutheran Astrologer," 199ff.; Müller-Jahnke, *Astrologisch-magische Theorie und Praxis*, 254.

13. Will-Erich Peuckert, *Die Rosenkreutzer: zur Geschichte einer Reformation* (Jena, 1928), 6 et passim.

14. T. Moller (Müller) 1592, D3/v.

15. See my essay "Der Herabstürzende Himmel," in Jakubowski-Tiessen, et al., eds., *Jahrhundertwenden*. In the same volume see also Hartmut Lehmann, "Weltende 1630" (Chapter 6, note 73).

16. On Nicolai, see my *Prophecy and Gnosis*, 206–07. On the double-advent idea see Kaufmann, "1600—Deutungen der Jahrhundertwende," 88–89.

17. Fischer 1596, C4; see my "Hope and Despair," 454–59. Claudia Brosseder points out that in the late sixteenth century, students of Melanchthon such as David

Chytraeus and Nikolaus Selnecker placed greater emphasis than their teacher on the stars as announcing not only divine law and wrath, but also the promise of God's grace: Brosseder, *Im Bann*, 275.

18. On Paracelsus's astrology in the context of his broader world of thought see Andrew Weeks, *Paracelsus: Speculative Theory and the Crisis of the Early Reformation* (Albany, 1997). Also valuable are the essays in Ole Peter Grell, ed., *Paracelsus: The Man and his Reputation, his Ideas and their Transformation* (Leiden and Boston, 1988). On Thurneisser: Juntke, "Über Leonhard Thurneisser zum Thurn" (see Chapter 5 note 95); also Rudolf Schmitz, "Medizin und Pharmazie in der Kosmologie Leonhard Thurneissers zum Thurn," in Bergier, ed., *Zwischen Wahn, Glaube, und Wissenschaft*, 141–66.

19. Bathodius 1594, A2, B6/v. Among other practica writers who showed strong signs of Paracelsian influence was Heinrich Winand, a teacher at Osnabrück. Winand 1590, 1594, 1595.

20. On the divide between Paracelsian and Melanchthonian astrology see Barbara Bauer, "Sprüche in Prognostiken des 16. Jahrhunderts," in Burghart Wachinger and Walter Haug, eds., *Kleinstformen der Literatur* (Tübingen, 1994), 165–203; here 185. On the Lutheran appropriation of Paracelsian ideas: Charles Webster, "Paracelsus: Medicine as Popular Protest," in Grell and Cunningham, eds., *Medicine and the Reformation*, 65.

21. Winckler 1599; Caesius 1596, 1598, 1600.

22. Bucha 1594; Krabbe, 1597, F. See Jole Shackelford: "Rosicrucianism, Lutheran Orthodoxy, and the Rejection of Paracelsianism in Early Seventeenth-Century Denmark," *Bulletin of the History of Medicine* 70, no. 2 (1996): 181–204; here 191. Cf. Carlos Gilly, *"Theophrastica Sancta": Der Paracelsismus als Religion im Streit mit dem Offiziellen Kirchen* (Stuttgart, 1994).

23. Westman, *The Copernican Question*, 384. On German Lutheran reactions to the series of comets and novas starting in 1572, see my *Prophecy and Gnosis*, 168–75 et passim.

24. Wilhelm Eo Neuheuser, *Tractatvs: De Nova Stella, Oder von dem newen Abent Stern Scheinende* (Strasbourg, 1604).

25. For background see Leigh T. I. Penman, "Unanticipated Millenniums: The Lutheran Experience of Millenarian Thought" (PhD dissertation, University of Melbourne, 2008). On Weigel and Arndt, see also my *Prophecy and Gnosis*, 152–53; 205–06.

26. On Poyssel, see my *Prophecy and Gnosis*, 197–98 et passim; also Carlos Gilly, "Las novas de 1572 y 1604" (note 27), 323–24. Volker Leppin assumes that Eustachius Poyssel was a pseudonym for Christoph Wilhelmi Walpurger (1548–1611), but the CERL Thesaurus does not make this identification, and at present it cannot be accepted as certain. See Leppin, *Antichrist*, 73ff.

27. The leading authority on Rosicrucianism is Carlos Gilly, whose recent works include "Las novas de 1572 y 1604 en los manifiestos rosacruces y en la

literatura teosófica y escatológica alemana anterior a la Guerra de los Trienta Años," in Granada, ed., *Novas y cometas*, 275–331. On the astrological dimensions of the Rosicrucian movement, see also Åckerman, "The Rosicrucians and the Great Conjunctions," in John C. Laursen and Richard H. Popkin, eds., *Millenarianism and Messianism in Early Modern European Culture* (vol. 4, Amsterdam, 2001), 1–8.

28. Thomas Birck, *Regenten Spiegel*, (Frankfurt a.M., 1607), 157–208. Opposition to attempts to reckon the time of the end had never ceased, but accelerated in the years around 1600; see e.g. Andreas Schoppe, *Christliche vnd Nötige Warnung für dem erdichten Lügen Geist der falschen Propheten vnd fürwitzige Leute . . .* (Wittenberg, 1596).

29. Philipp Fesel, *Gründtlicher Discvrs von der Astrologia Judiciaria* (Strasbourg, 1609), C3. On the Fesel-Schaerer exchange generally, see Brosseder, *Im Bann*, 301ff. On Fesel: Nils Lenke and Nicholas Roudet, "Philippus Feselius: Biographische Notizen zum unbekannten 'Medicus' aus Keplers 'Tertius Interveniens,'" in Karsten Gaulke, ed., *Kepler, Galilei, das Fernrohr und die Folgen* (Frankfurt a. M., 2010), 131–59; here 148.

30. Fesel, *Gründtlicher Discvrs*, B/v, B2; A4; C4/v; D/v; D4/v.

31. Schaerer 1609, A3. See Lenke and Roudet, "Philippus Feselius," 135ff.

32. Melchior Schaerer, *Verantwortung vnd Rettung der Argumenten vnd Vrsachen/ welche M. Melchior Scherer/in den Vorreden seiner zweyen Prognosticorum verschiener 1608. vnd 1609. Jahren . . . eingeführet* (N.p., 1611), 170, 220.

33. Johannes Kepler, *Tertius Interveniens. Das ist, Warnung an etliche Theologos, Medicos et Philosophos, sonderlich D. Philippum Feselium, das sie . . . nicht das Kindt mit dem Badt aussschütten . . .* (Frankfurt a. M., 1610). As Robert Westman notes, "even the most skilled practitioners found Kepler's work troublesome." *The Copernican Question*, 492.

34. Caspar Finck, *Kurtzer, Notiger vnd in Gottes Wort wolbegründter Bericht, Von dem Jüngsten Gericht, Ewigen Leben, Vnd Hellen . . .* (Giessen, 1612); Daniel Cramer, *De Regno Jesu Christi Regis Regum . . .* (Stettin, 1614).

35. N. E. Winckler 1606, 1613; see also Matthäus, "Zur Geschichte," 1073–74; On J. V. Andreae's turn against apocalyptic readings of the stars, see my *Prophecy and Gnosis*, 258.

36. Koestner 1605, A3–A4; Herlicius 1617; B3/v; Ev/v.

37. Herlicius 1591, preface.

38. Herlicius 1591. On Herlicius see Matthäus, "Zur Geschichte," 1049–55 et passim; also Brosseder, *Im Bann*, 72–77; Juntke, "Leonhard Thurneisser," (1980), 696–97; Kaufmann, "1600—Deutungen der Jahrhundertwende," 99–103; Leppin, *Antichrist*, 160f., 180f. et passim.

39. David Herlicius, *Astronomische vnd historische Erklerung des Newen Sterns oder vngeschwänzten Cometen, so Anno 1604 . . . erschienen* (Stettin, 1604); D. Herlicius, *Wahrhafftige vnd gründliche Widerlegung der grewlichen unbesonnen*

Schmekarten, welche im Junio 1606. Jahrs erst zu Lübeck publiciert vnd spargiert wurden (Stettin, 1606).

40. Herlicius 1610, preface.

41. Herlicius 1617, preface.

42. Herlicius, 1617.

43. Matthäus, "Zur Geschichte," 1096–98.

44. Marius 1615.

45. Marius 1612; 1615, A/v; C2.

46. Marius 1610.

47. Halbmayer (Albanus Marius) 1613, 1618. On Halbmayer see Matthäus, "Zur Geschichte," 1099–102; on Georg Kreslin 1102–03.

48. Christopher Cnoll, *Calendarium Generale Perpetuum. Ein Allgemeiner Calender, auff alle vnd jede Jahr bisz ans Ende der Welt* (Görlitz, 1616).

49. Leigh T. I. Penman, "Climbing Jacob's Ladder: Crisis, Chiliasm, and Transcendence in the thought of Paul Nagel (†1624), a Lutheran Dissident during the Time of the Thirty Years' War," *Intellectual History Review*, 20, no. 2 (2010): 201–26. See also by the same author: "'Repulsive Blasphemies': Paul Nagel's Appropriation of Unprinted Works of Jacob Böhme and Valentin Weigel in his *Prodromus Astronomiae Apocalypticae* (1620)," *Daphnis* 38, no. 3 (2009): 599–621. Also Penman, "Unanticipated Millenniums," 121ff., and my *Prophecy and Gnosis*, 177–80, 212–14, et passim. The *Astrologia Theologizata* appeared anonymously in 1617.

50. On the Lutheran Jubilee of 1617: Ruth Kastner, *Form und Funktion der illustrierter Flugblätter zum Reformationsjubiläum 1617 in ihrem historischen und publizistischen Kontext* (Frankfurt a.M., 1982); also Hans Jürgen Schönstädt, *Antichrist, Weltheilsgeschehen und Gottes Werkzeug: Römische Kirche, Reformation, und Luther im Spiegel des Reformationsjubiläums 1617* (Wiesbaden, 1978).

51. Penman, "Climbing Jacob's Ladder," 202.

52. See my *Prophecy and Gnosis*, 177–80; 212–14.

53. Penman, "Climbing Jacob's Ladder," 225; in my *Prophecy and Gnosis* I wrongly ventured that Nagel had died in 1621.

54. Georg Rost, *Prognosticon Theologicon Oder Theologische Weissagung, Vom Jüngsten Tage* (Rostock, 1620), D3/v-D4; Rost, *Heldenbuch vom Rosengarten. Oder Gründlicher vnd Apologetischer Bericht von den Newen Himlischen Propheten, Rosenkreutzern, Chiliasten vnd Enthusiasten* (Rostock, 1622), fol. 71. In his *Antinagelius* of 1622, Philipp Arnoldi willingly allowed that heavenly wonders were warning signs from God, but entirely rejected any reading of meaning in the regular motions of the stars. On Arnoldi's work see Penman, "'Repulsive Blasphemies,'" 617–19.

55. The excited commentators on the 1618 comet included Erasmus Schmidt, a member of the Wittenberg theological faculty. See my *Prophecy and Gnosis*, 173–74.

56. David Herlicius, *Kurtzer Discvrs vom Cometen, vnnd dreyen Sonnen . . . 1618* (Alten Stettin, 1619); Schaerer 1620, A4/v.

57. Huberin 1621; Halbmayer 1624.

58. Marius 1625, Preface, D; also Huberin 1629.

59. A touchstone for the modern scholarship is Walter Sparn, *Widerkehr der Metaphysik: die ontologische Frage in der lutherischen Theologie des frühen 17. Jahrhunderts* (Stuttgart, 1976).

60. Sascha Salatowsky, *De Anima: die Rezeption der aristotelischen Psychologie im 16. und 17. Jahrhundert* (Amsterdam, 2006), 283–93.

61. Balthasar Meisner, *Eines seligen Menschen Dreyfacher Schatz, Der Herr Christus, Christi heiliges Wort, Aus dem Wort geschöpffte Busse, Von welchen allen im Neunzehenden Psälmlein Davids gehandelt wird* (Wittenberg, 1624), 14–60. Jürgen Hoppmann agrees with Aby Warburg that by the time of the Reformation jubilee in 1617 Lutheran academics "finished off" the entire affair of astrology and the evangelical movement. The evidence suggests, however, that in 1617 this campaign to end the popular alliance was still at an early stage. See Hoppmann, *Astrologie der Reformationszeit*, 69.

62. See Kenneth Appold, "Academic Life and Teaching in Post-Reformation Lutheranism," in Kolb, ed., *Lutheran Ecclesiastical Culture, 1550–1675*, 65–116.

63. Henning Friedrich, *Gründliche Widerlegung der Abergläubischen Astrologorum, So ausz dem Gestirn, vnd desselbigen influents, prognosticiren, Geneses, oder Nativiteten stellen...* (Erfurt, 1624), 1–12.

64. Friedrich, *Gründliche Widerlegung*; passages on Aurifaber and Stoltz: 36–43 et passim; on the parallel between the astrologers and the Calvinists: 17, 26; on the parallel with the Papists: 50.

65. This is a central argument of Leppin, *Antichrist*; see esp. 264–92.

66. Brosseder, *Im Bann*, 300. Strong arguments for the enduring afterlife of astrology in England can be found in Patrick Curry: *Prophecy and Power: Astrology in Early Modern England* (Princeton, 1989). Mark S. Dawson argues for the persistence of the art in seventeenth-century England: "Astrology and Human Variation in Early Modern England," *Historical Journal* 56, no. 1 (March 2013): 31–53.

67. William Clark, "Der Untergang der Astrologie in der deutschen Barockzeit," in Hartmut Lehmann and Anne-Charlott Trepp, eds., *Im Zeichen der Krise: Religiosität im Europa des 17. Jahrhunderts* (Göttingen, 1999), 433–72; here 463. This essay should be read with caution; Clark sees no significant confessional differences in regard to astrology in the late-Reformation era. The seventeenth-century German scene in particular deserves much closer study. Wolf-Dieter Müller-Jahncke associates the decline of astrology rather too easily with "the decline of mythological thought"; see his *Astrologisch-Magische Theorie und Praxis*, 258ff.

68. Herlicius 1631.

69. Matthäus, "Zur Geschichte," 1049ff., 1055.

70. David Beineken, *Astrologische Wunder-Schrifft... In den jetzigen 1632. 33. unnd 34. Jahren* (N.p., 1633).

71. Matthäus, "Zur Geschichte," 1146ff.

72. Matthäus, "Zur Geschichte," 1147, 1148n.

73. On the use of figures such as Lichtenberger, Carion, and Paracelsus in the propaganda of the Thirty Years' War era see Carlos Gilly, "The Midnight Lion, the Eagle, and the Antichrist: Political, Religious, and Chiliastic Propaganda in the Pamphlets, Illustrated Broadsheets, and Ballads of the Thirty Years War," *Nederlands Archief voor Kerkgeschiedenis* 80, no. 2 (2000): 46–77. On Paul Gräbner, see Gilly, "Las novas de 1572 y 1604," in Granada, ed., *Novas y Cometas*, 275–331; here 309–21.

74. On the beginnings of newspapers see Hedwig Pompe, *Famas Medium: Zur Theorie der Zeitung in Deutschland Zwischen dem 17. und dem Mittleren 19. Jahrhundert* (Berlin, 2012); also Werner Faulstich, *Medien zwischen Herrschaft und Revolte: die Medienkultur der frühen Neuzeit (1400–1700)* (Göttingen, 1998).

75. Matthäus, "Zur Geschichte," 1147–49; Froehlich 1649.

76. Matthäus, "Zur Geschichte," 1230, 1223, 1006. The practice of binding the calendar and practica together was growing common already by the 1620s. Cf. Hellmann's assertion (*Wetterprognose und Wetterberichte*, 14) that this development came later, around 1640.

77. Matthäus, "Zur Geschichte," 1143–49; 1157–58.

78. To be sure, through the sixteenth century we find dedications both to city councils and to noble or princely patrons, and the growing prevalence of the latter followed an uneven pattern. But the overall decline in dedications to councils marks a significant trend.

79. Matthäus, "Zur Geschichte," 1075, 1103; Hartmut Sührig, "Die Entwicklung der Niedersächsischen Kalender im 17. Jahrhundert," *Archiv für Geschichte des Buchwesens* 20 (1979): 329–794; on Rhete: 452–53.

80. Melchior Schaerer died in 1624; Georg Kreslin in 1629; Christopher Cnoll around 1630.

81. On Rhumelius (Rummel): Matthäus, "Zur Geschichte," 1145–46.

82. Matthäus, "Zur Geschichte," 1055–63.

83. Matthaeus Lungwitz, *Des Seligen Mannes Gottes/ D. Martini Lutheri, So dann auch D. Davidis Herlitii, und anderer Iudicia Von der Grossen Conjunction und Zusammenkunfft der Obersten Planeten . . . welche geschehen seyn Anno 1524. Und 1583. Und welche jetzo wiederkommen in diesem 1642. Und folgendem 1643. Jahre/ Was davon zuhalten sey?* (Dresden, 1642). See also Brosseder, *Im Bann*, 298–99, and Matthäus, "Zur Geschichte," 1152, 1066.

84. Brosseder, *Im Bann*, 297–98; Matthäus, "Zur Geschichte," 1230ff.

85. Magirus 1651, A4/v et passim.

86. On the shifting forms and functions of calendars in the second half of the century, see Matthäus, "Zur Geschichte," 1235–68; also Hartmut Sührig, "Zur Unterhaltungsfunktion des Kalenders im Barock," in Wolfgang Brückner, Peter Blickle, and Dieter Breuer, eds., *Literatur und Volk im 17. Jahrhundert. Probleme populärer Kultur in Deutschland*, 2 vols. (Wiesbaden, 1982) vol. 2, 727–40.

POSTSCRIPT

1. Sachiko Kusukawa, "Aspectio divinorum operum: Melanchthon and Astrology for Lutheran Medics," in Ole Peter Grell and Andrew Cunningham, eds., *Medicine and the Reformation* (London and New York, 1993), 33–56; here 43; Ernst Troeltsch, *The Social Teachings of the Christian Churches*, trans. Olive Wyon, Vol. 2 (New York, 1931), 535.

2. For the argument that astrology helped fill a vacuum created by the Protestant rejection of Catholic ritual see Thomas, *Religion and the Decline of Magic*.

3. To be sure, scholars have challenged the traditional understanding. See for instance Siegfried and Annelore Müller, "Konfession, Bildverständnis und die Welt der Dinge: Überlegungen zu einem Problemfeld," *Archive for Reformation History* 93 (2002): 369–90.

Literature

The following is a core selection of secondary sources. It is restricted largely to books, and does not include numerous studies cited in the footnotes.

Allen, Don Cameron. *The Star-Crossed Renaissance: The Quarrel about Astrology and its Influence in England*. Durham, NC, 1941.

Andreas, Willy. *Deutschland vor der Reformation*. Stuttgart, 1959; first ed. 1932.

Bächtold-Stäubli, Hanns, E. Hoffmann-Krayer, and Gerhard Lüdtke, eds. *Handwörterbuch des deutschen Aberglaubens*. 10 vols. Berlin, 1927–1942.

Bailey, Michael D. *Magic and Superstition in Europe: A Concise History from Antiquity to the Present*. Lanham, MD, 2007.

Barnes, Robin B. *Prophecy and Gnosis: Apocalypticism in the Wake of the Lutheran Reformation*. Stanford, 1988.

Barton, Tamsyn. *Ancient Astrology*. London and New York, 1994.

Barton, Tamsyn. *Power and Knowledge: Astrology, Physiognomics, and Medicine under the Roman Empire*. Ann Arbor, 1994.

Becker, Peter Jörg, and Eef Overgaaw, eds., *Aderlass und Seelentrost: Die Überlieferung deutscher Texte im Spiegel Berliner Handschriften und Inkunabeln*. Mainz am Rhein, 2003.

Bellucci, Dino. *Science de la Nature et Réformation: La Physique au service de la Réforme dans l'enseignement de Philippe Mélanchthon*. Rome, 1988.

Bergdolt, Klaus, and Walther Ludwig, eds., *Zukunftsvoraussagen in der Renaissance*. Wiesbaden, 2005.

Bergier, Jean-François, ed. *Zwischen Wahn, Glaube und Wissenschaft: Magie, Astrologie, Alchemie und Wissenschaftsgeschichte*. Zurich, 1988.

Bezold, Friedrich von. *Aus Mittelalter und Renaissance. Kulturgeschichtliche Studien*. Munich and Berlin, 1918.

Bezold, Friedrich von. *Geschichte der deutschen Reformation*. Berlin, 1890.

Blume, Dieter. *Regenten des Himmels: Astrologische Bilder in Mittelalter und Renaissance*. Berlin, 2000.

Boll, Franz, Carl Bezold, and Wilhelm Gundel. *Sternglaube und Sterndeutung: Die Geschichte und das Wesen der Astrologie*. Darmstadt, 1966 (orig. ed. 1931).

Bollème, Geneviève. *Les Almanachs Populaires aux XVIIe et XVIIIe Siècles. Essai d'histoire Sociale.* Paris, 1969.

Borst, Arno. *The Ordering of Time.* Chicago, 1993.

Brod, Walter M. *Mainfränkische Kalender aus vier Jahrhunderten.* Würzburg, 1952.

Broecke, Steven Vanden. *The Limits of Influence: Pico, Louvain, and the Crisis of Renaissance Astrology.* Leiden and Boston, 2003.

Brosseder, Claudia. *Im Bann der Sterne: Caspar Peucer, Philipp Melanchthon und andere Wittenberger Astrologen.* Berlin, 2004.

Burmeister, Karl Heinz. *Achilles Pirmin Gasser 1505–77: Arzt und Naturforscher, Historiker und Humanist.* 3 vols. Wiesbaden, 1970–1975.

Burmeister, Karl Heinz. *Georg Joachim Rheticus, 1514–1574: Eine Bio-Bibliographie.* 3 vols. Wiesbaden, 1967–1968.

Cameron, Euan. *Enchanted Europe: Superstition, Reason, and Religion 1250–1750.* Oxford, 2010.

Campion, Nicholas. *History of Western Astrology.* Vol. 1: *The Ancient World.* London and New York, 2008; Vol. 2: *The Medieval and Modern Worlds.* London and New York, 2009.

Capp, Bernard. *Astrology and the Popular Press: English Almanacs, 1500–1800.* Ithaca, 1979.

Carey, Hilary M. *Courting Disaster: Astrology at the English Court and University in the Later Middle Ages.* Houndsmills, Basingstoke, 1992.

Céard, Jean. *La nature et les prodiges: L'insolite au XVIe siècle, en France.* Geneva, 1977.

Chrisman, Miriam U. *Lay Culture, Learned Culture: Books and Social Change in Strasbourg, 1480–1599.* New Haven and London, 1982.

Clair, Colin. *A History of European Printing.* London, New York, San Francisco, 1976.

Clemen, Otto. *Die Volksfrömmigkeit des ausgehenden Mittelalters.* Dresden and Leipzig, 1917.

Creasman, Allyson. *Censorship and Civic Order in Reformation Germany, 1517–1648: "Printed Poison and Evil Talk."* Farnham and Burlington, 2012.

Cumont, Franz. *Astrology and Religion among the Greeks and Romans.* New York, 1960; orig. ed. New York, 1912.

Cunningham, Andrew, and Ole Peter Grell. *The Four Horsemen of the Apocalypse: Religion, War, Famine, and Death in Reformation Europe.* Cambridge and New York, 2000.

Curry, Patrick, ed. *Astrology, Science and Society: Historical Essays.* Woodbridge, 1987.

Curry, Patrick. *Prophecy and Power: Astrology in Early Modern England.* Cambridge, 1989.

Debus, Allen G. *Man and Nature in the Renaissance.* Cambridge, 1978.

Debus, Allen G., and Michael T. Walton, eds., *Reading the Book of Nature: The Other Side of the Scientific Revolution.* Kirksville, MO, 1998.

Delumeau, Jean. *La Peur en Occident (XIVe-XVIIIe siècles).* Paris, 1978.

Dillenberger, John. *Protestant Thought and Natural Science.* New York, 1960.

Dresler, Adolph. *Kalender-kunde. Eine kulturhistorische Studie.* Munich, 1972.

École normale supérieure de jeunes filles. *Divination et Controverse Religieuse en France au XVIe Siècle: actes du colloque organisé à l'Université de Paris-Sorbonne le 13 mars 1986.* Paris, 1987.

Edwards, Mark U. *Printing, Propaganda, and Martin Luther.* Berkeley and Los Angeles, 1994.

Engelsing, Rolf. *Der Bürger als Leser: Lesergeschichte in Deutschland 1500–1800.* Stuttgart, 1974.

Evangelisches Predigerseminar, Lutherstadt Wittenberg, and Peter Freybe, eds. *"Wach auf, wach auf, du deutsches Land!" Martin Luther, Angst und Zuversicht in der Zeitenwende.* Wittenberg, 2000.

Frank, Günter. *Die Theologische Philosophie Philipp Melanchthons 1497–1560.* Leipzig, 1995.

Frank, Günter, and Stefan Rhein, eds. *Melanchthon und die Naturwissenschaft seiner Zeit.* Sigmaringen, 1998.

Fried, Johannes. *Aufstieg aus dem Untergang: Apokalyptisches Denken und die Entstehung der modernen Wissenschaft im Mittelalter.* Munich, 2001.

Friedrich, Johann. *Astrologie und Reformation: Oder die Astrologen als Prediger der Reformation und Urheber des Bauernkrieges. Ein Beitrag zur Reformationsgeschichte.* Munich, 1864.

Fuchs, Franz, ed. *Mathematik und Naturwissenschaften in der Zeit von Philipp Melanchthon: Akten des . . . 2010 veranstalteten Symposions in Nürnberg.* Wiesbaden, 2012.

Füssel, Stephan, ed. *Astronomie und Astrologie in der Frühen Neuzeit (Pirckheimer Jahrbuch, vol. 5).* Nuremberg, 1990.

Gantet, Claire. *Der Traum in der Frühen Neuzeit. Ansätze zu einer kulturellen Wissenschaftsgeschichte.* Göttingen, 2010.

Garin, Eugenio. *Astrology in the Renaissance: The Zodiac of Life.* London, 1983.

Gilly, Carlos. *Adam Haslmayr: Der Erste Verkünder der Manifeste der Rosenkreutzer.* Amsterdam, 1994.

Gilly, Carlos. *"Theophrastica Sancta": Der Paracelsismus als Religion im Streit mit den offiziellen Kirchen.* Stuttgart, 1994.

Goldammer, Kurt. *Der Göttliche Magier und die Magierin Natur: Religion, Naturmagie und die Anfänge der Naturwissenschaft vom Spätmittelalter bis zur Renaissance.* Stuttgart, 1991.

Grafton, Anthony. *Cardano's Cosmos: The Worlds and Works of a Renaissance Astrologer.* Cambridge, MA and London, 1999.

Grafton, Anthony, and William R. Newman, eds., *Secrets of Nature: Astrology and Alchemy in Early Modern Europe.* Cambridge, MA, 2001.

Granada, Miguel. *El debate cosmológico en 1588: Bruno, Brahe, Rothmann, Ursus, Röslin.* Naples, 1996.

Granada, Miguel Á., ed. *Novas y cometas entre 1572 y 1618: Revolución cosmológica y renovación política y religiosa.* Barcelona, 2012.

Grant, Edward. *Planets, Stars, and Orbs: The Medieval Cosmos, 1200–1687.* Cambridge, 1994.

Green, Jonathan. *Printing and Prophecy: Prognostication and Media Change, 1450–1550.* Ann Arbor, 2011.

Grell, Ole Peter, ed. *Paracelsus: The Man and his Reputation, his Ideas and their Transformation.* Leiden and Boston, 1988.

Grell, Ole Peter, and Andrew Cunningham, eds. *Medicine and the Reformation.* London, 1993.

Greyerz, Kaspar von. *Religion and Society in Early Modern Europe, 1500–1800.* London, 1984.

Greyerz, Kaspar von, and Thomas Dunlap, eds., *Religion and Culture in Early Modern Europe, 1500–1800.* New York and Oxford, 2008.

Greyerz, Kaspar von, and Thomas Kaufmann, et al., eds., *Religion und Naturwissenschaften im 16. und 17. Jahrhundert.* Gütersloh, 2010.

Grössing, Helmuth. *Humanistische Naturwissenschaft. Zur Geschichte der Wiener mathematischen Schulen des 15. und 16. Jahrhunderts.* Baden-Baden, 1983.

Grössing, Helmuth, and Gunther Hamann, eds. *Der Weg der Naturwissenschaft von Johannes von Gmunden zu Johannes Kepler.* Wien, 1988.

Gunnoe, Charles D. *Thomas Erastus and the Palatinate: A Renaissance Physician in the Second Reformation.* Leiden and Boston, 2011.

Harmening, Dietrich. *Superstitio: Überlieferungs- und theoriegeschichtliche Untersuchungen zur kirchlich-theologischen Aberglaubensliteratur des Mittelalters.* Berlin, 1979.

Hayton, Darin. "Astrologers and Astrology in Vienna During the Era of Emperor Maximilian I, 1493–1519." PhD dissertation, University of Notre Dame, 2004.

Heitz, Paul, and Konrad Haebler, eds. *Hundert Kalender-Inkunabeln.* Strasbourg, 1905.

Heitzmann, Christian, et al. *Die Sterne lügen nicht: Astrologie und Astronomie im Mittelalter und in der Frühen Neuzeit.* Wolfenbüttel, 2008.

Hellmann, Gustav. "Aus der Blütezeit der Astromeorologie. J. Stöfflers Prognose für das Jahr 1524," *Beiträge zur Geschichte der Meteorologie,* vol. I. Berlin, 1914.

Hellmann, Gustav. "Die Meteorologie in den Deutschen Flugschriften und Flugblättern des XVI. Jahrhunderts." *Abhandlungen der Preussischen Akademie der Wissenschaften* (1921, Nr. 1). Berlin, 1921.

Hellmann, Gustav. "Versuch einer Geschichte der Wettervorhersage im XVI. Jahrhundert." *Abhandlungen der Preussischen Akademie der Wissenschaften* (1924, Nr. 1). Berlin, 1924.

Herbst, Klaus-Dieter, ed. *Astronomie—Literatur—Volksaufklärung: Der Schreibkalender der Frühen Neuzeit mit seinen Text- und Bildbeigaben.* Bremen, 2012.

Hirsch, Rudolf. *Printing, Selling and Reading 1450–1550.* Wiesbaden, 1974.

Holl, Karl. *Gesammelte Aufsätze zur Kirchengeschichte.* 3 vols. Tübingen, 1921–1928.

Hoppmann, Jürgen G. H. *Astrologie der Reformationszeit: Faust, Luther, Melanchthon, und die Sterndeuterei* (Berlin, 1998).

Hotson, Howard. *Johann Heinrich Alsted, 1588–1638: Between Renaissance, Reformation, and Universal Reform*. Oxford and New York, 2000.

Hübner, Wolfgang. *Zodiacus Christianus. Jüdisch-christliche Adaptionen des Tierkreises von der Antike bis zur Gegenwart*. Königstein, 1983.

Instituto nazionale di studi sul Rinascimento. *Scienze, credenze occulte, livelli di cultura: Convegno internazionale*. Florence, 1982.

Jakubowski-Tiessen, Manfred, et al., eds., *Jahrhundertwenden: Endzeit-und Zukunfftsvorstellungen vom 15. bis zum 20 Jahrhundert*. Göttingen, 1999.

Jensen, Derek, "The Science of the Stars in Danzig from Rheticus to Hevelius." PhD dissertation, University of California at San Diego, 2006.

Kaufmann, Thomas. *Konfession und Kultur: Lutherischer Protestantismus in der zweiten Hälfte des Reformationsjahrhunderts*. Tübingen, 2006.

Kaufmann, Thomas. *Universität und lutherische Konfessionalisierung*. Gütersloh, 1997.

Keller, Hildegard Elisabeth, et al., eds. *Jakob Ruf: Leben, Werk und Studien*. 5 vols. Zurich, 2008.

Kitson, Annabella, ed. *History and Astrology: Clio and Urania Confer*. London, 1989.

Kjellgren, Martin. *Taming the Prophets: Astrology, Orthodoxy and the Word of God in Early Modern Sweden*. Lund, 2011.

Klibansky, Raymond, Erwin Panofsky, and Fritz Saxl. *Saturn and Melancholy: Studies in the History of Natural Philosophy, Religion, and Art*. London, 1964.

Klingner, Erich. *Luther und der deutsche Volksaberglaube*. Berlin, 1912.

Knappich, Wilhelm. *Geschichte der Astrologie*. 3rd ed., Frankfurt a. M., 1998.

Knopf, Jan. *Die deutsche Kalendergeschichte: Ein Arbeitsbuch*. Frankfurt a. M., 1983.

Koch, Ernst. *Das Konfessionelle Zeitalter: Katholizismus, Luthertum, Calvinismus (1563–1675)*. Leipzig, 2000.

Kolb, Robert, ed. *Lutheran Ecclesiastical Culture, 1550–1675*. Leiden and Boston, 2008.

Künast, Hans-Jörg. *"Getruckt zu Augsburg": Buchdruck und Buchhandel in Augsburg zwischen 1468 und 1555*. Tübingen, 1997.

Kurze, Dietrich. *Johannes Lichtenberger. Eine Studie zur Geschichte der Prophetie und Astrologie*. Lübeck, 1960.

Kusukawa, Sachiko. *The Transformation of Natural Philosophy: The case of Philip Melanchthon*. Cambridge, 1995.

Lehmann, Hartmut, and Anne-Charlott Trepp, eds. *Im Zeichen der Krise: Religiosität im Europa des 17. Jahrhunderts*. Göttingen, 1999.

Leinkauf, Thomas, ed. *Giordano Bruno in Wittenberg, 1586–1588*. Pisa, 2004.

Leppin, Volker. *Antichrist und Jüngster Tag. Das profil apokalyptischer Flugschriftenpublizistik im deutschen Luthertum 1548–1618*. Gütersloh, 1999.

Lindberg, David C., and Ronald L. Numbers, eds. *God and Nature: Historical Essays on the Encounter between Christianity and Science.* Berkeley, 1986.

Markowski, Mieczyslaw. *Astronomica et astrologica cracoviensia ante annum 1550.* Florence, 1990.

Matthäus, Klaus. "Zur Geschichte des Nürnberger Kalenderwesens: Die Entwicklung der in Nürnberg gedruckten Jahreskalender in Buchform." *Archiv für Geschichte des Buchwesens* IX (1969), 965–1396.

Maurer, Wilhelm. *Der Junge Melanchthon zwischen Humanismus und Reformation.* Göttingen, 1967.

Mazal, Otto. *Die Sternenwelt des Mittelalters.* Graz, 1993.

Mentgen, Gerd. *Astrologie und Öffentlichkeit im Mittelalter.* Stuttgart, 2005.

Methuen, Charlotte. *Kepler's Tübingen: Stimulus to a Theological Mathematics.* Aldershot and Brookfield, 1998.

Methuen, Charlotte. *Science and theology in the Reformation: studies in theological interpretation and astronomical observation in sixteenth-century Germany.* London and New York, 2008.

Midelfort, H. C. Erik. *A History of Madness in Sixteenth-Century Germany.* Stanford, 1999.

Montgomery, John Warwick. *Cross and Crucible: Johann Valentin Andreae 1586–1654, Phoenix of the Theologians.* The Hague, 1973.

Mueller, Markus. *Beherrschte Zeit: Lebensorientierung und Zukunftsgestaltung durch Kalenderprognostik zwischen Antike und Neuzeit.* Kassel, 2009.

Müller-Jahncke, Wolf-Dieter. *Astrologisch-magische Theorie und Praxis in der Heilkunde der frühen Neuzeit.* Wiesbaden, 1985.

Neumann, Hans-Peter. *Natura sagax—Die geistige Natur: Zum Zusammenhang von Naturphilosophie und Mystik in der frühen Neuzeit am Beispiel Johann Arndts.* Tübingen, 2004.

Newman, William, and Anthony Grafton, eds. *Secrets of Nature: Astrology and Alchemy in Early Modern Europe.* Cambridge, MA, 2001.

Niccoli, Ottavia. *Prophecy and People in Renaissance Italy.* Princeton, 1990.

North, John D. *Horoscopes and History.* London, 1986.

North, John David. *Stars, Minds, and Fate: essays in ancient and medieval cosmology.* London, 1989.

Nouhuys, Tabitta van. *The Age of Two-Faced Janus: The Comets of 1577 and 1618 and the Decline of the Aristotelian World View in the Netherlands.* Leiden and Boston, 1998.

Oestmann, Guenther. *Heinrich Rantzau und die Astrologie: ein Beitrag zur Kulturgeschichte des 16. Jahrhunderts.* Braunschweig, 2004.

Oestmann, Guenther, H. Darrel Rutkin, and Kocku von Stuckrad, eds. *Horoscopes and Public Spheres: Essays on the History of Astrology.* Berlin and New York, 2005.

Parish, Helen, and William G. Naphy, eds. *Religion and Superstition in Reformation Europe.* Manchester, 2003.

Penman, Leigh. "Unanticipated Millenniums: The Lutheran Experience of Millenarian Thought." PhD dissertation, University of Melbourne, 2008.

Peuckert, Will-Erich. *Astrologie: Geschichte der Geheimwissenschaften.* Stuttgart, 1964.

Peuckert, Will-Erich. *Die grosse Wende: Das apokalyptische Saeculum und Luther.* 2 vols. Darmstadt, 1966.

Peuckert, Will-Erich. *Die Rosenkreutzer.* Jena, 1928. Issued in revised and expanded form as *Das Rosenkreutz*, ed. Rolf Christian Zimmermann. Berlin, 1973.

Peukert, Will-Erich. *Gabalia: Ein Versuch zur Geschichte der Magia Naturalis im 16. bis 18. Jahrhundert.* Berlin, 1967.

Pfaff, Alfred. *Aus Alten Kalendern.* Berlin-Dahlem, 1943.

Pfister, Silvia. *Parodien astrologisch-prophetischen Schrifttums 1470–1590: Textform, Entstehung, Vermittlung, Funktion.* Baden-Baden, 1990.

Pilz, Kurt. *600 Jahre Astronomie in Nürnberg.* Nuremberg, 1977.

Plummer, Marjorie Elizabeth, and Robin B. Barnes, eds. *Ideas and Cultural Margins in Early Modern Germany: Essays in Honor of H. C. Erik Midelfort.* Farnham and Burlington, 2009.

Préaud, Maxime. *Les Astrologues à La Fin du Moyen Age.* Paris, 1984.

Pumfrey, Stephen, et al., eds. *Science, Culture, and Popular Belief in Renaissance Europe.* Manchester and New York, 1991.

Press, Volker, and Dieter Stievemann, eds. *Martin Luther: Probleme seiner Zeit.* Stuttgart, 1986.

Rohner, Ludwig. *Kalendergeschichte und Kalender.* Wiesbaden, 1978.

Rublack, Hans-Christoph, ed. *Die lutherische Konfessionalisierung in Deutschland.* Gütersloh, 1992.

Schmitt, Charles. *Aristotle and the Renaissance.* Cambridge, MA, 1983.

Schechner, Sarah J. *Comets, Popular Culture, and the Birth of Modern Cosmology.* Princeton, 1997.

Scheible, Heinz, ed. *Melanchthon in seinen Schülern.* Wiesbaden, 1997.

Schmidt, Heinrich. *Die Deutsche Städtechroniken als Spiegel des bürgerlichen Selbstverständnisses im Spätmittelalter.* Göttingen, 1958.

Schmitt, Charles, ed. *The Cambridge History of Renaissance Philosophy.* Cambridge, 1988.

Schöner, Christoph. *Mathematik und Astronomie an der Universität Ingolstadt im 15. und 16. Jahrhundert.* Berlin, 1994.

Scholz-Williams, Gerhild, and Charles D. Gunnoe, *Paracelsian Moments: Science, Medicine & Astrology in Early Modern Europe.* Kirksville, MO, 2002.

Schorn-Schütte, Luise. *Evangelische Geistlichkeit in der Frühneuzeit.* Gütersloh, 1996.

Schottenloher, Karl. *Flugblatt und Zeitung: Ein Wegweiser durch das Gedruckte Tagesschriftum.* Berlin, 1922.

Scribner, R. W. *For the Sake of Simple Folk: Popular Propaganda for the German Reformation.* Cambridge, 1981.

Scribner, R. W. *Popular Culture and Popular Movements in Reformation Germany*. London, 1987.

Scribner, R. W., and T. Johnson, eds. *Popular Religion in Germany and Europe 1400–1800*. London, 1996.

Sementowsky-Kurilo, Nikolaus von. *Der Mensch griff nach den Sternen. Astrologie in der Geistesgeschichte des Abendlandes*. Zurich, Stuttgart: 1970.

Smith, Pamela H. *The Business of Alchemy: Science and Culture in the Holy Roman Empire*. Princeton, 1994.

Smolinsky, Heribert. *Deutungen der Zeit im Streit der Konfessionen. Kontroverstheologie, Apokalyptik und Astrologie im 16. Jahrhundert*. Heidelberg, 2000.

Smoller, Laura A. *History, Prophecy and the Stars: The Christian Astrology of Pierre D'Ailly*. Princeton, 1994.

Soergel, Philip M. *Miracles and the Protestant Imagination: The Evangelical Wonder Book in Reformation Germany*. Oxford and New York, 2012.

Sondheim, Moriz. *Thomas Murner als Astrolog*. Strasbourg, 1938.

Stegemann, Viktor. *Aus einem mittelalterlichen deutschen astronomisch-astrologischen Lehrbüchlein: Eine Untersuchung über Entstehung, Herkunft, und Nachwirkung eines Kapitels über Planetenkinder*. Reichenberg, 1944.

Strauss, Gerald. *Luther's House of Learning: Indoctrination of the Young in the Lutheran Reformation*. Baltimore, 1978.

Strauss, Heinz Artur. *Der Astrologische Gedanke in der Deutschen Vergangenheit*. Munich and Berlin, 1926.

Sührig, Hartmut. "Die Entwicklung der niedersächsischen Kalender im 17. Jahrhundert." *Archiv für Geschichte des Buchwesens* 20 (1979), 329–794.

Talkenberger, Heike. *Sintflut: Prophetie und Zeitgeschehen in Texten und Holzschnitten astrologischer Flugschriften, 1488–1528*. Tübingen, 1990.

Tester, Jim. *A History of Western Astrology*. Woodbridge, Suffolk, and Wolfeboro, NH, 1987.

Thomas, Keith. *Religion and the Decline of Magic*. New York, 1971.

Thorndike, Lynn. *A History of Magic and Experimental Science*. 8 vols. New York, 1923–1958.

Troels-Lund, Troels. *Himmelsbild und Weltanschauung im Wandel der Zeiten*. Leipzig, 1908.

Van Dülmen, Richard. *Kultur und Alltag in der Frühen Neuzeit: Religion, Magie, Aufklärung*. Munich, 1994.

Veenstra, Jan R. *Magic and Divination at the Courts of Burgundy and France: Text and Context of Laurens Pignon's "Contre Les Devineurs" (1411)*. Leiden, New York, Cologne, 1997.

Vickers, Brian. *Occult and Scientific Mentalities in the Renaissance*. Cambridge, 1984.

Warburg, Aby. *Gesammelte Schriften*, 2 vols. Nendeln, 1969.

Webster, Charles, ed. *Health, Medicine, and Mortality in the Sixteenth Century*. Cambridge, 1979.

Weeks, Andrew. *Paracelsus: Speculative Theory and the Crisis of the Early Reformation.* Albany, 1997.

Wehrli, G. A. *Die Zürcher Stadtarzt Christoph Clauser und seine Stellung zur Reformation der Heilkunde im XVI. Jahrhundert.* Zurich, 1924.

Westman, Robert. *The Copernican Question: Prognostication, Skepticism, and Celestial Order.* Los Angeles, 2011.

Zambelli, Paola, ed. *"Astrologi Hallucinati": Stars and the End of the World in Luther's Time.* Berlin, 1986.

Zinner, Ernst. *Geschichte und Bibliographie der Astronomischen Literatur in Deutschland zur Zeit der Renaissance.* Stuttgart, 1964.

Zinner, Ernst. *Sternglaube und Sternforschung.* Freiburg and Munich, 1953.

Index